Why the Poor Get Richer and the Rich Slow Down

T0327474

W. W. Rostow

Why the Poor Get Richer and the Rich Slow Down

ESSAYS IN THE MARSHALLIAN LONG PERIOD

University of Texas Press, Austin

Publication of this book was made possible by a
grant from the Sid W. Richardson Foundation.

Requests for permission to reproduce material
from this work should be sent to Permissions,
University of Texas Press, Box 7819,
Austin, Texas 78712

Library of Congress Cataloging in
Publication Data

Rostow, Walt Whitman, 1916–
    Why the poor get richer and the rich slow
down.
    Includes bibliographical references and index.
    1. Economics—Addresses, essays, lectures.
2. Economic development—Addresses, essays,
lectures. 3. Business cycles—Addresses, essays,
lectures. 4. Neoclassical school of economics—
Addresses, essays, lectures. I. Title.
HB171.R674   330.1   79-20397
ISBN 978-0-292-72963-6

To Richard M. Bissell, Jr.

Contents

Charts

Tables

Preface

As the reader will perceive, these essays are unified by a pervasive judgment, namely, that modern economic theory must be extended to embrace systematically the factors at work in the Marshallian long period if it is to be a useful tool for either historical or policy analysis.

Alfred Marshall distinguished four periods in relating supply to price. Three of Marshall's periods assumed the following as fixed: technology, the size of the working force, tastes, and, with minor variation, productive capacity. They constituted variations on the short period. The fourth allowed for "very gradual or *Secular* movements of normal price, caused by the gradual growth of knowledge, of population and of capital, and the changing conditions of demand and supply from one generation to another." The definition of supply changes in terms of time periods permitted Marshall, in the first three cases, to assume diminishing returns and supply curves sloping upward to the right. With demand curves sloping downward to the right, under the assumption of diminishing relative marginal utility, unambiguous conditions of stable equilibrium could be defined in particular markets, and a good deal of economic theory could be translated with some elegance into mathematical terms. In the fourth, long-period case, supply curves could slope downward and to the right, reflecting increasing returns made possible by technological change or by large, discontinuous change in the supply of agricultural products and raw materials. Moreover, fundamental changes in supply (yielding, for example, cheap cotton textiles or the automobile) could play back on tastes and the shape and position of demand curves. Supply and demand were no longer independent of one another, and irreversible changes in both could occur. As Marshall was acutely aware, no stable equilibrium condition could then be defined. The simple elegance of mathematically formulated economic theory was gone. In the long period economists were plunged into a world where they confronted, in Marshall's phrases, "the high theme of economic progress," "organic growth," and "society as an organism."

The mainstream tradition of modern neoclassical economics has been to deal with the dilemma Marshall defined by confining itself primarily to propositions framed by short-period assumptions. When long-period problems were addressed, as in the Harrod-Domar and neoclassical growth models, changes in technology and population were introduced in highly aggregated, abstract forms.

But the deeper problem with Marshall's convenient but evasive formulation is that the actual flow of economic events and processes, historically or in the contemporary world, does not permit a valid separation of the short and long periods. At any given moment of time the economy is, in fact, being shaped by the long-run flow of demographic and technological change, as well as by short-period movements along fixed supply and demand curves or by short-run shifts in effective demand and supply. Contrary to Keynes' famous dictum—in the long run we are all dead—the long run is with us every day of our lives.

That is why, when I formulated the theoretical framework for my task as an economic historian, I called the book *The Process of Economic Growth* rather than *The Theory of Economic Growth*. I had concluded that there was no way serious economic historians could do their job without accepting the challenge of dealing with "the high theme of economic progress," "organic growth," and "society as an organism." This assessment was strongly reinforced by various experiences as a public servant, dealing with problems of economic policy.

The process of economic growth can also be conceived in equilibrium terms. But, in Allyn Young's phrase, it must be a "moving equilibrium," embracing irreversible changes in technology, the supply of basic commodities, population, tastes, and the quality of entrepreneurship. That is the kind of dynamic equilibrium concept which *The Process of Economic Growth* sought to outline and which suffuses this book, including explicit elaborations in Chapters 1, 2, and 4.

If it is to be truly serious, economics must be, then, a biological rather than a Newtonian science. Indeed, physicists, too, increasingly recognize that static equilibrium concepts are an inappropriate framework of analysis for a physical world in a state of 'instability, mutation, and diversification, where irreversible processes are constantly at work, and non-equilibrium is itself a source of dynamic order.'[1] In any case, this is the kind of world a student of economic growth or a policy maker inescapably confronts.

Chapters 1, 2, 4, 5, and 6 of the present volume apply this perception to four large analytic issues: theories of long cycles, the relation between technology and the economic process as a whole, the relation between money and prices in the pre-1914 world, and the tendency of per capita real income levels to converge as between early-and late-comers to modern economic growth.

Chapters 3 and 7 bring this perspective to bear on two policy issues where long-period factors are paramount: the potential role of energy-related investment in bringing the advanced industrial economies back to high, sustained growth rates; and the need to restructure multilateral economic negotiations between the more advanced and the developing nations if they are to prove fruitful.

These matters were touched on in *The World Economy: History and Prospect* and *Getting from Here to There*; but the proportioning of those books did not permit the more extended treatment of these themes that I believe their importance dictates.

Chapter 8 is the transcribed text of a talk delivered from notes and requires a special word. It justifies inclusion, perhaps, because it contains, to the best of my knowledge, the first application of Rousseau's notion of Le Contrat Social to incomes policy. Since the rate of productivity increase is a critical variable in determining the rate of inflation, the subject belongs legitimately in a book addressed to problems of the Marshallian long period. But the chapter also says a few things about economic policy in relation to the political and social behavior of societies I still believe to be relevant.

The occasion which yielded that talk is reflected in the text. As a member of the Inter-American Committee on the Alliance for Progress, visiting Argentina in February 1965, I was asked to speak at the University of Buenos Aires. I decided to discuss inflation and prepared some notes on the afternoon of the scheduled talk. A small but determined left-wing group created a sufficient disturbance and danger of violence at the meeting for the local authorities to call off my talk before it was delivered. Nine students sought me out at the United States Embassy to express their regrets. I invited them to a recording studio and said to them there what I had planned to say at the disrupted meeting. The talk was translated into Spanish, printed throughout Argentina, and, as a pamphlet, circulated widely in the Spanish-speaking world. It appeared in the *Department of State Bulletin*, March 29, 1965.

I would underline here what the text of Chapter 2 states: namely, that Michael Kennedy is a joint author of that chapter. It was, for me, a particularly pleasant collaboration. Faisal Nasr assisted in the development of Chapter 2; Frederick Fordyce, Chapter 6; and I thank them both.

I am grateful to the following for criticism of drafts or for other forms of assistance: Martin Baughman, Allan Davidson, William L. Fisher, J. Michael Gallagher, Wendell Gordon, Daniel Garnick, Charles Hitch, Irving Hoch, William W. Hogan, Milton Holloway, Nicholas Kaldor, David Kendrick, Charles P. Kindleberger, Simon Kuznets, William Miernyk, David Montgomery, Emmette Redford, Paul A. Samuelson, Anna Jacobson Schwartz, Robert Solow, Paul Uselding, and Jeffrey G. Williamson. Mrs. Schwartz' help was particularly appreciated. Chapter 5 is not exactly a monetarist tract; but, in the best tradition of academic life, she generously provided unpublished data as well as bibliographical suggestions and critiques of drafts which, if not wholly accepted, helped substantially to clarify my own views.

I am indebted to their respective editors for permission to reprint passages in Chapter 1 which first appeared in the *Journal of Economic History* and the bulk of Chapters 2 and 6, which first appeared in Vols. 3 and 4 of *Research in Economic History*. The University of Texas Press has permitted the inclusion of Chapter 4, the bulk of which first appeared in *Science and Ceremony: The Institutional Economics of C. E. Ayres*, ed. William Breit and William Patton Culbertson, Jr.

Chapter 6 uses extensively materials stored in the computer of the University of Texas at Austin by Project Mulhall, an economic history data base. Its initial mobilization was made possible by a grant from the National Endowment for the Humanities. It is now being expanded in a joint effort by a number of departments and research centers at the University of Texas at Austin. Project Mulhall is financed by grants from the Sid W. Richardson Foundation and HEW, whose generous assistance, along with that of NEH, I wish to acknowledge.

Mrs. Virginia Fay typed the various drafts of this book with her usual efficiency and good cheer. Miss Lois Nivens, as on many other occasions, was an indispensable editor and aide.

The dedication of this book to Richard Bissell acknowledges a major debt. Bissell, recently returned to the Yale Graduate School from a year at the London School of Economics, invited four undergraduate friends to participate in an informal seminar in modern economic theory during the autumn of 1933. The sessions took place, usually on Thursday evenings, in Bissell's rooms in Davenport College. I was then a sophomore majoring in history. Bissell's elegant and lucid exposition of what is now called micro- and macro-theory made a deep impression on me. It was during the academic year 1933–1934, directly influenced by this experience and strongly encouraged by Bissell, that I decided to build my professional career around the problem of bringing modern economic theory to bear on history. In 1934 I undertook my first such exercise: a testing of Keynes' *Treatise on Money* as a framework capable of explaining British inflation during the French Revolutionary and Napoleonic Wars. Its inadequacy set me directly on a path of analysis which led to the conclusions incorporated in Chapter 5 of the present volume.

W. W. ROSTOW

Austin, Texas
July 1979

Why the Poor Get Richer and the Rich Slow Down

1

The Long Cycle:
An Integrated View

I

The analysis of fluctuations longer than the nine-year business cycle has been somewhat confused by a failure to distinguish sharply and to relate three distinct phenomena: the forces set in motion by a leading sector in growth, stemming from the introduction and progressive diffusion of a new technology; the forces set in motion by changes in the profitability of producing foodstuffs and raw materials, whether from the side of prices or from technology, including their effects on investment in new territories and mines, on capital movements, interest rates, terms of trade, and income distribution; and the forces set in motion (notably in housing and urban infrastructure) by large waves of international or domestic migration or other forces changing the rate of family formation, housing demand, and the size of the working force. As the world economy unfolded after 1783, these three phenomena operated concurrently and related to each other in complex ways not easy to disentangle. Nevertheless, the substantial literature on long waves can be usefully clarified by distinguishing these phenomena more sharply than is sometimes done and then relating them to each other at particular times and places.

This theme is elaborated by first recalling how long waves (or trends) were dealt with in the imaginative, path-breaking excursions of N. D. Kondratieff, the early Simon Kuznets, and Joseph Schumpeter; and how their successors (including the later Kuz-

Note: Passages in this chapter first appeared in *Journal of Economic History* 35, no. 4 (December 1975).

nets) fragmented the problem into three components. Efforts to reintegrate the analysis of long cycles are then examined, including the outline of a general, disaggregated theory of production and prices capable of embracing the three types of phenomena involved. The chapter closes with some observations on the two opposing views of where the 1970's and 1980's stand in the rhythm of Kondratieff cycles.

II

Although he acknowledged two predecessors, N. D. Kondratieff is properly regarded as the father of the notion that capitalist economies are subject to cycles some fifty years in length.[1] He established an empirical case by finding two and a half cycles in a number of price, wage, interest rate, and other value-affected series, with troughs around 1790, 1844–1851, and 1890–1896; peaks at 1810–1817, 1870–1875, and 1914–1920. Production data were both sparse and recalcitrant when set into this cyclical mold. Nevertheless, Kondratieff believed that long-run cycles in output accompanied his cycles in prices and other value data. His image was one of a dynamic world economy moving forward in long oscillations around a more or less stable upward trend.

Kondratieff did not attempt directly to provide a theory of the long cycle; but he counterattacked critics who asserted that the phenomena he was examining reflected exogenous forces: changes in technology, wars and revolutions, the bringing of new countries into the world economy, and fluctuations in gold production. His counterattack asserted that none of these phenomena could be properly regarded as exogenous to the workings of a world capitalist system,[2] but he did not render them endogenous. He implied that a coherent explanation must exist; but, in his own phrase, he never developed "an appropriate theory of long waves." It is fair to say that his major net contribution was dual: to demonstrate long-period movements (or cycles) in prices, interest rates, and other value series and to pose for others to contemplate his empirical assertions that the upswings of his cycles tended to contain more years of (conventional) cyclical prosperity than the downswings, that agricultural depressions accompanied the downswings, that large numbers of inventions and discoveries were made in the downswings to be applied fully in the upswings, that the beginnings of the upswings were accompanied by both expanded gold production and the effective absorption of new areas into the world economy, and that the latter phase of the upswings brought with them "the most disastrous and extensive wars and revolutions." Above all, what Kondratieff did was to dramatize, in the most vivid and persuasive of his charts, the two and a half cycles between 1789 and 1920 in commodity prices (Chart 1-1).

Starting essentially from Kondratieff's dramatization of the long cycle in prices, Schumpeter tried to provide an "appropriate theory of long waves." He did so by linking price movements to the grand sequence of technological leading sectors, grouped in three batches: cotton textiles and iron; railroads, steam, and steel; electricity, industrial chemistry, and the internal combustion engine. The price link was achieved by assuming that the early, experimental phase of innovation involved an inflationary expansion of credit-financed investment not matched promptly by the cost-reducing results the innovation would ultimately

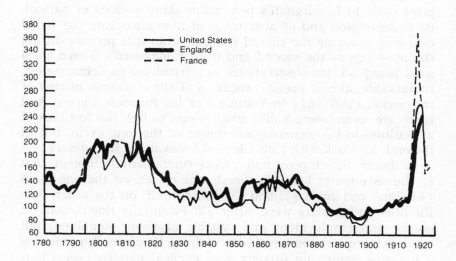

CHART 1-1. *Index Numbers of Commodity Prices, 1780–1922: England, United States, and France (1901–10 = 100).*

Source: N. D. Kondratieff, "The Long Waves in Economic Life," *Review of Economic Statistics* 17, no. 6 (November 1935): 106.

yield. The maturing and diffusion of the innovation brought cost reductions sufficiently powerful to bring down the aggregate price index.

This mechanism did not work very well on the upswings when confronted with the facts. The early experimental phase of cotton textile and iron innovation did not require credit expansion on a scale capable of inflating the British price level; and price reductions came promptly—even in the inherently inflationary setting of the Napoleonic Wars. Nor did the early days of the electricity-chemicals-automobile revolution provide a persuasive explanation for the price increase between the mid-1890's and 1914. The railroads and the price increase of the 1850's, in the upswing of the second Kondratieff, looked like the best case; but, as Schumpeter was uneasily aware, by the 1850's railroads were well beyond a possibly inflationary infancy, with major railroad expansion in the 1840's in Britain and the American Northeast, accompanied by relatively stagnant or falling prices. Railroads by themselves do not explain the price increase of the 1850's and the maintenance of a high range of prices down to 1873.

Schumpeter would have done better if he had tried to link the price cycle to Kondratieff's perception about periods of agricultural depression and of absorption of new areas into the world economy, weaving the role of railroads into that process during the upswings of the second and third Kondratieffs. There are a good many ad hoc observations on agriculture in Schumpeter's remarkable, almost poetic, evocation of the economic history of the period 1786–1913 in Volume I of his *Business Cycles.* And there are, even, some halfhearted efforts to link the fortunes of agriculture to his technological theory of the long cycle. But in the end, he stuck with technological innovations in industry.

In theory, Schumpeter had a more fundamental problem, that is, the asymmetry between the shorter cycles, on the one hand (Kitchins and Juglars), and the Kondratieff, on the other. The Kitchins and Juglars were, after all, essentially fluctuations in output and employment and capable of being combined; but when Schumpeter combined both with the Kondratieff, producing a majestic composite fifty-six year cyclical pattern (see Chart 1-2), what was the variable on the vertical axis? Schumpeter's visual image of the Kondratieff only made sense as a price or value cycle. As we shall see, this problem comes back to haunt

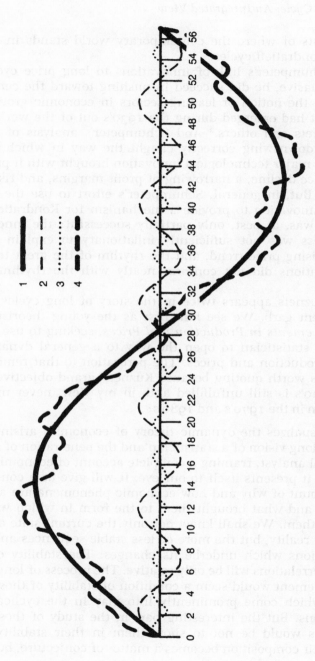

CHART 1-2. A Kondratieff, Juglars, and Kitchins: *Curve 1, Long Cycle; Curve 2, Intermediate Cycle; Curve 3, Short Cycle; Curve 4, Sum of 1–3.*

Source: Joseph Schumpeter, *Business Cycles* (New York: McGraw-Hill, 1939), vol. I, p. 213.

some analysts of where the contemporary world stands in the
rhythm of Kondratieff cycles.

While Schumpeter's link of innovations to long price cycles
was unpersuasive, he did succeed in pushing toward the center
of the stage the notion of leading sectors in economic growth.
This concept had emerged during the 1930's out of the work of
Simon Kuznets and others.[3] And Schumpeter's analysis of the
Kondratieff downswing correctly caught the way in which the
fruition of a major technological innovation brought with it pressures for price decline, a narrowing of profit margins, and rising
real wages. But, in general, Schumpeter's effort to use the dynamics of innovation to provide a mechanism for Kondratieff's
long cycles was, at best, only partially successful: the innovational process was not sufficiently inflationary to explain the
periods of rising price trend, and the rhythm of the great technical innovations did not conform neatly with the rhythm of
price trends.

Simon Kuznets appears twice in the story of long cycles, in
quite different garb. We see him first as the young theorist of
Secular Movements in Production and Prices, seeking to use the
tools of the statistician to open the way to a general dynamic
theory of production and prices. The peroration to that remarkable study is worth quoting because Kuznets' grand objective of
the late 1920's is still unfulfilled and, in my view, never more
relevant than in the 1970's and 1980's:

> One visualizes the dynamic theory of economics arising
> from the long vision of a statistician and the penetration of a
> theoretical analyst, framing a complete account of economic
> reality as it presents itself to our eye. It will give us a com-
> plete account of why and how economic phenomena are as
> they are, and what brought them to the form in which we
> conceive them. We shall know not only the current state of
> economic reality, but the more or less stable sequences and
> interrelations which underlie its changes. The stability of
> these interrelations will be only relative. The process of long-
> time movement would seem a condition of stability of those
> factors which come prominently into play in the cyclical
> fluctuations. But the interesting part in the study of these
> conditions would be not to show them in their stability,
> where their composition becomes a matter of conjecture, but

in their movement and flux where the hypotheses concerning their mechanism and forces can be tested. If we have a theory of economic changes in their different, discernible types we shall have a complete and general theory of dynamic economics.[4]

Kuznets was quite aware of the work of Kondratieff and others who interested themselves in economic movements which transcended conventional business cycles; but he was determined to proceed from a more solid statistical base than Kondratieff, even if that meant that all the phenomena Kondratieff identified could not be embraced in his conclusions. Whereas Kondratieff examined thirty-six series (finding long cycles in 25), Kuznets subjected some sixty-five production and thirty-five price series (drawn from five countries) to trend analysis. But, unlike Kondratieff, he confined himself mainly to the post-1865 period. His method was to establish a long-run primary trend, by clearing his data of short-run cyclical and other movements; then to establish secondary movements in production and prices around the primary trend; and, finally, to examine the relation between the rate of growth of a sector and the amplitude of the cycles it experienced.

Kuznets found that primary trends in production and prices reflected systematically the life cycle of a given technical innovation (or opening up of a new territory or natural resource), that is, a phase of rapid, then decelerating, increase in output and of rapid, then decelerating, decrease in price. Here, in Kuznets' phrase, was the path followed by the industries which "lead in development" as a revolutionary invention or discovery is applied to the industrial process.

The first thing Kuznets' analysis of primary trends demonstrated was that the cost-reducing effect of innovation was generally translated promptly into price reductions—a proposition Schumpeter failed to take into account. In fact, with the passage of time, price reductions were subject to retardation, just as were increases in output; and, in the post-1865 period he was primarily examining, a number of sectors saw marked deceleration in primary production trends accompanied, after the mid-1890's, by price increases. The cases of U.S. steel production and the price of steel rails (where the latter rises after 1898) and of Portland cement output and price (whose decline merely decelerates after

1900) illustrate the typical pattern Kuznets found in industrial sectors exploiting a major innovative breakthrough (Charts 1-3 to 1-6). Kuznets demonstrated that a version of diminishing returns operated with respect to a given innovative breakthrough with the passage of time and its progressive exploitation.

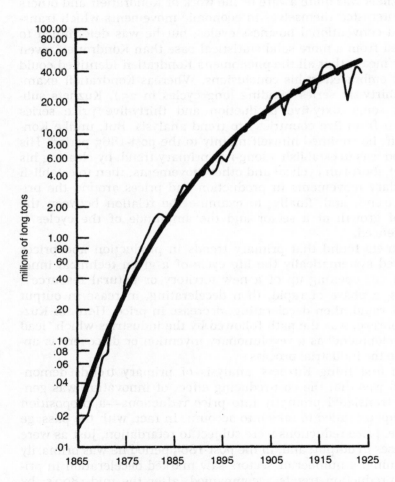

CHART 1-3. *Crude Steel Production, United States, 1865–1924: Original Data and Primary Trend Line.*

Source: Simon Kuznets, *Secular Movements in Production and Prices* (Boston and New York: Houghton Mifflin Company, 1930), p. 97.

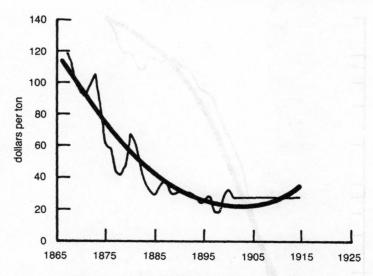

CHART 1-4. *Price of Steel Rails, United States, 1867–1915: Original Data and Primary Trend Line.*

Source: Kuznets, *Secular Movements*, p. 98.

As one would expect, similar paths were found in certain key agricultural and raw material sectors, as the American data for wheat, cotton, bituminous coal, and copper suggest (Charts 1-7 to 1-14). In these paths of decelerating increases in output accompanied by diminishing rates of price decrease—and then price increase—Kuznets had the materials in hand to proceed to a more satisfactory explanation than Schumpeter was to provide for Kondratieff's long cycles in overall price indexes. But he did not take that route. He stayed with the sectors.

Kuznets exhibited a similar reserve with respect to overall production. He did not link his insights into sectoral retardation to statistical data on the course of national output during the time period with which he dealt. But he contrasted in general terms the "fairly continuous march of economic progress" with the decelerating paths of the sectors, and he noted that the relatively steady overall rate of growth was sustained by a succession of leading sectors.[5]

In dealing with secondary movements in production and prices, however, Kuznets came seriously to grips in general terms with

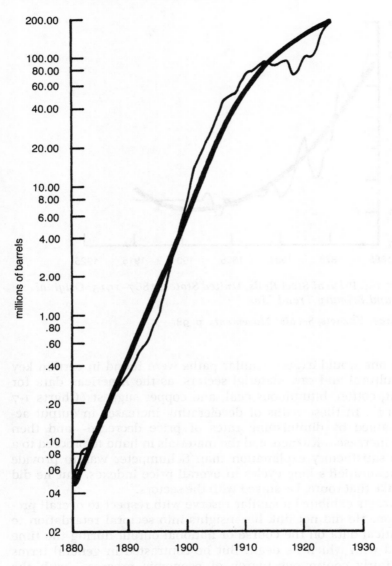

CHART I-5. *Portland Cement Production, United States, 1880–1924: Original Data and Primary Trend Line.*

Source: Kuznets, *Secular Movements*, p. 100.

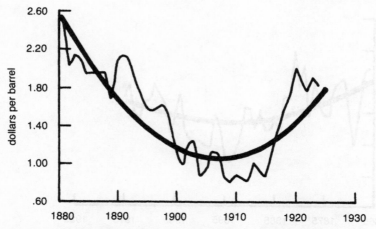

CHART 1-6. *Portland Cement, Factory Prices, United States, 1881–1924: Original Data and Primary Trend Line.*

Source: Kuznets, *Secular Movements*, p. 101.

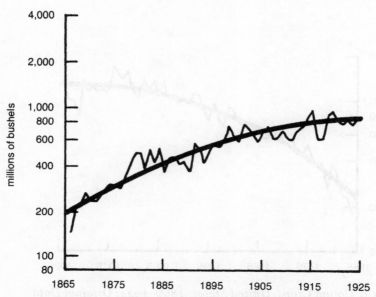

CHART 1-7. *Wheat Crops, United States, 1866–1924: Original Data and Primary Trend Line.*

Source: Kuznets, *Secular Movements*, p. 71.

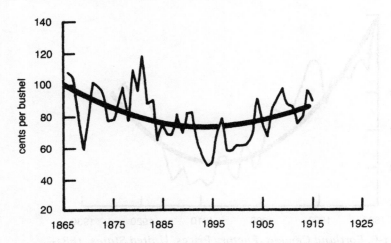

CHART I-8. *Wheat, December Farm Prices, United States, 1866–1915: Original Data and Primary Trend Line.*

Source: Kuznets, *Secular Movements,* p. 74.

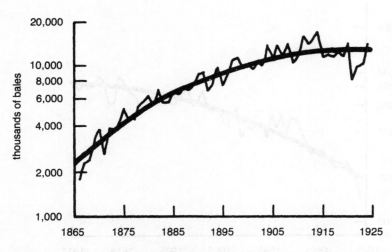

CHART I-9. *Cotton Crops, United States, 1866–1924: Original Data and Primary Trend Line.*

Source: Kuznets, *Secular Movements,* p. 83.

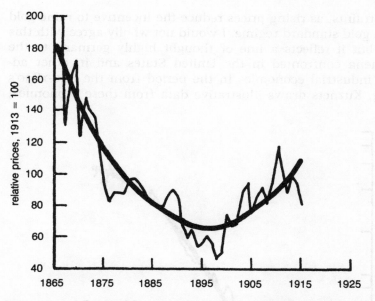

CHART 1-10. *Price of Raw Cotton, Upland Middling, New York, 1866–1915: Original Data and Primary Trend Line.*

Source: Kuznets, *Secular Movements*, p. 83.

the relations among output, prices, labor productivity, and real wages. He first demonstrated that secondary expansion and contraction in production around the primary trends were systematically preceded by price increases and decreases, suggesting clearly the role of price movements as a mechanism for shifting the direction of investment. In a sustained theoretical passage of some fifty pages, Kuznets then poses the question of why a period of rising prices should be, at once, a period of rapidly expanding output and of constrained real wages.[6] His answer is, essentially, that the downward relative shift in (urban) consumers' income, due to rising prices, is compensated for by reduced savings and by enlarged opportunities for employment in the production of capital goods, whose financing is rendered easier by the shift in income distribution from wages to profits. Kuznets then explores why an expansion phase of this kind should come to an end. He adduces a decline in labor productivity, as the working force in the rapidly expanding sectors is increased, combined with monetary restraints, as rising prices reduce the incentive to mine gold under a gold standard regime. I would not wholly agree with this model, but it reflects a line of thought highly germane to the phenomena confronted in the United States and in other advanced industrial economies in the period from the mid-1890's to 1914. Kuznets draws illustrative data from these economies;

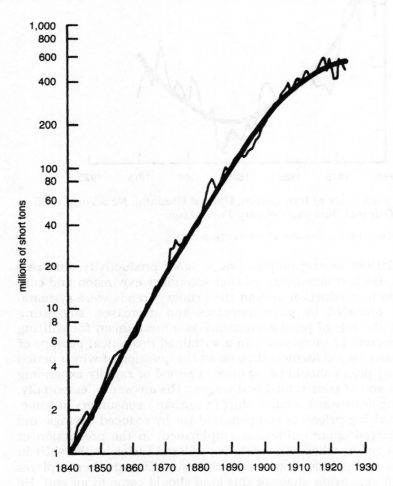

CHART I-11. *Bituminous Coal Output, United States, 1840–1924: Original Data and Primary Trend Line.*

Source: Kuznets, *Secular Movements*, p. 90.

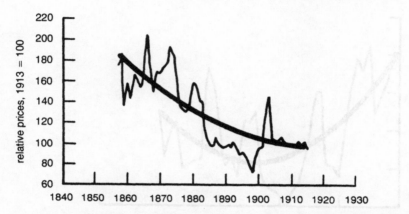

CHART I-12. *Bituminous Coal, Wholesale Prices, United States, 1857–1915: Original Data and Primary Trend Line.*

Source: Kuznets, *Secular Movements,* p. 91.

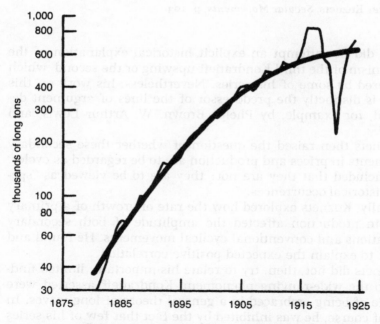

CHART I-13. *Copper Production, Smelter, Domestic Ore, United States, 1880–1924: Original Data and Primary Trend Line.*

Source: Kuznets, *Secular Movements,* p. 103.

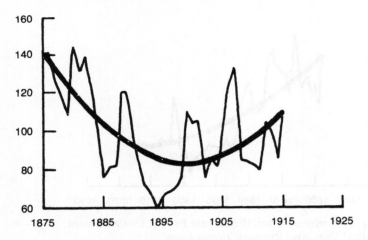

CHART I-14. *Price of Copper, United States, 1876–1915: Original Data and Primary Trend Line.*

   Source: Kuznets, *Secular Movements,* p. 103.

but he did not attempt an explicit historical explanation of the mechanism of the third Kondratieff upswing or the second, which is covered by some of his series. Nevertheless, his work on this period is distinctly the predecessor of the lines of argument developed, for example, by Phelps Brown, W. Arthur Lewis, and myself.

Kuznets then raised the question of whether these secondary movements in prices and production are to be regarded as cycles. He concluded that they are not: they are to be viewed as "specific, historical occurrences."[7]

Finally, Kuznets explored how the rate of growth of a primary trend in production affected the amplitude of both secondary fluctuations and conventional cyclical movements. He found and sought to explain the expected positive correlation.

Kuznets did not, then, try to relate his important, limited findings to the wide-ranging phenomena Kondratieff asserted were capable of being embraced in a general theory of long waves. In part, of course, he was inhibited by the fact that few of his series covered Kondratieff's century-and-a-quarter span. But, in any case, he wanted more flexibility in examining secondary fluctuations than acceptance of a fifty-year cycle would allow; and, besides, his secondary movements in production averaged twenty-two years; in prices, twenty-three.

In general, Kuznets regarded his book as a preliminary reconnaissance of the issues that had to be faced if a general dynamic theory of production and prices was to be built. Nevertheless, in its analysis of primary trends in a succession of leading sectors and in the lagged linkage he established between secondary trend movements in prices and production, this germinal study had a grip on two of the three key mechanisms I would regard as basic to an understanding of secular trends.

Kuznets then abandoned the world of refined sectoral analysis of production and prices for the highly aggregated field of comparative national income analysis. But he returned briefly to long waves in his *National Product since 1869*, in his essay "Levels and Variability of Rates of Growth," and at length in his celebrated paper of 1958, "Long Swings in the Growth of Population and in Related Economic Variables."[8] Here he elaborated suggestively a hypothesis which would link U.S. immigration to the pattern of investment—a hypothesis formulated in some detail by Brinley Thomas who, in turn, owed a good deal to A. K. Cairncross.[9] Kuznets asserted that the rhythm of American growth between the 1870's and the 1920's both attracted and was subsequently shaped by flows of immigration from abroad. As the most dynamic element in the rate of growth of U.S. population before its restriction in the 1920's, the scale of immigration substantially determined fluctuations in nonfarm residential construction; and its movement roughly coincided with fluctuations in capital expenditures for railroads. Trend fluctuations in other forms of investment were inverse to outlays on housing and railroads before the 1920's. Trend fluctuations in the per capita flow of goods to consumers tended to follow fluctuations in other forms of investment rather than outlays for nonfarm housing and railroads before the 1920's. Using overlapping ten-year averages, the peaks in population increase, nonfarm residential construction, and capital expenditure on railroads before 1914 come in the periods 1880–1890 and 1900–1910. For GNP (and GNP per capita) the peaks are 1875–1885 and 1900–1910. There is the familiar trough of the 1890's and evidence of some falling away in the pre-1914 decade. If one chooses to extend the analysis beyond 1914, despite two world wars and a uniquely severe depression, peaks emerge in 1920–1930 and 1940–1950 for population increase and GNP per capita.

This set of measurements is the proximate origin of a substantial part of the large literature on the "Kuznets cycle";[10] although Kuznets' quite legitimate claim to parenthood lies not in this line of thought, which is an extension of earlier formulations by others, but in the quite different mode of analysis that Kuznets used in his pioneering *Secular Movements in Production and Prices.*

We are dealing in Kuznets' 1958 essay with a narrow, straightforward hypothesis, essentially related to one economy over a relatively short period of time. It asserts, essentially, that a surge in population (and family formation) can have a significant effect on a major component of investment; and a surge in the size of the working force can produce a surge in output if not countered by excessive unemployment. Few would doubt this kind of linkage.

Empirically, the long-wave hypothesis was greatly strengthened by throwing in American railroads as a "population-sensitive" form of investment. This is how Kuznets did it: "Another 'population-sensitive' component of capital formation is capital expenditures by railroads, which reflect the long swings in population growth partly because they serve total population, partly because of concomitant swings in the volume of *internal* migration, either from the countryside to the cities or across the country's expanse. The long swings in capital expenditures by railroads are just as conspicuous as those in nonfarm residential construction, and even more closely related in timing to the long swings in population growth."[11]

As the leading sector in American growth from the 1840's to the 1880's, closely linked to the emergence of the steel industry after the Civil War, the railroads were surely connected in one way or another with immigration, population increase, internal population movement, and almost everything else that mattered in the American economy. And the waning of railroads as a leading sector in the 1890's is a significant factor in the protracted cyclical depression of that decade. But to designate the railroads as merely "population-sensitive" is to evade a good many basic analytic issues. Take, for example, the quite different economic motives for the railway booms of the 1840's and 1850's. The former linked industrial and commercial centers in the American Northeast, a direction of investment that commended itself (as in England) after the agricultural boom and bust of the 1830's in the American South and West. On the contrary, the railroad boom of the 1850's was positively related to the rise in the world wheat price and the attraction of opening up new wheat acreage in the Midwest. The motivation for the transcontinental lines built after the Civil War was still more complex. Then there is the problem of the decline of the railroads as a leading sector before 1914 (see Chart 1-15), at a time when immigration continued on a large scale. While, evidently, the sequence of great transport innovations—from turnpikes and canals to the trolley car, the automobile, and commercial aircraft—should have a major place in any analysis of the course of modern economic growth, we lose more than we gain by simply designating them as "population-sensitive."

There is a second characteristic of the Kuznets cycle in its later incarnation: prices disappear from the picture, except for a speculative observation—"One could also probably find long swings in price structures, i.e. in the relations of prices of various factors of production or of various groups of goods."[12] What one might call the orthodox Kuznets cycle school has focused primarily on establishing twenty-year cycles in a wide range of production and investment data.[13] In my view, the latter-day Kuznets cycle literature would have been greatly enriched and rendered more persuasive if it had been linked to the insights of the early Kuznets on price trends.

The exploration of long-period fluctuations over the past two decades has not been wholly dominated by the population-transport-infrastructure link. It has taken three directions.

First, there are those who have pursued and refined the demographic element which was at the heart of Kuznets' 1958 paper. Allen C. Kelley, for example, explored in Australia and elsewhere how a major change in the age-structure of a population, brought about by migration (or war), could set in motion waves in the rate of labor-force participation, in the formation of families (and housing construction), and in the savings rate.[14] Richard A. Easterlin, for example, using U.S. data, sought to clarify how an increased demand for labor could induce demographic change

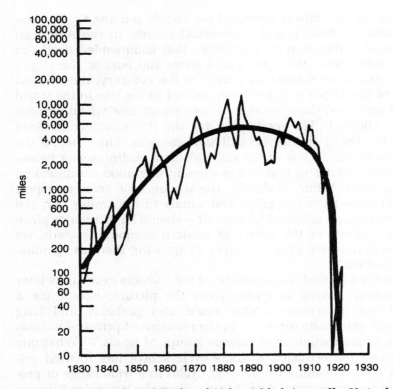

CHART 1-15. *Number of Railroad Miles Added Annually, United States, 1831–1922: Original Data and Primary Trend Line.*

Source: Kuznets, Secular Movements, p. 191.

(including fertility rates) and how this demographic change could then play back on the demand for housing and urban infrastructure, carrying this dimension of the Kuznets cycle analysis forward to the rise and collapse of the post-1945 U.S. baby boom.[15]

A second group of analysts looked for Kuznets cycles in a quite different direction: in flows of capital and trade balances rather than in flows of migrants. This raised questions about the motivation for international capital movements posed in the work of Thomas and Cairncross, but with a still older lineage reaching back at least to C. K. Hobson, to Frank Taussig and his distinguished pupils, and to others who explored what used to be called the transfer mechanism. Arthur I. Bloomfield used a long-cycle framework in reviewing fluctuations in international investment before 1914.[16] Country studies were done by Jeffrey G. Williamson and A. G. Ford, among others.[17] In the present narrow context, the point to be made is that these studies raised inevitably an issue posed by Kondratieff, explored by the early Kuznets (in his work on secondary movements in prices and production), but pretty well washed out by Schumpeter, the latter-day Kuznets, and their followers, that is, the relative abundance or scarcity of supplies of foodstuffs and raw materials. As Bloomfield noted: "A large but indeterminable part of the long-term capital that flowed to the 'newer' overseas countries before 1914 was undoubtedly stimulated directly or indirectly by the actual and prospective expansion of demand in the industrial centers for the primary products of these countries."[18] Bloomfield goes on to point out, quite correctly, that railroads and other foreign-financed infrastructure in these areas were often built for economic reasons that transcended a desire to expand exports and sometimes, even, for noneconomic reasons. But the flows of capital to Argentina, Australia, Canada, New Zealand, and (I would add) pre-1860 United States cannot be understood outside the context of the changing profitability of foodstuff and raw material production as decreed, on the one hand, by price movements of their export products and, on the other, by major developments in transport and other technology related to agriculture.

Behind the question of capital movements and price fluctuations in foodstuffs and raw materials lay deeper questions: What were the equilibrium levels of world output for foodstuffs and the various raw materials; what determined these levels; and what determined departures from them? What were the meaning and the consequences of the lagged price-output corrective mechanism caught by Kuznets in his measurement of secondary trends in foodstuff and raw materials, such as wheat, cotton, bituminous coal, and copper (see Charts 1-16 to 1-19)? International capital movements did not generally launch periods of expansion in foodstuff- and raw-material-producing areas. They moved in to exploit and support waves of prosperity already under way, triggered by the increased profitability of expanding output of particular foodstuffs and raw materials.[19] But they were palpably part of the process of balancing population expansion, urbaniza-

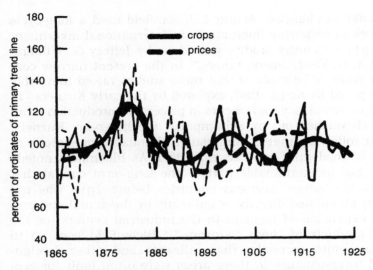

CHART I-16. *Wheat, Crops and Prices, United States, 1865–1925: Relative Deviations from Primary Trend Lines.*

Source: Kuznets, *Secular Movements*, p. 74.

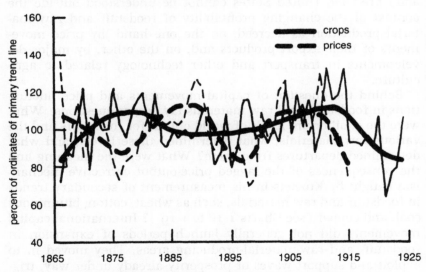

CHART I-17. *Cotton, Crops and Prices, United States, 1866–1915–1924: Relative Deviations from the Primary Trend Lines.*

Source: Kuznets, *Secular Movements*, p. 84.

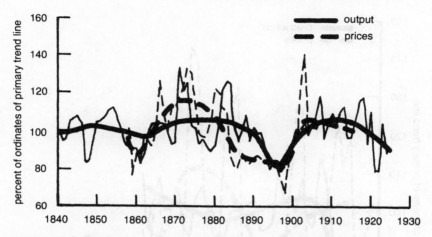

CHART 1-18. *Bituminous Coal, Output and Prices, United States, Output, 1840–1924; Prices, 1857–1915: Relative Deviations from Primary Trend Lines.*

Source: Kuznets, *Secular Movements*, p. 91.

tion, and the pace of industrialization with requisite increases in inputs. And changing prices and relative prices were critical to the whole clumsy effort to maintain dynamic equilibrium in the face of substantial lags. This is the perspective shared by W. Arthur Lewis' *Growth and Fluctuations, 1870–1913* and my *World Economy: History and Prospect.*

A third strand in latter-day Kuznets long-cycle analysis would link fluctuations in the rate of increase in output with the uneven sequence of major industrial innovations and consequent fluctuations in the capital-output (or capital-income) ratio. Here we return to the world of leading sectors—to Kuznets of primary secular movements, to A. F. Burns' study of sectoral retardation, and to Schumpeter's heroic innovations—linked, this time, to trend movements in production growth rates and productivity rather than to prices. E. H. Phelps Brown, S. J. Handfield-Jones, and Bernard Weber have evidently led the way in this mode of analysis,[20] which ultimately comes to rest on problems of productivity, real wages, and income distribution as well as fluctuations in overall growth rates.

Two final points should be noted about the intellectual history

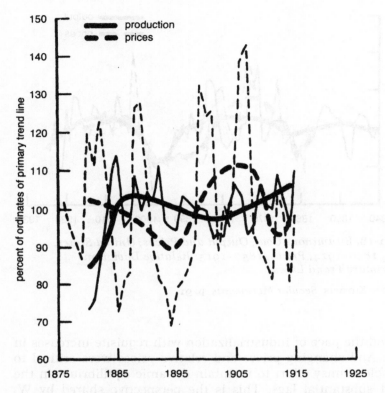

CHART 1-19. *Copper, Production and Prices, United States, 1880–1915: Relative Deviations from Primary Trend Lines.*

Source: Kuznets, *Secular Movements*, p. 104.

of Kuznets' cycle analysis. First, there emerges a growing awareness that what one is talking about in a latter-day Kuznets cycle
may be, simply, variation in the character of conventional business cycles (or Juglars) rather than an authentic cycle whose
rhythm and structure should supplant the concept of a Juglar.
Contrast, for example, these two observations of Moses Abramovitz made in 1961 and 1968, respectively:

> . . . continuing study has tended to cast doubt on the use-
> fulness of the Kondratieff and Juglar hypotheses and has
> concentrated attention on the postulated wave of intermedi-
> ate length.

These waves in growth rates are the smoothed reflection of the fact that at intervals of 15 to 20 years, the US economy suffered either a severe and protracted depression or else a period of pronounced stagnation in which business-cycle recoveries were disappointing and did not return the economy to full employment. In the intervening years, the economy experienced only mild and short recessions with expansions vigorous enough to make unemployment low at business-cycle peaks. One way to state the problem of the Kuznets cycles, therefore, is to ask why it is that America suffered unusually severe depressions, or protracted periods of milder recessions with disappointing recoveries, only at these long intervals, while in the interim employment remained at high levels subject to short mild recessions.[21]

Behind the latter proposition is the old notion, as A. F. Burns put it, that "the severity of a business depression is correlated with the intensity of the period of expansion preceding it."[22]

A second modification of the Kuznets cycle, suggested by Abramovitz in his "The Passing of the Kuznets Cycle," is that one ought to regard twenty-year waves in output as a phenomenon confined to the period "from about the 1840's to 1914." Certainly, if one builds the Kuznets cycle on migration, housing construction, and the railroads, it cannot be logically extended beyond 1914 in the United States. In fact, the railways, although still a massive outlet for investment, cease to be a leading sector before 1914. Over the period 1840–1914, there are two ambiguous and two clear cases of "severe and protracted depression": the ambiguous case of the late 1850's, merging as it did into the Civil War, which, without that circumstance, might well have proved neither severe nor protracted; the long and deep depressions of the 1870's and the 1890's; and the ambiguous case of the period 1909–1913, when the economy decelerated and unemployment was somewhat above the average of the period 1900–1907, but there was not "severe and protracted depression" in the same sense as in the 1870's and 1890's. Clearly, two cases do not justify a category of cycles. And one of them—the depression of the 1890's—is shadowed by the possible role of uncertainty about U.S. monetary policy in rendering the depression deeper and longer than it might otherwise have been.

I conclude, then, that the phenomena identified by Kondratieff were not brought by either Kuznets or Schumpeter within the framework of "an appropriate theory of long waves." Schumpeter tried but failed to link leading growth sectors to the upswings in long-term price cycles. The early Kuznets exposed some of the critical relationships among technology, prices, and production in the sectors but moved on to highly aggregated growth analysis before he achieved a synthesis responsive to Kondratieff's challenge. The later Kuznets dramatized long cycles in the United States related to immigration, housing construction, and railways; and he set others to work looking for long cycles elsewhere. But, under close examination, the phenomenon turned out to be more restricted in time and more limited in meaning than some first thought. Meanwhile, others looked to long-term capital movements and changing rates of increase in industrial production, related to the sequence of leading sectors, for partial insight into trends longer than conventional business cycles.

Putting aside my own earlier work on the subject, this was, roughly, the fragmented state of the literature when I confronted the task of dealing with long cycles (or trend periods) in the context of *The World Economy: History and Prospect*. I decided to apply a framework which could embrace the three phenomena generally examined separately in the work of Kondratieff's successors, that is, the sequence of leading growth sectors, the changes in the demand for and supply of foodstuff and raw materials and the changing pattern of investment they induced, and the relations between fluctuations in population, family formation, housing construction, and size of the working force.

III

We turn now to see how these three phenomena might be related to each other. It may be useful to begin this exercise in integration with a brief historical description of the phases of the Kondratieff cycle, starting with the first upswing from, say, 1790 to 1815. The role of each of the three phenomena will be indicated, along with the impact of war and peace and phases which violate the continuity of price and relative price trends.

1790–1815. The French Revolutionary and Napoleonic Wars (1793–1815) came after almost a half-century of gathering pressure of rising population on the British and European food supply. Britain, a food-surplus country early in the eighteenth century, gradually became a more or less regular importer of grain from Eastern Europe. The war broke out a decade after the British industrial revolution had begun in earnest, centered on the expansion of factory-made cotton textiles, the new methods of iron-making, and the diffusion of Watt's steam engine. There was, in the 1790's, a sharp rise in relative prices of agricultural products and raw materials. The claims of war on resources, and the necessity for expanding agriculture in Britain, damped the pace at which the major leading sector, cotton textiles, would otherwise have expanded. On the other hand, war conditions may have somewhat accelerated the expansion of the modern British iron industry. In the United States, war in Europe provided the new nation with an initial phase of high prosperity, based on the prices of its food and raw material exports. This interval of almost OPEC-like American prosperity not only eased the political problems of the new nation but also foreshadowed the dynamic process by which new nations and regions were to be drawn into the network of world trade by rising global requirements for food and raw materials. After 1807, Jefferson's embargo on foreign trade and the War of 1812 forced the United States to substitute its own manufactures for imports, which helped prepare the way for the post-1815 New England movement into modern industrialization. Some areas on the continent experienced similar forward movement in cotton textiles, but the British industrial lead as of 1793 had increased by 1815. Overall, the years down to 1815 were, for Britain and continental Europe, a period of relatively high food prices, which pressed down on real wages. The momentum of the leading sectors (notably, cotton textiles) cushioned this burden; but the combination of wartime diversions of resources and high food prices made the first Kondratieff upswing a difficult time for the urban worker.

There were no significant flows of immigration in this period, and, as usual, wartime conditions damped housing construction.

1815–1848. Here we have a classic Kondratieff downswing. With the coming of peace and normal access to Eastern European grain, agricultural and raw material prices broke sharply downward. The postwar abundance of grain and, after 1818, of cotton set a framework of relatively cheap foodstuffs and raw materials for the next decade. Cotton textile manufacture, the coming of the steamship on the rivers, and the diffusion of the steam engine to industry could proceed rapidly in this environment because basic commodities were relatively cheap. The 1830's broke the pattern temporarily. The pace of cotton industry expansion in the 1820's, in the United States and Western Europe as well as in Britain, yielded a raw cotton price explosion in 1833–1835. This made profitable the diversion of large U.S. and British capital flows to expand acreage in the American South; the West, too, absorbed substantial capital for transport development to make its agricultural products more marketable in the East. The great boom of the 1830's overshot the world market needs at existing prices. Prices and interest rates resumed their post-1815 trends in the 1840's, a period of rapid railroad and industrial expansion on both sides of the Atlantic: in the American Northeast and in Britain, Belgium, Germany, and France. This period experienced no significant diversions or distortions due to wars. But in the 1840's (notably, but not exclusively, in Ireland) there were signs that Europe's food-population balance was going awry. The potato crisis of 1845–1847 yielded a population push from land pressed too hard into European cities and across the Atlantic, leaving its mark to this day on populations as widely dispersed as New England, the upper Middle West, and Central Texas. Immigration begins to move up in the 1830's, drawn to the new areas opened up for cultivation and to industrializing New England; but a much stronger surge occurs in the 1840's, with Europe's food difficulties, continuing with minor interruption until late in the next decade. In the late 1830's we have the first appearance of a transatlantic rhythm which was to persist, more or less, down to 1914. The British contributed large capital flows to the American expansion of the first half of the 1830's. U.S. housing construction falls away from the peak in 1836, but Britain, no longer exporting capital to the United States, enjoys a second-stage construction boom running down to 1839–1840. In the 1840's, when agriculture prices were low, both countries enjoyed strong construction booms related to the laying down of railway lines on a large scale, as well as to a surge of immigration, in the case of the United States.

1848–1873. The price trends reverse sharply in this second Kondratieff upswing. As was the case for a few years after the Indian food crisis, 120 years later, the situation temporarily eased after the Irish potato famine. But the precarious balance in the Atlantic world between food and population increase yielded a sharp rise in grain prices in 1852–1854. Capital flowed lavishly from London and the American Northeast to open up the Middle West with a railway network. Cotton, after a decade's slack, also moved up in price, and acreage was opened up to the west as far as Texas. Urban real wages on both sides of the Atlantic came under severe pressure. The new leading sector—railroads—converged with food and raw material requirements, providing the means for bringing new acreage into production.

These agricultural demands for capital did not, however, prevent Western Europe from also moving forward rapidly with the railroads and the expansion of heavy industry down to 1873. The American Civil War, however, set back the United States and imposed transient constraints on the world's cotton supply, despite expanded cotton production in Brazil, Egypt, and India.

Between 1850 and the 1870's the much discussed inverse movement of British and American building cycles is quite marked and, to a degree, quite closely linked to the pace of immigration to the United States.

There was in the 1850's a major surge of immigration to the United States and a strong housing boom. Both variables fell off, as one would expect, during the Civil War, rebounding strongly thereafter until the cyclical peak of the early 1870's. Britain, on the other hand, experienced no great building expansion in the 1850's as immigrants and capital moved abroad and the Crimean War and Indian Mutiny contributed to high interest rates; but there was a major expansion in the 1860's which slackened off in the powerful capital export boom of the early 1870's. In the wake of the cyclical downturn, however, with interest rates reduced, Britain experienced some three years of strong building expansion, cushioning the general recession induced by sharply reduced exports.

The course of prices, interest rates, terms of trade, income distribution, and flows of capital in the world economy is distorted in this period by a series of minor wars and, for the first time, by the attractions of gold mining. The falling trend in prices since 1815 made gold a more attractive commodity because the price of gold was fixed in dollars and other currencies on the gold standard. Its real value, therefore, rose as the price level fell. A given amount of gold, commanding a fixed number of dollars, could purchase more goods and services. The incentive to find and mine gold increased; and, adventitiously or not (see below, Chapter 5, note 70), around mid-century prospectors struck it rich in California and Australia. The trans-Mississippi railroad extension after 1865 again drew (as in the 1850's) large flows of capital from London and the eastern American states. This process yielded in time enormous increases in grain exports, further cheapened by falling shipping rates. There was a transient energy crisis in the early 1870's, as the demand for British coal, at home and abroad, exceeded current mining capacity. An explosive rise in coal prices occurred; but accessible mines were quickly expanded. The framework was set for the second Kondratieff downswing, which was marked by strong downward trends in the prices of grain, coal, cotton, and most other raw materials.

1873–1896. In an interval of relative peace and abundance of foodstuffs and raw materials, as after 1815, the leading industrial sectors were driven forward in an uninhibited way. By the 1870's, railways had peaked out as a leading sector in most of the more industrialized countries. But they held up through the 1880's in the United States, where feeder lines and double-tracking were required to fill out and exploit the potentialities of the transcontinental railway structure earlier completed. Out of the railway's need for long-lasting rails had come, in the 1870's, cheap steel: the most powerful leading sector of the second Kondratieff downswing in the United States and Western Europe. Steel was soon being used for the construction of buildings and bridges, machine tools, ships, and more efficient steam engines. Meanwhile, electricity and new forms of chemicals began to move from laboratories to an early phase of application in the economy. But the railroad was not quite finished. In Canada, Australia, India, Argentina, and Russia it was beginning to transform the agricultural sectors—and not a moment too soon, for the limits of the American frontier were formally reached in the 1890's and the pull of the American agricultural and industrial economy in the post–Civil War period generated increases in population and urbanization which were about to limit the United States' grain export capacity with then existing agricultural technology.

In this period, the links among capital exports, immigration, and housing construction become more complex as Australia, Argentina, and Canada join the United States as "peripheral" regions. Britain experienced no substantial housing boom in the 1880's: in the early 1880's because the post-1873 boom had only recently subsided; in the mid- and late 1880's because there was substantial capital export and emigration to Canada and Australia; and in the late 1880's because of a major capital export boom centered on Argentina. A powerful housing construction boom occurred in the second half of the 1890's, when capital exports were low. On the other hand, the United States, after experiencing an extremely sharp decline in both immigration and housing in the post-1873 depression, underwent a building expansion throughout the 1880's, giving way to almost a decade of decline in the 1890's. Immigration, after peaking in the early 1880's, oscillated in a reasonably high range for the rest of the decade and collapsed in the depression of the mid-1890's.

From the early 1870's to the mid-1890's (as between 1815 and 1850), the trends in the world economy for prices and interest rates were down; real wage movements and income distribution favored the urban worker in industrial societies. As in the 1830's, there was a break in the continuity of these trends. The Argentine boom of the late 1880's and concurrent developments in South Africa drew large amounts of capital from abroad and stimulated the world economy in ways which triggered a brief inflationary interval. But in the first half of the 1890's, the post-1873 trend phenomena, notably falling prices and interest rates, reasserted themselves. Then came a reversal much like that of the early 1850's.

1896–1920. In this third Kondratieff upswing, relative shortages in foodstuffs and raw materials again emerged in an environment of small wars, enlarged military outlays, and then a great war. We are back in a period bearing a family resemblance to that of 1850–1873, including increased gold mining, notably in South Africa and Alaska. Large flows of capital to redress the balance in the world economy went this time not to the United States but to Australia, Argentina, southern Brazil, Canada, and Russia. All except Argentina experienced rapid industrial as well as agricultural expansion. Urban real wages in the older industrialized countries (e.g., Britain, United States, Germany) came under pressure, and profits did relatively well. The decline or deceleration of urban real wages contributed to the expansion of trade unions, to the rise of the British Labour party and the German Social Democratic party, and to pressure on democratic governments in the Atlantic world generally to allocate more resources to welfare purposes. In the United States, the forces generated by the third Kondratieff upswing helped strengthen the Progressive movement, as those feeling the constraint on real wages, imposed by the rising cost of living, turned to politics for redress.

The effects of the diversion of resources to agriculture (and to wider purposes in agricultural nations), to gold mining, to increased arms outlays, and to war were heightened by a transitional phase in the leading sectors of the more advanced industrial nations of the Atlantic world. The railroads were now an old and, at best, slowly expanding sector in these countries. Steel and all its related subsectors were still expanding; but expansion was at declining rates and, more important, with much diminished increases in productivity. As in the 1970's, there was in these pre-1914 years a general tendency for the rate of increase in productivity to slow down. Electricity, certain new chemicals, and the internal combustion engine were moving forward rapidly, but not at a rate sufficient to compensate for the decline in momentum and productivity of the older leading sectors. The net result of this tension between various diversionary capital and military outlays and the leading-sector transition was not uniform among the major industrial nations. It was most marked in Britain, where the Boer War was quite expensive; and it was followed by hitherto unprecedented levels of capital exports. It was a clear but less marked phenomenon in Germany and the United States, where the momentum of steel and all related to it, while decelerating, was sustained better than in Britain. In France, whose progress in the three preceding decades was relatively slow, there was some acceleration as the coming of electricity helped compensate for the lack of a Ruhr and the loss of Alsace-Lorraine in 1870. In a rough and ready way the links among British capital exports, immigration, and housing construction continued from the turn of the century down to the First World War. British housing construction slumped throughout this period, affected, successively, by the Boer War and, then, massive capital exports to Canada and elsewhere. Immigration to the United States remained high, as did housing construction, but with capital imports greatly diminished, as one would expect in a nation which had laid out its railway infrastructure, reached the end of its frontier, and moved briskly to industrial primacy. On the other hand, large flows of capital continued to Canada, Australia, Brazil, and Argentina which experienced strong surges in both immigration and housing construction.

In Europe, the First World War, on balance, accentuated and distorted the pattern of this trend period; that is, the character of the military conflict created artificially high requirements for steel and other heavy-industry products of the aging leading sectors, while also inducing a further expansion of agriculture in non-European areas which proved unprofitable after 1920. The United States and Canada shared, of course, in this transient agricultural expansion; but it was during the First World War that the United States moved solidly into the age of the mass automobile, with Canada in line astern, providing a strong leading sector for the prosperity of the 1920's. Britain became a net capital importer for the period 1915–1919, while flows of immigration from Europe were greatly attenuated during the period of conflict.

1920–1933. In 1920, the prices of agricultural products and raw materials broke sharply downward, in both absolute and relative terms. This movement, favorable to industrial societies and regions, lifted the real income of urban families but reduced the incomes and purchasing power of those dependent on the production and sale of food and raw materials. Stocks of these commodities built up in the 1920's and overwhelmed the markets when general depression struck the world economy in 1929. In the United States the new leading sectors of high mass-consumption (motor vehicles and electric-powered durable consumer goods) carried the economy forward at a rate consistent with high levels of employment; but the more advanced industrial nations of Europe did not fully recover in the 1920's. France from 1925 to 1929 did best, aided by a currency devaluation which strengthened its relative export and tourist positions. But, in general, the weakness of Europe's traditional pre-1914 export markets and a level of income per capita that was lower than in the United States converged to produce a situation where the new leading sectors of high mass-consumption did not move forward rapidly enough to bring the major economies back to sustained full employment. Then came the Great Depression, with catastrophic consequences in both industrial and basic commodity sectors.

There are, of course, many unique features to the interwar period, but, as compared to its predecessors (1815–1848 and

1873–1896), its central characteristic is that relatively cheap prices for basic commodities did not, in themselves, encourage a sufficiently accelerated diffusion of the new leading sectors to avoid a retardation of overall growth in the most advanced economies.

The pre-1914 pattern of immigration, capital flows, and construction cycles did not reassert itself in the post-1930 environment. Immigration to the United States was inhibited by law after 1924, and the relative prices of agricultural products did not encourage capital flows (or migration) on the previous scale. In Britain, housing construction, while still reflecting demographic forces, became substantially affected by public policy.

1933–1951. Here, again, we are in a time of relatively rising prices of basic commodities and the distortions of war. Recovery after 1932–1933 occurred against a background of reduced output of basic commodities which, at last, began to yield a reduction of the large stocks which had overhung the markets in the 1920's and early 1930's. From about 1936 rearmament accelerated. The war reduced agricultural production in most of Europe and increased it in overseas areas, as had happened a quarter of a century earlier. Relative shortages persisted, down to 1951, affected by the slower pace of European agricultural than industrial recovery and by the Korean War. Then, as in 1920, prices broke downward, relatively as well as absolutely.

1951—1972. This time the outcome for the world economy was quite different from that between the wars. The leading sectors of high mass-consumption moved forward rapidly in North America, Western Europe, and Japan, strengthened by cheap energy, food, and raw materials. There was another difference: despite weakened prices for basic commodities, especially in the 1950's, Asia, the Middle East, Africa, and Latin America also moved forward in earlier stages of growth. Their capacity to do so, in what might otherwise have been severely adverse circumstances, was assisted by the extraordinary and sustained boom in the advanced industrial nations which provided strong markets for their exports and by the provision of a substantial official flow of capital for development purposes, on concessional terms, in addition to considerable flows of private capital. For the first time in history, a large number of the nations of Latin America, Africa, the Middle East, and Asia sought systematically to modernize their economic and social life through development plans of in-creasing, if uneven, sophistication and effectiveness.

In the United States from the late 1950's, the automobile and durable consumer goods sectors (embracing also the movement to suburbia, massive road-building, etc.) began to lose their mo-mentum. They were superseded as a basis for growth by a rapid expansion of private and public outlays for education, health, and travel. These service sectors also expanded in Western Eu-rope and Japan where the automobile–durable consumer goods revolution continued swiftly down through the 1960's, but at a decelerating pace toward the end of the decade.

As the 1960's wore on, it was also evident, beneath the surface, that the rapid global expansion in food and energy requirements was altering the balance which had existed since the downward price turn in 1951. One region after another moved into a grain-deficit position or enlarged its imports: Latin America, Eastern Europe and the Soviet Union, Africa, and Asia. The United States, Canada, Argentina, and Australia were left virtually alone as food-surplus nations. Grain reserves as a proportion of annual global consumption fell away. A food crisis in India from 1965 to 1967 was a significant warning of what was to come. Similarly, the pace of energy consumption in the United States converged with a reduction of American gas and oil reserves to require a rapid in-crease in U.S. oil imports. In 1972 the food situation came to crisis; in 1973, OPEC (Organization of Petroleum Exporting Countries), perceiving its monopolistic leverage in a world where the United States was no longer a potential energy exporter, moved to exploit that leverage by a fourfold increase in prices. In a sense, the second Kondratieff downswing was ended by the United States reaching the end of its agricultural frontier, given existing agricultural prices and technologies; the fourth Kondra-tieff downswing was ended by the United States reaching the end of its gas and oil frontier, given existing energy prices and technologies.

1972–1979. The price revolution of 1972–1979, like its four predecessor Kondratieff upswings, altered the terms of trade, in-come distribution, and the rate of inflation in familiar ways. Its effects on the balance of payments position of the industrial world also set in motion a severe recession in 1974–1975, bringing to an end the great post-1945 boom. It struck directly at the leading sectors: the automobile, durable consumer goods, and a new range of chemicals (e.g., plastics and synthetic textiles). All were energy intensive. The recession, combined with continued inflation, struck at both real tax revenues and, even more, the willingness of taxpayers to continue to allocate an increasing share of their income to public services. In the United States, its impact was particularly severe in the northern industrial states. In the developing world, the direct impact was most severe among the poorest nations; but virtually all, except the oil monopolists, were hit by the stagnation of the advanced industrial world, as well as by the higher costs of oil imports. A recovery began in 1975–1976, but the prospects were for lower growth rates in the OECD world (and higher unemployment) than in the Kondratieff downswing of the 1950's and 1960's; this probability diminished also the prospects for the developing nations which did not command oil surpluses.

IV

The sequence outlined above would be, I suspect, more or less accepted as a summary statement of historical fact. The analytic challenge has been to relate some or all components of this pattern to each other in a coherent and persuasive way.

Brinley Thomas has been a pioneer in this kind of analytic effort. His early work on migration and investment was, as noted above, one of the foundations on which the latter-day Kuznets cycle was built. In the second (1973) edition of his *Migration and Economic Growth*, he presents the most sophisticated version of his theory. It rests on the following hypotheses for a two-country model:

(i)   Each is divided into two sectors, home construction and export.

(ii)   C exports capital goods and D food and raw materials.

(iii) Migration depends on the difference in real wages which can be approximated by the difference in real incomes.

(iv)   Export capacity is generated through population-sensitive capital formation, i.e., the building of infrastructure—railways, roads, land clearing, ports, houses, public utilities, etc.—and this investment has a relatively long gestation period. There is an inter-temporal relation between a country's infrastructure investment in one period and its export capacity in the next period.

(v) The level of activity of a country's export sector depends on the expected marginal efficiency of investment in the construction sector of the other country. The marginal efficiency of investment is the marginal physical product of capital multiplied by the ratio of the price of output to the price of capital input. Applied to exported output, this means that the marginal efficiency of investment depends on the expected future purchasing power per unit of factor input, i.e., the "single factoral terms of trade."

(vi) A major fraction of total capital formation is population-sensitive, i.e., varying with the rate of change in population growth and internal migration.

(vii) The population growth rate is a function of population structure (i.e., a vector showing proportions of population in various age and sex groups) and the external migration balance.

(viii) The countries are linked by a gold standard with specie currency.[23]

Thomas then proceeds to test these hypotheses, mainly over the period 1878–1913, with formal statistical evidence and historical narrative covering the U.S.-U.K. interaction, as well as the Canadian and Australian cases.

Without entering into a detailed critique of Thomas' system, three characteristics should be noted:

1. Migration, set in motion by perceived differences in real wages, is the engine which sets in motion the sequence of cyclical interaction between creditor and peripheral countries. Except for his reference to the single factoral terms of trade, the role of relative prices hardly appears in Thomas' system. In his view the terms of trade shift as a result of the flows of migration and capital to peripheral countries, not as an initiating cause of such flows (pp. 256–258, 261, and 264). Thomas supplies no explanation for the price trends in the period he examines, and, indeed, his valuable statistical appendixes contain no price series.

2. Thomas accepts Kuznets' concept of "population-sensitive"

investment which lumps together housing construction, directly related to demographic change, and transport investment, often related to the believed profitability of opening up new agricultural and raw material producing areas.

3. Thomas does not attempt to deal with the rhythm of technological innovations in relation to the course of productivity, although he makes some brief, highly aggregated observations on productivity trends (pp. 283–287). Gold production is referred to in a few episodic asides. Wars are treated mainly in terms of their impact on migration.

I conclude that Thomas' analysis captures important aspects of the relation between industrial, capital-exporting regions and peripheral agricultural regions. I believe he is quite correct in protesting against excessively nationalist and parochial analyses of long cycles (p. xxiv). In terms of the issues explored in this chapter, he links, to a degree, two of the three elements in long-cycle analysis, that is, the opening up of peripheral areas and the forces set in motion by migration. And I share his emphasis on the importance of disproportionate lags in the investment process in peripheral regions. But Thomas' system is weakened by his failure to deal with relative price movements and the technological and political changes which, in fact, determined at various times the expected rate of return over cost for investments in basic commodities. This failure, in turn, helps explain the quasi-autonomous role migration plays in his construct and the unhelpful lumping together of housing construction and transport investment as "population-sensitive."

Thomas' monetary views are considered in Chapter 5.

W. Arthur Lewis, like Thomas, is concerned with interactions between the core and the periphery over the period 1870–1913. His wider-ranging analysis, as incorporated in *Growth and Fluctuations, 1870–1913*, differs from Thomas' in a number of important respects:

1. He places shifts in industrial prices relative to agricultural prices firmly at the center of the stage. It is the engine which determined not only capital flows and, to a significant degree, patterns of migration but also the course of real wages in the core areas. As I do, he takes movements in relative prices to be the key variable determining the cycles that Kondratieff identified but did not explain.

2. Lewis also provides an analytic rationale for cycles in rela-

tive prices. He does so by examining systematically the demand for and supply of the products of peripheral regions. This leads him into calculations of the rate of growth and pattern of fluctuations in industrial production in the core region, as a surrogate for the demand for agricultural products and raw materials; a rationale for Kuznets cycles, which he views as a sequence of stronger and weaker (Juglar 8-year) business expansions, deeper and shallower depressions; and a systematic review of alternative theories of the Kondratieff cycle, including those of the monetarists.

3. Unlike Thomas, Lewis takes into account the dynamics of pre-industrial development in the tropical regions, including the role of Indian and Chinese migration.

4. Lewis directly confronts the question of the deceleration in productivity in the core countries in the pre-1914 years and concludes that it is mainly the consequence of reduced hours of work. The deceleration in real wages in the core countries he attributes primarily to the unfavorable shift in the terms of trade.

In my view, Lewis' analytic structure embraces more of the relevant phenomena than does Thomas'. My major difference with Lewis' formulation is its overaggregated treatment of the productivity deceleration in the core countries in the pre-1914 period, which fails to capture the rapid deceleration of the old leading sectors not adequately compensated for by the emergence of new leading sectors with rapid momentum but insufficient weight in the economy as a whole.

I would also offer this reflection on all the analyses which attempt to trace out the impact of a substantial shift in the terms of trade, including my own previous work in the field. It is, I believe, helpful to separate out more explicitly than we generally do the following four distinct elements in the impact of a favorable shift in the terms of trade in a peripheral region:

1. *A direct real income effect.* By permitting a larger quantity of imports to be acquired with a fixed quantum of exports a favorable shift in the terms of trade directly raises real income.

2. *An increase of immigration.* Population is likely to flow to the country experiencing the lift in real income brought about by a favorable shift in the terms of trade, a lift heightened with the passage of time, by the forces delineated in elements 3 and 4.

3. *An expansion of investment and acceleration of growth.* The investment rate in the country experiencing favorable terms of trade is likely to rise for three distinct reasons: to supply housing

and urban infrastructure for the migrants; to supply infrastructure and other capital to expand output of the commodities whose relative rise in price has caused the favorable shift in the terms of trade; and to exploit disproportionately high profit possibilities through increased capital imports.

4. *A possible acceleration of industrialization.* If the peripheral society experiencing the expansionary impulses set out in elements 1–3 is otherwise prepared to absorb new technologies efficiently, the forces set in motion by a favorable shift in the terms of trade can yield a surge of industrialization. This happened, for example, in pre-1914 Canada, Australia, and southern Brazil. It is happening now in a good many OPEC countries as well as in the western mountain region of the United States. It did not happen in pre-1914 Argentina, nor the tropical countries, which benefited to a degree from the increased real income provided by their expanding plantation sectors but did not move on, at that time, into sustained industrialization.

V

What is the lesson of this review for the "appropriate theory of long waves" that Kondratieff defined as the objective, but which his successors have never quite achieved?

I believe the lesson is that long cycles or trends can only be explained on the basis of a general, disaggregated dynamic theory of production and prices. It must be capable of embracing the three major trend phenomena explored here and relating them to each other. But a system capable of explaining and relating the pace and characters of technological change, relative price movements, and population movements can be not much less than the grand dynamic theory the young Kuznets envisaged in the passage quoted earlier in this chapter.

Evidently, I cannot elaborate fully here the terms of such a theory, but I can suggest its character as it bears on the three major phenomena examined in this chapter and the general problem of secular trends:

1. A satisfactory dynamic theory of production and prices must render substantially endogenous the sequence of major inventions and innovations—the leading-sector complexes—as well as the incremental improvements in productivity embraced under the case of increasing returns, as conventionally defined. (We

consider this problem in Chapter 4.) It follows that the allocation of resources to science and invention must be treated as part of the investment process, and the quality of entrepreneurship must be specified.

2. It must deal with birth and death rates—the demographic transition—as part of the economic process, as well as education (as it affects the quality of the working force) and both domestic and international migration.

3. It must deal with the determinants of the level of investment.

4. It must, above all, specify the determinants of the sectoral composition of investment.

It is not difficult to conceive of a theoretical optimum path of overall growth from formal assumptions (or statistical data) which tell us the rate of increase in population, the size and quality of the working force, the scale and productivity of capital investment. But such models (and highly aggregated statistical exercises based on them) give us no grip on long cycles, for these cycles are inherently sectoral phenomena, although reflected in aggregate production and price indexes.

What we need, therefore, is the concept of optimum levels of sectoral prices and output, related to the level and rate of increase of output as a whole, that is, related to demands set up by the level and rate of increase of consumers' income (with given tastes); to the level, character, and rate of increase in required industrial inputs, including transport; and to the supply conditions in the sectors, including not only agricultural acreage and raw material resources but also the changing state of technology and entrepreneurship. An optimum sectoral pattern of investment would flow directly from this concept of optimum sectoral paths. Price movements would signal deviations away from the optimum sectoral paths and by altering profit possibilities (along with technological change) would alter also the pattern of investment and thus bring the sectoral structure of production back toward dynamic equilibrium. (We try to capture something of this process, in a formal way, in Chapter 2.)

If we are to dynamize a Walrasian price-output system, we must, then, set aside diminishing returns as a general, ruling assumption. We must permit changing technology, expanding high-productivity agricultural and raw material resources, and increasing returns. We are, thus, talking about a formidably complex model: in effect, a fully dynamic multisector model, sufficiently disaggregated to catch all changes in production functions actually introduced into the economic system. At first glance, it seems an impossible dream.

But, in fact, the task is intellectually manageable, as indicative planners have demonstrated in advanced industrial countries and development planners in less advanced economies. They have, in practice, roughly calculated optimum sectoral paths linked to the overall rate of growth, the dynamics of consumers' demand, the input requirements of industry, and the potentialities of the resources and technologies available to them. And they have tried to persuade their governments and induce their private sectors to approximate them. Their success has, of course, varied; but they have demonstrated that, in reasonable approximation, the job can be done.

For our limited purposes in exploring secular trends, we can, at some risk of oversimplification, limit our disaggregation to four kinds of sectors:

—*The leading-sector complexes*, that is, those centered historically on factory-manufactured textiles, the steam engine, modern iron technology, the railroads; steel; electricity; the major branches of the modern chemical industry; the automobile; the aerospace complex; the service sectors (notably, higher education and health services) which expanded so rapidly in real terms during the 1950's and 1960's. Historically, these technologies unfolded in a sequence generated by a mixture of the income elasticity of consumers' demand and the evolving requirements of industry and transport. In the contemporary world of developing nations they are drawn from the pool of existing technologies and are productively absorbed in a sequence related to private and public demands and the technical absorptive capacity of particular economies. At any period of time the industrial structure of an economy which has moved beyond take-off will consist, in part, of old leading-sector complexes as well as new ones, with the latter moving forward at high rates while the former decelerate, level off, or even absolutely decline. By and large, sectoral rates of productivity increase are related to the sector's rate of growth. The average rates of productivity increase in industry have thus been sustained by the supplanting of old leading sectors with new ones.

—*The agriculture sector*, excluding agricultural inputs to industry. Here the link is to the population increase, the rate of increase of private income per capita, and the income elasticity of demand for food in general and for specific types of food.

—*Inputs to the industrial system*, that is, energy, raw materials, and products of agriculture. Here the link is to the rate of increase of industrial output, whose composition, in turn, is determined mainly by the stage of growth of the system, its leading sectors, and the composition of its exports.

—*Housing and infrastructure*. Here the link is to the rate of family formation as decreed by population increase, domestic and international migration, and factors determining the rate of urbanization—since social overhead capital outlays tend to be greater per capita in urban than rural areas.

To convert a disaggregated sectoral model of this kind into one which yields an approximation of secular movements in production and prices, one must make four assumptions:

—The proportion of income invested within a national post–take-off economy, if not absolutely fixed, varies within relatively narrow limits. As Kuznets wrote of the United States, in noting the inverse correlation between railroad and nonfarm residential construction, on the one hand, and other forms of capital formation, on the other, there seemed to be "some limits to *total* capital formation in the country, perhaps largely on the savings side."[24]

—The dynamic system does not adjust instantaneously. There are lags between the appearance of a profit possibility (due to price movements, discoveries, or new technology) and an effective flow of new investment; between the initiation of investment and its completion; between its completion and its full contribution to the flow of goods and services to the economy. And these lags may vary significantly with different types of investment—a critical aspect of the formal model of the Kondratieff cycle presented in Chapter 2.

—Current investment decisions tend to be made on a micro-basis, responding to current indicators of future profitability; and there is a follow-the-leader tendency in capital markets. This fact, plus inherent lags in the investment process, produces a systematic tendency to overshoot the sectoral optima once evidence of profitability in a major line of investment is recognized and acted upon.

—The system is international, in the specific sense that flows of migration and of capital are possible, and that a wide range of prices are determined by demand and supply situations throughout the world economy.

Without formulating the matter in these terms, what Kondratieff, Schumpeter, and the early and late Kuznets were getting at —and all the others who have analyzed trend movements—were the forces set in motion by the imperfect effort of the world economy to approximate, under these four conditions, an optimum pattern of growth in these four kinds of sectors. Looked at in this way, we are not examining different theories of secular movements in prices and production but aspects of the dynamic adjustment process in particular national economies within a more or less interconnected world economic system.

At certain times and places the march of the leading sectors and the requirements for inputs of foodstuffs and raw materials converged, notably with the coming of the railroads and more efficient steel ships. Within national economies, however, these four demands for investment resources more usually competed. For example, pre-1914 Canada, and other nations and regions undergoing a similar experience, not only had to expand acreage but also had to invest in housing and urban infrastructure as the immigrants flowed in and large-scale internal migration occurred. And in that process, an expansion of industry also became profitable. When Britain invested massively abroad, the resources available to build houses and urban infrastructure at home were attenuated. Thus, the housing boom which followed the crisis of 1873 down to 1877 and the rush of home railways, gas works, and water companies into the capital market during the slump of 1908. Within this framework of competing demands for a limited volume of national (and international) investment resources, how were priorities established and how did they change? Leaving inventory cycles aside, the normal form of adjustment by which the investment process proceeded down to the post-1945 era was the medium cycle, or Juglar. Generally speaking, the key sectors leading expansion in each Juglar varied from cycle to cycle. Overshooting in one cycle temporarily exhausted profitability in those directions, but prior neglect or new technology yielded profitability in a batch of somewhat different key sectors in the next upswing. Thus, the rather elegant rhythm of the American economy between 1815 and 1860, with booms primarily focused on agriculture and on industry following each other in sequence until they fully converge in the 1850's. After the Civil War, we have the three majestic Juglars peaking in 1872, 1882, and 1892, combining, as in the 1850's, extensive agricultural expansion and industrial development, the former involving investment with relatively long periods of gestation. From the mid-1890's to 1914, industrial development clearly dominates, with shorter periods of gestation, a fact which may account for the shorter and generally less volatile fluctuations down to 1914, excepting the acute but short-lived collapse of 1908.

What, then, of the price and investment trends which persisted for longer periods—for it is these that Kondratieff dramatized and on which a great deal of the long-cycle and trend literature comes to rest.

Although subject to Juglars, two of our four sectors are controlled by forces with a longer life than nine or ten years: the leading-sector complexes and that form of generating agricultural and industrial inputs that involved the opening up of large new unexploited areas.

The paths of (say) textiles, railroads, and the diffusion of the automobile leave their mark not on one Juglar but, in increasing and then receding degree, on a sequence of Juglars. And the transition from one leading-sector complex to another can have consequences for the overall rate of growth as, for example, in Britain, Germany, and the United States from the mid-1890's to 1914; in interwar Western Europe; and during the sluggish interval in the United States in the late 1950's.

But the dynamics of opening up a peripheral region could also involve time periods longer than a Juglar. The period of gestation of investment tended to be longer than in industry or older agricultural areas; the period before investment yielded its full productive contribution to the economy could also be longer than was normal elsewhere. Thus, the incentive to continue to invest in a given area could persist, even if temporarily broken from time to time by the rhythm of the Juglars. This is essentially what happened in the progressive opening up of the American West. In effect, it took three post-1865 Juglars to open up and consolidate the trans-Mississippi area. It was the momentum of that process, reflected in the relatively mild Juglar depression of the mid-1880's, which accounted for the virtually unbroken rise of the building index, the continuity of net capital imports, and the brief setback to immigration of the mid-1880's. Similar protracted periods were required to open up and consolidate Australia, Argentina, and Canada between 1880 and 1914. The attraction of opening up these areas was by no means uniform year by year or even cycle by cycle; but domestic and (sporadically) foreign capital were drawn to the task until the efficient absorption into the international economy was complete.

It was in the periods of rising foodstuff and raw material prices after the mid-1840's and mid-1890's that the time lags involved in such enterprises had their greatest effect. Rising prices drew resources to the peripheral regions, but the lagged and complex process of their development helped reinforce the upward price trend until their increase in commodity output yielded overshooting which helped set the framework for the Kondratieff downswings after 1873 and, with the added distortion of war, 1920.

As we have seen, international migrations as well as capital movements are linked to this process. In general, international migration movements appear to be of three types. First, there have been movements from more developed to less developed areas, when the latter have attractive population-resource balances and relatively high real incomes. This is the kind of movement on which Brinley Thomas concentrates. Second, there have been movements from less developed to more developed industrial areas, when the latter are enjoying periods of short-run prosperity and high secular growth rates relative to others, for example, the movement of labor from south to north in Europe of the 1950's and 1960's. The flow of immigrants to the United States in the period 1902–1914 must be accounted primarily an example of this type of international migration. Third, there have been movements from low productivity pre-industrial nations to higher productivity pre-industrial nations, for example, the flow of Indians to East and South Africa and the flow of Chinese to Southeast Asia.

The interweaving of the leading-sector complexes and the agricultural sector, linked in different ways to the overall path of growth and relative price movements and setting in motion between them the major flows of capital and migrants, thus explains most of the phenomena isolated for study in the literature of sectoral trends. From Kondratieff's initial list of possibly relevant variables, we are left with gold and wars. We shall deal with gold in Chapter 5.

As for war, it strongly reinforced the first Kondratieff upswing in prices and the abnormal expansion in British agriculture. Agricultural prices were rising disproportionately before 1793, but there is no doubt that the attentuation of supplies from Eastern Europe imposed by war exacerbated the underlying problem. In the second upswing, we have the Crimean War, the Indian Mutiny, and the American Civil War, as well as Bismarck's three ventures. In the third, the Spanish-American and Boer Wars and the Russo-Japanese and Balkan Wars, climaxed by that of 1914–1918. In the fourth, the Second World War and the Korean War occur. All these conflicts reinforce the inflationary tendency at work in the Kondratieff upswings; but in all cases it is possible to demonstrate that they did not initiate them.

But Kondratieff implied not that wars caused or contributed to long-cycle price increases but that, somehow, long-cycle upswings led to wars. All the wars just cited involved issues of relative national power. Most of them involved, also, physical control over territory. But only the American Civil War can be linked in any coherent way to the expansion process decreed by the rising prices and increasing demands for food, which are the mark of the Kondratieff upswing. These asserted themselves in the 1850's and helped induce the extensive railroad expansion of that decade. The westward march of the railroad in the 1850's and the foreseeable absorption into the Union of all that lay between the Mississippi and California did, indeed, force onto the political agenda the constitutional issues that led to war, although those issues were rooted, of course, in slavery. That is all one can rationally make of the causal linkage Kondratieff implied between long-cycle upswings and wars. But the tensions that exist or might develop over scarce or prospectively scarce resources in the period which began in 1972 suggest that we might take Kondratieff's observation as a warning against the dangerous potentialities of the neomercantilism which is one possible outcome of the fifth Kondratieff upswing.

VI

Or, is it a Kondratieff downswing? As the contours of the world economy changed so disconcertingly in the 1970's, after a generation of rapid and easily attained growth, people sought in various directions an intellectual framework capable of explaining what had happened to the structure of the world economy and of foreshadowing what lay ahead.

In the English-speaking world the first revival of the Kondratieff cycle applied to the 1970's was incorporated by James B. Shuman and David Rosenau in *The Kondratieff Wave*, published in 1972. Writing before the price explosion, which began at the end of that year, and viewing the past in terms of overall price indexes rather than the prices of basic commodities relative to industrial products, they saw the 1950's and 1960's as part of a long upswing that began in the 1930's, which was giving way to a downswing as the 1970's began. They were quite insensitive to the more than 20 percent favorable shift in the terms of trade for advanced industrial countries which played such a substantial role in the boom of the 1950's and 1960's. They accepted wars as an integral part of the Kondratieff cycle, without explaining the economic mechanism of their detonation, and viewed the war in Southeast Asia as a "peak war" like the First World War. They envisaged the 1970's as a kind of return to normalcy, explicitly analogous to the situation of the United States in the 1920's: "The 1970's, therefore, will be characterized by federal expenditures reduced in relation to the gross national product, federal surpluses, stable prices or mild deflation, high prosperity, and no inflation. It will be a time when material wants, long denied by years of war and inflation, will be filled—years when American industry will produce goods to fill those needs rather than produce consumables for war."[25] After this amiable interval the authors predicted for the 1980's a long and severe depression, analogous to that of the 1930's.

Shuman and Rosenau extended their cyclical observations and predictions over a wide range: attitudes toward religion and sex, types of popular music, art, dress, and so on. They provided no theory of long cycles, however, beyond some observations on the self-reinforcing processes set in motion by falling and rising prices and profit margins. Some of their predictions appear, with hindsight, prescient; others, including their basic analogy between the 1920's and 1970's, less so. Indeed, the proportion of GNP allocated by the United States for military purposes has fallen sharply in the 1970's; and, for reasons the authors did not envisage, strong pressures are at work to contain or reduce the proportion of public outlays to GNP. They failed to perceive the underlying forces operating in the 1960's which produced the massive unfavorable alteration in the terms of trade in 1972–1974. The situation in the 1920's was, of course, quite contrary; it was marked by extremely favorable terms of trade for industrialized societies. It is on this fundamental point that the Shuman-Rosenau analogy fails.

Ernest Mandel's *Late Capitalism* reaches similar apocalyptic conclusions by a far more sophisticated analytic route. It was published in German in 1972; in English, updated to a degree, in 1978. In its latest version, it is a massive study of over six hundred pages.[26] It seeks to explain in unadulterated Marxist terms the main features of modern economic history, especially the post-1945 boom in the advanced industrial countries of the non-communist world and the reasons "it would be followed by another long wave of increasing social and economic crisis for world capitalism, characterized by a far lower rate of overall growth." Mandel argues that multiple forces are tending to reduce the rate of profit; that these are compounded by the pressure of wage demands in excess of productivity increases which can only be contained by incomes policies which he counsels labor to resist; and that the inner contradictions of late capitalism will force the bourgeoisie into armed violence to protect surplus-value. The primary cause of declining profits, however, is distinctly Schumpeterian: the waning capacity of the great innovations of the previous upswing (which he takes to be the electronic and nuclear power industries) to carry forward the growth process in a setting of capitalism.

Putting aside Mandel's political pamphleteering, the structural weakness of his system is that it is a two-sector model which (like neoclassical growth models) fails to take into account fluctuations in the relative abundance or scarcity, relative prices and profitability of investment in agricultural products, raw materials, and energy. They are embedded in Mandel's system somewhere in Marx' Department 1 (capital goods). He misses, therefore, a good deal that is central to all the Kondratieff long upswings he examines; misses the critical role of declining relative prices for basic commodities in the boom of the 1950's and 1960's; and fails to introduce adequately in this 1978 edition the meaning of the price revolution of 1972–1978.

As we shall see, this failure bears significantly on Mandel's assessment of the prospects for democratic capitalist societies.

There are ample opportunities and need for productive investment in the generation ahead in resource-related fields, for example, energy production and conservation, the control of pollution, agricultural output to match the population bulge in the developing regions, raw material development, transport, research and development over a wide front. For our times, investments of this kind are the equivalent, say, of those required to open up the American West in the third quarter of the nineteenth century, during the second Kondratieff upswing, and those in Canada, Australia, and Argentina in the pre-1914 generation which experienced the third Kondratieff upswing. Although the rate of growth of urban real income may be less than in the 1950's and 1960's, the time ahead need be neither a period of stagnating real income nor one of chronic unemployment.

As the accompanying chart ("The Kondratieff Wave") makes clear, the notion that the world economy entered the fourth Kondratieff downswing in the 1970's persisted despite the contra-Kondratieff behavior of prices in this decade.

In that chart prices go on rising in the 1970's but the Idealized Kondratieff Wave turns down. Historically, either the idealized curve is a stylized price (or interest rate or money-wage) index, or it is false. Except for price and the other value-linked trends, the course of production and real wages in the world economy in no sense followed the downward path of the curve from 1814 to 1843 and from 1874 to 1896. Those who argue that the world economy is in a fourth Kondratieff downswing simply ignore the movements of prices, interest rates, and money-wages on which Kondratieff originally focused.

Jay W. Forrester and his colleagues also argue that the contemporary world is gripped by a Kondratieff downswing. Forrester weaves together his view of the limits to growth and his interpretation of the Kondratieff cycle.

The mechanism of the Forrester long-wave model is wholly physical. Prices, interest rates, and money-wages disappear. Like Mandel, Forrester uses a two-sector model, outlined as follows:

> . . . a long-wave behavior can arise from the physical structure connecting consumer-goods sectors and the capital sectors. A sufficient cause for a 50-year fluctuation lies in the movement of people between sectors, the long time to change production capacity of capital sectors, the way capital sectors

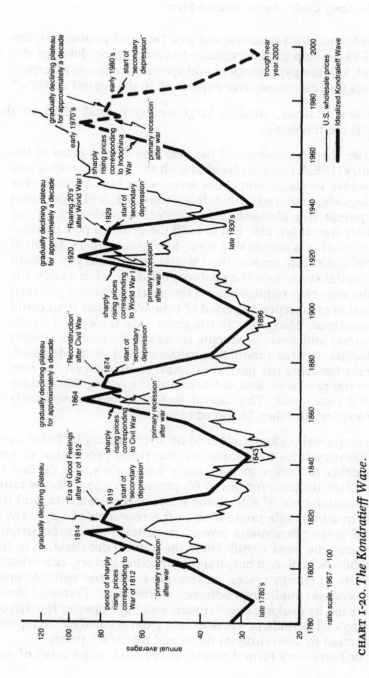

CHART 1-20. *The Kondratieff Wave.*

Source: *Media General Financial Weekly*, June 3, 1974.

provide their own input capital as a factor of production, the need to develop excess capacity to catch up on deferred demand, and the psychological and speculative forces of expectations that can cause over-expansion in the capital sectors.[27]

The key analysis, yielding large excess capital plant in the 1970's, is the following:

> After the Depression and the War, the capital plant of the country [U.S.A.] was depleted at both the manufacturing and consumer levels. Automobiles were worn out, housing was inadequate, commercial buildings were old, and production equipment was obsolete. The physical capital stock of the country was at low ebb. But to refill the depleted pool of physical capital in a reasonable time, like twenty years, required a production rate greater than would be necessary to sustain the capital stock once the pool was filled. In other words, the production rate required to replenish the depleted physical capital in an acceptable period of time was higher than could be sustained. Moreover, as the order rate for capital in the consumer and goods-producing sectors of the economy began to decline, desired production in the capital sector declined, thereby lowering the need for capital equipment on the part of capital producers and accentuating the falling demand for capital equipment. The capital sectors would consequently over-expand and then be forced to retrench.[28]

The empirical evidence adduced for overcapacity includes 1975 office vacancy rates in Manhattan, the rising production of corporate debts to profits in the 1950's and 1960's, the decline in capital plant utilization rates to 65 percent in 1975, excess tankers, the peaking out of school and hospital requirements, and the decline in automobile production in the recession of 1974–1975. Some of these phenomena proved transitory; others, persistent. In my view, the most significant is the natural deceleration in the automobile, school, and hospital construction sectors, exacerbated by the rise in energy prices, on the one hand, and political pressures to contain public expenditures, on the other. Forrester closes this passage by evoking explicitly an analogy between the 1930's and 1970's as periods of gross excess capital capacity, incapable of correction by conventional fiscal and monetary policy.

As for Forrester's formal model, as opposed to the array of empirical evidence assembled, I would make two observations. First, there is no reason to believe that the backlog of demand for durable consumer goods built up during the Second World War required a quarter century to satisfy. The lags are simply not that long. What happened, in fact, is that the dynamics of the post-1945 years yielded a rapid rise in consumers' real income, notably after the relative decline of basic commodity prices set in from 1951. The income elasticity of demand for durable consumer goods was high as was the demand for education, health services, and travel. These leading sectors (and those related to them) were, like all leading sectors of the past, subject to deceleration. The impact of the unfavorable shift in the terms of trade since 1972, combined with stagflation, has further weakened their potential role in generating overall economic expansion in the decades ahead.

Second, by choosing capital and durable consumer goods as the two sectors for his model, and leaving out basic commodities, Forrester, like Mandel, missed critical insights for both analysis and policy: the role of favorable terms of trade for industrialized countries in driving forward the boom of the 1950's and 1960's and their reversal in creating stagflation; and the potential stimulus of investments required to deal with the problems of energy, the global food-population balance, and other resource-related sectors.

These analyses, which view the world economy as having entered a Kondratieff downswing in the 1970's, evidently vary in their framework of analysis and in their complexity. What they all share is a sense that the rate of profit is under downward pressure and profitable investment opportunities for the private sector have diminished, as compared to the 1950's and 1960's—a theme elaborated in Chapter 3. Stripped of their subtleties, these analyses are reasserting, in one way or another, versions of the secular stagnation theory widely applied at the time as an explanation for the Great Depression of the 1930's. In a rough and ready way they derive a good deal from Schumpeter's explanation of the disappointing Juglar expansion after the trough of 1932, although they do not all make clear the distinctions Schumpeter elaborated in the closing pages of *Business Cycles*.[20] Schumpeter asserted, essentially, three propositions. First, in the very long run the world economy might well move gradually toward a steady state, for a variety of possible reasons operating on both the supply and demand for capital. Second, as of the late 1930's that time had not arrived; the three great innovational sectoral complexes of the twentieth century (electricity, automobiles, and chemicals) had not yet lost their capacity to drive forward the process of growth; and there was, objectively, no shortage of investment and innovational possibilities. But, third, deep societal changes "hostile to the industrial bourgeoisie" had diminished the confidence and innovational zeal of the private entrepreneur and had yielded the weakness of the response of the private sector to investment opportunities and to the stimulus provided by increased government expenditure to aggregate effective demand. Only in this latter "subjective" sense did Schumpeter accept the notion that investment opportunities had diminished. Schumpeter's was, then, a political, sociological, and psychological explanation for secular stagnation, and, to a degree, he believed it would prove transient. His two-volume study closed with a quite prescient prediction: ". . . if our schema is to be trusted, recovery and prosperity phases should be more, and recession and depression phases less strongly marked during the next three decades than they have been in the last two. But the sociological drift cannot be expected to change."[30]

Mandel does introduce some of the noneconomic factors at work on the environment of the private entrepreneur and his profit expectations, although there is a strong technological strand in his explanation for an alleged declining trend in profits. Forrester confines himself to the concept of prior overinvestment and currently diminished investment opportunities. But neither examines seriously the prospects for leading growth sectors in the future beyond Mandel's view that capitalism is incapable of exploiting the potentialities for automation and Forrester's introduction of physical limits of growth constraints.

Almost by definition, those arguing that the 1970's are to be viewed as a Kondratieff downswing do not explore the implications of the relative price movements which have occurred since 1972, including their implications for investment opportunities.

In one sense, my argument meets head on the perspective of those who believe we are in the fourth Kondratieff downswing; that is, if we deal with our resource problems, investment outlays would bring high sustained growth rates within our grasp. In another sense, my argument evades two significant questions raised by some analysts about the future prospects for capitalism.

Both hark back to the debates of the 1930's about secular stagnation.

The first question is technical. Do diminishing returns apply to the application of basic science and technology, and, as some claim, are we now on the decelerating slope of an S-shaped curve symbolizing the creation of productive new technologies? Do the rising marginal capital-output ratios and slackened rates of productivity increase of advanced industrial economies since the second half of the 1960's demonstrate that this time, unlike in the 1930's, we are moving into a phase of secular technological deceleration if not true secular stagnation? Put another way, it would be possible to admit that large resource-related avenues for investment exist and still hold that the long-run path of growth will be depressed by a gradual decline in the productivity of investment due to diminishing returns from new inventions.

I explore these matters in two chapters of my *Getting from Here to There* and evidently cannot repeat here the full argument. A survey of the state of the basic sciences suggests unparalleled momentum in biology, physics, chemistry, and the understanding of the human brain. All these activities are strengthened by remarkable improvements, including prospective improvements, in our capacity to measure. We cannot predict the oblique consequences for invention of these formidable scientific efforts, but they are likely to be substantial. As for inventions actually in the pipeline, there appears to be great momentum not only in new forms of nuclear energy and photovoltaic cells but also in computers, communications, laser applications, new agricultural technologies, and other fields. Somewhat in the vein of Schumpeter's final words in *Business Cycles*, I tentatively conclude in *Getting from Here to There*: "It is . . . in the domain of private innovation and its relation to public policy, rather than in the alleged deficiencies of science or invention, that the greatest danger to the future appears to lie."[31]

Charles P. Kindleberger carries further the question of nontechnical, noneconomic forces at work. In a wide-ranging, lively, and imaginative essay, he asks whether the advanced industrial societies are capable of the kind of adaptation and innovation required to sustain momentum in the environment they now confront.[32] He argues that the past is not easily discarded, "especially not the collective memories that inhibit, or the groups with *positions acquises* that fight to resist loss of income and especially of status." He evokes by implication the image of nations which may prefer to go down in the style to which they have become accustomed, their citizens squabbling meanly among themselves for shares of a diminishing pie. He can point to Nicholas Kaldor's argument for tariff protection for aging economies like Britain's and other suggestions for insulating the advanced industrial economies from the rigors of adjustment they otherwise face. He concludes that we may not need "the moral equivalent of war" to pull us out of our yearning for a past that will never return but require, perhaps, the "Sociological Equivalent of Defeat"; for, in his view, defeat destroys old vested interests and habits, and inhibiting collective memories, clearing the way for innovators and a resilient process of adaptation to new realities.

Whether the West has the collective will and wit to adjust and go forward is, surely, the right question to pose; and none of us can be dogmatic about the outcome. It is palpable that the advanced industrial societies command the resources and the technical potentialities to cope with the tasks of the fifth Kondratieff upswing. But looking at the dishevelled state of the Western world, there is little present evidence of a pervasive will to confront those tasks and mobilize the resources and technical potentialities which lie to hand. There is no objective basis at the moment for optimism.

But I would temper Kindleberger's implicit pessimism with three observations:

—A part of the problem lies in the minds of our reigning economists and the politicians who depend on them. The theoretical constructs of conventional economists and related conventional modes of policy analysis are geared to the understanding and manipulation of aggregate effective demand. They have not yet reorganized the main body of economic theory to deal with a supply-oriented world. Of course, economists also develop *positions acquises* which they surrender or alter only slowly and painfully. But such changes have occurred in the past and should not prove impossible to bring about; with the economists providing more relevant insights, politicians and policy should respond.

—Crises short of the trauma of defeat have proved capable of producing significant changes in policy, including the acceptance of new modes of operation by powerful vested interests, for example, British policy after 1931, U.S. policy after 1933, French acceptance of indicative planning after 1946.

—Perhaps most important, there is the saving dynamics of the generations. It is often conventional to talk about societies as if their life were continuous; and there are, of course, powerful continuities of the kind Kindleberger emphasized—continuities in the form of ideas and institutions, laws, habits, and vested interests, including vested interests in existing technologies and industrial structure. But each generation comes forward with a significant degree of resistance to these continuities. In fact, as commentators have noted, from Plato down through Thomas Mann (in *Buddenbrooks*) to analysts of the youth of the 1960's, there is a built-in tendency of succeeding generations to take for granted what the previous generation has achieved, to refuse to be weighed down by its obsessions and failures, and to strike out in new directions believed relevant to their own time. Something like this process helps account for the surprising momentum of advanced industrial societies, both victorious and defeated, after the Second World War. It is by no means sure—but it is by no means ruled out—that, as we move into the 1980's, those coming forward to responsibility will break out of the inhibiting patterns of thought and action of the 1950's and 1960's and confront with vigor the agenda before them.

But, analytically, I would conclude on this matter of secular stagnation much as I did in *The Process of Economic Growth*:

> The same outcome might emerge [secular stagnation] if one assumes that, with a rise in income, any of the underlying propensities are weakened, that is, the propensities to develop fundamental science, to seek innovations, to apply them, to respond to profit possibilities, to consume, or to have children. This approach would cover the view that secular stagnation may result from a population decline or from a decline in the propensity to consume; and it would introduce the less familiar notion that secular stagnation may result from a fundamental failure to respond to the challenges and opportunities of growth by sufficient allocations to science or applied science, by a sufficient degree of acceptance of possibilities offered, or by a sufficient desire to achieve further material advance.

It may well be that, as our knowledge increases, we will lay greater stress than is now conventional on the possibility that secular stagnation may result from a decline in the propensities rather than from a decline in the yield from additional outlays of investment in various directions. The evidence for long-run diminishing returns from accretions to science and applied science is, indeed, so dubious, as is evidence for a trend toward capital-saving innovations, that in the end it is to social and political behavior that we may look for analyses of economic stagnation and decline.[33]

2

A Simple Model of the Kondratieff Cycle with Four Variations

I

One key conclusion of Chapter 1 is that trend periods, or Kondratieff cycles, were primarily caused by periodic undershooting and overshooting of the dynamic optimum levels of capacity and output for food and raw materials in the world economy. Optimum levels were defined as those which would have been attained in a continuous dynamic equilibrium where capacity was smoothly adjusted to rates of increase in population and income, the income elasticity of demand, the rate and changing structure of industrial growth, and the pace and character of technological change. These gross deviations of actual from optimum capacity were caused, in turn, by three distinctive characteristics of certain major forms of investment in foodstuffs and raw materials: a relatively longer lag between the emergence of a profit possibility and the investment decisions designed to exploit it, as compared to manufactures; a relatively longer period of gestation, caused, in part, by large prior infrastructure outlays before production could begin; and a longer time period between the completion of the investment and its maximum efficient exploitation, often involving large domestic or international migration. All three characteristics arose because such investments usually required the opening up of whole new areas for agricultural production, large new mines, oil fields, and so on. Production capacity could not be expanded in as small increments as in manufactures. It increased

Note: The bulk of this chapter was first published in Research in Economic History 4 (1979).

by more discrete, large steps; and these discontinuous increases in capacity involved long time lags.

Protracted upward shifts in the relative prices of basic commodities were seen as the catalyst setting in motion the over-shooting process, by inducing enlarged investment in capacity capable of producing such commodities; consequent protracted periods of decline in relative prices, and, in some cases, the build-up of stocks, led to a decline of investment in the capacity to produce basic commodities. Since demand for these commodities increased more steadily than did capacity, in response to the continued expansion of population and the trend expansion of industry, the relative neglect of investment in basic commodities ultimately caused undershooting and a reversal of relative price movements when surplus capacity (including stocks) was worked off. The general price level, interest rates, income distribution within and among nations, and paths and scale of migration, as well as patterns of investment, reflected this erratic cyclical process which can now be traced back for almost two centuries.

The course of events in the world economy since the close of 1972 has made trend-period analysis highly relevant to an understanding of what has happened in the past six years and to the design of appropriate public policy: both to re-achieve high and regular growth rates and to restore structural equilibrium in the face of problems of energy, food and water supply, raw materials, and containment of air and water pollution. As indicated at the close of Chapter 1, I would characterize the period 1972–1979 as the early phase of the fifth Kondratieff upswing. There is, of course, much unique about the price revolution of 1972–1979, as there was in each of its four predecessor periods which started in the 1790's, 1850's, 1890's, and 1930's. But the major variables in the world economy have moved in ways similar to their movement in the early phase of the other Kondratieff upswings. The principal exception is the phenomenon of higher average unemployment levels than in the 1960's. We shall have something to say about this phenomenon in Section III, below.

Without entering into sterile debate about method, it is a simple fact that the evolution of modern neoclassical and neo-Keynesian economic theory has made it difficult for its practitioners to deal with the phenomena involved in the trend-period process. In particular, the formal growth models developed over the past generation were generally marked by the following characteristics which ruled out, in effect by assumption, the trend-period phenomena:

—The availability of resource-bearing land for the production of energy, food, and raw materials is either aggregated out of such models or implicitly assumed to appear as an automatic function of the level or rate of growth of demand—a theme elaborated in Chapter 4. This casualness about the supply of basic commodities is, perhaps, an understandable reflection of the fact that most such models were designed by economists in the advanced industrial world during a period of falling or relatively low prices of basic commodities (1951–1972).

—The two sectors isolated in neoclassical growth models were generally capital goods and consumption goods, produced by varying proportions of capital and labor. Therefore, the problem of relative prices and income distribution emerged as the question of the relative marginal return to capital and labor. There was no awareness that, historically, shifts in income distribution were mainly brought about by periods of relative abundance or scarcity of foodstuffs and raw materials, and consequent changes in the relative prices of basic commodities.

—Changes in the capital stock were viewed as incremental: no variations in periods of gestation were envisaged, if, indeed, such lags were introduced at all.

The negative outcome was not surprising. Economists working this terrain were not exploring the trend-period problem. They were, mainly, trying to define the conditions for a dynamic, full-employment equilibrium, assuming technological change, with varying capital-labor (and capital-output) ratios.

With a variable for progress in technology inserted, with a stable consumption function, and with entrepreneurs assumed to choose their technologies in ways which kept inventions Harrod-neutral, such models yield a balanced equilibrium path with per capita GNP growing steadily at the rate of technical progress.

The shock of the energy crisis of 1973–1974 produced some imaginative innovations in the world of model-building and econometrics, of which the most elaborate was the Hudson-Jorgenson model.[1] It aimed to combine the techniques of econometric models focused on effective demand with the structural apparatus of input-output analysis. As opposed to neoclassical growth models, recent formal analyses of the energy problem have the virtue of relating changes in the relative price of a basic commodity to the overall course of output in the economy. But they do not deal with problems of lumpiness in capacity and the period of gestation; nor do they explain well the fact of stagnation. The latter weakness stems from the conventional assumption of continuous full employment introduced not only for formal convenience but also to contrast various long-run growth paths under alternative assumptions concerning the relative price of energy or alternative energy policies.[2]

A two-sector model capable of illuminating the Kondratieff cycle must focus not on capital and consumer goods but on industrial production and the production of basic commodities (food, raw materials, and energy). It must, in addition to capital and labor as factors of production, include "land," that is, natural resources, to which diminishing returns will apply unless new technologies or new high-productivity exploitable resources are found. It must provide for changing directions of investment as between the two sectors as well as changing relative prices. And, above all, it must allow for the possibility of gross discontinuities in the expansion of capacity to produce basic commodities and for differing periods of gestation and exploitation between the two sectors.

To get at the trend-period problem we must, then, relax certain conventional basic assumptions in formal growth analysis, for our situation in economic theory is not unlike that which led John Williams, a half century ago, to go into revolt against the classical theory of international trade: "The classical theory assumes as fixed, for purposes of reasoning, the very things which . . . should be the chief objects of study."[3]

I set about, therefore, to outline a model with two sectors: I (industrial goods) and B (basic commodities); deviations of actual from optimum sectoral capacity would be reflected in relative prices; the direction of investment as between the two sectors would be determined by relative prices; and investment in increments to B capacity would be subject to lumpiness and multiple lags not shared in the I sector. As a reader, but not a practitioner, of mathematical economics, I recruited Faisal Nasr as an assistant. We were soon joined by Michael Kennedy, already engaged on original elaborations of the formal relations between energy supply and economic growth. The characteristics of the formal models which emerged—and their results—are set out in Section II below. Section III relates them to the historical sequence of Kondratieff cycles and to the contemporary scene.

In Section II we proceeded in six stages:

Model 1 (BG: Balanced Growth). This is a model in stable dynamic equilibrium—in effect, a neoclassical model in which the two sectors are *I* and *B* rather than consumer goods and capital goods.

Model 2 (K: Kondratieff). This is a Kondratieff cyclical model (forty years) in which new, lumpy increments to *B* capacity are introduced into Model 1 (BG), subject to lags not shared in the *I* sector.

Model 3 (S: Schumpeter). We introduce Schumpeter models (S1 and S2) in which variations of the average rate of technical progress in the *I* sector are permitted, in differing sequences, as the productivity of major technological innovations waxes and wanes.

Model 4 (W: War). This is a war model, in which international conflict suddenly reduces *B* capacity; there is expanded investment subject to diminishing returns in residual *B* capacity; and, with a lag, the postwar brings overshooting when *B* capacity revives. It is, in effect, an arbitrarily induced and foreshortened version of Model 2 (K).

Model 5 (SF: Stagflation). This is a variation on Model 2 (K) in which money-wage and money-supply frictions introduce the possibility of unemployment on both a Kondratieff upswing and downswing.

Model 6 (LG: Limits to Growth). This is a degenerative limits-to-growth model, with diminishing returns operating on a fixed amount of land in the *B* sector. It might as well have been called a Malthusian or Ricardian model.

Although we designed and worked over these exercises together, Section II is primarily the work of Michael Kennedy.

As we shall see in Section III, we can use these models in various combinations to approximate, but then only incompletely, the great complexity and irregularity with which Kondratieff cycles actually unfolded in history.

II

We now describe the basic, underlying model (BG) which we will use with variations for exploring the sectoral foundations of the relative price changes associated with the Kondratieff cycle as we interpret it. In its analytical form, the model is essentially a multisector–general equilibrium model of the type explored by Paul A. Samuelson,[4] with dynamic properties, such as those described by Hirofumi Uzawa.[5] Its novelty lies in the time path for the formation of factors of production which permits us to examine certain cyclical phenomena in the sectors with implications for the aggregate performance of the economy.

There are three factors of production in the economy: labor (L), capital (K), and resource availability (N). We will sometimes use the word *land* as shorthand for resource availability. There are two kinds of output. Basic goods (B) are produced, under technical conditions of constant returns to scale, from capital, labor, and available resources; that is, a proportionate increase in the amount of labor, capital, and land of constant quality will produce an equal proportionate increase in output. The general phenomenon of diminishing returns arises when the amount of land is held constant or not increased in proportion to the other factors of production. The severity of the impact of a restriction on land is a function of the assumed elasticities of substitution of labor and capital for land. Industrial goods (I) are produced from labor, capital, and intermediate inputs of B, again under conditions of constant returns to scale. GNP is composed of the net outputs of B and I; part of GNP is consumed and part is devoted to capital formation for use in future periods.

It is well known in the growth literature that (a) if the GNP demand-relations have unitary income elasticities, (b) if L grows at a constant rate (say λ), (c) if saving is a constant proportion of GNP, (d) if Harrod-neutral technical progress occurs at a constant rate (say v) in the production relations governing gross output of B and I, and (e) if land is superabundant (i.e., has a marginal product of zero), then the economy will admit a balanced growth path at rate $\mu = \lambda + v$, with all per capita quantities growing at rate v and all relative prices constant, with the exception of the real wage, which grows at a rate v. Furthermore, if land is scarce but grows at rate μ, then a similar balanced growth path exists in which resource owners receive a nonzero but constant rent.

The sequence of models developed here investigates the implications of other patterns of land availability for the growth of quantities and the time paths of relative prices in the economy. In particular, we examine a scenario in which resource availability grows at a rate μ over the long run but becomes available in discrete lumps and needs a certain amount of social overhead capital in place before any output is forthcoming.

Mathematics of the Model

STATIC CONDITIONS

1. Production Relations
   We first define the following variables:

   X_B gross output of B
   X_I gross output of I
   Y_B net output of B
   Y_I net output of I
   L_B labor devoted to production of B
   L_I labor devoted to production of I
   K_B capital devoted to production of B
   K_I capital devoted to production of I
   N land

   The production functions are
   $$X_B = f_B(e^{vt}L_B, K_B, N) \tag{1}$$
   and
   $$X_I = f_I(e^{vt}L_I, K_I) \tag{2}$$
   (f_B and f_I are homogeneous functions of degree 1).
   The input-output relations are
   $$Y_B = X_B - a_{BI}X_I, \tag{3}$$
   where a_{BI} is a constant input-output parameter, and
   $$Y_I = X_I. \tag{4}$$
   There is thus no intermediate input of I goods into B goods production.

2. Factor Availability
   $$N = \overline{N} \tag{5}$$
   $$L_I + L_B = \overline{L} \tag{6}$$
   $$K_I + K_B = \overline{K} \tag{7}$$
   In the short run, all factors are fixed in supply.

3. Income Formation and Disposal
   We define the following variables:

   Y nominal GNP
   w nominal wage
   r nominal rental of capital
   n nominal rental of resource areas

C_B consumption of B
C_I consumption of I
S saving=investment, composed totally of I goods
P_B price of B
P_I price of I

The prices of output goods are competitively determined through the total cost relations:

$$P_B = g_B(e^{-vt}w, r, n), \qquad (8)$$

and

$$P_I = g_I(e^{-vt}w, r) + a_{BI}P_B \qquad (9)$$

(g_B and g_I are the unit cost functions associated with f_B and f_I);[6]

$$Y = P_I Y_I + P_B Y_B = wL + rK + nN. \qquad (10)$$

Nominal GNP equals the value of net output, which in turn equals total factor payments:

$$P_I S = \sigma Y. \qquad (11)$$

Nominal saving is a constant fraction of nominal GNP:

$$C_B = C_B((1-\sigma)Y, P_B, P_I) \qquad (12)$$

and

$$C_I = C_I((1-\sigma)Y, P_B, P_I). \qquad (13)$$

C_B and C_I are demand functions derived from utility maximization; they satisfy $P_I C_I + P_B C_B = (1-\sigma)Y$.

Along with the factor demands implied by the first partial derivatives of the cost functions (8) and (9), equations (1)–(13) determine all the variables in the static solution of the economy. Relative but not absolute prices are determined in this nonmonetary model.

DYNAMIC CONDITIONS

The dynamic behavior of the economy depends on the time paths of availability of factor supplies, that is, the time paths of $\bar{L}, \bar{K}$, and $\bar{N}$. Letting subscripts denote time, we assume

$$\bar{L}_t = e\lambda \bar{L}_{t-1}, \qquad (14)$$

or labor grows exponentially at rate λ. In neoclassical simulations we have

$$\bar{K}_t = S + (1-\delta)\bar{K}_{t-1}. \qquad (15)$$

Here δ is the depreciation rate. This is the traditional capital-accumulation relation. In most of our simulations, however, we will deduct from the available directly productive capital stock certain social overhead investments which will only become productive, and *then* added to the stock, after a certain gestation lag.

In a balanced growth case, we have

$$\overline{N}_t = e_\mu \overline{N}_{t-1}. \tag{16}$$

As described above, in our basic simulations, land becomes available in discrete lumps, although averaged across the very long run it follows equation (16).

NUMERICAL ASSUMPTIONS

The arbitrary numerical values chosen for the parameters of the model are:

$$\lambda = .01$$
$$v = .02$$
$$\mu = (\lambda + v) = .03$$
$$\sigma = .15$$
$$\delta = .10$$

Although these parameters are arbitrary, we think they are not unreasonable. The production functions are *CES* with an elasticity of substitution of .25. The distribution parameters were chosen so that the following share relations hold in balanced growth. (Here ρ_{JK} is factor *J*'s total payment as a share of the total revenue from production of good *K*.)

$$\rho_{LB} = .40 \qquad\qquad \rho_{KB} = .30 \qquad\qquad \rho_{NB} = .30$$
$$\rho_{LI} = .18 \qquad\qquad \rho_{KI} = .42 \qquad\qquad \rho_{BI} = .40$$

The consumer-demand functions are derived from a *CES* utility function, here with elasticity of substitution .70. Distribution parameters were chosen so that, in balanced growth, the share of *B* in consumption expenditure is .30, and the share of *I* is .70.

As described above, in balanced growth all per capita quantities grow 2 percent per year, the real wage grows 2 percent per year, the labor force grows 1 percent per year, and the real returns to capital and land, as well as the relative price of *B* and *I*, are constant. These results conform, of course, to the neoclassical growth model.

Two Basic Simulations

We first present the results of two basic runs of the model. These runs are designed to illustrate the fundamental role of the availability of resources (the factor of production N) in determining the functioning of the economy.

Accordingly, all the exogenous inputs in these two runs are identical, except for the amount of the N factor available to the economy. Chart 2-1 shows the differences in the availability of this factor in the runs. (All runs are done over a forty-year time span, as indicated in the abscissa of Chart 2-1.) The line marked BG represents the neoclassical, or *balanced growth*, case. In this case, resource availability grows at the underlying growth rate of the economy as a whole, μ, or 3 percent per year. Thus, at the end of the forty-year cycle, resource availability is $(1.03)^{40}$, or 3.26 times its original level.

The line marked K reflects Model 2. It exhibits the assumed pattern of resource availability in the Kondratieff case. Technically, this shows the level of the factor N that can be used in the production function for basic goods in each year. Its path can be simply summarized in four stages, corresponding to the four decades of the cycle:

First decade: Fixed availability, or no increase at all
Second decade: Slow growth in availability (less than 3% per year) staying below the neoclassical path
Third decade: A sharp spurt, moving up toward the neoclassical path
Fourth decade: Slowed growth, converging to the BG path

Our rationale for, or interpretation of, this path is based on the scenario for the introduction of new resource areas into a growing economy, suggested in Section I of this paper. At the end of each cycle, the economy is in essentially neoclassical balance, with adequate supplies of the N factor available for short-run sectoral equilibrium to lie on the long-run balanced growth path. However, any new supplies of the N factor that can be exploited are located physically apart from current centers of economic activity. These new resource areas, where additional supplies of N factor are to be found, may be distant potential farming ground (the American Midwest or Australia), mineral fields (Swedish, Brazilian, or Liberian iron ore), or oil deposits (the Middle East or Alaska). Before these new areas can be effectively introduced into the economy, so as to contribute fruitfully to its output, three sorts of lags must be overcome. (Technically, this means these three lags must be overcome before a higher avail-

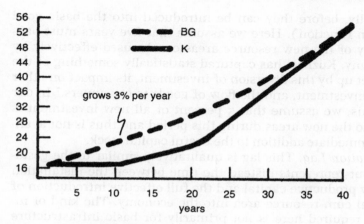

CHART 2-1. *Availability of "Land."*

ability of the N factor can be introduced into the basic good production function (1).)

Recognition Lag. This lag lasts for about half the first decade and represents the time that passes before economic decision makers, investors in particular, realize that the resource areas currently being exploited are insufficient to supply basic goods to the growing economy *at unchanged relative prices.* It is, in fact, the phenomenon of rising prices for basic goods, coupled with rising rents on resource areas, that causes this recognition. Given the order of magnitude of the investment required and the length of the period of gestation, investors must become convinced that the relatively higher prices of B will persist. In the contemporary world, as suggested in Section III, the recognition lag involves political processes where the force of inertia has proved strong.

Gestation Lag. This lag begins when investors decide to exploit new resource areas. However, the necessity of supplying adequate infrastructure capital to the new areas prevents their output from becoming available immediately to the economy. Examples of this kind of capital are transportation, communications, and dwelling installations. In fact, during this period the new areas are a drain on investment goods output, which must be supplied to the new areas before they are capable of producing anything (technically, before they can be introduced into the basic good production function). Here we assume that five years must pass before any of the new resource areas can be used effectively by the economy. Kuznets has captured statistically something of the process set up by this diversion of investment, its impact on other forms of investment, and the flow of goods to consumers.[7] In our simulations, we assume that 5 percent of all new investment is drawn into the new areas during this period and thus is not available for immediate addition to the useful capital stock.

Exploitation Lag. This lag is qualitatively similar to the gestation lag but represents instead the time between the installation of directly productive capital and the full effective introduction of the capital cum resource area into the economy. The kind of investment required here is not primarily for basic infrastructure but for the new production units themselves, for example, farms, mines, double-tracking and feeder roads, oil fields. Characteristic of this period is a slowly increasing availability of factors for productive use. We represent this period by the second decade of slow but steady increase in the N factor's availability. During this period of the simulations, and across five more years, the investment drained off during the gestation lag becomes available in equal yearly doses for directly productive use with the new land.

The third decade then models the full introduction of the new resource area into the economy, and in the fourth it is producing at full capacity as part of the B sector.

We now examine the results of simulating Models 1 (BG) and 2 (K) under the two time paths of resource availability just described: neoclassical, steady 3 percent growth, and the Kondratieff path outlined above. In particular, we examine the time paths, over a forty-year period of four key endogenous variables: real GNP, the real wage, the relative price of basic to industrial goods, and the real rate of rent in resource areas.

Real GNP. Chart 2-2 shows the paths of real GNP in each case. Line BG, of course, simply indicates smooth exponential growth at 3 percent, in accordance with the neoclassical model.

Growth in real GNP in the K case closely parallels resource availability. GNP lags behind the neoclassical path in the early part of the cycle, overshoots this path toward the middle, and converges toward it at the end of the cycle.[8] Growth rates of real GNP and resource availability throughout the cycle are:

Years	GNP Growth per Annum	N-Factor Growth per Annum
1–11	1.8%	0.0%
11–21	3.1%	2.8%
21–31	4.1%	5.6%
31–41	3.3%	3.7%

Real Wage. We now look at the real wage, one indicator of the effects of dynamic resource availability on income distribution. Line BG on Chart 2-3 shows the neoclassical result: in the absence of resource constraints, the real wage grows smoothly at a rate λ, in this case 2 percent. By the end of our simulation, it has reached a level $(1.02)^{40}$, or 2.21 times its original level.

Line K in Chart 2-3 shows the real wage pattern in the Kondratieff case. Real wages fall steadily throughout the first decade, reaching 75 percent of their original level. This occurs as labor compensation is reduced, first by resource scarcity and then by the need to put long-gestation, thus not immediately productive, investment into new resource regions. After this period, however, wages grow steadily faster than 2 percent for the remainder of the cycle, as the benefits of the new resource regions accrue to the

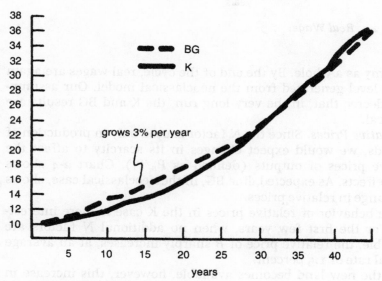

CHART 2-2. *Real GNP.*

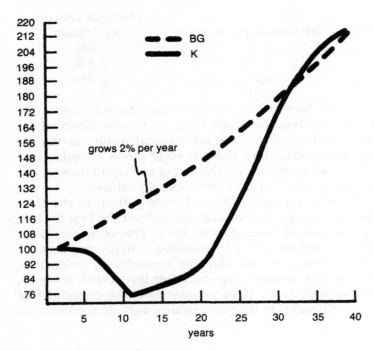

CHART 2-3. *Real Wage.*

economy as a whole. By the end of the cycle, real wages are again at the level generated from the neoclassical model. Our assumptions decree that, in the very long run, the K and BG results are identical.

Relative Prices. Since the N factor is used only in production of B goods, we would expect changes in its scarcity to affect the relative prices of outputs (defined as P_B/P_I). Chart 2-4 shows these effects. As expected, line BG, in the neoclassical case, shows no change in relative prices.

The behavior of relative prices in the K case is more interesting. For the first few years, when no additional N factors are available, the relative price of B sharply increases, at an average annual rate of 1.5 percent.

As the new land becomes available, however, this increase in relative prices slows and prices increase at only 0.8 percent per year, reaching a peak of 26 percent above their original level. At year 21 we see a sharp break in relative prices, and they fall sharply for the next ten years. It is in this phase that the new land is rapidly increasing its output of *B* goods, forcing their price down. Finally, the course of relative prices in the K case converges to that in the BG case, and the relative price is equal in the last period to its value in the base period.

Rent on Land. Chart 2-5 shows the time path of the real rental value of a unit of land over the cycle. This chart is similar to Chart 2-4, except that changes in magnitudes are much larger. Of course, in the BG case real rents, like all other aspects of income distribution, are unchanged. Rents in the K case follow the path of relative prices described above: a rapid rise (7.5% annual rate in the first decade), ten years of a slower rise (1.8%), a sharp break, and a gradual convergence to the values of the BG case. The peak level is 148 percent above the original level.

Variations on a Theme

We have identified four major cyclical phenomena that occur solely as a result of Kondratieff assumptions about the availability of resources (or the *N* factor) as opposed to neoclassical, balanced growth assumptions: (*a*) real GNP *grows relatively slowly* over the first part of the cycle, then spurts ahead to catch the balanced growth path; (*b*) the real wage *falls* for a certain

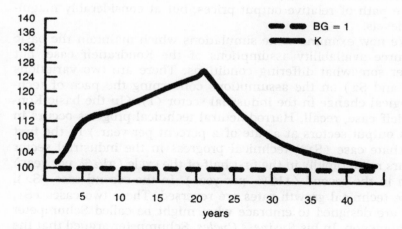

CHART 2-4. *Relative Output Price:* $\frac{PB}{PI}$.

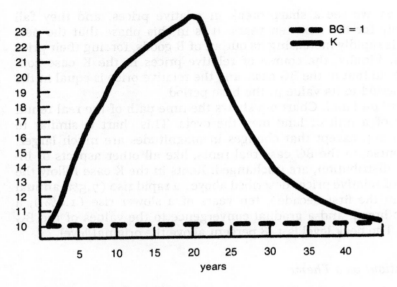

CHART 2-5. *Real Rent on "Land."*

period, then it too spurts ahead to catch the neoclassical path; (*c*) the relative price of basic goods to industrial goods grows sharply, then more slowly, and then breaks sharply down toward the neoclassical level; (*d*) the real rent on land follows the qualitative path of relative output prices, but at considerably magnified levels.

We now examine some simulations which maintain the basic resource availability assumptions of the Kondratieff case, but under somewhat differing conditions. There are two variations (S1 and S2) on the assumptions concerning the pace of technological change in the industrial sector (*I*). (In the basic Kondratieff case, recall, Harrod-neutral technical progress occurs in both output sectors at a rate of 2 percent per year.) In the first alternate case (S1), technical progress in the industrial sector occurs more rapidly in the first half of the cycle (2½% per year) than in the second (1½% per year). In the second case (S2), these technical growth rates are reversed. These two cases (S1, S2) are designed to embrace what might be called Schumpeter phenomenon. In his *Business Cycles*, Schumpeter argued that the process of introducing and diffusing major industrial and transport innovations into the economy involved an initial phase when there were large credit-financed capital outlays, but the innovation did not contribute fully its cost-reducing, productivity-increasing effects to the economy. This was the assumption by which he sought to link the inflations of the Kondratieff upswing to the process of innovation. When major innovations matured and were diffused, their cost-reducing effects then yielded the falling price trend of the Kondratieff downswing. This possibility is caught in Model S2.

This construct has been challenged by the judgment that the capital outlays required in the early stages of innovation were not sufficient to produce generally inflationary effects on the economy and that a good many major innovations produced their cost-reducing effects promptly; for example, the cotton textile and iron innovations of the late eighteenth century tended to damp inflation in Britain during the French Revolutionary and Napoleonic Wars.

On the other hand, it has long been observed that the rate of productivity increase in a new innovational sector is subject, after a time, to retardation. This possibility is caught in Model S1. In both cases, S1 and S2, technical progress continues to occur at a uniform 2 percent rate in the basic-goods sector.

Finally, we introduce a war case (Model 4: W) in which 25 percent of resource availability is destroyed or otherwise removed from the economy in the first period. Additions are then made to resource (or the N factor) availability proportional to addition levels in the K case, but in large enough amounts to bring resource availability at the end of the period equal to that in the K case. In this case, we essentially assume that part of available land is devastated or otherwise taken off the world market at the beginning of the cycle and brought back rather slowly into the productive sphere when peace comes.

Table 2-1 shows the results of these variations in assumptions. The cases are arrayed in increasing severity of cyclical effects. The cyclical peak value of the relative price of basic to industrial goods is lowest in the S1 case, increases slightly through the K and S2 cases, and is considerably higher in the W case. The increase in the rent rate and the initial dip in the real wage follow similar patterns.[9]

TABLE 2-1. *Results for Variations on a Theme*

Case	S1	K	S2	W
GNP Growth Rates				
Year 1–20	2.4%	2.4%	2.5%	2.0%
Year 21–40	4.0	3.7	3.4	4.2
Overall	3.2	3.1	2.9	3.1
Real Wage Path				
Trough	.77%	.75%	.73%	.44%
Year	11	11	11	11
Relative Price Path				
Peak	1.23%	1.27%	1.30%	1.66%
Year	22	21	21	11
Rent Path				
Peak	2.29%	2.46%	2.62%	4.48%
Year	22	21	21	11

Unemployment Cases

All the simulations discussed so far have assumed full employment of factors of production or, more generally, instantaneous adjustment of wages, rents, and prices so as to eliminate any excess supplies that occur. Given the rather sharp adjustments in prices needed to keep this economy on an equilibrium path and the notorious stickiness of some prices, such as nominal wages, this assumption will now be modified. To do this, we must append a macromonetary framework to our predominantly sectoral equilibrium model.

The macroframework we use is quite simple and is based on two fundamental assumptions: (*a*) constancy of the velocity of money, which means that the time path of the money supply determines the time path of nominal GNP and, along with real quantities, determines all nominal prices; (*b*) downward immobility of the nominal wage, which means that, if the *real* outcome of the economy, along with the behavior of the money supply, dictates a fall in the nominal wage, unemployment (and a higher than equilibrium real wage) will result. The two assumptions just listed lead to this result. For any given array of real conditions in the economy (factor availabilities, technical progress rates, etc.), there exists a minimum money supply growth rate (and ensuing inflation rate) high enough to lead to full employment; and for money supply growth rates below this, the monetary authorities can trade inflation off against unemployment.[10]

The cases we report here have identical input assumptions, except for varying growth rates of the money supply. All real assumptions are those made in the basic K case. We report results for annual money supply growth rates of 8, 6, 4.5, and 3 percent, as seen in Table 2-2.

TABLE 2-2. *Results of Unemployment Cases*

	K Case			
	(M=.08)	M=.06	M=.045	M=.03
GNP Growth				
Year 1–20	2.4%	2.4%	2.4%	2.2%
Year 21–40	3.7	3.7	3.7	3.9
Overall	3.1	3.1	3.1	3.0
Real Wage Path				
Trough	.75%	.82%	.84%	.99%
Year	11	14	17	5
Relative Price Path				
Peak	1.27%	1.26%	1.25%	1.21%
Year	21	21	21	21
Rent Path				
Peak	2.46%	2.43%	2.42%	2.02%
Year	21	21	21	21
Unemployment Path				
Peak	0	4.9%	5.9%	10.5%
Year	—	11	11	11–21
Inflation Rate				
Peak	6.8%	5.1%	4.0%	2.5%
Year	7–11	7–11	7	7–11
Average	4.8%	2.8%	1.4%	0.0%

From Table 2-2 we see the following results:

1. A money supply growth of 8 percent, leading to an inflation rate of approximately 5 percent (since the real economy grows 3% per year on average), is sufficient to guarantee full employment.

2. The shape of the implicit Phillips curve of the model is that shown in Chart 2-6, and a zero inflation policy leads to very high unemployment for a protracted period.

3. A high unemployment (or low money supply growth) policy mitigates the fall in the real wage for those employed (as is well known) and also mitigates the relative price increase of basic goods and the real rent increase through the cycle. However, the impacts on nonwage prices are small.

4. Impacts on the growth of GNP across the cycle from differing monetary policies are small.

The Importance of the Elasticity of Substitution and the Limits to Growth

All the results reported so far have assumed elasticities of substitution of .25 among capital, labor, and (in basic good production) resources. This elasticity of substitution is on the low side of reported elasticities among these factors (see Hudson and Jorgenson; Humphrey and Maroney).[11] The elasticity of substitution represents the ease with which various factors of production can be substituted for each other. In our case, it represents the degree to which more labor- and capital-intensive working of

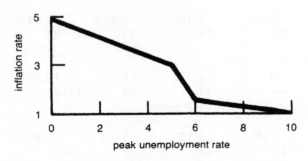

CHART 2-6. *Phillips Curve: Unemployment Cases.*

existing resources can compensate for the lack of additional new resources.

We did an alternate run of the K case with these elasticities of substitution set at .50 instead. This gave results that were qualitatively identical, but the quantitative cyclical phenomena were sharply mitigated. In particular, the following three differences emerged:

1. The relative price of basic goods peaks at only 10 percent above its original level, as opposed to 26 percent in the first case.

2. The rental rate peaked at 61 percent above its original level, instead of 146 percent.

3. The real wage fell to only 97 percent of its original level, instead of 75 percent.

Thus, a change of the value of the elasticity of substitution well within our current uncertainty about its true value causes a significant change in the quantitative nature of the results. Any higher level of this elasticity (from .50 to infinity) would result in further mitigation of the cyclical phenomena, but these phenomena would continue to occur at any finite elasticity.

The importance of this parameter can be seen further in a final set of simulations performed: Model 6 (LG). These simulations were to illuminate some aspects of the "limits to growth" controversy, which essentially concerns itself with the implications of a rigid quantitative limit on the amount of resources available. All input assumptions in these cases were identical with those of the K case, except that resource availability throughout the period was limited to that available in the first period. (For further comparison, note that, in the K case, resource availability for the first ten years is held at the level of the first year. In the "limits" cases, this condition continues throughout the entire forty years.)

With an elasticity of substitution of .25, these assumptions lead to drastic results indeed. Real GNP growth throughout the cycle falls from 3 percent per year to 1 percent, leaving a zero growth in per capita GNP. Income distribution effects under competitive factor pricing and full-employment assumptions are even more pronounced. The real wage falls to 8 percent of its original level, while real rents increase 740 percent. An economy under these conditions is clearly not viable.

Assuming an elasticity of substitution of .50, however, gives a considerably different picture. After a forty-year period, with the same fixed land conditions, real GNP has grown at an average annual rate of 1.8 percent, leading to an 0.8 percent increase in per capita GNP. More important, the real wage has fallen to only 93 percent of its original level. Evidently, the nonland factors of production have not been impoverished.

III

We are now in a position to suggest the relationship of the six stylized models elaborated in Section II to an array of historical and contemporary situations. We shall first briefly comment on each model and then make some observations on what they illuminate or fail to illuminate in the historical sequence of Kondratieff cycles. For these purposes, we shall alter somewhat the sequence of exposition in Section II.

Model 1 (BG) is, of course, a two-sector neoclassical dynamic equilibrium model. Its purpose is merely to expose the structure, assumptions, and basic relationships which are varied in subsequent models in an effort to approximate elements in the Kondratieff cyclical process.

Model 6 (LG) injects the classic assumption of diminishing returns to land and other natural resources. Its purpose is to exhibit the triggering mechanism, in the form of rising relative prices of basic commodities, which sets in motion the struggle against diminishing returns by increasing the proportion of investment in the B sector. In Model 6 the effort fails because there is no new land (B). The economic system progressively degenerates. In fact, a successful struggle against diminishing returns to land and natural resources was conducted for two centuries and more by a combination of expansion into new land and development of new technology in the exploitation of natural resources—the latter process suggested, at least, by our final assumption of a .50 elasticity of substitution among the factors of production. Historically, the only major failure to overcome diminishing returns was in forestry, where the protracted rise in the relative price of timber was countered by substitution and economy in timber use. The pattern was set in the eighteenth century when the relatively rising price of wood induced an expansion in the use of coal for house and other heating purposes and a relatively rising price of charcoal helped stimulate the switch to coke in the manufacture of iron. We do not attempt in this chapter to deal in the B sector with the generation of new technology and the manner in which necessity, as reflected in relative price movements, has been the mother of invention. (That theme is pursued in Chapter 4.) We believe it would be quite easy to modify this model to illuminate that linkage. It appears in the I sector in the bland form of a constant rate of increase in productivity, modified, however, to deal with major industrial innovations in our two versions of Model 3 (S1, S2).

Model 6 also exhibits starkly one of the two key mechanisms used in Dennis Meadows' *Limits to Growth* computer runs to bring on catastrophe to industrial civilization: that is, the manner in which diminishing returns to land force an increasing proportion of a relatively fixed percentage of income invested to be directed, in a losing game, into the effort to maintain agricultural and raw material production. Meadows' other principal instrument for cataclysm is the assumed rise in pollution as global industrial output expands, in effect, a contraction in certain key subsectors (air and water) within the B sector.

Model 2 (K) presents our view of the central Kondratieff mechanism. The key assumptions are that the expansion of capacity into new high-productivity land in the B sector is possible but is subject to lags not shared by the I sector; that capacity can only be expanded in large increments; and that "old" B capacity is subject to diminishing returns because it is fixed in size. The I sector proceeds forward under constant returns to scale and a fixed rate of productivity increase. With the insertion of appropriate and not unreasonable values, Model 2 not only yields a cycle of the approximate length of those Kondratieff observed (40–50 years), but also reproduces approximations of these other empirically observable characteristics of Kondratieff cycles: an initial sharp rise in the relative price of B in the wake of the lower turning point; a sharp initial fall in the relative price of B, after the upper turning point; and a deceleration of the relative decline in the price of B as the Kondratieff downswing proceeds toward its lower turning point. Further, it exhibits the shifts in the proportions of investment, as between I and B sectors, which, in fact, accompanied Kondratieff cycles, and the shifts in income distribution as among real wages, profits, and rents. The rate of increase in GNP moves cyclically, with its lowest rate in the first decade and its highest in the third, when new *B* capacity pours into the economy after the overshoot of the sectoral long-run optimum is at its maximum.

In fact, the contours of the first four Kondratieff upswings were affected by war, as well as by what might be called natural undulations in the relative supply-demand relationship for output from the *B* sector. We have, therefore, developed Model 4 (W), a war case. For these purposes, war was assumed to remove from the economy (through trade blockages as well as physical destruction) a portion of the *B* sector. Compensatory increase of investment in the residual *B* sector, responding to a relative rise in *B* prices, is assumed to be subject to diminishing returns. A postwar lag is assumed before *B* capacity, damaged or disrupted by war, is fully restored. The consequent increase in *B* capacity, in combination with expanded wartime *B* capacity, then yields an overshoot of requirements and a sharp relative decline in *B* prices, as in 1815, 1920, and 1951. Model 4 is, then, a foreshortened version of Model 3.

As we shall see, Models 2 and 4 must be combined to approximate the historical course of events in the first four Kondratieff upswings.

Model 3 introduces the role of leading sectors, or the Schumpeter strand in the story of Kondratieff cycles. As noted above, Schumpeter sought to build a general theory of the Kondratieff cycle around the sequence of major innovations: cotton textiles, Watt's steam engine, and Cort's iron made from coke; the railroads and steel; and the internal combustion engine, electricity, and modern chemicals. He did so by assuming that in the upswing the introduction of the new technologies was inflationary. The pioneering entrepreneurs drew on credit resources and expanded effective demand but were not yet contributing to the economy the full cost-reducing results of the inventions they were introducing into the economic structure. In the downswing, the innovations were widely diffused and achieved full efficiency. Their net effect was deflationary with respect to the price level but caused a rise in real wages as well as a narrowing of profit margins. In Schumpeter's view, particularly severe depressions came when the rate of increase of productivity (and profits) within these now massive but aged sectors had decelerated to a point which reduced the marginal productivity of capital as a whole (1840's, 1890's, 1930's).

As noted earlier, Schumpeter's hypothesis does not work well for the Kondratieff upswings because the amount of capital required and/or the short period before the new innovations yielded their cost-reducing results are incapable of explaining the strong inflationary tendency of such intervals. On the other hand, an element of Schumpeter's hypothesis has a legitimate place in the Kondratieff process. The stage at which the major innovations stood in relation to movements of relative prices of B helped determine the outcome for real wages, but the rhythm of the leading sectors and the rhythm of relative price movements were not necessarily identical. Therefore, we include Model 3 (S1). For example, in the first Kondratieff upswing the rapid technological progress of cotton textile production (including the effect of the cotton gin on raw cotton prices) helped damp the rise in the cost of living decreed by relatively high food prices and thereby limited the downward pressure on real wages. Similarly, the coming in of the railways in the second Kondratieff upswing damped the downward pressure on real wages that relatively high food prices decreed. On the other hand, the failure of the new sectors of the third (pre-1914) Kondratieff upswing to overcome the deceleration of the older leading sectors (notably, steel) added an element of downward pressure on real wages to that imposed by the relatively high prices of basic commodities and the diversion of capital flows to the B sector. Something of the same process may be at work in the contemporary fifth Kondratieff upswing, with its tendency toward rising marginal capital-output ratios in the advanced industrial economies.

To formalize this element in the story of Kondratieff cycles, Model 3 allows for fluctuation in the rate of productivity increase in the I sector. Periods of high productivity increase are meant to reflect times when new leading-sector technologies are being efficiently introduced on a scale sufficient to lift the average; periods of lowered productivity increase reflect times when diminishing returns are operating in those sectors not overcome by the positive effects of new leading-sector complexes.

Model 5 (SF) is meant to capture the possibility that a Kondratieff upswing can be marked by both inflation and abnormally high unemployment, the reality of which has been enforced upon us since 1974. Stagflation has been the most difficult piece of historical experience to approximate in this series of models. This is so because of a general and a specific problem.

The general problem is that Models 1–4 are, in the Harrod-Domar and neoclassical traditions, full-employment models. This characteristic flows directly from the assumptions introduced about the continuity of the flow of investment, the identity of the wage rate with the marginal productivity of labor, and the perfect mobility of labor and capital. One major limitation of Models 1–4 (and Model 6, as well) is, of course, that they so deal with these variables as to rule out the business cycles which have, in fact, marked the relatively modern portions of the world economy since 1783, at least. Stagflation, from 1974 to 1979, was not, strictly speaking, a trend phenomenon, although it may emerge as such if the directions of investment do not come more nearly to approximate their dynamic optimum pattern. Stagflation took the form of an abnormally deep recession, by post-1945 standards, accompanied by continued price increases (1974–1975), followed by an abnormally weak revival marked by higher rates of inflation than those typical of the period, say, 1951–1972 (the fourth Kondratieff downswing). Our general problem is, then, that we are trying to introduce unemployment into an inherently noncyclical model.

The specific problem centers on which variable in Model 1 to modify in order to produce the phenomenon of stagflation. We have chosen what might be called a Keynesian-monetarist solution; that is, we assume that the money-wage rate is sticky and fails to respond to the fall in the real wage decreed by the coming of the fifth Kondratieff upswing and that this stickiness is not compensated for by a sufficient expansion in the money supply. This is the best we could do in a simple, formal modeling procedure. As we shall see below, in the discussion of the fifth upswing, the mechanism that has, in fact, operated to produce abnormally high unemployment levels in the oil-importing advanced industrial economies has been a good deal more complex than that.

Against this background, we shall now comment briefly on each Kondratieff cycle in its unique historical context.

First Kondratieff Cycle: 1790–1848

We require Models 2 (K), 3 (S1), and 4 (W) to illuminate—not to reproduce—the first Kondratieff upswing, 1790–1815. The circumstances of protracted war heightened an underlying tendency for the relative prices of food and raw materials to rise. In Europe the relative price of grain had been rising since, roughly, the mid-eighteenth century. Britain moved to increasing reliance on grain imports. The relative rise in agricultural prices was accentuated by wartime interruptions in the Baltic trade as well as by high shipping and insurance rates. The downward pressure on real wages was mitigated by a factor isolated in Model 3 (S1), that is, the highly productive stage of the innovational leading sectors of the time: cotton textiles, iron, and Watt's more efficient steam engine on which the diffusion of both partially depended. Between 1790 and the year of maximum strain on agricultural supplies (1812), the ratio of agricultural to industrial prices rose from 100 to 172. Relatively high agricultural prices induced large increases in investment in British agriculture and provided, down to Jefferson's Embargo Act of 1807, an erratic period of almost OPEC-like prosperity for the United States.

Although there was an initial rise in prices after war broke out in 1793, the brief interval of intense inflation, typical of the first phase of a Kondratieff upswing, came in 1798 to 1801, when more than half the total price increase of the period 1790–1815 occurred.

There was also a typical sharp downward break in prices as the first Kondratieff downswing (1815–1848) began, followed by a shallower downward trend. This interval is, in general, marked by all the classic features of a Kondratieff downswing: falling agricultural prices, a rising tendency in real wages, rapid industrial progress, with railways supplementing after 1830 the diffusion to Western Europe and the United States of the technologies Britain had earlier pioneered in cotton, iron, and the steam engine. Model 2 takes care of the first Kondratieff downswing fairly well. But the historian, as opposed to the model builder, faces a problem here. The *I* sector for the industrial economies, and the individual national economies, did not move forward at constant rates of productivity increase. For example, productivity increase in the American and British cotton textile industries rapidly decelerated from the early 1830's, as the major gains from the application of the power loom were absorbed. And, for this period, cotton textiles was certainly the most dynamic industrial sector in the Atlantic world. The railroads began to come in during the 1830's, but we simply do not know to what extent their multiple productivity effects countered the deceleration in cotton. There are similar problems in agriculture, whose expansion was not wholly dependent, as in our models, on the expansion of acreage. Farm machinery, improved draining methods, and the systematic use of fertilizers emerge toward the end of the first Kondratieff downswing, although their full exploitation occurs in the second. Our ability to deal with the problem of variations in the productivity of the I sector is limited by the fact that we have available for this period only a relatively few serious productivity studies, confined to particular sectors in particular economies. From what we do know, however, it is unlikely that the average rate of productivity increase in the I sector was constant; and we must bear in mind that, even in the first Kondratieff cycle, new technology as well as acreage (and other resource) expansion was at work in the B sector.

There is also a significant exception to the Kondratieff downswing pattern centered on the story of the cotton price and the expansion of cotton acreage in the United States. In a world at peace, the expanded demand for American cotton produced a price rise of over 60 percent between 1814 and 1818. U.S. receipts from the sale of cotton lands rose from about $100,000 to over $9 million, and the price of slaves about doubled between those years. But the period of gestation in opening up new cotton acreage was relatively short because the new acreage was no great distance from the old and because no massive infrastructure investments were required before the land could be brought into production and the market. In this respect the dynamics of American cotton and wheat differed. By 1819 supply had overshot demand, and all three variables had reversed. By the late 1820's, however, there were signs that the demand for raw cotton, enjoying still a high trend rate of expansion, was catching up with supply from existing acreage. The proportion of British cotton consumption to stocks began to rise from 1828, as did the sale of cotton lands in the United States. The cotton price ceased to fall after 1827. The price of slaves, then 20 percent below the peak of the previous cotton boom, a decade earlier, began to rise again in 1829–1830. Against this background, the sharp cyclical expansion of Britain, starting in 1833 and shared throughout the Atlantic community, yielded a mini-Kondratieff upswing; that is, investment flowed to expand cotton capacity, and, briefly, all the other key variables reversed their trend course. As we all learned from our school-day expositions of the Jackson era, it did not take long for the overshoot to occur. By 1835, U.K. cotton consumption, as a proportion of stocks, began to fall, and the cotton price broke sharply in 1836. We are back in the environment of a typical Kondratieff downswing, which persists to the end of the 1840's: the farmers complain, capital flows to industry and the expansion of railways in Britain and the American Northeast, and real wages rise.

There was, however, a typical warning of change before the second Kondratieff upswing began: the Irish potato famine of 1845–1847 and less acute food supply problems on the European continent signaled the likelihood of a change in relative prices, as population growth pressed against existing acreage. In its timing, the food crisis of 1845–1847 bears the same relation to the coming of the second Kondratieff upswing as the Indian food crisis of 1965–1967 bears to the beginning of the fifth. Each warning crisis was followed by a transient easing in the strain on food supplies. The periods of convulsive rise in food prices come in 1852–1854 and 1972–1974, respectively.

Second Kondratieff Cycle: 1848–1896

The second Kondratieff upswing is conventionally dated from the deep business cycle trough of 1848, although, as just noted, the sharp initial rise in agricultural prices occurs in 1852–1854. Almost three-quarters of the total rise in the British price level in this Kondratieff upswing took place in that two-year span. Again we have an element of Model 4 (W) as well as Model 2 (K) at work, that is, the Crimean War. And war continues to play an episodic role throughout the second Kondratieff upswing: the Indian Mutiny (1857–1858), the American Civil War, and the three Prussian campaigns that ended with the defeat of the French in 1870.

The sharp rise in the wheat price induced the opening up with railways of the American Middle West in the 1850's, drawing large capital imports (as well as migrants) to the United States. The transcontinental link was completed after the Civil War. High food prices led also to expanded investment in European agriculture which incorporated the technologies that had emerged toward the close of the first Kondratieff downswing. And the railroads worked their magic not only in new *B* areas but also by accelerating the commercialization of European agriculture.

Speaking of the impact of the railway on French agriculture, John Clapham wrote: ". . . forces were set free vastly more powerful than had ever played upon it, forces capable of doing in decades what under all previous conditions might have taken centuries."[12]

The wheat price began to decline in the late 1860's, but its rapid descent (in terms of international prices) comes after 1873.

As in the first Kondratieff upswing, the operation of Model 3 (S1) is relevant and a damping factor on the inflationary process. The convergence of the great leading sector of the period (railroads) with the requirements for expanding B capacity down to the early 1870's is evident; and the railroads, by cutting transport costs, had diffuse but powerful effects in containing the rise in the cost of living.

It should, perhaps, be noted that the world confronted a brief energy crisis of sorts in the boom of 1871–1873. The British coal price doubled in the face of a capacity shortage, but additional coal seams were accessible, investment promptly responded, and the coal price was soon in rapid decline along with most other prices.

The second Kondratieff downswing (1873–1896) is, like the first (1815–1848), relatively unbroken by war and fairly well covered by Model 2 (K). Its central feature is, from our perspective, the convergent effects on urban real wages of the grain oversupply from the new B area of the prior Kondratieff upswing (the American West) and the cost-reducing consequences of the steel revolution—a phenomenon covered by Model 3 (S1). Among its other effects, it rendered long-distance steel ships efficient. Ocean freight rates about halved between 1873 and the mid-1890's. The price of steel rails fell by 80 percent in the United States.

The old wheat-producing areas in Europe either went out of production (in Britain and Denmark) or sought refuge in protection (Germany and France), but rising real income made meat and dairy production profitable in many parts of Europe. Meanwhile, the railroads spread to certain potential new agricultural export areas, notably Canada, Australia, Russia, India, and Argentina. In the latter case, a major boom occurred in the late 1880's which broke the continuity of the second Kondratieff downswing, as the American cotton boom of the 1830's broke the continuity of trends in the first. Once the pampas were cleared of Indians and barbed wire permitted fencing, that rich area was judged profitable for development despite the falling trend in agricultural prices. This preparation of new areas for expanded grain output proved fortunate; for the rate of increase in the American demand for grain, reinforced by large immigration and rapid urbanization, was high, and the rate of increase in American wheat production rapidly decelerated from the 1890's, in the wake of the ending of the frontier. For a time the American capacity to export grain narrowed sharply, but the process was more general than grain; *B* prices rose relatively along a broad front from their troughs in the mid-1890's.

Third Kondratieff Cycle: 1896–1933

Like its two predecessors, the third Kondratieff upswing was marked, even before 1914, by military conflict on a considerable scale as well as by increased proportions of GNP allocated to military purposes by the major powers of the time. The major pre-1914 conflicts were the Spanish-American, Boer, Russo-Japanese, and Balkan wars. But the forces at work on the *B* and *I* sectors were, evidently, deeply rooted and would have left Model 2 (K) marks on the world economy even in the absence of the wastages of war and expanded arms outlays.

With respect to the *B* sector, the rise of agricultural and raw material prices after the mid-1890's led, as Model 2 suggests, to large capital flows to Canada, Australia, Russia, and Argentina. They played in the third Kondratieff upswing a role similar to that of the American West in the second; and all except Argentina enjoyed rapid industrial expansion as well. The rise in food prices again yielded rising urban costs of living which reduced or decelerated the rise in real wages—most markedly in Britain, but also in Germany and the United States. Extremely high British capital exports to new *B*-sector countries in the decade after the end of the Boer War contributed to the result.

There was, however, a strand in this third Kondratieff upswing not shared in the first and second; that is, Model 3 (S1, S2) operates in a different way. The old leading sectors (notably steel) had come to a stage of diminishing rates of productivity increase, and the new leading sectors (notably the automobile and electricity) had not achieved sufficient scale to compensate for the retardation in steel. Thus, in the older industrial economies, there is evidence of rising marginal capital-output ratios in the pre-

1914 decade or so. This Model 3 element contributed in those economies a significant strand to the retardation of real income per capita and real urban wages.

The First World War is a classic Model 4 case in the B sector; that is, the wartime loss of B capacity is at least partially made good by compensatory expansion outside the war-affected areas, and two years of postwar revival of production and trade in the war-inhibited areas yield a massive overshooting in B capacity and a sharp reversal in the relative prices of B goods. The formal upper turning point occurs in the second quarter of 1920, but a year-long plummeting of raw material prices begins in the fourth quarter. The third Kondratieff downswing was under way.

Although it is legitimate to deal with the interwar years in trend-period terms, its complexities and pathology make Model 2 (K) a less satisfactory abstraction of economic history than in the two earlier cases. One reason is that the First World War had a special impact on the I sector: it changed quite radically the distribution of industrial production as compared to the pre-1914 years. When Europe had re-attained what passed for normalcy between the wars (1926–1929), the United Kingdom, France, and Germany were producing about 28 percent of the world's industrial output as opposed to 35 percent in 1913; the United States, 44 percent versus 38 percent; Japan and the rest of Asia, including the Middle East, 7 percent versus 3 percent. This outcome did not flow primarily from the fact that the United States and Asia escaped physical damage. Round about 1916, the United States entered, with high momentum, the age of the mass use of the automobile. This momentum proceeded forward down to 1929, carrying with it virtuosity in a wide range of industries: strip steel, light electronics, rubber tires, oil refining. Japan, on the other hand, had not merely captured a number of European export markets in Asia but had also moved forward in steel, metalworking, chemicals, and other sophisticated industrial sectors. Western Europe—Britain, above all—had thus lost export markets; its residual export markets were weakened by the relatively low range of B commodity prices in the 1920's, and its difficulties were compounded by its return to the gold standard in 1925 at the excessive pre-1914 exchange rate. But high unemployment was endemic in Western Europe of the 1920's. This made it difficult to generate the expansion in real consumer income necessary to move into the automobile age at a pace sufficient to absorb the chronically unemployed in the old export-related leading sectors (steel, shipbuilding, textiles, coal).

Under these circumstances, large stocks of B commodities built up, overhanging the markets until the depression after 1929, when they contributed to a massive further collapse in B prices.

Agricultural prices and incomes were also relatively weak in America of the 1920's, as they were in Europe in the second Kondratieff downswing (1873–1896); but the dynamism of the new leading sectors in the United States, with a higher income per capita, was sufficient to overcome the drag and maintain relatively full employment down to 1929. Western Europe was not able to achieve this.

Then came the unique pathology of the Great Depression which, obviously, cannot be explored here. But its depth and protracted character do relate, in part, to the impact on incomes in the B sector of the collapse of relative prices after 1929. They also relate to the fact that the leading industries within the I sector required direct stimulus to consumer income before they could regather momentum. With respect to Model 3 (S2), it may be useful to point out that, contrary to widely held views at the time, the leading sectors of the period had not come to a stage of maturity and low productivity. Once an environment of full employment was established after 1945, they exhibited a decade of continued high momentum in postwar United States, two decades in postwar Western Europe and Japan.

Fourth Kondratieff Cycle: 1933–1972

The turning point into the fourth Kondratieff upswing was, of course, triggered by the global revival which began in 1932–1933. After 1929, B production stagnated or declined, in response to reduced demand and, in some cases, government policies of restriction on the production of food and raw materials. Nevertheless, stocks generally continued to rise during the depressed years; but with recovery, stocks fell and prices began to lift, some responding strongly to the rearmament boom which got under way in 1936.

The Second World War had the usual impact of major conflict on relative B prices. There was also the usual postwar delay in the revival of B production, yielding a continued rise in relative B prices after 1945. There was a tendency toward stabilization in

1948–1949, but then the Korean War yielded a second sharp rise in relative B prices. Between 1938 and 1951 the prices of manufactured goods in world trade rose by 106 percent; the prices of food and raw materials, by 257 percent. The terms of trade for developed market economies fell between those two years from 98 to 89 (1963 = 100); for developing market economies they rose from 79 to 128 (excluding petroleum).

The distinctive characteristic of the fourth Kondratieff upswing is that it did not involve the opening up of large new agricultural areas. The wartime and postwar increases (down to 1947–1948) in U.S. production were, essentially, from existing agricultural areas. But a powerful productivity revolution was gathering momentum, centered on new seeds, chemical fertilizers, pesticides, and more efficient farm machinery, including the mechanical cotton picker. Output of wheat per acre rose by 38 percent between 1932 and 1948; of corn, by 61 percent. Overall, farm production per man-hour, which had increased at an annual average rate of 1.2 percent in the period 1919–1929 and 2.1 percent for 1929–1937, increased at 4.5 percent from 1937 to 1948. On the other hand, the post-1945 development of Middle East oil belongs in the great tradition of the mid-nineteenth-century opening up of the Middle West and the expansion of agriculture in Canada, Argentina, and Australia in the pre-1914 generation.

The fourth Kondratieff downswing (1951–1972) has, with one major exception, many of the characteristics of the first and second: a sharp initial downward break in relative B prices followed by a leveling off; a concentration of investment in the I sector, where the leading industries moved strongly forward (automobiles, durable consumer goods, chemicals, electronics); favorable terms of trade for industrialized countries and a rapid rise in urban real wages within them; and anticipatory warnings, as the downswing came toward its close, of a likely turn in relative prices (notably in grain and energy). The major exception is that this is the only Kondratieff downswing with an overall inflationary trend. There was some absolute fall in B prices in the 1950's; but the uniquely low average levels of unemployment maintained in this neo-Keynesian period, combined with the failure of public policy to cope with wage-push inflation, imparted an inflationary cast to the period as a whole. Indeed, as a matter of trend, the rate of inflation accelerates, in part because the relative decline in *B* prices, which damped inflation in the 1950's, ceases in the 1960's. Otherwise, Model 3 works pretty well.

As for the role of Model 3, the various parts of the industrialized world experienced different rates of productivity increase in the *I* sector, depending on the time at which they began efficiently to absorb on a mass-production basis the technologies of the leading sectors at the stage I have called high mass-consumption. The United States, having pioneered these industries, moved most slowly after 1945; postwar northwestern Europe enjoys a rate of output per unit input 2.24 times higher than that of the United States; the Japanese rate is, of course, still higher. But toward the end of the 1960's there is, in varying degrees, the suggestion of a general deceleration in the rate of productivity increase and rise in capital-output ratios as the leading sectors of high mass-consumption move toward maturity. Like the industrial world in the pre-1914 generation, the United States, Western Europe, and Japan entered the fifth Kondratieff upswing at a time when the previous leading sectors were decelerating in both growth rate and rate of productivity increase.

Fifth Kondratieff Upswing, First Phase: 1972–1979

Despite the unique role of OPEC, as an effective cartel with control over an important *B*-sector price, the world economy's entrance into the fifth Kondratieff upswing bears a clear family relation to the four predecessor equivalent phases: sharp rises in grain and energy prices against the background of a prior period of decline in the proportion of reserves to consumption; a sharp, brief rise in relative *B* prices (1972–1974), not sustained but not giving way to prior relative price levels; the usual shifts in terms of trade and income distribution within and among nations; severe pressure on urban real wages; and accelerated general inflation.

What is unique about the first phase of the fifth Kondratieff upswing is that it led also to an interval (1974–1979) when unemployment levels were higher than those typical of the prior period (say, the 1960's), despite the recovery from the trough that took place in 1975.

This brings us to the problem abstractly but inadequately captured in Model 5 (SF). Historically, Kondratieff upswings were marked by cycles with normal or perhaps even lower than normal average unemployment levels. The expanded investment in the *B* sector, induced by the upward relative shift in *B* prices, led to expanded exports from regions (or countries) containing the *I* sector. These expanded exports were often accompanied by expanded capital exports. Real wages in *I*-sector countries were damped; but employment in the export component of the *I* sector was high.

To a degree, that certainly happened in the period 1974–1977; that is, there was an enormous shift in global exports to the OPEC countries (from 6.6% in 1972 to 14.5% in 1974), and, to a degree, that enlarged flow of goods and services helped sustain the level of employment in the industrialized exporting countries. But only a limited part of that flow, enforced by the monopoly price, was devoted to expanding the world's energy production capacity.

Monopoly control over this critical *B*-sector price counseled that production (notably, in Saudi Arabia) be constrained and production capacity expanded at less than the maximum potential rate. In a less dramatic way, there was a shift of relative income and capital to the energy-producing states within the United States, as well as to Norway and Scotland. But, in general, the energy-importing nations were slow to react to the shift in the relative price of energy by enlarging their own investments in energy and energy conservation. In the United States, notably, energy prices were not permitted to reflect the changed state of things; and this desire to go on in the style of the fourth Kondratieff downswing (when the relative price of energy fell by 23%) was reinforced by environmental and other legal and administrative obstacles to an expansion of energy production. Poor public policies have made the "recognition lag" of Model 2 (K) much longer than it should have been. Since the income and employment multiplier effects of exporting to OPEC countries and importing a margin of their excess capital were less than for domestic investment in energy and energy conservation, the level of employment suffered in the energy-importing OECD countries.

This effect was compounded by the price—as well as income—elasticity of demand for the products of the leading sectors in the prior period of rapid growth. Automobiles, durable consumer goods, modern chemicals, and the movement from central cities to suburbia were all energy intensive. Their momentum was damped by the relative rise in energy prices and further damped by the decline or deceleration in the expansion of urban real wages in energy-importing countries or regions. This is a sectoral phenomenon not captured in our models.

All this had its effects on the scale and pattern of world trade. In the fourth Kondratieff downswing the extraordinary expansion of world trade was mainly among the most advanced industrial countries. The volume of that trade declined or decelerated after 1972, only partially compensated for by expanded trade with the OPEC countries. The non-OPEC developing nations also suffered retardation or worse. This happened because of high oil import prices and the deceleration of growth rates in the United States, Western Europe, and Japan. These pressures on their foreign exchange availabilities were only partially compensated for by enlarged foreign aid or private borrowing abroad.

One consequence of this complex process as a whole was a further deceleration in the rate of productivity increase in the world's *I* sector. It was caused by operations short of capacity; by the continued rise, already to be observed in the late 1960's, in capital-output ratios; and by efficiency losses due to efforts to economize energy. Recently installed environmental regulations may have somewhat accentuated this tendency.

This incomplete and stylized explanation for the deceleration of growth rates and higher than average unemployment in the developed industrial countries of the world since 1974 is meant to indicate the difficulty of capturing, in a simple model, the reasons for the six years of relative stagnation experienced in the advanced industrial countries in the period 1973–1979.

At the core of the difference between the fifth and the first three Kondratieff upswings (the fourth occurred during revival from the pit of the Great Depression of the 1930's) is, I believe, this fact: public policy has either obstructed or failed to encourage sufficiently the shift of investment flows to the *B* sector. This failure was particularly marked with respect to non-OPEC investment in energy production and conservation.

Benedetto Croce once observed: ". . . whilst it is possible to reduce to general concepts the particular factors of reality which appear in history . . . it is not possible to work up into general concepts the single complex whole formed by these factors."[13] That, we take it, is the large meaning of the exercise this chapter incorporates. It is quite possible to set up models which capture elements in the trend behavior of the world economy over the past two centuries; these models can illuminate lucidly processes not fully developed in either conventional economic history or contemporary economic theory. We also believe they may have some significance for the design of effective economic policy now and over the coming generation. But they fall considerably short of re-creating economic history. And we take it that it is the duty of model builders to be as conscious of what their fabrications fail to embrace as they are of the piece of reality they capture.

3

Energy, Full Employment, and Regional Development: The American Case

I

This chapter brings to bear the perspective elaborated in Chapters 1 and 2 on a major issue of public policy: energy policy in the United States. It seeks to demonstrate a relationship little perceived by conventional macroeconomists, that is, the link between the solution to a key sectoral problem and the aggregate performance of the economy. The link is the expansion of energy-related investment required to reduce oil imports. Although the analysis is confined to the United States and its major regions, the analytic framework and method are, I believe, highly relevant to Europe, Japan, and other countries.

Most policy-oriented analyses of the energy problem of the United States begin by assuming a national rate of real growth consistent with relatively full employment; calculate the energy requirements needed to sustain it, under stated assumptions about the potentialities for energy saving and policies to exploit those potentialities; and then proceed to estimates of the optimum mix of domestic energy production required to balance the growth-energy equation, at some viable level of oil and gas imports. President Carter's National Energy Plan of 1977 (NEP), for example, assumed an annual average real rate of growth of GNP of about 4.3 percent between 1976 and 1985; proposed policies that would permit that growth rate to continue with an annual average increase of 2.25 percent in energy consumption, rather than the 3.0 percent otherwise assumed necessary; and then proceeded to the supply balance sheet and the policies believed necessary to generate the production and switch in energy sources that balance sheet demanded, if oil and gas imports were to be reduced by 1985 to about the equivalent of 6 million barrels of oil per day (mboed). The macroeconomic consequences of the plan, including its effects on investment, income, and employment, were dealt with in an extremely brief, fragmentary passage.[1] Its central theme was: "The macroeconomic impacts of the Plan would be quite small in a $2 trillion economy."[2]

That is also the central theme of the various longer-term models designed to examine the effects of alternative energy policies on the real rate of growth over periods extending beyond 1985.[3]

I doubt that the macroeconomic consequences of a serious national energy plan will be "quite small." On the face of it, an effective national effort to contain oil imports at the level of, say, 6 mboed, when the present level is almost 9 and expected to rise in the early 1980's; when energy consumption is rising at 2–3 percent per annum and the decline in energy production is not yet reversed; when we must shift massively out of natural gas to coal, changing the locus of energy sources and the nation's transport requirements; when we must drill and find new oil and gas reserves at a rate sufficient to overcome a steady decline in production from old reserves (including Alaska) at a rate of about 5.5 percent per annum for oil, 7.5 percent for gas—such an effort is bound to have large macroeconomic effects on the economy.

Quite aside from the massive investments required to damp the rate of increase in energy consumption, the NEP called for the development of 22.6 mboed in new domestic energy resources over the nine years between 1976 and 1985, if the declining trend in production from existing oil and gas fields is taken into account. This figure compares with the average for all nine-year periods since 1920 of 3.3 mboed.[4] The maximum increase for any nine-year period since 1920 was 9.0 mboed, over the years 1962–1970, during which the North Slope Alaska reserves were added to the nation's energy production capacity. As shall emerge, we are talking about an increase of two to three times in the relative flow of resources to a sector which, before 1974, normally absorbed, at a minimum estimate, about 16–20 percent of nonresidential fixed business investment, 1.7–2.0 percent of gross national product (Table 3-5, below). We were confronted, then, with the need for a massive as well as rapid change in the structure of the economy and the disposition of investment resources over a nine-year span, and two of those years passed with little progress. In addition, we must engage in substantial efforts (in research, development, and the early stages of commercial production) if, in fact, the post-1985 technologies (shale, synthetics, geothermal resources, etc.) are to play their predicted role in future energy supply.

Against that background of prima facie argument, this chapter explores the following questions:

—How would the aggregate performance of the economy as a whole be affected by a successful effort to achieve the approximate goals set out in the NEP?

—How would the major regions be affected?

As always when relatively new questions are being posed, the data are not available in the form necessary to permit firm answers. But the systematic posing of these two questions and an effort to find approximate answers may be useful as a preliminary canvassing of a field about which, I believe, we are destined to learn a great deal more than we now know.

I shall proceed as follows:

—First, evoke some historical evidence of shifts in the direction of investment, responding to a rise in the relative prices of one or more basic commodities, and briefly outline some of the consequences of such shifts.

—Second, discuss the extent to which existing models attempting to relate the energy sector to the macroperformance of the economy are relevant to the two key questions posed.

—Third, suggest by what routes the relative rise in the price of energy and expanded energy-related investment bear on the problem of achieving and maintaining a high sustained rate of growth and relatively full employment.

—Finally, discuss some of the possible regional implications of the analysis as a whole.

II

As indicated in Chapters 1 and 2, the history of the world economy over the past two centuries has been marked by four irregular cycles in the relative prices of foodstuffs and raw materials. Since 1972 the world economy has experienced the probable beginning of a fifth upswing. The cyclical upswings were characterized by an overall inflationary trend (including money wages and interest rates); a relative shift of income to producers of foodstuffs and raw materials; and deceleration or decline in real wages. In the downswings, the movements were, of course, obverse. The upswings began round about 1790, 1848, 1896, 1933, and 1972; the downswings, 1815, 1873, 1920, 1951.

For our limited purposes, the heart of the matter is the change in the direction of investment induced by these shifts in relative prices and, therefore, in profitability. Here, we are in a field where historical data are scarce, indeed. But a few examples where we have some statistical insight may be helpful in illuminating the process set in motion by the sustained rise in the relative price of a significant basic commodity.

In the first cycle (say, 1790–1848), there is considerable evidence that, responding to the course of agricultural prices, agricultural investment in Britain increased on the upswing and fell away relatively on the downswing. In the period 1788–1792, parliamentary acts of enclosure averaged annually 35; 114 for the peak period of agricultural prices (1808–1814); and by the early 1840's the figure was 16.

Estimates of total agricultural investment are more difficult to establish. The best calculations we have exhibit a rise from £3.6 million ca. 1790–1793 to £5.3 million ca. 1815 and a decline to £4.6 million ca. 1830–1835.[5] Despite a sharp rise in the proportion of total investment in machinery over these years, as one would expect in the decisive initial phase of the industrial revolution (12.5% ca. 1790–1793 to 15.8% ca. 1815 to 20.0% ca. 1830–1835), the proportion of agricultural to total investment roughly held its own in the upswing, but fell away from 21.1 percent ca. 1815 to 11.5 percent ca. 1830–1835.

These shifts in the direction of investment were, to a degree, made possible by a second effect of the movement in relative prices: an income, or terms-of-trade, effect. In the upswing, the judgment of historians is that British farmers were, by and large, notably prosperous; in the downswing, many were borne down by lower prices, although productivity improvements cushioned the position of the more enterprising in the 1830's and 1840's. This familiar generalization is hard to demonstrate rigorously. For part of the upswing (1806–1815) we have some fragmentary evidence as a result of the wartime income tax. When the yield of that tax, under its several schedules, is analyzed by regions, the expansion of agricultural incomes emerges clearly.[6] That expansion, in turn, permitted the increase in investment. Speaking of agriculture, Arthur Hope-Jones concluded: "Under the threat of war, food shortage and rising prices 'progress' became a patriotic duty and a profitable investment."[7] A good many new or expanded country houses, as well as enclosed and well-drained fields, flowed from this rise in income. We lack equivalent evidence for the downswing, but the complaints of the agricultural community and pressures for tariff protection suggest that a relative shift in income occurred, a trend validated by the rising trend in urban real wages. And this shift in income distribution is undoubtedly related to the shift in the direction of British investment away from agriculture toward industry and (after 1830) the laying down of the highly productive British railway net.

Aspects of the American pre-1860 experience illustrate the same network of relationships. Although the role of industry increased over the period 1815–1860, the United States was still primarily an agricultural nation, its exports dominated by cotton, with wheat exports increasing their role in the fifteen years before the Civil War. The American terms of trade are, therefore, a fair reflection of movements in the relative prices of agricultural products and manufactures.

The terms of trade exhibit three intervals of increase: 1815–1817, 1828–1835, and 1845–1851, although fluctuations persist at a high level until 1857.[8] For most of the 1820's and the first half of the 1840's, the terms of trade were, relatively, low.

The related shift in the direction of investment can be traced in two rough indicators: the purchase of federal lands and capital imports. Both exhibit high levels in the three periods of favorable terms of trade; both fall away in the 1820's and 1840's.[9] As one would expect, real wages rise in the 1840's and come under downward pressure in the 1850's.[10] This passage in American history introduces a further variable: immigration. The data, which begin at 1820, exhibit only a modest rise down to 1831, a sharp increase in the boom of the 1830's, a relative decline or deceleration down to 1845, and movement to a peak in 1854. The annual average figure for 1840–1844 was 80 thousand; for 1850–1859, 384 thousand.

The case of Canada from 1896 to 1914 permits one to observe this mechanism at work, plus an additional potential dimension of the process. There is, as in the United States of the 1830's and

1850's, a shift in relative prices favorable to a producer of wheat and raw materials, a favorable movement of the terms of trade, a large influx of capital from abroad, and a massive increase in immigration.[11] The new dimension to be observed here is that the combination of forces at work in Canada in the two pre-1914 decades lifted that nation into its first sustained phase of modern industrialization.[12] Since 1868 a number of developments, including considerable railroadization and the expansion of processing industries, had prepared the way for the Canadian takeoff. The point to be made here is that, when other conditions are propitious, an expansion of real income initiated by a favorable export price environment can have a significant expansionary effect on industry, over a wide front, as well as on the production of agricultural products and raw materials.

What of the fate of capital exporters under these circumstances? Britain was the largest supplier of capital to pre-1914 Canada. In the long run, Britain benefited as the laying of the Canadian railway network to the wheat areas of Western Canada opened up a new and necessary supply of imported grain to supplant the attenuated supplies from the United States. While the Canadian boom was under way, British export industries gained, as did those in Britain deriving income from interest and profits. But the unfavorable shift in the British terms of trade, which, in effect, initiated the Canadian boom, was accentuated by the scale of the expansion in Canada and the concurrent expansions in Argentina and Australia. These were triggered by the same mechanism as that which set off the Canadian boom and were also sustained substantially by British capital exports. The result was downward pressure on British real wages and a lower level of domestic investment in Britain than would otherwise have occurred. In the period of high capital exports (1903–1913) gross domestic fixed capital formation in Britain fell from about 11 percent of GNP to 6–7 percent.[13] Net investment abroad rose from £43 million (1903) to £235 million, that is, from 2 percent of GNP to 8.6 percent. Thus the proportion of total investment to GNP rose, despite the fall in domestic investment. Other decelerating forces were at work in the British and other advanced industrial economies of the time, but the scale of British capital exports rendered that deceleration more marked than in, say, Germany and the United States.[14]

One of the most dramatic reflections of the relation between a relative price movement and the pace of overall economic development is incorporated in the story of per capita income of the American South in relation to that of the rest of the country. Table 3-1 shows relative real income per capita for all the American regions from 1840 to 1975. Between 1840 and 1860 the cotton South experienced a decade of relative deceleration (1840–1850) followed by a decade of relatively high prices and prosperity. It lost, nevertheless, a little ground to the rapidly industrializing North. By 1880, however, the South's position had radically deteriorated. This was not the result merely of war destruction and Reconstruction but also of a decline of the cotton price from 43 cents per pound in 1866 to 12 cents in 1880. The decline continued to a trough of 6 cents in 1898. This trend was accompanied by a global deceleration in the cotton textile industry and the volume of U.S. cotton exports. Thus, the value of U.S. cotton exports exceeded its 1866 level in only one year (1887) down to 1899. Meanwhile, industrialization in the South proceeded slowly, indeed. The relative lift in cotton prices reversed to a degree the relative income position of the South down to 1920: the cotton price was less than 7 cents per pound in 1899; 13 cents in 1913; 34 cents in 1920. But, substantially influenced by the subsequent decline in cotton prices, the relative income position of the region sagged away in the 1920's and, of course, during the period of acute depression, 1929–1933.

After 1933, once again the cotton price lifted; but this time the South, like Canada forty years earlier, was ready for sustained industrialization. With a large backlog of available technologies to apply, it moved forward over a wide front, gaining relatively on the more mature industrial states as it modernized its agriculture, developed an increasingly diversified industrial structure, and rapidly urbanized its social life. That process proceeded despite the relative setback to its basic commodity prices between 1951 and 1972. The relative upward shift in agricultural and energy prices since 1972 accelerated the narrowing of the income gap, as well as the flow of migrants to the South. The large flow of Negroes to the northern cities began to reverse. No doubt, if we had such data, we would find that the flow of external capital to the South also accelerated.

The link of relative price to income movements is underlined

TABLE 3-1. Per Capita Income as Percentage of U.S. Total, by Regions: 1840–1975

Year	USA	New England	Middle Atlantic	East North Central	West North Central	South Atlantic	East South Central	West South Central	Mountain	Pacific
1975	100%	108%	108%	104%	98%	90%	79%	91%	92%	111%
1970	100	108	113	105	95	86	74	85	90	110
1965	100	108	114	108	95	81	71	83	90	115
1960	100	109	116	107	93	77	67	83	95	118
1950	100	106	116	112	94	74	63	81	96	121
1940	100	121	124	112	84	69	55	70	92	138
1930	100	129	140	111	82	56	48	61	83	130
1920	100	124	134	108	87	59	52	72	100	135
1900	100	134	139	106	97	45	49	61	139	163
1880	100	141	141	102	90	45	51	70	168%	204%
1860	100	143	137	69	66	65	68	115	—	—
1840	100%	132%	136%	67%	75%	70%	73%	144%	—	—

Sources: 1840–1970: Historical Statistics of the United States, Colonial Times to 1970 (Washington, D.C.: Department of Commerce, 1975), p. 242. 1975: Survey of Current Business 56 (August 1976): table 2, p. 17.

by recent trends in population and relative income in the energy-rich states of the Mountain West and, of course, Alaska, as Table 3-7, below, suggests.

As in the case of pre-1914 Britain, the states of the Northeast and industrial Middle West lost ground, relatively, at an accelerated rate since the disproportionate rise in energy prices. The number of manufacturing jobs declined absolutely in the Northeast and industrial Middle West; unemployment was higher than the national average in the recession of 1974–1975, remaining so in the years of limited recovery, 1976–1977.[15] Lacking internal balance of payments data for American states and regions, we cannot measure the probable increase in capital flows to the energy-producing states, but the movement of population to those states has been impressive.

The reason for evoking these brief historical illustrations is to suggest something of the dynamic process and its dimensions which a shift in relative prices, of the kind we now confront in energy, can set in motion. As among nations and within nations, we confront not merely terms-of-trade (or direct income) effects, but also changing investment and population flows, triggering in some cases far-ranging alterations in the pace and character of economic and social development. These forces operate both on regions enjoying the advantage of high-priced basic commodities and on those experiencing unfavorable terms of trade, from which capital and population may flow.

III

Against this background, we turn now to what the energy-economy models tell us and fail to tell us about the links of energy to the performance of the economy.

They start with four empirical and, as nearly as we know, correct assumptions:

1. There is no foreseeable physical limit on the U.S. energy supply over, say, the next half-century; that is, coal, shale, and advanced forms of nuclear power could supplant the probable decline in oil, natural gas, and uranium reserves, even without large-scale solar or fusion power.

2. The marginal (and average) cost of energy will rise; that is, for some time we can expect the real cost of replacing a unit of

energy consumed to exceed its present average price. We do not know with confidence what the rise in the real price of energy will prove to be.

3. The total cost of energy in the U.S. economy as a proportion of GNP is relatively small, say, 5 percent in 1975. Therefore, even a quite substantial rise in the price of energy will yield only a modest damping in the rate of increase of real GNP, assuming GNP continues to rise regularly at rates not grossly dissimilar to those we have experienced since the end of the Second World War.

4. We cannot estimate reliably, on the basis of past experience, what the price elasticity of demand for energy will prove to be in the face of a gross alteration of energy prices over a long period of time; nor can we estimate reliably long-period changes in taste and in the income elasticity of demand for energy, as real income per capita rises; nor can we estimate reliably what the long-run elasticity of substitution of other factors of production for energy will prove to be. Therefore, in striking long-run demand-supply balances, considerable ranges are appropriate.

With this framework of empirical assumptions, a good many energy-economy models have been developed and applied to long-run energy policy issues. They all derive, in one fashion or another, from the neoclassical growth models evolved over the past generation from the Harrod-Domar model.

The neoclassical models have these basic characteristics shared by current energy-economy models:

—Since both neoclassical and energy-economy models are, essentially, closed systems, the balance of payments and the level of energy imports are dealt with in casual ad hoc observations, if at all.

—Since these models are highly aggregated and closed system or national in their structure, neither differential regional effects within the United States nor the impact of U.S. energy performance on other regions of the world economy is dealt with systematically.

—They are long-run, full-employment models, assuming either competitive market conditions or public policies which approximate such conditions.

—The rate of technological progress is exogenously determined, although some energy-economy analysts speculate, at least, on the damping effect of higher energy prices on the average rate-of-productivity increase.

—A stable consumption function is assumed, although some energy-economy analysts speculate, at least, about a possible rise in the proportion of energy-related investment required and a possible rise in the proportion of GNP invested if their growth and full-employment assumptions are to be fulfilled.

—Since these models are long term, the period of gestation of energy-related investment is not explicitly dealt with.

As always, then, we get out of models what we assume in the first place. The energy-economy models tell us that the United States commands the resource and probable technological capacity to weather, under the assumed conditions, a period of transition to higher-cost energy sources with a relatively slight aggregate deceleration in GNP as compared to a situation where the real price of energy remained constant; that the potentialities of coal and shale give us considerable flexibility in exercising the nuclear option, and vice versa; and that the precise long-run outcome will be affected significantly by what the various relevant elasticities prove to be.

If our central analytic task in the field of energy economics was to prove that a simple limits-to-growth view was incorrect, the energy-economy models might be judged helpful. By underlining that the United States, at least, commands the resources and technologies to meet its likely energy requirements over the long term, that the central problem is a rise in the real cost of energy, and that the low proportion of energy outlays to GNP makes that rise consistent with a continuing expansion in real per capita income, something useful might be accomplished for those who believe the contrary, although a good many advocates of the limits-to-growth view are unlikely to find the techniques of energy-economy models accessible or particularly persuasive.

On the other hand, the energy-economy models are substantially misleading both as an approximation to the energy problem confronted by the United States as of early 1979 and as a guide to current U.S. energy policy. In effect, these models wash out by assumption the critical features in our current situation.[16]

Specifically:

1. The peaking out of OPEC production capacity in the 1980's, perhaps as early as 1983, imposes a critical time constraint on

U.S. energy policy, if the analyses of the CIA, MIT, and OECD experts are roughly correct, which I believe them to be (Chart 3-1).* The crucial factors here are two: (*a*) the explicit decision of Saudi Arabia to expand production capacity slowly at a time when production capacity in some other substantial OPEC nations will begin to decline; (*b*) limitations on energy conservation

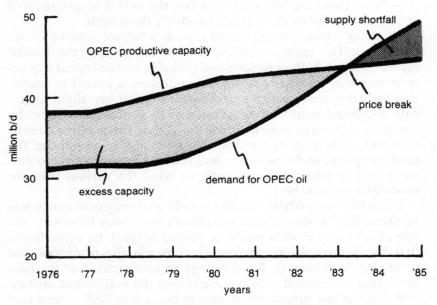

CHART 3-1. *Projection of Demand and Capacity in OPEC Production.*

Source: "The International Energy Situation: Outlook to 1985," Central Intelligence Agency, April 1977. A much more ominous prediction of OPEC's production ceiling in the 1980's is made by the U.S. Department of Energy, appearing in Energy Information Administration, *Annual Report to the Congress, Vol. II,* 1977 (Washington, D.C., April 1978), pp. 80–81. The April 1977 CIA estimate for OPEC production capacity in 1985 was 43.6–44.3 mbod; the DOE estimate a year later was 36.8–38.8, and, given developments in 1979, this may well prove also to have been excessively optimistic.

* Since this passage was written in early 1978, two events have brought about lower OPEC production capacity and lower production than was then envisaged: the direct and indirect effects of the Iranian crisis of 1978–1979 and the downward revision of Saudi Arabian production capacity. The consequence is to heighten the urgency of the argument in this paragraph.

which decree a quite substantial annual rate of growth of energy consumption if relatively full employment is to be sustained. The significance of the emergence of such an OPEC production capacity ceiling is heightened by the fact that Western Europe, taken as a whole, and Japan (as well as many developing countries) lack the potential alternative energy resources and technologies available to the United States. And, as in the United States, political forces are inhibiting the full exercise of the nuclear option. It is not an exaggeration of current reality to describe the increasing dependence of the United States, its allies, and others on a limited source of external energy supply as the key economic and, potentially, strategic fact on the world scene— the latter proposition underlined by Secretary of Defense Harold Brown on October 26, 1977.[17] Even the narrowly economic dimensions of this constraint are not captured in current energy-economy models. The pace at which the United States succeeds in reducing its energy imports will affect not merely the possibility of sustaining relatively full employment and high steady growth in the OECD world, but also the bargaining power of the importers vis-à-vis OPEC and the real price of imported oil itself. The implications of the required U.S. 1985 oil import level (up to 16 mboed), which will result from the shortfall many analysts believe is implicit in the implementing arrangements of the Carter Energy Plan, are not dealt with in energy-economy models (see Table 3-2).

2. The real or believed differential impact of energy policy on the various regions of the United States has, almost certainly, been the greatest political obstacle to the acceptance of effective national courses of action with respect to energy prices, the settlement of energy-environment trade-offs, and the government role in energy-related investment. The energy-economy models merely assume that, soon or late, these issues will be resolved on optimum dynamic equilibrium terms. The costs and consequences of a failure to achieve such resolutions are not systematically explored either for the aggregate performance of the economy or for the major regions.

3. Similarly, the stubbornly high level of unemployment in the OECD world since 1974 and the slackened average growth rates, as compared to the 1950's and 1960's, are neither noted nor explained in the energy-economy models. The failure of public policy to permit or achieve by purposeful action the energy prices

TABLE 3-2. *Various 1985 Projections of Domestic Energy Production and Shortfalls Relative to NEP Goals and Requirements (millions of barrels per day in oil equivalents [mboed])*

	Coal		Oil, Gas, & Liquids		Nuclear		Imports
	Projected Production	Shortfall	Projected Production	Shortfall	Projected Production	Shortfall	Projected
Congressional Research Service, Library of Congress	Low 8.6 Med 9.3 High 10.4	5.9 5.2 4.1	Most likely 17.3	2.1	Low 3.0 Base 3.8	.8 0	Base case 13.0
Office of Technology Assessment, U.S. Congress	12.1	2.4	18.4 to 16.4	1.0 to 3.0	3.2	0.6	Median or probable 15.9
U.T. Council on Energy Resources			Low 14.4 Median 15.9 High 17.2	5.0 3.5 2.2			16.5
General Accounting Office (excluding natural gas)							11.9–12.9
Independent Petrol. Assoc. of America			16.2	2.3			

Source: Council on Energy Resources, University of Texas at Austin.

the energy-economy models call for is, occasionally, noted; but the implications of that failure for levels of energy-related investment and employment are not explicitly explored.

4. The rising tendency in capital-output ratios (and declining per-hour labor productivity) since the late 1960's in the OECD economies is neither examined nor explained, nor are the means to enlarge the proportion of GNP invested which some of these analyses require for long-run dynamic full-employment equilibrium.

5. Finally, the dangers to the American and world economy implicit in the periods of gestation set out in Chart 3-2 are not considered. If the CIA analysis of the OPEC production capacity ceiling and its judgment about the level of global demand for OPEC oil are roughly correct, all but a few new sources of enlarged U.S. energy production (onshore and Gulf oil and gas, surface coal mining on private lands) carry with them present periods of gestation too long to avoid a serious global supply restriction by 1983. Energy conservation lead times can also be quite long; for example, some seven years are required to turn over the existing stock of automobiles.

As presently formulated, then, the energy-economy models systematically fail to capture the major features of the energy problem confronted by the United States and the world economy—now and over the decade or so ahead. They grip neither the urgency of the task nor its international and regional dimensions nor its linkage to the costly retardation of the American, OECD, and non-OPEC developing economies since 1974. As I wrote some years ago in another context: "It is an old story in the history of economic thought that the variables assumed as fixed or given, for purposes of formal exposition or convenience, tend to disappear from consideration among the objects of policy."[18]

IV

In turning now to the relation of energy investment to the level of employment, I shall not proceed by systematic modification of one or another energy-economy model. I am inclined to believe that portions of the argument that follows are capable of translation into modified formal growth models, along the lines of the exercise elaborated in Chapter 2. And it would, surely, be useful if some of the practitioners of the art would try to render their

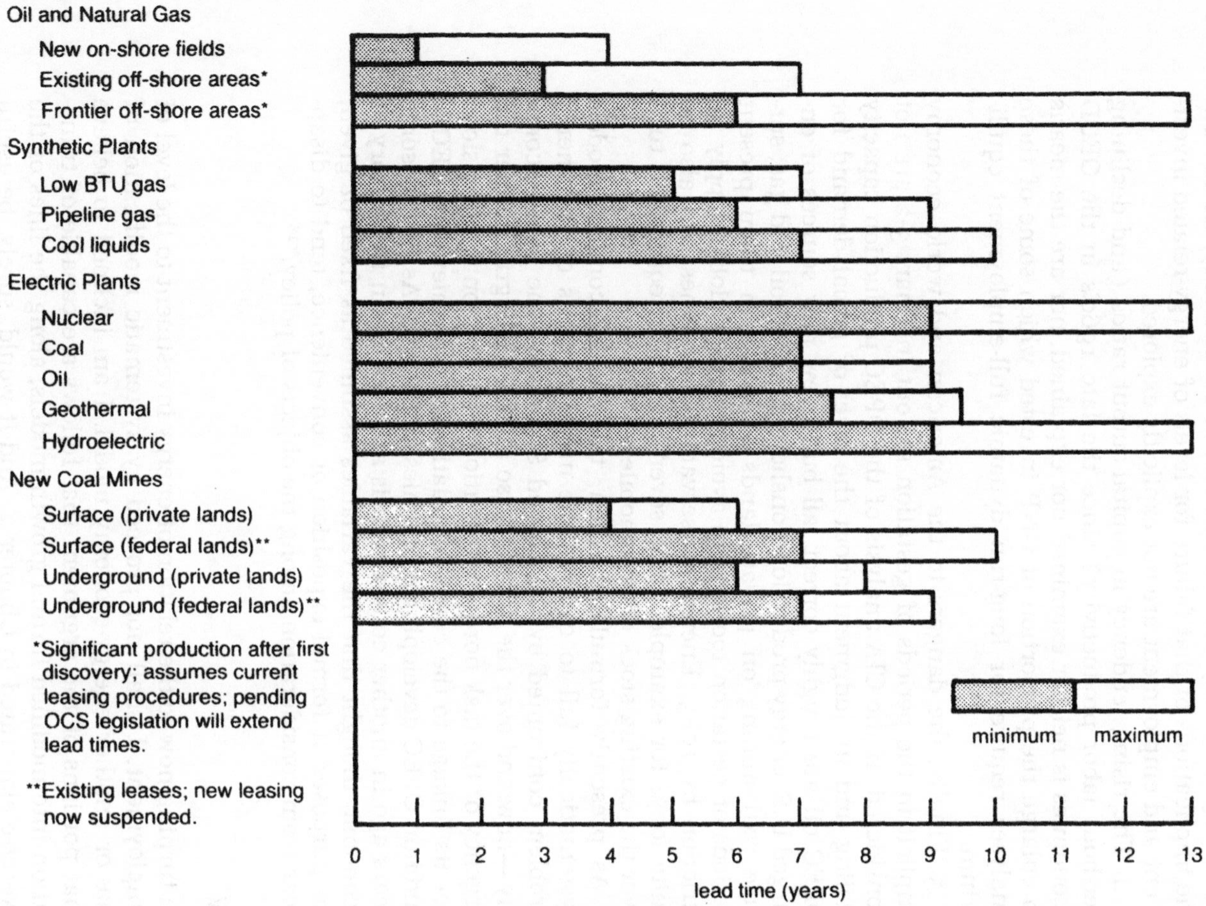

CHART 3-2. *Lead Times in Domestic Energy Development.*

Source: Modified from National Academy of Engineering (1973) and U.S. Geological Survey (1975) by Bureau of Economic Geology, University of Texas at Austin.

models more realistic and relevant. But I shall here approach the problem through more conventional economic analysis.

The argument can be summarized as follows: the relative stagnation of the OECD economies is the result of a failure of investment to revive to the extent that it did during the cyclical recoveries of the 1950's and 1960's; this failure is related to the impact on the rate of increase of real private income of the rise in energy prices; in the United States, at least, the order of magnitude of the energy-related investment required between now and 1985 to reduce U.S. oil imports to something like 6 mboed is sufficient to bring the American economy back to relatively full employment; the regional locus of this investment would be such as to mitigate some, at least, of the problems of the hard-pressed Northeast and industrial Middle West, as well as to accelerate the rapid expansions under way in the Mountain and West South Central states. The effects on the South Atlantic, East South Central, and Pacific Coast states (excepting Alaska), which have a stronger underlying momentum than the states of the industrial North, fall somewhere in between.

Chart 3-3 catches vividly the failure of investment in the six major OECD economies to recover from the recession of 1974–1975 with the resilience exhibited in previous cyclical expansions. This phenomenon stems from the anatomy of the great OECD boom of the previous two decades. In economic jargon, investment was driven forward in this period by the accelerator. The rapid increase in real income per capita, strengthened after 1951 by falling or relatively low prices for energy and other basic commodities, permitted the income elasticity of demand to express itself strongly in these directions: the further diffusion of the private automobile, durable consumer goods, the migration to suburbia, and the expansion of higher education, medical services, and travel.[19] The rapid expansion of these sectors, in turn, stimulated investment over a wide front in North America, Western Europe, and Japan. Thus, it was the accelerator which lay the basis of the great boom of the 1950's and 1960's in the OECD world: a powerful expansion of investment based on an expansion of real income sustained, in part, by falling or relatively low prices for basic commodities.

The radical upward shift in the prices of energy (and, to a degree, other basic commodities) after 1972 struck at the pillars of this majestic expansion in three ways. First, some of the leading

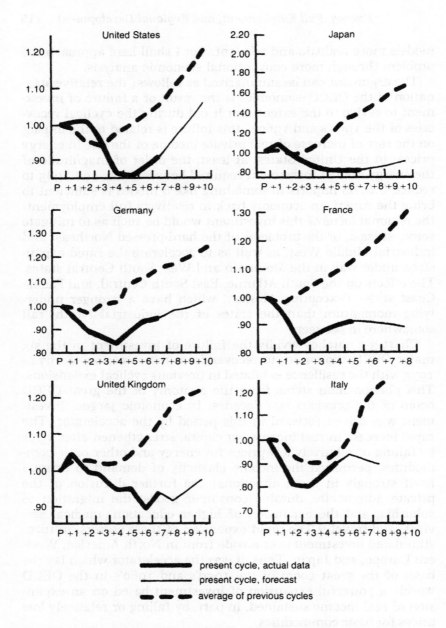

CHART 3-3. *Cyclical Behavior of Nonresidential Investment in Six Major Countries, 1955–1978 (half years, volume indices, peak 100).*

Source: OECD Observer, no. 87 (July 1977), p. 23.

sectors were energy intensive and were affected by the price elasticity of demand. Second, the expansion of real income was decelerated, as a matter of trend, by the unfavorable shift in the terms of trade for the OECD as a whole, despite the good fortune of Norway, now Britain, and the U.S. energy-producing states. Between 1972 and 1975, the price of agricultural exports in world trade rose by 83 percent, minerals (including fuels) by 213 percent, industrial products by 54 percent. The value of OPEC's exports rose from 6.6 percent of the world total to 13.4 percent.[20] Third, the slowness of the adjustment of public policy to the new trend period yielded an incomplete cyclical revival from the 1975 cyclical trough, which compounded the effect on the path of personal real income of the unfavorable shift in the terms of trade. Thus, we can observe what is now becoming chronic, substantial idle industrial capacity in the OECD world, notably acute in the steel industry.

It is not unfair, I believe, to characterize the plan of the Carter administration to return to full employment as a kind of attempted replay of the great neo-Keynesian economic expansion of the Kennedy-Johnson years, this time without a large expansion in military expenditures but with what might be called a Ray Marshall addendum in the form of a substantial public services job program.

I am sceptical that it will work. I am sceptical because this is not the early 1960's. At that time energy, food, and raw material prices were relatively low. The real expenditures of consumers were rising rapidly—at about 5 percent a year. Between 1971 and 1977—two comparable years in terms of the business cycle—the rate was only 3.7 percent. The real outlays by consumers for energy-intensive automobiles and durable consumer goods rose at an annual rate of 10 percent between 1961 and 1965. The figure for 1971–1977 was about 6 percent. Fixed investment in residential housing rose at an annual rate of over 5 percent in 1961–1965; for 1971–1977 the figure was 1.4 percent, rising above the 1971 level only in the latter year. In 1961–1965 the total real government outlays for education, health, and other goods and services rose at an annual rate of 3.5 percent; for 1971–1977 the figure was 1.4 percent. It was against this background that real private fixed business investment rose at an annual rate of almost 8 percent in the first half of the 1960's, whereas it increased at an average rate of only 3 percent between 1971 and 1977, despite revival from the trough of the 1974–1975 recession.

The conventional neo-Keynesian remedy for this situation would be expansionary fiscal and monetary policy. One can, of course, conceive of some increased level of consumers' income, induced by extravagantly lowered taxes, extravagantly unbalanced federal budgets, and a rapid increase in the money supply that would permit automobile production and use, expanded sales of energy-intensive durable consumer goods, and a general overriding of high energy prices. Theoretically, incomes could be expanded enough for the income elasticity of demand to override to a considerable degree the price elasticity of demand for energy-intensive products. But retribution would certainly come in three forms: an accelerated increase in oil imports and severe balance of payments difficulties; accelerated inflation; and currencies gravely weakened on international exchanges, for floating exchange rates by no means wholly free domestic economic policy from external constraints as the experiences of pre–North Sea oil Britain and Italy suggest, as well as the current weakness of the U.S. dollar.*

The alternative to a self-defeating, conventional neo-Keynesian effort to expand effective demand is at once obvious and difficult.

It is obvious if one breaks out of neo-Keynesian economics and asks the simple question: Where are the nation's great problems that require large investments? The answer is, surely, in these fields:

—Energy production and conservation

—Water development, conservation, and transfer

—Investment in the transport system to deal with energy problems, to provide cost-effective urban mass-transit systems (perhaps, simply, buses), and to rehabilitate obsolescent parts of the transport network

—Land rehabilitation and forestry development (including development for biomass energy) and the modernization of rural regions of the South

—Reduction of air and water pollution

—Expanded research and development in energy and other

---

*This analysis is, of course, confirmed by the effort to induce a recession in the autumn of 1979 through a restriction of the money supply, a policy backed by the Carter administration.

resource fields as well as other measures to accelerate the lagging rate of productivity increase

The data are not now adequate for confident estimation of investment requirements in these fields. But from surveying the data that can be mobilized, I, at least, emerge with considerable confidence that the means to full employment are at hand, if we address vigorously resource problems which will become progressively more serious with neglect.

Why, then, is the problem difficult? It is difficult for related intellectual and institutional reasons. Intellectually, our leading economists of what is sometimes called the mainstream, be they Republican or Democratic, are experts in manipulating effective demand. Children or grandchildren of John Maynard Keynes, they are awkward in handling the kind of resource and supply problems which have marched to the center of the stage so disconcertingly in the 1970's but which have no formal place in neo-Keynesian models. Institutionally, we do not yet have the tools to mount large investment programs in these resource fields. We know how to raise or lower the Federal Reserve discount rate and the rate of expansion of the money supply. We know how to enlarge or diminish the federal budget deficit. Since the 1930's, we have learned how to carry out public service job programs. But we lack the institutions for mounting the kind of public and private sector collaboration required to increase investment in some of the necessary directions; and, with respect to the conventional sources of energy and energy conservation, the democratic process in the United States has been unable to fulfill the price assumptions underlying energy-economy models or to settle firmly the energy-environmental trade-offs.

In broad terms, the expansion of investment in the directions listed above should constitute, in the generation ahead, the equivalent, say, to the opening up of the American West in the third quarter of the nineteenth century or the development of the resources of Canada, Australia, Argentina, and the Ukraine in the two decades before 1914. We would be evoking the multiplier as the catalytic instrument to move us back to full employment to supplant a weakened accelerator.

For present purposes, the narrower question then arises: To what extent can we measure, even roughly, the extent to which an effective national energy program would close the gap in investment which now prevents in the United States a return to sustained full employment?

The gap on which we are focusing emerges from Table 3-3. It would be misleading to draw fine-grained conclusions from the numbers in Table 3-3. Evidently, the role of annual inventory fluctuations has affected the varying gap between total and fixed private domestic investment. Residential investment has fluctuated over a considerable range, even putting aside the post-1972 years. Perhaps the best way to approximate roughly the investment shortfall, as it bears on full employment, is to put inventory fluctuations aside and compare the proportion of fixed private investment at the 1973 peak with that for 1977. The shortfall is 1.3 percent of GNP, roundly $24 billion (1977). Depending on the multiplier chosen, an expansion of investment of that order of magnitude would go a considerable distance toward closing the full-employment GNP gap now estimated in the range of $100–120 billion. If the multiplier were 2, about half the full-employment gap would be covered. If the shortfall is taken at 2.1 percent (the 1973–1977 difference for gross private domestic investment as a whole), a filling of the gap would, of course, bring the economy still closer to full employment. The measurement of

TABLE 3-3. *Gross Private Domestic Investment as a Proportion of GNP: Selected Years (1972 U.S. $)*

	Gross Private Domestic Investment			
	Total	Fixed	Non-residential	Residential
1952	13.9%	13.2%	8.9%	4.5%
1956	15.4	14.5	9.7	4.8
1965	16.2	15.0	10.3	4.7
1968	15.2	14.3	10.3	4.1
1972	16.1	15.3	10.0	5.3
1973	16.8	15.4	10.6	4.8
1974	15.0	14.3	10.6	3.7
1975	11.6	12.6	9.3	3.2
1976	13.6	12.9	9.1	3.7
1977	14.7	14.1	9.7	4.3
Shortfall: 1973–1977	2.1%	1.3%	0.9%	0.5%

Source: Bureau of Economic Analysis, Department of Commerce, *Business Conditions Digest*, various issues.

the gap is also sensitive to the level of unemployment regarded as "full employment." Average unemployment in 1973 was 4.9 percent. Some would regard that figure as a minimum for the 1970's, given recent changes in the structure of the working force. If, say, 4 percent unemployment is taken as a norm for "full employment," the 1972 investment gap would be still larger.

Taking the arbitrary figure of 1.3 percent of GNP as a benchmark, the next question is whether a successful effort to fulfill something like the targets of the NEP would enlarge energy-related investment on a scale capable of closing that gap, assuming that gap is a structural phenomenon which will persist if not corrected.

There have been a good many estimates made of energy investment requirements for both production and conservation since 1974. They were made for different time periods and under varying assumptions. They are well summarized in *National Energy Outlook, 1976*.[21] But, certainly, the first recommendation I would make is that some branch of the federal government decide on a standard definition of energy-related investment; recalculate historical data in terms of that definition, both nationally and regionally; and publish regularly current estimates disaggregated by various types of energy production and conservation. Evidently, such data are highly relevant to the macroperformance of the U.S. economy and regional paths of development, as well as to the energy situation and its evolution. As shall emerge, the prospects are for energy-related investment to approximate in the decade ahead at least the proportion of GNP now allocated to residential housing construction, an item sedulously followed by macroeconomists and prognosticators. They should certainly be of interest and concern to the Council of Economic Advisers.

Despite varying definitions (and occasional vagueness in specifying them), a rough consensus nevertheless emerges on requirements down to 1985, when energy investment is narrowly defined, mainly in terms of plant and equipment requirements. The consensus is that, to reduce U.S. oil imports to something like 6 mboed by 1985, outlays of the order of some 700–800 billion in 1976 dollars will be required between 1977 and 1985. As we shall see, estimates with broader definitions yield figures up to 60 percent higher for energy-related investment down to 1985.

Table 3-4 presents one such estimate falling at the lower end of the conventional range. It approximates, for example, the estimate of the Federal Energy Agency (FEA) for the ten-year period up to 1985 when the latter is converted into 1976 prices and reduced to a nine-year basis. The FEA figure comes to $792 billion, also including some downstream expenditures. Allen Davidson and Martin Baughman calculated their investment figure for conservation for 1977 by first approximating a figure for the whole period 1977–1985 and then arbitrarily assuming a 4 percent per annum expansion rate over the nine-year span. It is virtually certain that the 1977 figure ($18.5 billion for both household and business conservation investment) is somewhat too high and that the growth rate required to achieve the conservation investment target will have to be higher than 4 percent. But one simple conclusion emerges from Table 3-4 and, indeed, from all other such calculations; namely, that, if the United States deals seriously with its energy problem, energy-related investment will constitute a leading growth sector over the next decade and, almost certainly, beyond. The point can be made most simply by comparing the annual average rate of growth of energy investment in Table 3-4 (7.4%) with the assumed real rate of growth of GNP (4.3%).

The question then arises: Is the energy sectoral complex a sufficiently large part of the economy so that its expansion at some such rate would narrow significantly the current investment gap?

TABLE 3-4. *U.S. Energy Investment, 1977–1985, to Fulfill 1985 NEP Targets (billions of 1976 U.S. $)*

	1977	1985	1977–1985
Oil & gas	$19.6[a]	$52.4[a]	$304[a]
Electric utilities	24.8	33.0	230
Coal	2.9	4.6	35
Residential conversion			46
Industrial/commercial	18.5	26.5	201 · 155
Conservation			
Total	$65.8	$116.5	$770

[a] Includes downstream expenditures of $6.5 billion in 1977; 9.3 in 1985; 70 for the period 1977–1985.

Source: Allen Davidson and Martin L. Baughman, "Regional Patterns of Energy Investment, 1977–1985," in *National Energy Policy: A Continuing Assessment* (Austin: Council on Energy Resources, University of Texas at Austin, January 1978), where sources and methods are indicated.

Table 3-5 presents the latest estimates compiled by the Energy Information Administration (EIA) on investment in energy production, with a column added showing the percentage of energy investment to gross national product.

The following should be noted:

1. The EIA estimates are stripped of all downstream and infrastructure outlays associated with energy investment. They represent, as nearly as possible, plant and equipment outlays. For example, the 1974 figure is about 10 percent less than previous U.S. government estimates which included some downstream investment.

2. After falling from and rising back to about 21 percent of nonresidential fixed business investment (NFBI), between 1960 and 1972 (about 2% of GNP), the percentage of energy-production investment to both categories rose by about 20 percent between 1972 and 1977, that is, by 0.4 percent of GNP. Although it has not been generally remarked by macroeconomists, it is evident that the recession of 1974–1975 would have been considerably more severe than it was and the recovery of 1975–1978 less vigorous if the relative role of energy-production investment in the economy had not expanded in this substantial way. The proportionate rise in 1976–1977 is particularly significant, since other types of investment were increasing quite rapidly in the recovery from the 1975 cyclical trough. This shift occurred in the face of all manner of obstructions and uncertainties with respect to national energy policy, notably, policies which kept domestic energy prices below the price of imported oil and which failed to settle definitively conflicts between energy and environmental criteria.

3. The EIA has not yet developed regular calculations for energy-conservation investment. This category, virtually new since 1974, almost certainly expanded substantially over the past six years relative to total investment. Total energy-related investment (including conservation, downstream, infrastructure, and research and development) must have increased significantly more than the EIA estimates for plant and equipment suggest.

In a manner described in the Appendix to this chapter, EIA has undertaken energy-investment projections down to 1985 under three possible future circumstances. Their cases unfortunately do not include a national effort to achieve a reduction of oil and gas imports to 6 mboed by 1985. These scenarios yield 1985 energy

TABLE 3-5. *Historical Capital Expenditures in Energy-Producing Industries (billions of current dollars)*

	Coal Mining	Utilities		Total
		Electric[a]	Gas & Other	
1960	$0.22	$3.62	$1.62	$5.24
1961	0.21	3.55	1.45	5.00
1962	0.21	3.53	1.38	4.91
1963	0.23	3.67	1.31	4.98
1964	0.26	3.97	1.51	5.48
1965	0.29	4.43	1.70	6.13
1966	0.39	5.38	2.05	7.43
1967	0.47	6.75	2.00	8.75
1968	0.38	7.66	2.54	10.20
1969	0.38	8.94	2.67	11.61
1970	0.43	10.65	2.49	13.14
1971	0.46	12.86	2.44	15.30
1972	0.60	14.48	2.52	17.00
1973	0.53	15.95	2.76	18.71
1974	0.83	17.63	2.92	20.55
1975	1.32	17.00	3.14	20.14
1976	1.64	18.80	3.47	22.27
1977[d]	$2.04	$21.74	$4.40	$26.14

NA = Not available.

[a] Includes capital expenditures on generation, transmission, and distribution by investor-owned utilities.

[b] Includes capital expenditures on oil and gas exploration and production, natural gas liquid plants, and additions to refinery capacity. Excludes downstream capital expenditures on pipelines, tankers, chemical plants, marketing, and others.

[c] Includes geological and geophysical expenses and lease rentals.

[d] Preliminary estimates subject to revision.

imports of 11.2–11.9 mboed. The EIA conclusion is that, under the circumstances assumed, the proportion of investment in energy-producing industries to NFBI would be less than the average figure for 1974–1977 (24.2%). For reasons set out in the Appendix—stemming from the EIA assumptions about the rela-

Oil & Gas			Total Capital Expenditures in Energy	Total Non residential Fixed Business Investment (NFBI)	Percentage Energy Total to NFBI	Percentage Energy Total to GNP
Production[b]	Other[c]	Total				
$4.10	$0.62	$4.72	$10.18	$47.70	21.3%	2.0%
3.89	0.60	4.49	9.70	47.01	20.6	1.8
4.35	0.58	4.93	10.05	51.25	19.6	1.8
3.98	0.60	4.58	9.79	53.60	18.3	1.6
4.31	0.65	4.96	10.70	59.66	17.9	1.7
4.36	0.61	4.97	11.39	71.25	16.0	1.7
4.55	0.65	5.20	13.02	81.42	16.0	1.7
4.80	0.61	5.41	14.63	82.08	17.8	1.8
5.73	0.71	6.44	17.02	89.27	19.1	2.0
5.70	0.73	6.43	18.42	98.95	18.6	2.0
5.41	0.67	6.08	19.65	100.46	19.6	2.0
4.43	0.72	5.15	20.91	104.06	20.1	2.0
6.81	0.74	7.55	25.15	116.83	21.5	2.1
8.49	0.85	9.34	28.58	135.98	21.0	2.2
13.23	1.13	14.36	35.74	150.61	23.7	2.5
$11.48	$1.20	12.68	34.14	149.11	22.9	2.3
NA	NA	16.38[d]	40.29	161.95	24.9	2.4
NA	NA	$18.50	$46.68	$185.60	25.1%	2.5%

Sources: Energy Information Administration, *Annual Report to the Congress*, 1977, vol. II, pp. 50–51, with percentage of GNP added from *Business Conditions Digest*, various editions. Coal data: *Historical Capital Expenditures and Related Data* (rev.), Mimeo (New York: McGraw-Hill, June 1977). Utilities data: "New Plant and Capital Expenditures," *Survey of Current Business*, various issues. Oil and gas data: Chase Manhattan Bank, *Capital Investments of the World Petroleum Industry*, annual, various issues. Nonresidential fixed business investment data: National Income and Product Accounts, *Survey of Current Business*, various issues.

tion between feet drilled and new oil and gas reserves found—I believe their calculations involve a gross underestimate of investment levels required to achieve even the rather unambitious import targets incorporated in their projections. And, on the face of it, a relative slackening of the U.S. energy effort seems an improbable response to the rising real price of energy that the EIA assumes between 1977 and 1985.

The critical point for the analysis conducted in this chapter, however, is simply that, by these most recent government calculations, energy-production investment alone, even under rather restrictive definitions, is a sufficiently large figure that, say, a doubling in its relative scale would, indeed, close the 1977 investment gap. For example, if an average 4.3 percent real growth rate is maintained down to 1985 and if the fixed investment proportion rises back to its 1973 level of 15.4 percent, 1985 energy-related investment would constitute 4.7 percent of GNP, 30.6 percent of gross fixed private domestic investment, if the import goal of 6 mboed were to be achieved. As compared to our 1.3 percent of GNP investment shortfall, energy-related investment would have increased by about 2 percent of GNP as compared to 1977.

Roughly speaking, then, conventional plant and equipment estimates of the necessary increase in energy-related investment involve something just short of a doubling of its proportion to GNP by 1985, as compared to, say, 1974; and the enlargement covers a significant proportion of (or exceeds) the current full-employment investment gap, depending on the multiplier and the size of the gap assumed.

Table 3-6 presents energy-investment estimates in the higher range. For purposes of easy comparison, the Davidson-Baughman estimates in Table 3-4 are repeated. The totals in Table 3-6 would require a rise in the average proportion of energy-related investment to total fixed investment, over the period 1977–1985, of between 29.2 percent and 40.5 percent, assuming that the 1973 rate of 15.4 percent of GNP is re-established.[22] These estimates suggest that energy-related investment would average over the period somewhere in the range between 4.4 percent and 6.1 percent of the GNP. If we take the average within this range (5.25%), we are talking about approximately a doubling in the proportion of energy-related investment to total investment and GNP over the whole period 1977–1985 as opposed to the situation in 1974.

For our limited purposes, it is not necessary to isolate precisely the differences between the estimates in Tables 3-4 and 3-6. Table 3-6 includes a considerably higher figure for utilities (conversion plus nuclear), as well as a significant item for synthetic

TABLE 3-6. *Estimated Energy Investment, 1977–1985, to Fulfill 1985 NEP Targets (billions of 1976 U.S. $)*

	Low	High	Davidson-Baughman Estimate
Conservation Program			
Residential insulation	53	147	46
Residential solar	5	15	—
Industrial/commercial insulation	125	200	155
Transportation—auto/truck/bus	?	?	—
Federal insulation program	2	2	—
Subtotal	185	364	201
Energy Supply Investments			
Oil & gas	250	320	304
Federal strategic reserve—oil	6	8	—
Utilities industry—conversion	240	250	230 (including nuclear)
Coal	36	49	35
Nuclear power	108	143	—
Synthetic fuels, shale, & other	10	25	—
Subtotal	650	795	569
Grand total	835	1,159	770

Source: George Kozmetsky and Eugene B. Konecci, "National Energy Plan and Investment Analyses" in *Preliminary Assessment of the President's National Energy Plan* (Austin: University of Texas at Austin, May 11, 1977), p. 354, where sources and methods are described.

fuels, shale, and so on and the cost of the strategic reserve. It also includes rough first approximations for infrastructure outlays by state and local governments, the building industry, and transport required in direct support of energy-related investment calculated conventionally as plant and equipment. In the case of coal, for example, this procedure increases the range of required investment from $24–30 billion (1976), for plant and equipment, to $36–49 billion. Whatever the precision of the figures, energy-related investment should conceptually include such direct-support infrastructure outlays.

If a large commercial synthetics program should develop, the figure for that item in Table 3-6 would greatly expand, as would the estimate for investment in coal production. On the other hand, the nuclear power investment estimate may prove less than suggested in the table.

Whatever the imperfection of these pioneering calculations in a somewhat new and uncertain field, it is palpable that the necessary rise in energy-related investment down to 1985 is of an order of magnitude sufficient to close or exceed the investment shortfall in the U.S. economy as of 1977, if the United States were to succeed in bringing its oil imports down to 6 mboed.

To put the order of magnitude we are examining into perspective, it may be useful to recall that in the great boom of the 1850's gross railroad investment accounted for about 15 percent of gross capital formation, reaching almost 25 percent at the peak in 1854. The gross investment rate in these years may have approximated 18 percent, so that railroad investment averaged about 2.7 percent of GNP, reaching 4.5 percent at the 1854 peak. During the years 1870–1895, the railroads accounted for something like 13 percent of aggregate gross investment, about 1.7 percent of GNP, with a peak in the early 1870's of perhaps 5.75 percent of GNP. To cut U.S. oil imports back to about 6 mboed by 1985 may prove to be, proportionately, a bigger effort than the railroadization of the American West.

The order of magnitude of increased energy-investment requirements, when measured in some such way, has, in various analyses, led to the question of a possible capital shortage, that is, demands for capital which cannot be met from current savings rates at relatively full employment.

In terms of the argument thus far developed here, the capital shortage issue might be put as follows: What problems are posed for the execution of an effective national energy plan if, in fact, the private investment gap of 1974–1977 disappeared, on its own, without radically increased energy investment; or (which is quite possible) rising investment requirements for transport, water development, pollution control, raw materials, and in other resource-related fields yield total capital requirements which, along with those for energy, bring about the need for investment priorities if acute demand-pull inflation is to be avoided?

In terms of method, the most satisfactory treatment of this problem is that of Barry Bosworth, James S. Duesenberry, and Andrew S. Carron.[23] They ask, in effect, if an assumed shift in the proportion of energy investment to total nonresidential investment from 24.6 percent in 1973 to 32.6 percent in 1980 can be accommodated without a capital shortage or an increase in the proportion of GNP invested. Their answer, as of the time of their study, was that only a slight increase in the overall investment proportion would be required if the following major conditions were fulfilled:

—The economy resumed promptly its full-employment path
—The proportion of resources absorbed in residential investment, the interstate highway system, and education declined
—The federal government generated a budget surplus
—There were no new starts in social programs

To approach rationally the possible priority problem we shall face, evidently we need sectoral investment-requirement estimates in a number of resource fields, aside from energy. My own best guess is that, if the energy, water, transport, and other resource-related problems, where degeneration is now under way, were to be successfully confronted by the United States, either our problem would, indeed, become one of priorities or the U.S. investment rate, markedly lower than that of most European countries or Japan, would have to be raised. In either case, the unemployment problem as we have known it since 1974–1975 would disappear. For an economic historian, this conclusion is no surprise. By and large the other four periods of sustained relatively high prices for basic commodities have also been periods of relatively low unemployment.

V

We turn now to an area where data and analysis are even less well formulated than in the case of energy-investment requirements, that is, the regional impact of a successful effort to approximate the NEP targets. I shall set aside the direct income-transfer effects of the array of taxes and rebates proposed to the Congress in 1977 by the Carter administration, for their fate is still undecided as this chapter is written. I shall concentrate on attempting to sketch the possible rough directions of change under the headings set out in Section II of this chapter, that is, effects on income, investment, population movements, and industrial structure.

It may be, first, useful to give some quantitative form to a fact of which we are all instinctively aware, namely, that growth rates have varied widely in the various regions over recent years. As noted earlier (Section II, above), the normal catching-up process of the South and Southwest since the 1930's was accelerated by the relative price movements since the close of 1972. The result is seen in Table 3-7, which exhibits the average annual increase in real earnings for the period 1971–1976 and population change by regions. Data do not permit calculations of gross state or gross regional income; but changes in real earnings are a reasonable surrogate, although the national rate of increase in real earnings from 1971 to 1976 was slightly less (2.4%) than for real GNP (2.7%).

In a large continental economy, one would not expect uniform regional growth rates. But a spread of regional real income growth rates over a range of almost 9 to 1 is an impressive phenomenon. It underlines the inadequacy of national macrodata, macromodeling, and macropolicy. With respect to population, the United States contains regions with virtually stagnant populations and others with populations expanding as fast or faster than those in developing nations.

For our purposes, these data underline the prima facie case for linking energy to growth. Putting aside the vertiginous figure for Alaska, the highest growth rates are in the two regions containing large energy resources exploitable at current prices: the Southwest and Rocky Mountain states. Although here placed in the Southeast, Louisiana enjoyed a rise of 4.71 percent in real earnings. The figure for Wyoming (8.84%) is the highest for any state except Alaska.

The rise of real income in these states is, of course, compounded of the three related elements delineated in Section II of this chapter: the terms-of-trade (or income) effect, population expansion, and increased investment. I, at least, do not command the data to decompose these elements and assign them relative weights, although their analytic interconnection should be underlined.[24]

Before turning to estimates of approximate regional distribution of energy-related investment, in an effective national energy program, it is worth underlining a few general propositions.

First, of course, there is, despite the strong forces at work in the various regions, a complex set of interconnections within the national economy. Rapid expansion or deceleration in one region

TABLE 3-7. *Annual Average Percentage Growth in Real Earnings by Regions: 1971–1976; Percentage Population Change between 1970 and 1975 (calculated from data in 1972 U.S. $)*

	Real Earnings	Population	
	Annual Average Change	Total Change, 1970–1975	Annual Average Change
New England	0.94%	2.9%	0.57%
Middle Atlantic	0.60	0.1	0.03
East North Central	1.84	1.8	0.35
West North Central	2.20	2.2	0.44
Southeast	3.65	9.9	1.67
Southwest	5.26	7.9	1.54
Mountain	5.05	16.4	3.08
Pacific	3.14	6.2	1.20
(Alaska)	(23.81)	—	—
U.S. National Average	2.415%	4.8%	0.94%

Source: Growth in real earnings from data calculated by Daniel Garnick, Bureau of Economic Analysis, Department of Commerce; population change, Bureau of the Census.

affects all the others. A general cyclical expansion or recession in the national economy leaves its mark, in different degrees, on all the regions. A weakening or strengthening of the dollar alters import prices throughout the economy.

Second, so far as energy is concerned, the greatest stake is one that is universally shared by all the regions, namely, that a reduction in U.S. oil imports permits the OECD world (including the United States) and the developing countries which import oil to experience low levels of unemployment and rapid growth. A period of international and domestic energy rationing (or a brutal struggle for scarce supplies) is likely to be a time of extreme tension and frustration. Moreover, it is a phase which would, almost certainly, see a marked further rise in real international oil prices, as the CIA has predicted. In short, there is a large negative interest in avoiding a global energy crisis in the 1980's shared by all the American regions.[25]

Third, a successful effort to conserve and to expand production sufficiently to reduce imports sharply by 1985 would have the general effect of assuring energy supplies throughout the country, including the energy-importing states and regions. There is evidence that the believed unreliability of energy supplies is one (among other) reason for the shift of manufacturing capacity toward energy-producing states.

Nevertheless, as Table 3-8 indicates, quite distinctive regional effects are likely to flow from an effective national energy production plan.

The total energy-production investment figure for the UT (University of Texas) model was built up mainly from regional estimates; the Bechtel estimate is the FEA Reference Case, 1976–1985, reduced to a nine-year basis. Both estimates are, essentially, for construction costs, excluding interest during construction, lease costs, operating capital, and so on, which, the Bechtel analysts estimate, could add about 35 percent to their figure.

To some extent the differences between the two production-in-

TABLE 3-8. *Energy Production Capital Requirements by Regions to 1985: Nine Years (billions of 1976 U.S. $)*

	UT Estimate	%	Bechtel Estimate	%
New England	$ 6.8	1.4%	$13.5	2.5%
Middle Atlantic	31.9	6.4	56.2	10.6
South Atlantic	48.0	9.6	54.9	10.3
East North Central	44.8	9.0	77.0	14.5
East South Central	44.4	8.9	45.5	8.5
West North Central	37.6	7.5	38.8	7.3
West South Central	155.9	31.3	125.4	23.6
Mountain	76.6	15.4	42.9	8.1
Pacific	52.2	10.5	77.6	14.6
Total	$498.2	100.0%	$531.8	100.0%

Sources: The "UT Estimate" was calculated by Davidson and Baughman, in "Regional Patterns of Energy Investment." The "Bechtel Estimate" is that of J. Michael Gallagher and Ralph G. J. Zimmermann in *Regional Requirements of Capital, Manpower, Materials, and Equipment for Selected Energy Futures* (San Francisco: Bechtel Corporation, November 1976). The regional breakdowns have, in this comparative table, been reconciled; and the Bechtel estimate, converted from third quarter 1974 to 1976 dollars (using the deflator for fixed private nonresidential investment) and from a ten- to nine-year basis.

vestment estimates stem from differing assumptions about the energy production mix over the next decade. The difference in assumed oil and gas drilling costs almost certainly explains, for example, the difference in the investment figure for the West South Central region in Table 3-8. The higher electric utilities figure in the Bechtel estimate (since reduced), as well as its figure for coal synthetics and shale, would also alter the regional investment proportions.

Turning to conservation, the FEA estimated that energy-conservation investment would add about $250 billion (1975) to energy-related capital outlays, which converts to $236 billion (when converted into 1976 dollars and put on a nine- rather than ten-year basis; see Table 3-9).[26] The Bechtel estimate does not include conservation investment. The UT analysts did attempt a regional breakdown of a somewhat lesser total ($201 billion) by proportioning residential conservation investment by number of households; commercial-industrial conservation investment, by value added in manufacturing (1972). The results are set out in Table 3-10.

Total energy-related investment (production plus conservation) by regions, per household, and per dollar-value added in manufacturing is given in Table 3-11. With these rough data in hand, two broad conclusions can be drawn about the regional impact of a successful NEP.

First, energy-conservation investment emerges as a major category, of the same order of magnitude as investment in utilities (including nuclear) and oil and gas. Moreover, its regional allocation is quite different from the production categories, and its inclusion produces an overall energy investment pattern less skewed toward the producing states, as a comparison between the percentages in Tables 3-8 and 3-9, as well as between Tables 3-8 and 3-10, suggests. The difference flows, of course, from the proportioning of energy-conservation investment by households and value added in manufacturing. The mitigation of skewness is further strengthened by the fact that energy-conservation investment starts, as it were, from near zero. It is, virtually, a new category since 1974. The outlays for energy conservation will, therefore, be substantially incremental.

Second, evidently the major energy-producing regions will experience (relative to population or households) much higher levels of energy-related investment than the others, notably,

TABLE 3-9. *Energy-Production Capital Requirements by Sector to 1985: Nine Years (billions of 1976 U.S. $)*

	UT Estimate	Bechtel Estimate
Electric utilities		
(including nuclear)	$230.25	$275
Oil & gas	230.60	210
Coal	35.17	42
Coal synthetics & shale	—	5

Source: Same as for Table 3-8.

TABLE 3-10. *Energy-Conservation Investment by Regions, 1977–1985 (billions of 1976 U.S. $)*

Census Region	Residential Conservation	Industrial & Commercial Conservation	Total Expenditures for Conservation	Percentage by Region
New England	$2.65	$ 9.81	$12.46	6.2%
Middle Atlantic	8.58	30.78	39.36	19.6
South Atlantic	6.84	19.45	26.29	13.0
East North Central	8.98	43.86	52.84	26.2
East South Central	2.81	9.32	12.13	6.0
West North Central	3.74	10.36	14.10	7.0
West South Central	4.31	10.81	15.12	7.5
Mountain	1.83	3.20	5.03	2.5
Pacific	6.07	17.29	23.36	11.6
Alaska & Hawaii	0.20	0.25	0.45	0.2
Total	$46.01	$155.13	$201.14	99.8% *

*Due to rounding, total not equal to 100.
Source: Davidson and Baughman, "Regional Patterns of Energy Investment."

Alaska, the Mountain states, and the West South Central region.

Putting broad generalizations aside, what can be said more directly about the relation of an effective national energy plan to the fate of the regions?

The Northeast and East North Central States. This region, taken as a whole, includes half the U.S. population. In 1960 it contained 61 percent of the nation's manufacturing jobs; in

1975, 52 percent. This decline, which was absolute as well as relative in the first half of the 1970's, was accompanied, as we all know, by acute fiscal problems in many cities, pressures to reduce public services, a rise in the proportion of obsolescent plants, and a deteriorating transport system. The region is also experiencing severe chronic unemployment among minorities in the central cities. As Table 3-7 indicates, the average growth rate in real earnings for each of its subregions was below the national average in the period 1971–1976. Only Maine and New Hampshire, enjoying the flight from the metropolitan areas, experienced growth rates higher than the national average.

The question is, therefore, to what extent could an effective national energy policy help arrest the process of deterioration and revitalize the industrial north, taken as a whole?

TABLE 3-11. *Total 1977–1985 Regional Energy Investment: per Household and per Dollar-Value Added in Manufacturing**

Census Region	Total Energy-Related Investment		Total Expenditure per Household	Expenditure per Dollar-Value Added
	(Billions of 1976 U.S. $)	Percentage by regions		
New England	$19.28	2.8%	$ 5,286	$ 0.86
Middle Atlantic	71.22	10.2	6,017	1.01
South Atlantic	74.26	10.6	7,869	1.67
East North Central	97.60	14.0	7,603	0.98
East South Central	56.51	8.1	14,614	2.66
West North Central	51.74	7.4	10,042	2.20
West South Central	171.03	24.5	28,741	6.95
Mountain	81.63	11.7	32,420	10.96
Pacific	67.33	9.6	9,887	1.70
Alaska & Hawaii	8.64	1.2	30,638	14.85
Total				
United States	$699.24	100.1%**	$11,022	$ 2.09

* Household and value-added figures used are for the year 1974.
** Due to rounding, total not equal to 100.
Source: Davidson and Baughman, "Regional Patterns of Energy Investment." The total figure for energy-related investment is an estimate of outlays required to fulfill NEP targets.

The Northeast governors have already decided that energy-related investment could play a major role to that end, and they have thrown their weight behind an Energy Corporation for the Northeast. Hearings will be held in 1979 on the project (and other regional development banks) in the Congress. A special study done for the project estimates energy-related investment required in the region for the period 1977–1985 in the range of $100–$120 billion. This figure is somewhat higher than that in Table 3-10 ($90.5 billion); but, if related infrastructure is included, the total could easily reach $120 billion. The major fields identified for investment by the corporation are these: coal conversion, cogeneration and district heating, infrastructure to increase long-term coal supply, residential retrofit program, solid waste recovery, and solar and alternative energy resources. A major accelerated commercial synthetics program would increase this figure, notably in Pennsylvania. Through public-private collaboration in areas where private profit incentives may not be sufficient, it is hoped that the corporation might invest over the period something of the order of $8 billion, which, with the incentive thus provided, might increase total investment by over $20 billion, providing about twice that figure in increased income and perhaps an extra 40,000 jobs per annum.

Behind the thrust of this initiative are two judgments. First, that while the battle for additional federal revenues will be fought, an extra margin of such funds is not likely to induce a regenerative process in the Northeast. Only a large self-reinforcing and sustained increase in investment will do the job; and, in present circumstances, this requires new forms of public-private collaboration in the region. Second, the problem of severe unemployment in the central cities can only be significantly ameliorated in a setting where the region as a whole regathers momentum and the demand for labor is high and rising. Without that condition, additional funds channeled directly to the central cities will be pushing on a string. No one believes that the hard-core problem of central city unemployment can be totally and promptly eliminated by a sharp expansion of regional investment, but there is ample evidence that it could be substantially reduced; and, in such a framework, where the hard-core problem was reduced and isolated, more narrowly targeted programs might have a chance to yield benign results over a longer time span.

The larger objectives of the energy effort envisaged in the Northeast, aside from additional employment, are to reduce dependence on imported oil; to assure a reliable regional energy supply and thereby remove one of the inducements for movement of facilities to energy-production regions; to reduce, by conservation, the income (or terms-of-trade) burden of high energy prices; and to acquire, by increased energy production, some of the income (or terms-of-trade) advantages of such production in an era of high-priced energy.

It should be noted that the Northeast governors were the first public officials to recognize the connection between a vigorous attack on the energy problem and the problem of chronic unemployment and slow growth.

With one addition, a similar rationale would apply in the industrial Middle West where the governors threw their support behind a regional development bank in August 1977. The additional dimension in the region flows from the fact that it contains vast deposits of Devonian shale. If these resources can be brought into commercial production, perhaps with some initial public subsidy, the economic prospects for the industrial North as a whole and the nation would be altered substantially for the better.

As an economic historian, I would note that rapid increases in productivity and reductions in cost of production have generally followed the introduction into commercial production of new methods and the exploitation of new raw material sources.

The Northeast and industrial Middle West have a further stake in the acceleration of what are conventionally referred to as post-1985 technologies. Aside from nuclear power, coal is the major regional energy source. Its enlarged use is likely to increase the substantial air pollution problems of the region despite environmental regulations. In situ conversion of coal and shale as well as the conversion of coal into synthetics would, it is to be hoped, mitigate this problem.

If national policy faces up to the acceptance of marginal cost energy pricing and establishes machinery for the prompt settlement, on national terms, of energy-environment trade-offs, I am inclined to believe regional development banks can perform a powerful catalytic role. That role would be in accelerating the solution to research and development problems and in overcoming uncertainties which inhibit commercial production from so-called post-1985 energy technologies, for example, deep lignite, shale, synthetics, geopressurized methane, and geothermal resources.

The Mountain States. The rise in energy prices is producing in the Mountain states all four of the phenomena which emerged from the historical cases briefly summarized in Section II of this chapter: an income (or terms-of-trade) effect, enlarged investment, accelerated immigration, and the beginning of a new phase of energy-related industrialization. It is not surprising that Denver is being referred to as the new Houston.

A good deal of the momentum in the region flows, of course, from the beginnings of the exploitation of the massive coal deposits of the northern Mountain states. A preliminary analysis indicates that "moderately firm plans" in four centers of coal development in Montana, North Dakota, and Wyoming will lead to an expansion of population in those sites between 1970 and 1985 by some 64,000 people (185%).[27] This includes some calculation of working force required for supporting private and public services, including transport. Overall, the annual average rate of population growth of these three states was 1.34 percent between 1970 and 1975, 3.1 percent for the Mountain states as a whole. If that rate were to persist for another decade, their population would rise from 9.6 to 13.0 million.

The relative rise in incomes, investment levels, and population in the region, already evident in Tables 3-7 and 3-8, is likely to be accompanied, over a period of time, by a new phase of industrialization based on the reliability and accessibility, with low transport costs, of energy supply.

As in other regions that have struck it rich in the past, the boom in the Mountain states will transform the way of life of a good many now thinly populated parts of the region, impose considerable environmental costs, and set up strains between the old and new lines of economic activity. State severance and other taxes are designed to tap off some current income from the exploitation of natural resources both to support public infrastructure requirements and to cushion the environmental impact of accelerated development.

The scale of the available coal reserves of the region provides a base for a long-term process of development, in which a working force mobilized initially to build infrastructure, synthetic plants, and such is likely to have the opportunity to move over into industrial employment and the services required to support it.

The West South Central States. This region, containing a good deal of the conventional oil and gas reserves of the country, faces a somewhat more complex future than the Mountain region. In one way or another it is likely to experience, for a time, a rise in domestic energy prices, enlarged investment flows, and continued rapid in-migration. The prospect is heightened by the delay since 1974 in establishing a viable national energy plan. That delay makes it probable that the nation will require a very rapid expansion of conventional onshore and Gulf reserves, since these have relatively short periods of gestation (see Chart 3-2, above). These reserves are, however, believed to be limited—more limited than, say, the coal reserves of the Mountain states. The industrial structure of the oil- and gas-producing states is built substantially around energy-intensive industries historically dependent on a reliable regional energy supply.[28] Forty percent of the natural gas consumed in the United States for industrial purposes, for example, is consumed in Arkansas, Louisiana, Mississippi, and Texas. Evidently, these energy-intensive industries are important to the national, rather than merely the regional, market.

One central task in the region is, therefore, to build an alternative energy base for the longer future. That process is already under way as a result of Texas' precocious conversion of utilities from natural gas to coal. A free intrastate market price for natural gas plus a state regulation (Docket 600) set in motion a rapid expansion of local lignite production starting in 1972. By 1985 the utilities industry in Texas may be using some 98 million tons of coal of which 40 million tons will be imported from the Mountain states. Gas-generated electricity will have been reduced from 90 percent to 25 percent or less of the total.[29] This process will impose some deterioration in air quality. With the passage of time, however, the oil- and gas-producing states of the Southwest will have to exploit not only their surface lignite but also try to render cost effective the development of their deeper lignite deposits, geothermal gas, abundant supply of solar energy, and acquisition of oil by tertiary recovery methods. The rapid rate of growth of population and income in the region may also require extensive resort to nuclear energy and the full exploitation of the region's uranium resources.

It will be a considerable strain on both resources and policy to play the critical short-run role in the national energy plan that the region's resources dictate while also laying the basis for the region's long-run viability in an era when conventional oil and gas reserves will have been run down. Although the region commands a much more sophisticated and diversified economy than the members of OPEC, its underlying challenge—to make the most of a period of transient high income in ways which will permit continued long-run growth—bears a family relation to theirs.

The Southeast States. The southern states (South Atlantic and East South Central regions) confront the future energy problem with an underlying advantage over New England and the mid-Atlantic states; that is, they are still enjoying some of the momentum of late-comers catching up with early-comers to industrialization, as Tables 3-1 and 3-6 suggest. Their coal resources and utility requirements, moreover, should induce considerable energy-related investment. Measured per household (Table 3-10), the South Atlantic investment requirement approximates that of the East North Central states; the figure for the East South Central states is higher due to the presence within that region of Louisiana. Because of the lesser role of industry in the two regions, the expenditure per dollar-value added in manufacturing is higher.

Recent analyses have emphasized that within the Sunbelt a distinction is emerging in the growth rates of energy-importing versus energy-exporting states; and this is, of course, to be expected, given the terms-of-trade effect and the order-of-magnitude difference between energy investment in the West South Central states and the others (except Louisiana).

Like the states of the Northeast and East North Central regions, the South contains a major structural poverty problem. The excellent report of the Task Force on Southern Rural Development has recently measured the scale and character of poverty in the South relative to the rest of the country. In 1974 there were still 10.8 million poor southerners and 13.5 million poor outside the South. Relative to population, the southern poverty problem is, evidently, much greater than in the rest of the country. But the southern poor are less visible: 54 percent are rural; only 38 percent of the poor are rural outside the South.

Like the central city problems of the North (and parts of the South), more than a high level of aggregate growth is required to reduce radically hard-core rural poverty. But a background of high growth rates in the region is a necessary condition.

Although it should be emphasized again that considerable differences exist among the states of the region—and even within states—the South Atlantic and East South Central regions should be able to continue in the time ahead to narrow the gap between their levels of real income per capita and the national average, if a serious national energy program is mounted and high average growth rates are maintained.

The Pacific States. In terms of per capita income, the Pacific region, even putting Alaska aside, remains relatively one of the richest in the country (Table 3-1); and it continued to do better in growth between 1971 and 1976 than the national average of 2.4 percent (Table 3-7). Energy-related investment down to 1985, putting aside Alaska, falls in an intermediate range, a bit below the national average (Table 3-11). Aside from Hawaii, California, much the most populous state of the region, did least well in the period 1971–1976, with a growth rate in real earnings of 2.87 percent versus the regional average of 3.14 percent. With hydroelectric resources and the energy flow from Alaska and, perhaps, Mexico, the region's energy supply is reasonably well assured. The pace and fruitfulness of off-shore drilling in the Pacific will, evidently, affect the region's income, investment, and growth pattern to a degree. It may be that other resource problems (e.g., water supply, air pollution, agricultural productivity) may prove more acute in the Pacific region over the next decade.

VI

Seven large conclusions flow from this analysis.

1. The effects of a shift in the relative price of energy must be analyzed, internationally and by regions, in terms of four routes of impact: on income (or the terms of trade), investment, migration, and industrial structure, including in the latter the effect on the momentum of leading growth sectors of the price elasticity of demand for energy. Current energy-economy models are designed in ways which preclude their gripping this process as a whole. They have also focused primarily on the long-term U.S. energy problem, that is, the path to the year 2000 or thereabouts.

2. The most acute phase of the energy problem, however, is upon us now and will continue over the next five to ten years when the United States and other energy importers must strive with great intensity to accommodate themselves to the probable

OPEC production ceiling of the 1980's by reducing oil imports. The urgency of the problem is heightened by the long lead times at work in various key types of energy production and conservation.

3. There is a solid convergence between such an intensive effort and the task of returning the United States and other OECD economies to relatively full employment and high, sustained growth rates. The required expansion in energy-related investment is of an order of magnitude in the United States to make this sector a leading growth sector in the economy, supplanting the consumer-oriented leading growth sectors, now decelerated, which drove forward the great OECD boom of the 1950's and 1960's, and filling the investment gap which, in the United States and elsewhere, is the basis for decelerated OECD growth rates. The current investment gap for the United States is of the order of 1.3–2.1 percent of GNP: the expansion of energy-related investment required between 1977 and 1985 to reduce imports to, say, 6 mboed is, at the minimum, of the order of magnitude of 2 percent of GNP and probably a good deal higher.

4. If we deal vigorously with the energy problem and face up also to other resource problems with degenerative characteristics (e.g., water supply, pollution control, transport, soil rehabilitation), the nation's central economic problem will cease to be unsatisfactory levels of unemployment and rates of growth and will become one of investment priorities and/or an increase in the overall investment rate.

5. Contrary to the impression imparted by some rhetoric, energy conservation (except nonuse) is capital intensive. Energy-conservation investment falls, in various calculations, in the range of 22–32 percent of total energy-related investment required over the period 1977–1985 to reduce imports to about 6 mboed by 1985.

6. Regional growth rates, rates of population expansion, and the structural problems the regions confront are extremely diverse. The impact upon them of an effective national energy plan will also be diverse, although the large role of energy-conservation investment mitigates the skewness which would exist if the nation's task were merely to expand energy production. Among the regions, the most acute problems lie in the Northeast and industrial Middle West. Their difficulties have not been caused by the energy crisis but thus far have been exacerbated by it. An effec-

tive national energy plan, vigorously pursued in those regions through public-private sector collaboration, could substantially mitigate their energy and deeper structural problems, including, especially, a massive synthetics program based on coal and shale. Each of the other regions, including those producing and exporting energy, also faces difficult structural challenges.

7. The analysis as a whole would suggest:

a. Energy-economy model builders should move away from long-run, full-employment, equilibrium models toward models which would capture the anatomy of the transition confronted over the years immediately ahead, including the time dimension imposed by the probable OPEC production capacity ceiling and by energy-production and conservation lead times, the role of energy-related investment in moving the national economy back to full employment and sustained growth, and the regional dimensions of the energy-economy problem.

b. Macromodel builders and prognosticators, including the Council of Economic Advisers, should introduce systematically the role of energy-related investment into their calculations, disaggregate their analyses by regions, and relate regularly the role of now-degenerating resource sectors to their macrocalculations.

APPENDIX. *A Comparison of Investment Estimates for the National Energy Plan and Energy Information Administration Projections to 1985.*

The purpose of this Appendix is to effect a rough comparison of investment requirements for energy production presented in Chapter 3 with those developed by the Energy Information Administration (EIA). The comparison is difficult for a variety of reasons but above all because the production projections of the EIA differ from those earlier presented by the Carter administration.

The projections published by the Carter administration in April 1977 contrasted the situation in 1985, absent the National Energy Plan (NEP) then presented to the Congress, with the situation which would prevail if the NEP were adopted (*The National Energy Plan*, Executive Office of the President, Energy Policy and Planning, April 29, 1977, especially pp. 95–96). Although a number of analysts expressed serious doubts that the legislation proposed would achieve the production and reduced import targets defined in the NEP, the setting of the target for reduced net energy imports (about 6 mboed—about 14 quads— by 1985) proved a stimulus to analysts outside the government to clarify the implications of actually achieving some such result by 1985. That is the framework, for example, of Chapter 3.

In April 1978, the newly created EIA, in its first annual report to the Congress, presented projections down to the year 1985 (and beyond) based on a quite different procedure (vol. II, pp. 27–28).

So far as legislation was concerned, its analysts merely assumed "continuation of present energy policy as expressed in existing legislation and actual practice." This understandable but inherently unrealistic assumption, for a period of some seven years, is overcome by the presentation of a matrix of cases (Table 3-12): high, medium, and low rates of economic growth (and therefore in energy demand); high, medium, and low rates of increase in energy supply; plus mid-level projections for both energy demand and supply under the assumptions of a constant and a rising real price for world oil.

Table 3-13 contrasts the hopeful NEP outcome with EIA's Case C (medium demand, medium supply) for major categories. The real growth rate for the economy is slightly lower in Case C than the NEP projection (4.1% per annum versus 4.3%); the growth rate for energy consumption is considerably higher (3% per annum versus 2.25%).

The critical differences in the two projections are, evidently, that Case C assumes about 15 quads less U.S. energy production by 1985 (an 18% shortfall) and 9 quads more energy imports (56% higher). Case B (high demand, low supply) yields a still higher level of imports for 1985 (28.3 quads); and, indeed, as Table 3-2 indicates, some projections suggest a U.S. energy import requirement of 34 quads (about 16 mboed) if present trends continue. NEP calculated a 1985 import requirement of 27 quads, if existing trends continued and its proposals were not adopted.

Against this background, we turn to a comparison of the investment estimates for required energy production generated by EIA with those presented in Chapter 3.

Certain characteristics of the EIA investment estimates should first be noted:

—They are for the seven-year period, January 1, 1978, to January 1, 1985. The Chapter 3 estimates are for the nine-year period, 1977–1985, inclusive. In Table 3-14 the EIA data are, therefore, extended to nine years on a proportional basis.

—The EIA estimates are in 1978 U.S. dollars; the Chapter 3 estimates, 1976 U.S. dollars. A correction of 13 percent has been applied to deflate the EIA estimates in Table 3-14.

—There are a number of differences in the categories of investment included in the EIA estimates, the most important being the exclusion of downstream investment outlays (e.g., marketing and distribution, lease bonuses, and transport facilities). These constitute, for example, $70 billion (or 23%) of the oil and gas estimate of Davidson and Baughman for the period 1977–1985.

Table 3-14 compares the EIA investment estimates for energy production, corrected for time period and price, with the Davidson-Baughman estimates presented in Chapter 3. It should be noted that the EIA has made no estimates for investment in energy conservation.

Evidently, the major difference between the two estimates lies in the oil and gas production estimates. Even if we add 23 percent to the EIA estimate for downstream investments, the difference is $127 billion, or 42 percent ($177 versus $304 billion). A dif-

TABLE 3-12. *1975 and 1985 Energy Supply/Demand Balance (quadrillion [quads] Btu per year)**

Projection Series 1975	A High Demand, High Supply	B High Demand, Low Supply
Domestic Production		
Crude oil	17.9	20.3	17.7
NGL & butane	2.6	2.2	1.8
Shale oil	0	0.2	0.1
Natural gas	19.0	19.4	16.0
Coal	14.6	23.0	23.8
Nuclear	1.8	6.2	6.2
Hydro & geothermal	3.2	4.2	4.2
Total domestic production	59.1	75.5	69.8
Imports		
Crude oil	8.7	15.5	19.3
Petroleum products	3.8	6.6	6.9
Natural gas	1.0	1.6	2.1
Total imports	13.5	23.7	28.3
Total supply	72.6	99.2	98.1
Domestic Consumption		
Oil	32.8	44.4	45.4
Natural gas	20.0	21.0	18.1
Coal	12.8	21.1	21.9
Nuclear	1.8	6.2	6.2
Hydro & geothermal	3.2	4.2	4.2
Total domestic consumption	70.6	96.9	95.8
Exports		
Coal	1.8	1.9	1.9
Refinery Loss	0.2	0.4	0.4
Total consumption & exports	72.6	99.2	98.1
Domestic Consumption by Sector		
Residential	14.7	19.3	19.0
Commercial	11.3	13.8	13.5
Industrial	26.0	42.0	41.5
Transportation	18.6	21.8	21.8
Total domestic consumption	70.6	96.9	95.8

* A quad equals the equivalent of 0.472 mbod.
Source: EIA, *Annual Report to the Congress,* 1977, vol. II, p. 27.

C Medium Demand, Medium Supply	D Low Demand, High Supply	E Low Demand, Low Supply	F High Oil Price	NEP
19.0	20.3	17.7	19.5	22.5
2.0	2.2	1.7	1.9	—
0.1	0.2	0.1	0.1	—
17.2	19.2	15.6	17.5	18.6
23.1	22.2	22.8	23.6	30.7
6.2	6.2	6.2	6.2	8.0
4.2	4.2	4.2	4.2	4.9 (other)
71.8	74.5	68.3	73.0	84.7
16.5	16.0	17.5	17.0	14.8
6.7	3.2	5.7	4.3	—
1.9	1.2	2.0	1.9	1.3
25.1	20.4	25.2	23.2	16.1
96.9	94.9	93.5	96.2	100.8
43.9	41.5	42.3	42.4	
19.1	20.4	17.6	19.4	
21.2	20.3	20.9	21.7	
6.2	6.2	6.2	6.2	
4.2	4.2	4.2	4.2	
94.6	92.6	91.2	93.9	98.3
1.9	1.9	1.9	1.9	2.5
0.4	0.4	0.4	0.4	—
96.9	94.9	93.5	96.2	100.8
19.0	18.9	18.6	18.6	
13.5	13.4	13.1	13.2	
40.7	39.9	39.1	40.9	
21.4	20.4	20.4	21.2	
94.6	92.6	91.2	93.9	98.3

TABLE 3-13. *Case C and NEP 1985 Projections (quadrillion [quads] Btu per year)*

	Case C	NEP
Total domestic energy production	71.8	84.7
Total energy consumption	94.6*	98.3
Exports	1.9	2.5
Imports	25.1	16.1

* Refinery loss excluded (0.4).

TABLE 3-14. *Energy-Production Investment Requirements, 1977–1985 (billions of 1976 U.S. $)*

	Davidson-Baughman	EIA (Case C)
Oil & gas	304	144
Coal	35	23
Electric utilities*	230	232
Others	—	8**
Total	569	407

* Includes nuclear and conversion.

** A category (embracing synthetics, solar, geothermal, etc.) not included in Davidson-Baughman estimates.

Source: The EIA figures were converted from the C Case, EIA, *Annual Report to the Congress*, 1977, vol. II, p. 54.

ference of this order of magnitude cannot be accounted for by the difference in the 1985 production estimates: Davidson-Baughman assumed the 1985 NEP target figure for gas and oil production (41.1 quads); Case C estimates a somewhat lower figure (38.3 quads). The 1975 production figure was, in fact, 39.5 quads. These differences are of a trivial order of magnitude compared to the order of magnitude of investment required to find new oil and gas reserves sufficient to overcome the rapid annual fall in production from old reserves. Differing assumptions used to relate feet drilled to new oil and gas reserves found mainly determine, in this case, differences in energy-investment requirements as between Davidson-Baughman and EIA.

The Davidson-Baughman estimates are based on calculations made by the Bureau of Economic Geology, University of Texas at

Austin (see William L. Fisher, William E. Galloway, and Robert A. Morton, "National Energy Production Requirements and Projections," in *National Energy Policy: A Continuing Assessment* [Austin: Council on Energy Resources, University of Texas at Austin, January 1978], pp. 63–120). The data exhibit a quite stable relationship between footage drilled and new reserves of oil and natural gas found over the period 1952–1970; a different, less productive relationship emerges after 1970 as Charts 3-4 and 3-5 indicate. The Davidson-Baughman investment estimates are based on the post-1970 correlation, as were the calculations of the FEA, down to February 1977.

At that time officials of the Carter administration decided that the post-1970 figures were an aberration caused by changes in the character of oil and gas drilling, responding, in turn, to the sharp increase in energy prices since November 1973 (see Department of Energy, Office of the Assistant Secretary for Policy and Evaluation, *An Analysis for the National Energy Plan: An Evaluation of Some Criticisms*, June 22, 1978, especially pp. 13–24; also Mark J. Fredericksen, *An Analysis of the Productivity of Domestic Petroleum Exploration Activities*, Energy Information Administration, Office of Energy Industry Analyses, July 1978 [Analysis Memorandum AM/EI/78-14]). At its core, the Department of Energy (DOE) argument (still supported by the EIA) is that a sharp rise in oil and natural gas prices would lead wildcat drillers to concentrate their drilling in previously discovered reservoirs (so-called development drilling), where risks are low but the relation between feet drilled and new reserves found is also low. The rise in price, according to this argument, makes profitable the exploitation of known reserves not worth development at lower prices. Such development drilling is believed to occur at the expense of higher risk but potentially higher yield exploratory drilling to establish new reservoirs. The DOE experts believed they had detected evidence of this kind of economically motivated shift in the character of drilling in the years since the oil embargo of 1973. They concluded that "as soon as the population of passed-over, newly economically attractive prospects are fully pursued, the industry will likely return to its more traditional exploratory activity with concomitant higher returns" (*Analysis for the National Energy Plan*, p. 19).

On the basis of this conclusion, finding rates in the NEP were

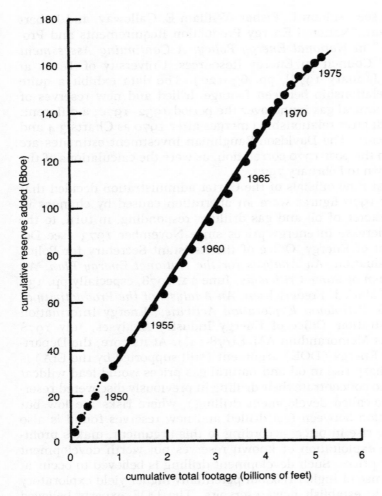

CHART 3.4. *Historical Trend of Reserve Additions, National Data,*
1947–1977.

projected down to 1985 on the basis of a regression calculated
over the twenty years preceding 1977, ignoring the change of
slope round about 1970. This period embraces, incidentally, two
anomalies which further distort the DOE's image of likely finding

rates, both relating to the period 1960–1963. In those years finding rates actually rose in the face of declining current drilling
rates due to (*a*) the lagged effects of high drilling rates in the
1950's and (*b*) the initial prolific reserve findings associated with
the early stage of off-shore development in the Gulf of Mexico.
The resultant DOE curve thus yields a markedly more optimistic
result than the projection of the slopes from 1970 forward in
Charts 3-4 and 3-5. Since the assumptions relating average price
to feet drilled are similar in the two analyses, the DOE projection
yields by 1985 about 40 percent more reserves found for the rate
of drilling both analyses assume would prevail if the pricing and
tax policies advocated in the NEP were adopted by the Congress.
It was this optimistic assumption about finding rates which led

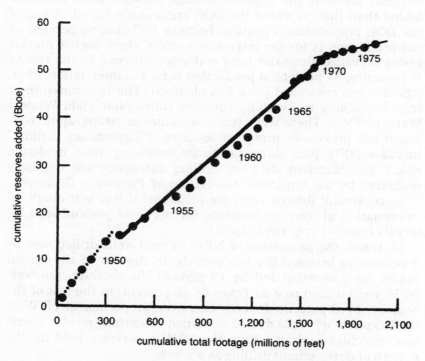

CHART 3.5. *Historical Trends of Reserve Additions, Texas Data,
1947–1977.*

the Carter administration to argue that its price incentives were sufficient to reconcile the low investment rates and high production levels assumed for oil and natural gas in the NEP of 1977. The shallower slopes of Charts 3-4 and 3-5 led to predictions of either shortfall in production or higher required investment rates if the Carter reserve and production targets were to be achieved.

There are two fundamental criticisms to be made of the line of argument adopted by the DOE. First, it is palpable that the downward trend in finding rates antedates the elevation of oil prices, as Charts 3-4 and 3-5 and Table 3-15 indicate. They suggest that we confront, as a matter of trend, a case of classic diminishing returns as increasing amounts of capital (i.e., feet drilled) are applied to a fixed geologic resource.

Second, as is often the case in economics, overaggregation conceals important analytic linkages. In this case, disaggregation suggests precisely the opposite linkage between price and risk-taking than that on which the DOE argument is based. A test of the DOE proposition is possible because in Texas 70 percent of gas production is for the intrastate market where higher market prices prevailed since the 1973 embargo, whereas, in the rest of the country, 81 percent of production is for the interstate market, where a low controlled price has obtained. The best measure of high risk-taking is a drilling category called New Field Wildcat Wells (NFW). These wells test a structure or stratigraphic condition not previously proved productive. ("Exploratory drilling" includes NFW plus three categories involving more moderate risk.) The standard data on drilling categories are regularly mobilized by the American Association of Petroleum Geologists.

Since annual figures vary, the most useful test is through an examination of average behavior for pre- and postembargo intervals (1967–1973; 1974–1978).

In Texas, the proportion of NFW to total wells drilled rose by 2 percent as between the two periods; in the rest of the United States the proportion fell by 18 percent. In absolute numbers, NFW wells drilled rose in Texas by 56 percent; in the rest of the country, by 6 percent. In both cases the proportion of NFW to total exploratory wells drilled remained essentially stable. Therefore, conclusions drawn from the NFW experience hold for the pattern of development drilling as a whole.

Thus, the hypothesis that a substantial price increase leads to a disproportionate shift to development drilling at the expense of

TABLE 3-15. *Finding Rates for Total Domestic New Field Wildcat Exploration, Excluding Prudhoe Bay, Alaska (barrels of oil equivalent found per new field wildcat foot drilled)*

Year		Year	
1966	23.00	1972	13.11
1967	26.01	1973	16.89
1968	14.20	1974	18.15
1969	12.14	1975	18.70
1970	19.52	1976	9.56
1971	13.08	1977	14.77

Source: Mark J. Frederiksen, *An Analysis of the Productivity of Domestic Petroleum Exploration Activities*, Energy Information Administration, Office of Energy Industry Analyses, July 1978 (Analysis Memorandum AM/EI/78-14), p. 7, where detailed sources are indicated.

exploratory drilling is not sustained; and, until solid evidence to the contrary emerges, prudence requires that we accept, as a geologic probability, the relation between feet drilled and new reserves found which has emerged since 1970. This means that the higher Davidson-Baughman energy-production investment requirements for oil and gas (Table 3-14) are to be regarded as more credible than those developed in EIA (Case C).

4

Technology and the Price System

The recurrent unifying themes of Chapters 1–3 are the problems of dealing systematically with deviations of capacity in the production of basic commodities away from dynamic optimum levels and of dealing systematically with major changes in technology. Both have proved extremely difficult to absorb within the conventional body of economic theory. In considering how and why modern economics has failed to deal successfully with the role of changing technology, it is useful to begin with Clarence Ayres, for, almost uniquely, he put the expansion of technology at the center of his analysis of society.

As Ayres made scrupulously clear, he drew upon the insight of many of his contemporaries: Dewey and Veblen, above all, but also Sumner, Freud, Durkheim, Pareto in his phase of sociology, and Keynes of the *General Theory*, among others. But no one can study Ayres without knowing that he constructed out of his environment a private vision of man in society, informed by deeply held private values. Ayres read widely in history as well as the social sciences. He rejected that branch of institutionalism which retreated into shapeless empirical investigations. He sought a general theory which would embrace it all—from the elements of human nature to how the economy really worked. In the phrases of Alfred Marshall, to which we shall return, Ayres

Note: The bulk of this chapter was first published in *Science and Ceremony: The Institutional Economics of C. E. Ayres*, ed. William Breit and William Patton Culbertson, Jr. (Austin: University of Texas Press, 1976), pp. 75–113.

addressed himself directly to "the high theme of economic progress" in the context of "society as an organism."[1]

Technically, Ayres was an economist in revolt against classical theory. In *Toward a Reasonable Society* he describes vividly how he "felt the heavens falling" when, at Amherst, Walton Hamilton responded to his question about when he would get around in his undergraduate course to some ideas about marginal utility with the reply: "I'd do so at once if only I understood them myself."[2] And soon Ayres followed Hamilton as a disciple of Veblen. But he did more than protest against "the dogma of the classical tradition." He was both a general theorist of society and a pamphleteer on behalf of the future of man and Western civilization.

In theory, he rejected the legitimacy of demand curves and the concept of the unique individual with private values. Tastes and income distribution were, in his view, the arbitrary product of culture and mores. He believed Darwin had erased the notion (Ayres attributed to Descartes and Kant) that scientists could be scientists and still be men. But, paradoxically, he built his synthesis and projected his view of its meaning as a unique scientist and a quite particular man of a special integrity.

Ayres hammered out his system with such intense clarity that it is not difficult to summarize.

Man acts in terms of his culture: there is no meaning to individuality outside this frame of reference.

How man gets his living is simply a part of his culture: the economy must be put in its full cultural context.

The economic aspect of a culture is shaped, in turn, by the tools man has and those he develops: the tools determine both how man gets his living and the social structure and mores (ceremonies) he elaborates.

There is an eternal clash between the introduction of new tools and the existing ceremonial structure of society.

What distinguishes Western culture is the process of progressive development of new tools, a process Ayres attributed (following Pirenne) to the fact that Western Europe was a frontier area which received the cumulative scientific and technological achievement of the ancient and Eastern worlds but where the mother culture was incompletely installed. Therefore, the inhibitions to technical change were less than in the older civilizations, where the power of ceremony was greater and more stifling.

Technical change has been the motor of Western civilization;

progress and value can only be defined as the continuity of technical development permitting a more effective organization of the whole life process. Technical progress has been real, reducing humbug, cruelty, and squalor; further progress will overcome war and poverty, yielding abundance and a world state.

From this perspective, the price system is not central to the economic system. The price system is a moving picture of a deeper process that conventional economics fails to analyze. Equilibrium analysis is a misleading technique in this dynamic setting and is also shot through with implicit but wrong moral values. Capitalism, and the commercial revolution, is a product, not the parent, of the technological revolution. The holding of private financial claims on physical capital assets, and the right to inherit them, is the product of ceremony rather than a legitimate function in modern societies. The institutions of property (like the nation-state) require, therefore, profound modification.

When he came to specific prescription, Ayres' proposals were relatively moderate: a Naderesque consumerism and income redistribution, justified on both ethical and Keynesian grounds. But his analysis was radical.

I would agree with parts of this vision and creed and disagree with others. Here I shall deal only with a limited but fundamental segment of Ayres' system, that is, the place of technology in economic theory—the place it has occupied and something of the place it should occupy.

II

In a curious way, Ayres' analysis shares two fundamental weaknesses of the classical tradition, stretching from *The Wealth of Nations* to Nicholas Kaldor's "The Irrelevance of Equilibrium Economics." The first is a failure to examine satisfactorily the character of the linkages among science, invention, and innovation.[3] The second is a failure to explore satisfactorily the linkage of these three variables to the price system.

In Ayres the development of technology is an autonomous aspect of Western culture unfolding more or less at a geometric rate, as tools multiply and are combined in new ways. He spends little time on the relation of science to invention and virtually none on innovation. The three activities are lumped together. He places the total process of technological advance at the center of his system; he sets it in motion with his analysis of the peculiar historical nature of medieval western Europe. But, once the creative explosion of the fifteenth century occurs (notably, printing), technological change, as it were, looks after itself. Ayres was not particularly interested in the coming in of particular technologies and did not explore the extent to which necessity, as reflected in the price system or the demands of the state, was the mother of invention.

Classical theory is equally casual about the relations among science, invention, and innovation. And the process of technological change is mainly dealt with in either of three ways: first, by exclusion, as in Marshallian short-period partial equilibrium analysis and Walrasian general equilibrium analysis; second, by assuming it is a simple function of an expanding overall level of demand or of investment, as in Adam Smith and Kaldor; or, third, by assuming it is an exogenous variable, as in Harrod-Domar and neoclassical growth models. Thus, Ayres and the classical economists of the nineteenth and twentieth centuries were asserting a similar if not identical proposition. Ayres pounded the table in demanding that the automatic process of technological change built into Western culture be recognized as the heart of the economic as well as the social and political process; classical price and production theory and Keynesian income analysis said, in effect: "Why, of course. But it is an automatic long-run function of increasing demand; let us, therefore, concentrate on how things unfold from day to day, and on maintaining steady high levels of employment."

Links of technology to the price system do emerge in classical economics, primarily in the theoretically troublesome partial equilibrium case of increasing returns; and these we shall examine. Moreover, from Adam Smith to the present, classical analysis also included the recurrent, haunting theme of long-run diminishing returns to land, natural resources, and, perhaps, capital itself. And the notion of diminishing returns continues to underlie many of the most important propositions in contemporary economic theory. But in the past it was left mainly to economic historians, a narrow group of specialists on the absorption of technology, and occasional bold exercises, like Schumpeter's treatment of the Kondratieff cycle, to try to relate the unfolding of technology to the economic process, including the price system. In recent times, as we shall see, theorists of development plan-

ning have begun to address themselves head-on to some of the
difficult issues involved.

III

But economists come to the task with an awkward heritage. The
trouble started with Adam Smith's assertion that "the division of
labor is limited by the extent of the market." If this famous dictum is taken to mean that the widening of the market is a sufficient condition for major technological change, the proposition
is false. It is simply not the case, in eighteenth-century Britain—
before or since—that commercial expansion led on automatically
to regular and substantial technological innovation.[4] Certainly,
the emergence of modern experimental science, interweaving in
complex ways with the processes of invention and innovation, is
what distinguishes the early modern history of Europe from the
many prior periods of economic expansion, when agricultural,
commercial, and industrial activity increased without significant
technological change. Put another way, without the scientific
revolution and all its complex, ramified consequences, the great
expansion of trade in Asian and American groceries and bullion
that we call the commercial revolution would have yielded not an
industrial revolution but, as in the past, a long cycle. Students of
the vital ancient empires would agree with Dwight H. Perkins'
dictum: "There is no natural or irresistible movement from commercial development to industrialization. The experience of China
is alone testimony to this."[5] And, one can add, so is the experience of the southern half of the world in the nineteenth and a
good part of the twentieth centuries, where commercial expansion proceeded for long periods without generating sustained industrialization. Ayres was notably emphatic on this point in his
foreword to the 1962 edition of *The Theory of Economic Progress*,
perhaps overdoing it a bit by making the commercial revolution
of the sixteenth to the eighteenth century a simple function of
the technological revolution.[6]

Smith was, indeed, a historian, philosopher, analyst, and
pamphleteer of the commercial rather than the industrial process.
The Wealth of Nations was published in precisely the interval
between the acceleration of British inventive effort, after the end
of the Seven Years' War, and the first phase of rapid innovation

in textiles, iron, and steam power, after the end of the American War of Independence. Smith exhibited no awareness of the momentous changes germinating around him: "There was not a line in his book anticipating such transformations as were to take place."[7] He did perceive that specialization of function could increase the productivity of labor with, essentially, constant or marginally improved technology; and he also perceived, in the case of the woolen industry, that three "capital improvements" had taken place since the end of the fifteenth century.[8] But there is no inkling of how rapid, discontinuous technological change fitted his system; nothing about the new textile machines, the new developments in iron, and the steam engine; and not even a reference to the concurrent wave of English canal building.

Koebner finds Smith's myopia about technological change a result of the timing of his work and, especially, its main purpose—that is, an attack on the mercantile system. In this view, the economics of technological change would have been an excessive diversion from his main theme. But it may be that, like his successors, Smith perceived that the introduction of discontinuous technological change would have disrupted the elegance of the price system, which emerged on the basis of competition, and the incremental technical improvements a widening of the market under competitive assumptions might yield. It would also have led him into the inevitable elements of monopoly, involved both directly in a patent system and indirectly in the real if transient advantage of early innovators. Smith was in no mood in *The Wealth of Nations* to suggest that private monopoly might serve constructive purposes.

In any case, Smith's successors, living in times when technological change was an inescapable, massive, and central fact in the world economy, have generally followed his lead: they made technological change a function of expanding demand (or a widening of the market); they viewed it as a diffuse, incremental process that could be assumed rather than examined; and they did not explore the interactions among science, invention, and innovation and their place in a general theory of production and prices.

Smith's most significant successor, Alfred Marshall, was, to a degree, an exception, for Marshall understood better than any economist in the classical tradition the depth of the problem posed by technological change for equilibrium price theory. In a passage that Ayres might have written (or, at least, applauded) Marshall said this:

> The theory of stable equilibrium of normal demand and supply helps indeed to give definiteness to our ideas; and in its elementary stages it does not diverge from the actual facts of life, so far as to prevent its giving a fairly trustworthy picture of the chief methods of action of the strongest and most persistent group of economic forces. But when pushed to its more remote and intricate logical consequences, it slips away from the conditions of real life. In fact we are here verging on the high theme of economic progress; and here therefore it is especially needful to remember that economic problems are imperfectly presented when they are treated as problems of statical equilibrium, and not of organic growth. For though the statical treatment alone can give us definiteness and precision of thought, and is therefore a necessary introduction to a more philosophic treatment of society as an organism, it is yet only an introduction.
>
> The Statical theory of equilibrium is only an introduction to economic studies; and it is barely even an introduction to the study of the progress and development of industries which show a tendency to increasing return. Its limitations are so constantly overlooked, especially by those who approach it from an abstract point of view, that there is a danger in throwing it into definite form at all.[9]

Marshall then refers the reader to Appendix H, where the case of increasing returns is formally examined.[10]

In dealing with increasing returns Marshall is, of course, posing the question of the relation between demand and supply over substantial periods of time. He distinguishes four concepts of supply, each related to different time intervals:

> As regards *market* prices, Supply is taken to mean the stock of the commodity in question which is on hand, or at all events "in sight." As regards *normal* prices, when the term Normal is taken to relate to *short* periods of a few months or a year, Supply means broadly what can be produced for the price in question with the existing stock of plant, personal

and impersonal, in the given time. As regards *normal* prices, when the term Normal is to refer to *long* periods of several years, Supply means what can be produced by plant, which itself can be remuneratively produced and applied within the given time; while lastly, there are very gradual or *Secular* movements of normal price, caused by the gradual growth of knowledge, of population and of capital, and the changing conditions of demand and supply from one generation to another.[11]

In his fourth time interval, and in other observations on the case of increasing returns, Marshall argues that a shift in demand and a short-period rise in price will yield in time an increase in efficiency as well as in scale of production, granting a price lower than that which preceded the initial shift in demand. (Here Marshall evokes a sudden fashion for watch-shaped aneroids.) There is some implication that technological change is induced by the initial outward shift in demand and increase in price. But this insight—linking the course of technology to the price system—is not systematically pursued. It is in an institutional section of the *Principles of Economics* devoted to industrial organization (bk. 4, chap. 9) that Marshall deals with machinery; and there we are out of the price system and back with Adam Smith, the widening of the market, and the division of labor. In fact, there is no index reference to invention in Marshall's *Principles*; and inventions are considered in *Money, Credit, and Commerce* only in the context of their disruptive effect on employment and how to cushion it (pp. 244–245, 260).

Despite his sensitivity to the problem posed by increasing returns, his distinction between internal and external economies, and his appendixes and diagrams, Marshall never addresses himself satisfactorily to "the high theme of economic progress," "organic growth," or "society as an organism." Like *The Wealth of Nations*, Marshall's work contains long discursive passages on history and institutions, labor, and even education. Appendix A in the *Principles* is an essay entitled "The Growth of Free Industry and Enterprise," but Marshall's greatest admirers would agree that it is an indifferent account of how the industrial revolution came about. This is the case not only because of its curious racial cast but also because Marshall had no firm grasp on the relation between the market process and the emergence and application of new technologies. Indeed, in creating his celebrated device of "the representative firm," reconciling declining long-period marginal costs with a gradual increase in demand, Marshall explicitly excluded from view "any economies that may result from substantive new inventions."[12] Thus, as in Adam Smith, technical change in Marshall is a matter of incremental adjustment: to use his own language, changes "which may be expected to arise naturally out of adaptations of existing ideas."[13] He never asked or answered the questions Where did the "existing ideas" come from? What was the impact on the economy of their introduction? Thus, although he was acutely aware of the limits of short-period partial equilibrium analysis, there is a rude justice in the fact that his refinements in this branch of economics were his major residual contribution. Marshall had, in the end, little fruitful to say about the process of economic growth.

Allyn Young took a quite serious crack at the unresolved problems left by Marshall in his famous presidential address of September 10, 1928, "Increasing Returns and Economic Progress."[14] Building on Adam Smith, as well as Marshall, Young advanced the analysis by challenging the notion that increasing returns could be analyzed or understood in terms of a single industry with its representative firm. He argued that economic progress took the form of specialization, which created new industries rather than merely new, narrow tasks within an industry. (His illustration is the transformation of the old printing trade to a complex of industries embracing pulp and paper, inks, type metal and type, presses, etc.) He argued, also, that progress within an industry involved increasingly roundabout methods of production, which led to specialized plants, "which, taken together, constitute a new industry"; and, thus, the concept of the representative firm "dissolves." Finally, like Ayres he perceived that new technology could lead to a widening of the market, as well as vice versa.

Aside from these specific conclusions, there was a distinctive general thrust in Young's paper toward the creation of a dynamic general theory of production and prices:

> . . . the counter forces which are continually defeating the forces which make for economic equilibrium are more pervasive and more deeply rooted in the constitution of the modern economic system than we commonly realize. Not only new or adventitious elements, coming in from the out-

side, but elements which are permanent characteristics of the ways in which goods are produced make continuously for change. Every important advance in the organization of production, regardless of whether it is based upon anything which, in a narrow or technical sense, would be called a new "invention," or involves a fresh application of the fruits of scientific progress to industry, alters the conditions of industrial activity and initiates responses elsewhere in the industrial structure which in turn have a further unsettling effect. Thus change becomes progressive and propagates itself in a cumulative way.

The apparatus which economists have built up for the analysis of supply and demand in their relations to prices does not seem to be particularly helpful for the purposes of an inquiry into these broader aspects of increasing returns.[15]

And Young throws out, at one point, the evocative observation that "the appropriate conception is that of a *moving* equilibrium."[16] But Young did not try to grapple with major discontinuous technological breakthroughs. Like Marshall, he confined himself to "such new ways of organizing production and such new 'inventions' as are merely adaptations of known ways of doing things, made practicable and economical by an enlarged scale of production."[17] This is the confining assumption built into Young's much-quoted dictum: "Even with a stationary population and in the absence of new discoveries in pure or applied science there are no limits to the process of expansion except the limits beyond which demand is not elastic and returns do not increase."[18] Young was aware that there was more to technological progress and increasing returns than this. In assessing the influences which make for increasing returns, he observed: "The discovery of new natural resources and of new uses for them and the growth of scientific knowledge are probably the most potent of such factors. The causal connections between the growth of industry and the progress of science run in both directions, but on which side the preponderant influence lies no one can say."[19] But this fundamental question Young did not pursue. On balance, he held to the view that the commercial revolution yielded the industrial revolution; and, subsequently, the expansion of the market (or its potential expansion) was the engine that drove forward the refinement of technology and business organization.

Young's effort to reconcile classical partial equilibrium price and production theory with the dynamics of economic progress was not pursued by others. The Great Depression came, followed by the Keynesian revolution, the war, and postwar European reconstruction and growth. The center of the stage was taken over by the study of short-period fluctuations in national income and employment. The refinement of aggregative income analysis did, however, involve two problems which brought back the question of invention, innovation, and economic progress. First, there was the analysis of business cycles in terms of the interaction of the multiplier and the accelerator. This exercise required a distinction among investment which expanded capacity with existing techniques (motivated by expected increases in output), investment incorporating new technology, and investment motivated by profit possibilities looking beyond the current rate of increase in output.[20] Formally, the problem was solved by introducing the concept of "autonomous investment," organized in some mysterious and irregular way by innovators, coming along from time to time to set the multiplier-accelerator machine into motion. But, as Richard M. Goodwin observed: "No analytic solution can be given if $\phi(t)$ [autonomous investment] is taken, as it must, to be an arbitrary, historically given function."[21]

Harrod-Domar models of growth also posed the question of how to deal with technological change and innovation, as well as population increase. Again, the formal problem was solved by arbitrary assumption: in Harrod's model, by taking as given population growth, the flow of inventions into the production process, their productivity, and their neutrality with respect to the saving of labor and capital.[22] Such models, and their more sophisticated neoclassical successors, contributed little to our understanding of growth, although they may have added something to the case for public policy addressed to the task of maintaining relatively full employment.

To see where we had come by the late 1960's, it is instructive, by way of example, to examine the references to increasing returns, invention, and innovation in Professor Paul A. Samuelson's textbook *Economics* (page references are to the seventh edition):

—A simplified version of the multiplier-accelerator model is presented on pages 248–251, with a casual reference to "technical progress" in the last paragraph.

—On pages 369–370 supply under three of Marshall's four time periods is illustrated, the case of decreasing cost dealt with in an appendix (pp. 386–387) along Marshallian lines (of demand-supply interaction) but diagrammed in terms of a downward shift in cost curves rather than movement along a downward-sloping cost curve.

—On page 446 it is noted that internal decreasing costs for a firm lead to monopoly and that external economies, notably social overhead capital, can shift downward a firm's cost curves, a point elaborated on pages 450–451.

—On page 579 it is noted that new inventions and discoveries "are constantly being made"; and these have thus far offset diminishing returns to capital and maintained the rate of interest, a point made again on pages 716–718 in dealing with productivity and real wage trends in advanced, growing economies and in demonstrating how the capital-output ratio has remained low. Labor- and capital-saving inventions are explored on pages 720–722, after which an appendix discusses various development theories, including the Schumpeter and Harrod-Domar models.

—On page 743 it is noted that, in dealing with developing nations, "the phenomenon of increasing returns can make it possible for dramatic spurts and accelerations to occur in economic development"; but this possibility is solely illustrated by the impact of external economies induced by enlarged social overhead capital.

—On pages 751–754, there are a few paragraphs dealing with the transfer of existing technology to developing nations, the possible embodiment of technology in capital investment and replacement, and an admonition on the importance of creative innovation.[23]

These are all, essentially, peripheral references. What we have here is a lucid and faithful summary of neo-Marshallian value theory and neo-Keynesian income analysis. (Walrasian general static equilibrium is well but briefly summarized on pages 606–608.) The strengths and ambiguities of these cumulative achievements are all there. Nowhere are the relations among science, technology, and innovation dealt with fully or as a working part of a modern economic system. Major technological change remains exogenous, in both value and growth theory, dealt with in the case of the former by ad hoc illustration; in the latter, by means of highly aggregated flows whose average productivity offsets diminishing returns to land and capital. Problems of development are treated as an afterthought, in no way linked structurally to the corpus of received economic theory.

In the past several years this way of looking at the economic system has come under increasing attack. The mood is well summed up by the title of Janos Kornai's study, *Anti-Equilibrium*, which, after examining the weaknesses in the received tradition of theory, calls for "a broader synthesis."[24] One effort in revisionism is Kaldor's article "The Irrelevance of Equilibrium Economics."[25] Kaldor takes as his platform a mixture of Adam Smith on the division of labor, Allyn Young on increasing returns, Keynesian income analysis, and Kornai's specification of the arbitrary and unrealistic assumptions underlying Walrasian general equilibrium theory. His mood is almost Ayresian: ". . . without a major act of demolition—without destroying the basic conceptual framework—it is impossible to make any real progress."[26] He believes economics went wrong in the middle of the fourth chapter of Book One of *The Wealth of Nations*, when Smith abandons his examination of the relation between the extent of the market and the division of labor and becomes fascinated with money and price theory. From that point on, the theory of value took over the center of the stage, with its constraining and unrealistic assumptions about production functions.

Kaldor believes that Young's treatment of increasing returns rendered incremental technological change endogenous. Young's consequent judgment about the elasticity of supply, combined with his assumption that demand curves were adequately elastic, yields a chain reaction "between demand increases which have been induced by increases in supply, and increases in supply which have been evoked by increases in demand."[27] Kaldor indicates his respect for this intuitive pre–*General Theory* insight, but believes that, without Keynesian assumptions about the course of total expenditure (as opposed to increased expenditure on a particular commodity subject to increasing returns), Young's system does not guarantee steady overall economic progress. He turns, therefore, to a specification of the conditions required for Young's demand-supply interaction to yield self-sustained growth.

His conditions are these:

—With respect to primary commodities (subject to diminishing returns), merchants' expectations about future price prospects must be sufficiently inelastic so that they will increase the value of their stocks in the face of a phase of excess supply and falling prices.

—With respect to manufactured commodities (subject to increasing returns), entrepreneurs' expectations about the future volume of sales must be sufficiently elastic so that an increase in demand yields increased investment in both working and fixed capital.

—The monetary and banking system must be sufficiently permissive (or passive) to respond to these inducements to expand investment, generating the required savings out of the consequent increment to production and income.

At the close of an appendix to his paper, Kaldor observes that the task before us is to replace "the 'equilibrium approach' with some, as yet unexplored, alternative that makes use of a different conceptual framework."[28] His initial contribution to that objective does not, in my view, take us very far. It is wholesome that, like Kornai (and Marshall, Robertson, and Young), he underlines the arbitrary and unrealistic assumptions underlying partial and general equilibrium theory and the explosive meaning of increasing returns. But when he turns to self-sustained growth, his treatment of technological change suffers from the same weakness as his predecessors'. In Kaldor it is a diffuse incremental process, related to (and encouraging) a Smithian widening of the market, governed by no defined principles except a linkage to the scale of industrial investment. In his analysis, investment induces increasing returns in three ways: by an enlargement in the scale of plants; by the simplification and specialization of production methods, yielding "embodied technical progress"; and by cumulative improvements resulting from the number of plants constructed per year. There is no more in Kaldor than in Smith or Marshall about the interplay of science, invention, and innovation. There is not even Marshall's awareness that his treatment of increasing returns excluded "any economies that may result from substantive new inventions" or G. T. Jones' awareness that it was necessary to exclude from the Marshallian case the "epoch-making discoveries" that created "new industries rather than economies reaped from the growth of the old."

In the end, as in Harrod-Domar growth models, Kaldor is simply trying to refine marginally our knowledge of what is required on the demand side to guarantee growth under conditions of full employment. He evades the critical historical question with a bland projection backward of Youngian supply-demand inter-action: "It is a hen-and-egg question whether historically it was the growth of commerce which continually enlarged 'the size of the market' and thereby enabled increasing returns to be realized, or whether it was the improvement of techniques of production and the improvement in communication which led to the growth of commerce. In the process of the development of capitalism the two operated side by side."[29] That is not an adequate answer for a serious historian. More important, the treatment of technology by Kaldor—and his predecessors back to Smith—is an inadequate basis on which to build the dynamic theory of production and prices required to supersede Walrasian and other static equilib-rium formulations.

IV

Well, then, how should we proceed if we are to build a dynamic theory of production and prices, embracing the flow of technology as an endogenous variable and facing up to the complexities of in-creasing returns? I believe we face four distinct but related tasks. First, we must bring science, invention, and innovation within the bounds of economic analysis, as forms of investment. Second, we must expand the concept of increasing returns to embrace the case of "substantive new inventions" and "epoch-making dis-coveries"; third, we must construct a concept of dynamic sectoral equilibrium embracing not only the dynamic cases of increasing returns but also older sectors where progress is slow and incre-mental, nil, or where diminishing returns may apply; and, finally, we must relate this dynamic map (from which flows the concept of an optimum pattern of investment) to aggregative income analysis, the foreign balance, and the lags and frictions of the real world.

I can only suggest here—and briefly—how these objectives can be accomplished. But if I am right, it is possible to salvage more of traditional price and production theory than Ayres' (and Kal-dor's) analysis would suggest, while meeting the thrust of Ayres' argument by moving technological change toward the center of the stage, without quite dominating it.

V

First, the connections among science, invention, and innovation.[30]

Science and invention represent forms of investment within a society. Men devote time and current resources to produce new knowledge or new, more efficient ways of doing things. A decision is required to forego some other activity and accept the risk of failing to achieve a result valued by the market or public authorities or sought by the scientist or inventor in personal fulfillment.

Viewed in this way, the volume of resources (including human talent) devoted to fundamental science and to invention in a given society at a particular period of time can be symbolized by quite conventional supply and demand curves. A demand curve would exhibit the expected yield to be derived from the application of additional resources to the pursuit of fundamental science, with the existing scientific stock given. Since the results of pure science do not enter directly into the private economy (except in certain contemporary sophisticated industries with great laboratories), the demand for scientific achievement may reflect the premium in prestige and academic status a given society attaches to such achievement or public subsidy. A supply curve would exhibit the volume of resources actually offered by a given society to the pursuit of fundamental science. Some men are driven to search for new knowledge by inner compulsions not closely related to external reward; but for substantial numbers of human beings one can expect that talent would be responsive in degree to the rewards, financial and otherwise, a society offers for scientific achievement.

A similar pair of curves would exhibit the demand for inventions and the supply of talent and resources offered in response to the expected yields. Here we are closer to the market place. Therefore, for invention, one can probably presume somewhat greater elasticity of supply in relation to expected yields. But, we are also dealing with men with an instinct to express a creative talent, and the shape of the supply curve for inventors may also reflect nonmaterial rewards.

The purpose of viewing science and invention in these static supply and demand terms is extremely limited. It is to suggest that the actual volume of talent devoted to these enterprises within a society at any given time is the result, on the side of demand, of the premium, economic and/or otherwise, that the private market and the public authorities attach to these activities; and, on the side of supply, of the extent to which the system of education, social opportunity, and values within a society lead men of potential scientific and inventive gift to offer their talents in these directions—for achievements in science and invention are cumulative, and the numbers engaged matter. The simple point here is that the numbers can be increased if the demand curve shifts to the right, since some elasticity in supply is likely; but the numbers can also be increased if the supply curve shifts to the right, under the impact of a change in social circumstances, social values, or the intellectual and philosophical environment.

So much for a simple, static picture. Over a period of time, the demand curves and supply curves lose their independence and interact: a demand curve that shifts steadily to the right can shift the whole supply curve to a new position. It can induce a substantial increase in the numbers of talented men devoting themselves to science and invention; and, in turn, the achievements of such men can stimulate an interest in and awareness of their potentialities which increase the effective demand for their efforts; that is, it can shift the position of the demand curve.

How do science and invention evolve if, in fact, increased numbers of talented men devote themselves to these activities?

We assume that progress in science is cumulative and is a function of the volume of talent and resources applied to the solution of particular problems. Therefore, the development of a particular branch of science through time might be shown as a curve exhibiting, after an episodic start with low yields, a period of gradually increasing returns; a rather dramatic breakthrough, bringing together in a new and striking way the insights previously accumulated; then a period of refinement, framed by the new paradigm, ultimately subject to diminishing returns to additional applications of talent and resources, as in Chart 4-1.[31]

For fundamental science as a whole, the experience of the past three centuries does not permit us to predict diminishing returns. Its overall course (like that of production in growing economies) would sum up movements in numerous sectors, some in a phase of increasing returns, others in a phase of diminishing returns; some expanding rapidly, others less so, or even stagnating or declining. The marginal yield from fundamental science would

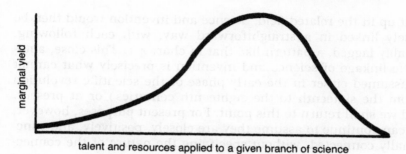

marginal yield

talent and resources applied to a given branch of science

CHART 4-1. *Marginal Yield in a Branch of Science.*

exhibit a gradual rise (with breakthroughs averaged out), level-ing off, at some point, when fundamental science (on a world basis) became a sufficiently massive effort to exploit economies of scale and when, in a rough-and-ready way, marginal returns were equated as among science, invention, and other forms of investment of talent and resources. Chart 4-2 exhibits these characteristics.

Curves of similar general shape to Chart 4-1, reflecting phases of increasing and diminishing returns, would characterize the yield from the application of talent and resources to particular lines of invention, where dramatic breakthroughs generally oc-curred against the background of much cumulative effort by many hands; and a curve like that in chart 4-2 would show the yield from invention as a whole.

We can regard, then, the pursuit of science and invention as a form of investment by societies or, as knowledge moved more freely across international boundaries, an international society. Like other forms of investment, they appear to have been subject to certain general patterns which decreed in the modern era phases of increasing and diminishing returns in particular sectors and relative overall stability in the profit rate, when the quantum of resources applied reached a certain point.

Now, how are science and invention related? The simplest as-sumption would be that invention in a given sector is the applica-tion to practical matters of a particular branch of fundamental science. In that case the productivity of talent cumulatively ap-plied to invention in a given field would rise, with an appropriate time lag, as the stock of fundamental scientific knowledge was built up in the related field. Science and invention would then be closely linked in a straightforward way, with each following, suitably lagged, a pattern like that in chart 4-1. This close, automatic linkage of science and invention is precisely what cannot be assumed either in the early phase of the scientific revolution (from the sixteenth to the eighteenth centuries) or at present. And we shall return to this point. For present purposes, however, we can continue to assume they are closely, positively, and functionally connected, without specifying the nature of the connection.

If we take that view, what determines the areas of science and invention to which talent and resources are applied? The answer, in simple economic terms, would be that men devote their creative scientific and inventive talent to solving the problems whose solution will yield the greatest profit, as determined in the market place or by public authorities. In short, we can assume, formally, that necessity, as reflected in profitability or public policy, is the mother of science and of invention, in the sense that it determines the areas of science and the kinds of inventions developed at particular periods of time, with suitable lags required for the creative processes to work their way to solutions.

With respect to invention, there is an important element of truth in this proposition which has long been recognized,[32] although necessity (or profit) is, in itself, no guarantee that human knowledge and ingenuity will always provide a fruitful response. The link of necessity to fundamental science is less clear. The sequence in which modern science developed (mathematics, as-

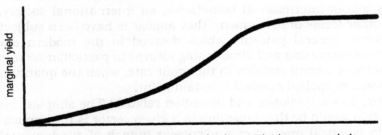

CHART 4-2. *Marginal Yield from Science as a Whole.*

tronomy, physics, botany, chemistry, etc.) is related to ease of observation and tools for experiment and measurement.[33] Moreover, fields of science have an inner life of their own, in which the participants carry forward their work, debating and probing contrapuntally, relatively insulated from the demands of the active world. At different times and places external demands have played their part in shaping the lives and activities of scientists and, to a degree, affected their work. But we are dealing with a linkage less powerful, more remote than that which shapes the pattern of invention.

I have examined elsewhere the links between science and invention in the critical period from Copernicus to the great innovative breakthroughs at the end of the eighteenth century.[34]

I conclude that there were three powerful but oblique linkages: philosophical ties, the ties of scientists to toolmakers, and osmotic ties (like those of James Watt to Professor Joseph Black) which strengthened the inventor's hand in significant but indirect ways. Jacob Schmookler arrived at similar conclusions about the linkage in twentieth-century America:

> The negligible effect of individual scientific discoveries on individual inventions is doubtless due to the orientation of the typical inventor, even those well trained in science and engineering, to the affairs of daily life in the home and industry rather than to the life of the intellect. The result, however, does not mean that science is unimportant to invention, particularly in recent times. Rather it suggests that, in the analysis of the effect of science on invention, the conceptual framework of the Gestalt school of psychology is perhaps more appropriate than is that of the mechanistic, stimulus-response school. The growth of the *body* of science conditions the course of invention more than does each separate increment. It does this by making inventors see things differently and by enabling them to imagine different solutions than would otherwise be the case. The effect of the growth of science is thus normally felt more from generation to generation than from one issue of a scientific journal to the next.[35]

In the end, then, the growth of the stock of scientific knowledge does relate to the productivity of inventive activity, although the connection is not the simple one postulated earlier in this section, for purposes of stylized exposition. Despite the quasi independence of science and the limitations on the proposition that necessity is the mother of invention, the pool of scientific knowledge and the pool of inventions can be regarded as productive stock on which a society can draw. But until the innovating entrepreneur acts, science and invention represent potential, not actual, increases in the productivity of the economy.

The number of existing inventions actually incorporated in the current volume of investment at any period of time can be presented in various ways. Perhaps the most useful is to modify the familiar Keynesian marginal efficiency of capital curve by drawing above it a theoretical optimum curve in which the current demand for investment would contain within it all existing profitable inventions. The gap between the actual and optimum curves would exhibit for any society, at a particular period of time, the propensity to innovate or the quality of entrepreneurship. The level of investment (and the degree to which inventions were incorporated in the capital stock) would be determined, in the Keynesian world, by the intersection of the rate of interest (as set by the intersection of a liquidity preference curve and the supply of money) and the actual marginal efficiency of capital curve. The point to be made here is, simply, that with a given stock of inventions available, the quality of entrepreneurship—the number of entrepreneurs willing to take the risks of innovation—will help determine the productivity of actual investment outlays and the progress of the economy. This factor, like the numbers engaged in science and invention, can be influenced by noneconomic as well as economic factors at work in a given society at a particular period of time; and it may be subject to significant sectoral (as well as interregional and international) variation.

We conclude, then, that the scale of scientific activity in the world economy is a function of a recognizable investment process, although its sectoral composition is related in only a partial and dilute way to current demand; the cumulative stock of science is obliquely but significantly related to the productivity of current invention; the scale and sectoral composition of inventive activity are, like other forms of investment, significantly related to profit possibilities signaled by the price system; the innovative zeal of entrepreneurs cannot be assumed automatically to exhaust all potentially profitable inventions: the quality of innovative entrepreneurship must be specified by sectors.

VI

Now, what happens if an innovation in a particular sector is pursued over a period of time? How does the notion of rising and then declining yields from a particular inventive breakthrough (Chart 4-1) translate itself into economics? Here there are two familiar and closely related formulations: the case of increasing returns, if we are prepared to apply it to a major change in production functions, and the concept of a leading-sector complex in the growth process.

Breaking from the now-hoary tradition of segregating major innovations from incremental technical change (or external economies), I. D. Burnet has applied the concept to a leading sector in take-off. Using the diagram in Chart 4-3, Burnet describes the outcome as follows: "Contrary to one's first impression, [Chart 4-3] is representative of an explosion rather than an equilibrium. Starting, for example, from P_1Q_1 in period T_1, industry decides to expand production in period T_2 to Q_2, which reduces costs to P_2, which inspires industry to expand production to Q_3 . . . and so on. The only constraints to the explosion are the time lags involved in accumulating capital, refining technology, acquiring tastes, training the work force and so on."[36]

After citing some famous cases of explosive growth in particular sections (from the Model T Ford to ball-point pens), he asserts: "The entrepreneur lucky enough to discover a virgin field of consumer demand can look forward to a golden age of self-generating growth."[37]

In fact, Burnet's falling supply curve must level off for any given breakthrough which lowers costs with an increase in output. Ultimately, constant or diminishing returns will set in; for trees do not grow to the sky and deceleration is inevitable, as his reference to a succession of innovations implies.

Translated from Burnet's world of the lucky entrepreneur to the path of an industry which has seized on a major technological innovation, we find that, after a possible phase of acceleration, deceleration becomes the normal path of increases in output and decreases in price. This was the powerful insight of Simon Kuz-

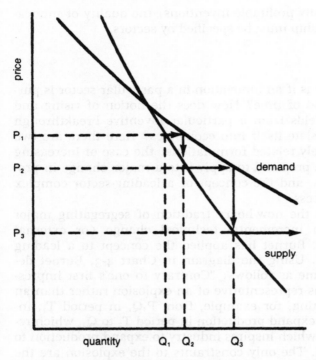

CHART 4-3. *The Case of Increasing Returns.*

Source: I. D. Burnet, "An Interpretation of Take-Off," *Economic Record: Journal of the Economic Society of Australia and New Zealand* (September 1972), p. 425.

nets in his *Secular Movements in Production and Prices* as he concluded: "As we observe the various industries within a given nation system, we see that the lead in development shifts from one branch to another. The main reason for this shift seems to be that a rapidly developing industry does not continue its vigorous growth indefinitely, but slackens its pace after a time, and is overtaken by industries whose period of rapid development comes later. Within any country we observe a succession of different branches of activity leading the process of development, and in each mature industry we notice a conspicuous slackening in the rate of increase."[38]

At any period of time a growing economy is characterized by a few accelerating sectors and many decelerating sectors moving forward (or declining) at different trend rates, when cleared of short-period fluctuations. In a rough-and-ready way, these rates tend to be related to the time of the last major technological breakthrough which granted them a phase of increasing returns. The pace of deceleration for a national industry can be affected by a wide range of factors: the likelihood that technological change, after an initial breakthrough, will yield diminishing marginal reductions in cost; the possibility that the quality of entrepreneurship will decline after an industry's heroic generation of innovation; the chance that diffusion of technology abroad may reduce a given national industry's share of the world market; the possibility that price and income elasticity of demand may diminish with expanded consumption and incomes; and so forth.

The sectors enjoying high rates of growth and increasing returns link backward to those which supply them with machinery and raw materials; laterally, they stimulate the growth of cities and regions where they take hold; and they link forward through externalities and the creation of bottlenecks which it becomes profitable to widen with new inventions and innovations. The multiple impact of a new leading sector thus requires one to think in terms of a leading-sector complex, rather than a single sector.

In the end, then, one economic result of the bringing together of sustained scientific, inventive, and entrepreneurial effort is the emergence of a powerful case (or cases) of increasing returns and of a leading-sector complex capable of lifting the economy into a new stage of growth. Self-sustained growth requires, *inter alia*, a continued flow of creative effort in these three domains— science, invention, and innovation—yielding new cases of increasing returns and new leading-sector complexes as the older impulses inevitably lose their power to lower costs and expand total production.

From its beginnings, modern economics has contained another case of increasing returns. It was recognized that, in opening up a new agricultural region or source of raw materials, a certain minimum quantum of effort and scale of acreage or of exploitation were required before the maximum marginal yield could be obtained. There was, in short, a phase of increasing returns before classic diminishing returns set in. This process, too, has its place in a dynamic theory of production.

VII

With these concepts and tools we turn now to the outline of a dynamic, disaggregated general theory of production and prices. At this stage, we shall assume that full employment is steadily maintained and that the rate of population increase and its composition (as it affects the size of the working force) are given, and the consumption function, as well.

In accordance with the previous analysis we shall assume that the available stock of scientific knowledge is being steadily built up. The sectoral composition of current scientific effort is determined partially in response to potential profit signals from the market place and the political process and partially on an autonomous basis, but it is constrained and shaped in both cases by what we might call the Rosenberg reservation; that is, the limits and possibilities of scientific advance are set and opened up by available tools and devices for experiment. The rate of buildup of the scientific stock is determined by the numbers at work in the various fields of science on a global basis (assuming scientific knowledge is fully communicated); and the numbers, in turn, are determined by a recognizable market process, including public as well as private incentives. By oblique routes the stock of scientific knowledge helps determine the productivity of the flow of inventions.

The scale of the flow of inventions is determined by the numbers engaged in the inventive process, again on a global basis, although the availability of inventions is more inhibited (and costly) than the transmission of scientific knowledge. The composition of the flow of inventions is a function of profitability (necessity) as determined by the private market system, supplemented by public incentives (e.g., aerospace requirements).

The path of sectoral evolution in both science and invention is assumed to follow that set out in chart 4-1, and we assume the scale of total effort in both domains has reached the yield plateau in chart 4-2.

The economic system is assumed to equate net marginal value product in all uses of resources (including fundamental science and invention) and to equate relative marginal utility in the disposition of private income (with income distribution given). Corrections for major elements of private monopoly must be made, and for the functions of public policy: in helping determine full employment; income distribution via the tax system; direct and indirect subsidy to science, invention, and other sectors; and provision of social overhead capital. Where relevant, direct government operation of productive segments of the economic system must be specified.

The quality of entrepreneurship, as it determines the proportion of inventions actually incorporated in the current flow of investment, must also be specified; and this variable must be assumed to vary by sectors.

On the side of demand, tastes are given, as well as the income elasticity of demand.

A system of this type yields not only an aggregate level of GNP and its overall rate of increase but also optimum sectoral paths for each sector and, therefore, an optimum pattern of current investment, when both the market process (with all its imperfections) and the political process (with all its imperfections) are granted legitimacy.[39] In concept, this is a formidably complex system: in effect, a fully dynamic multisector economic model, sufficiently disaggregated to catch all changes in production functions actually introduced into the economic system, including external economy effects, other spreading effects, organizational changes, and so forth.

In fact, however, it permits in a manageable way some critically important aspects of economic progress to be isolated which are impossible to grip with either static equilibrium models or overaggregated models of the Solow-Denison type.

—First, leading sector complexes. The grand sequence of major inventive breakthroughs becomes a part of the system—that is, factory-manufactured textiles, the steam engine, modern iron metallurgy, the railroads, steel, electricity, the various major branches of chemicals, the automobile, the aerospace complex, the postautomobile age service sectors which are expanding rapidly in real terms, and so forth. In partial equilibrium analysis, we no longer need to exclude major inventive breakthroughs from the case of increasing returns. They become induced phenomena, brought about by the sustained effort of many hands, focused on the task by incentives set up by the economic system, supplemented in some cases by incentives created by public policy.

—Second, the technologically older, slower-growing sectors. As Kuznets noted, the major technological changes tend to be bunched in the early years after a great inventive breakthrough.[40]

Thus, along with other factors which decree deceleration as the normal path of a given sector, provides a significant element of shapeliness and order to a dynamic theory of production, as Kuznets' logistic curves for a wide variety of sectors demonstrated.

—Third, declining sectors. Major inventive breakthroughs can significantly displace older vital sectors, as the automobile displaced the railroad, since the broad categories of final and intermediate demands (food, shelter, clothing, transport, power, etc.) can be satisfied in a variety of ways. Moreover, for a given economy, the international diffusion of inventions can shift the locus of production, sending a vital national sector into decline, when the pace of technological change fails to compensate for lower wage rates abroad. Such declines in production are usually accompanied by a decline in the quality of entrepreneurship, including a failure to introduce new technology becoming available. This process may open up at some stage the possibility of new entrepreneurs moving in to exploit profitably the gap between current costs and potentially lower costs. This happened, for example, in the British railroads and in the coal industry, with government as entrepreneur. In theoretical terms, this case illustrates the requirement of specifying by sectors the quality of entrepreneurship.

—Fourth, the inputs of foodstuffs and raw materials. In general, the evidence suggests, as we are all brought up to believe, that the production of foodstuffs and raw materials is less subject to productive technological change than manufactures.[41] On the other hand, these input sectors are by no means subject to a simple, protracted operation of Ricardian diminishing returns. Indeed, major breakthroughs can occur not only through the opening up of new acreage and mineral discoveries but also from the application of new technology—for example, the application of chemical fertilizers, pesticides, new seeds, and new methods of organization in agriculture.

—Fifth, social overhead capital. As we all know, a very high proportion of investment in all modernizing societies goes into housing, other forms of construction, transport, and electric power. Housing has been, historically, a sector of low productivity increase; transport has experienced a series of great inventive breakthroughs subject to retardation; electric power has followed a similar course, with significant incremental productivity improvements in the use of fuels.

From the perspective of a dynamic theory of prices, production, and investment, the point to make here is that a great deal of economic history (and, indeed, current economic activity and policy) is centered on the forces set in motion by increasing population, incomes, and urbanization, as they affect the demand and prices for foodstuffs, housing, transport, and a portion of power requirements; and by increased industrialization, as it affects the demand for raw materials, transport, and the balance of power requirements. In theory and in practice the composition of investment (including investment in inventions and exploration) cannot be understood without taking into account the incentives set up through the price system by these derived demands for the basic inputs to an advancing industrial system.

At one point, in discussing increasing returns, Dennis H. Robertson put a cogent question and gave his long-considered reply: "Can we really, even if we are careful to correct for the effect of major inventions which clearly did not depend on the scale of the industry, ever hope to get beyond what is really simply an historical record of the way costs have fallen as output has risen? . . . after a period of revolt, I am now of the opinion that the concept of a true falling long-period supply curve is one which we cannot do without, though we must handle it carefully."[42]

I am asserting a similar but not identical proposition. The structure outlined here would embrace major inventions (and leading-sector complexes) within the system, and it would shift the treatment of increasing returns from firms to sectors. But, like Robertson, I conclude that we need to deal formally with the dynamic case of increasing returns, in the wide sense used here, if we are to have a serious theory of production and prices; for in a modern dynamic economy, all sectors are, in fact or potentially, subject to increasing returns.

I would go further. It is precisely the kind of dynamic sectoral map outlined here—with implicit or explicit notions of optimum sectoral paths—which intelligent economic planners carry in their heads in both socialist and mixed economies. As planners set their sectoral targets and formulate their investment programs, what else are they doing but seeking to define optimum sectoral paths and to guide the economy along them? And, if they are wise, they initiate action (sometimes by inducing private capital imports, but by other means as well) to improve the quality of entrepreneurship in critical sectors, including the introduction of major new technologies. A good development planner knows the leading-sector complexes appropriate to his nation's stage of growth and nurtures them; is concerned to avoid a falling off in the quality of entrepreneurship in older, slower-growing or declining sectors; and provides for the requisite foundation of supporting inputs from agriculture, raw material sources, and social overhead capital, seeking always greater efficiency in these sectors where productivity increases are harder to come by. In mixed economies he is also concerned that elements of monopoly in the private sector (including those induced by excessive protectionism) do not distort the price system and frustrate the full utilization of capacity and the optimum flow of innovation. He will also be using the government's influence over the flows of credit and capital to back not only the sectors which require expansion but also, within them, the entrepreneurs of greatest quality. In command economies, burdened with trying to plan the whole, he will be struggling to create the equivalent of a competitive pricing system (in part as the basis for an optimum allocation of capital to the sectors) and to establish a system of incentives and rewards to elevate the quality of entrepreneurship.

In advanced economies like those of the United States and Western Europe, after postwar reconstruction, the planners have mainly (not wholly) confined their attention to the environment of aggregate demand, the rate of inflation, and the foreign balance. And we shall comment on these familiar matters at a later point. The implicit assumption was that optimum dynamic sectoral paths, including the optimum scale and composition of invention, would be generated by the competitive private sectors within this framework. And in the stage of high mass-consumption, where the diffusion of the automobile, a suburban house, and a standard package of durable consumer goods to a large proportion of the population constituted the leading-sector complex, this was a tolerably realistic way to proceed, leaving for the state the primary task of providing the requisite roads, schools, and public utilities, as well as the other social services decreed by the political process. But as we move into a time when the inputs of food, energy, air, water, and, perhaps, basic raw materials are in question, we shall face—and, indeed, already are facing—the need for more explicit sectoral planning on a national and international basis.

In short, we have been talking prose for some time; that is, while the main body of formal economic theory has gone its way in terms of essentially static micro- and macrotheory, plus over-aggregated growth models of limited relevance, those charged with shaping national economies, including the major institutions providing external assistance, have been operating in terms of dynamic, disaggregated sectoral models which carry with them implicit if not explicit notions of optimum sectoral paths. If rendered explicit, those models would approximate that outlined here.

VIII

And, in fact, a redoubtable band of planning theorists and econometricians have been working their way toward such a disaggregated, dynamic model since the mid-1950's, spurred on by the challenge of providing a rigorous framework for policy in and toward developing nations where, palpably, many assumptions of classical equilibrium analysis do not apply.[43] From the special perspective of this chapter, two of their lines of approach have particular significance.

One line of approach is illustrated by Larry E. Westphal's *Planning Investments with Economies of Scale.* He introduces the possibility of economies of scale into a dynamic input-output model of the economy of South Korea and explores the optimum timing for two industrial plants which require a high proportion of total investment: a petrochemical complex and an integrated steel mill. Here the question of increasing returns is directly addressed. The central issue is when, in relation to assumed time-paths of domestic demand, the plants should be built, with prior reliance on imports and rapid movement into export markets for the period until domestic demand catches up with capacity, in order to exploit the advantages of increasing returns that go with full capacity utilization.

A second line of approach is incorporated in Hollis Chenery and Lance Taylor's "Development Patterns: Among Countries and Over Time," published in the *Review of Economics and Statistics,* November 1968. They break away from the tyranny of overaggregation (in the form of primary versus industrial sectors) and correlate the relative importance of various types of industries (in terms of share of GNP) with the rise of GNP per capita for a large group of contemporary nations. They group the industrial sectors in terms of "early," "middle," and "late" industries. As noted in Appendix B of the second edition of my *Stages of Economic Growth* ([Cambridge: At the University Press, 1971], pp. 230–233), these groupings roughly approximate the leading sectors for take-off, the drive to technological maturity, and high mass-consumption.

If further developed and related to each other, these two approaches could move us further toward a fully dynamic system. Specifically, the Chenery-Taylor approach requires further disaggregation so that the typical paths of industrial expansion are revealed in the detail required for, say, an investment planner in a developing nation. These would constitute a kind of planner's guide, like the ex post optimum sectoral paths considered in *The Process of Economic Growth* (see note 39). They would also represent a generalization of the sectoral time paths presented in Kuznets' *Secular Movements in Production and Prices*.

In fact, of course, the optimum sectoral path for any particular economy will not be identical with these ex post Chenery-Taylor averages. In David A. Kendrick's phrase, realistic model building "is more of an art than a science."[44] Certainly a realistic model for a particular economy over a particular period of time must be approximated sensitively in terms of its unique features. Nevertheless, a more disaggregated version of the Chenery-Taylor calculations would help.[45]

With Chenery-Taylor curves sufficiently disaggregated and adjusted for the unique circumstances of a particular economy and time period, the kind of sectoral and project analysis of investment represented by the work of Westphal and Kornai would have a firmer base than at present. In fact, a theoretical optimum pattern of industrial investment would flow directly from such curves, when interdependencies were taken into account, which, up to a point, present computer technology permits model builders to do.

In general, then, the imperatives of investment planning in developing nations have led to major advances in dynamic theory, which embrace some aspects of technological change, including significant aspects of the case of increasing returns. Important limitations, of course, remain. For example, the existing pool of technology is taken as given. These models do not deal with the dynamic interplay of science and technology. The quality of entrepreneurship is either not dealt with or embraced in interesting but rather abstract and overaggregated calculations of absorptive capacity. Partly because they lack a refined Chenery-Taylor sectoral map, they do not make clear the role of leading sectors in growth; and the spreading effects that go with a fast-moving leading-sector complex are inadequately measured in present multisectoral models—for example, what I call lateral spreading effects are not taken into account. But, in the long history of economic thought, the planning econometricians are beginning to make a serious dent on problems long set aside or swept under the rug by empty devices of formal elegance.

IX

In the end, of course, a dynamic disaggregated sectoral model on a national basis must be linked to neo-Keynesian income analysis and to the imperatives of balance-of-payments equilibrium.[46] The imperatives of avoiding inflation and controlling the foreign balance impose constraints on the planner. In a dynamic developing nation he must establish priorities in sectoral investment, foregoing or postponing desirable low-priority outlays to avoid inflation, with a given consumption function. He may have to constrain imports below the level he would like and allocate more resources to the generation of exports. If there is substantial unemployment or partial unemployment, he faces a challenge: to expand outlays (hopefully, productive labor-intensive investment) in ways compatible with the stability of the foreign balance.

In this familiar terrain of economic analysis and policy, I would underline only one point which flows from the mode of analysis developed here. It is conventional in contemporary income analysis to focus on the overall level of investment. In multiplier-accelerator analyses of business cycles, for example, the upper turning point comes about because the rate of increase in total output tapers off when full employment is approached, reducing the level of investment, and/or there is a tendency to slide down the curve of the marginal efficiency of capital, as total investment expands, or for the marginal efficiency of capital curve to shift inward. In Kaldor's analysis of increasing returns, for example, it is the volume of investment which determines those increases in efficiency included within his definition of the case.

In fact, neither the path of business fluctuations nor the path of growth (including the course of productivity in the economy) can be understood without reference to the composition of investment. Historically, business cycles have each been marked by definable leading sectors, often also leading sectors in growth (e.g., cotton textiles, railroads, etc.), but sometimes supporting sectors, requiring expansion for balance in the system, whose profitability is signaled by relative price movements (e.g., the opening up of new agricultural areas, housing, etc.). The downturns can only be understood in terms of an expected decline in profitability in those leading sectors: costs rise as relatively full employment approaches, while increased capacity, brought about by prior investment in the leading sectors, also reduces the expected profitability of further investment in those particular directions. Similarly, the scale of investment at a particular period of time (as well as its composition) is often determined by the attractiveness of investment in certain key sectors, as determined by new technologies or the possibility of absorbing efficiently into the economy already existing technologies. The possibility of major technological change can determine the direction and, even, the scale of investment. In Britain and continental Europe, for example, the proportion of income invested rose during the railway age; and in Europe of the 1950's, the scale as well as the pattern of investment were affected by the arrival of levels of per capita income which permitted the technologies associated with high mass-consumption to be absorbed efficiently in the automobile and related industries.

Thus, the exercise of even the most familiar and most widely accepted elements of Keynesian income analysis requires a degree of disaggregation and a degree of explicit attention to the interplay between the sectors and the aggregates which is not yet conventional.

X

To return to my central theme, Ayres anticipated well the current phase of disabuse with static equilibrium analysis of prices and production. He was also correct in arguing that the flow of technological change be brought toward the center of the stage in any modern economic theory worthy of the name.

But it is not sufficient to inveigh against static equilibrium analysis and to list in a sadistic or masochistic spirit the formidable array of unrealistic assumptions required for its logical exposition. The complications which must be introduced to render economic analysis realistic are considerable, but not insurmountable; and, without excessive strain, the complex process which lies behind the flow of technology into a modern economic system can be rendered substantially endogenous, if we are prepared to widen the frame within which we view the economy. A dynamic post-Walrasian general theory of production and prices is not an impossible dream, if we are prepared to sacrifice margins of elegance for essential elements of realism. Indeed, as I have noted, economic planners and planning theorists, as well as economic historians, have been able to make considerable sense of a world of changing production functions and increasing returns without abandoning important segments of conventional price and production theory. But we could do better. In the current debate on the future of economics it would be well to break through Marshall's painful frustration and, together, with our various insights and tools, address directly "the high theme of economic progress."

As I wrote on another occasion:

> It follows from this notion of sectoral patterns that there is, in theory, an optimum balanced sectoral map which an economy would follow in dynamic equilibrium, and an optimum balanced pattern of investment.
>
> But in real life economies do not work out their destinies by following neat balanced equilibrium paths. These paths are distorted by imperfections in the private investment process, by the policies of governments, and by the impact of wars. They reflect business-cycles and trend-periods. Nevertheless, the economic history of growing societies takes a part of its rude shape from the effort of societies to approximate the optimum sectoral paths . . . They seek an equilibrium never attained.[47]

This dynamic disaggregated mode of analysis, linked to modern income and balance-of-payments analysis, is, I believe, the correct road to Allyn Young's "moving equilibrium," to Kornai's "broader synthesis," and to Kaldor's "different conceptual framework." It is also an appropriate response to Clarence Ayres' insistence that economic theory cease to be Hamlet without the Prince.

5

Money and Prices

". . . human discourse is intrinsically addressed not to natural existing things but to ideal essences, poetic or logical terms which thought may define and play with. When fortune or necessity diverts our attention from this congenial ideal sport to crude facts and pressing issues, we turn our frail poetic ideas into symbols for those terrible irruptive things. In that paper money of our own stamping, the legal tender of the mind, we are obliged to reckon all the movements and values of the world."

—George Santayana,
*Character and Opinion
in the United States*

I

My earliest research in economic history led me, *inter alia,* into the problem of explaining periods of trend increase and trend decrease in the level of British and world prices.[1] I discovered promptly, in trying to apply Keynes' *Treatise on Money* to the period of inflation during the French Revolutionary and Napoleonic Wars, that analyses focused on the demand side did not suffice. The Marshallian long-period factors operating on supply were critically important. That insight was reinforced in further work on the period down to 1914. The views I developed have, over the intervening years, been re-affirmed by the work of some of my colleagues, criticized by others. Among the latter it has been argued that my judgments have been overtaken by later scholarship, notably the well-known studies of René P. Higonnet, Milton Friedman and Anna Jacobson Schwartz, and Phillip Cagan.[2] I reviewed the whole question of trend-period (or long-cycle) phenomena, including the monetary interpretations, while preparing to write *The World Economy: History and Prospect.*[3] I concluded that, in determining the course of production and prices, during cycles, trend periods, and the process of growth itself, nonmonetary forces were "paramount. . . . Men and societies have devised and evolved monetary systems which more or less met their deeper needs and purposes as they conceived them. Different monetary policies, at different times and places, might have yielded somewhat different results than history now records. The same could be said with equal or greater strength about fiscal policies. But down to 1914 modern concepts of monetary and fiscal policy did not exist, except, perhaps, in a few unorthodox minds; and prevailing notions rendered the monetary system substantially passive and responsive."[4]

I return here to this matter because the debate over the determination of price trends has been marked for some 170 years (since, say, Thomas Tooke argued against David Ricardo) by a curious dialogue-of-the-deaf quality. By and large, monetarists use their vocabulary; nonmonetarists use theirs. There is a good deal of shouting, notably between the Keynesians and the monetarists, but no accepted synthesis. In Santayana's phrase, each side has stayed with the "paper money of [its] own stamping." As for those concerned with price trends rather than short-period price movements, there was and is no agreed exchange rate and virtually no trade between the two intellectual domains.

As a young economic historian I tried but, evidently, failed to force a bringing together of the two vocabularies and the theories which inform them. The impressive scholarship in monetary statistics and analysis of recent decades has, with all its virtues, if anything, further polarized the argument, for reasons which will emerge. In now explicitly taking that scholarship into account, I shall, therefore, try again, without excessive optimism, to contribute to responsive dialogue and reconciliation.

I shall proceed in three steps:

—First, restating my view of the relation between real and monetary factors in the determination of price movements, between 1793 and 1914

—Second, examining, in the light of that restatement, the

analyses and judgments of others who have taken a different view in recent decades

—Third, reflecting briefly on the theoretical implications of the debate

II

By a route I shall later describe, I concluded that the pre-1914 world of more advanced economies had the good sense not to permit itself to be crucified on a cross of gold—or silver; that is, as a matter of trend, the monetary systems of the major advanced economies were sufficiently flexible to adjust to the requirements for money as determined by other factors at work in the world economy or in national economies. The gold standard in particular and monetary and financial mechanisms in general did, indeed, impose disciplines on the world's economies at certain times, notably close to and immediately after turning points at the peak of business cycles. This happened even during periods of suspension of the gold standard, for example, in Britain from 1797 to 1821 and in the United States from 1861 to 1879. As we learned again rather painfully in the 1970's, floating exchange rates are not a panacea releasing domestic economic policy from the interdependence of a world economy. And, of course, money was important when business declines and/or good harvests eased demands on the monetary system, helping set the framework for business expansions. But my positive analysis of price trends was and is framed by the conclusion, empirically established, to my satisfaction at least, that the monetary systems were passive and flexible over a sufficiently significant range to avoid imposing, from the monetary side, the quite powerful trend decreases or increases in prices that we observe in the historical data. (We shall deal with gold mining a bit later.) And I would emphasize, here at the beginning, that the historical analyses in which I engaged did not ignore the monetary and financial mechanisms. In attempting to account for cyclical and trend behavior of prices and production, I have systematically examined these mechanisms as an evidently significant part of working modern economies.

Relative Prices and "the Price Level"

If the assumptions of passivity and flexibility are valid, upward or downward movements of the relative prices of major com-

modities could affect that statistical abstraction of our own creation that we call "the price level." Take, for example, the carefully constructed domestic price index presented in the Gayer
study of Britain over the period 1790–1850.[5] The weight given
wheat and oats, subject to the vicissitudes of domestic harvests,
is 43 percent of the total. Direct dependence on current harvests
decreed that this component of the price index was subject to
greater amplitude than most other items, for example, iron and
coal prices. The upshot of weight and amplitude was that the
sections of the Gayer study which sought to explain the course
of the domestic price index (and, indeed, the combined domestic
and import index) became, substantially, a history of British
grain prices. It was only in the import index and the course of
certain particular prices (e.g., iron) that one could observe clearly the impact of cyclical fluctuations of aggregate demand.

Put another way, a disproportionate rise (or fall) in the price
of wheat was not the movement of a relative price, compensated
for by the contrary movement of other prices, within a fixed
money (or money income) ceiling: it yielded a rise (or fall) in
"the price level." Such changes translated themselves quite
promptly, on a damped basis, into movements of cost-of-living
indexes larger than those in money wages. Therefore, the sections
of the study addressed to the short-term course of real wages are
also suffused with references to the harvests and consequent
movements in grain prices.

Trend movements in grain prices over longer periods than year-
to-year harvest fluctuations also leave a clear imprint on the
course of the price level and real wages, notably, the trend rise
from 1792 to 1812 and the trend decline from 1812 to 1822.[6]

Similarly, over longer periods of time, trends in ocean freight
rates, whether up or down, had substantial effects on trends in
import prices which were transmitted to the price level in countries where foreign trade represented a significant proportion of
national income. And so also with technological innovations affecting sectors of the economy with heavy weight from the side
of costs, for example, cotton textiles, railroads, steel.

The approach to price-level changes, through large changes in
the prices of major commodities and services, with substantial
weight and/or large amplitude of movement, without fully com-
pensating changes in other prices, might be called the Tooke approach. It is a quite legitimate approach if, in fact, the monetary

system is passive and sufficiently flexible not to impose a monetary ceiling (or expansion) which, in effect, forces the compensatory price decreases (or increases) required to maintain a constant price level. Although Tooke himself had a good deal to say of great interest about the behavior of the money supply in the periods of rising and falling price trends about which he wrote,[7] he did not address himself explicitly to the issue of relative prices versus the price level because the issue was not then posed as it now tends to be. For example, Anna Jacobson Schwartz recently took issue, in retrospect, with the view we once jointly held in these terms, which put the central analytic issue very well:

> The cost-push or cost-pull explanation offered in the present study for secular price change stresses demand and supply conditions in individual markets. Rises in costs are associated with poor harvests, obstructions in supply conditions—including wartime blockades—increases in foreign exchange, insurance, freight and interest costs. Declines in costs are associated with good harvests, improved transportation facilities, discovery of new foreign sources of supply, technological improvements, and reduced foreign exchange, insurance, and interest costs.
>
> These factors are all highly relevant to the price of one item *relative* to the price of others. But, for movements in general prices, the cost explanation begs the question of the source of the autonomous increase or decrease in costs. The explanation is generally *ad hoc*, relying on different factors in different circumstances and typically confusing effects on absolute costs. Moreover, even if this basic defect is overlooked and we suppose an autonomous increase or decrease in money costs, a valid application of the cost explanation would have to demonstrate how the increase in money costs increased either money supply or velocity or both or how a decrease in money costs decreased either money supply or velocity or both. We gave no such demonstration.[8]

In accepting a modified version of the Tooke approach in the Gayer study, we argued from evidence certain critical propositions which do, indeed, constitute a "demonstration." We took the view that an increase or decrease in money costs increased or decreased the demand for money to conduct a given volume of transactions; and we went to work to find out how the financial and monetary system responded: Did it respond with deflationary or inflationary impulses sufficient to maintain a constant price level? Or, did it permit rises and declines in money costs to translate themselves into rising and falling price levels?

On the period 1790–1915, we concluded on the basis of a painstaking year-by-year analysis of the workings of financial mechanisms: ". . . it may be said that the banking system, behaving, for the most part, passively, supplied the commercial, industrial, and government demands that confronted it."[9] On the period 1815–1850, we concluded: ". . . it is our contention that none of the significant secular characteristics of the years 1815–50 can be traced to the money supply; in both secular periods the banking system was sufficiently flexible to permit the expression of the more profound underlying forces. That view, it should be emphasized, cannot be derived or disproved simply from an examination of the secular movements in financial data, but depends intimately on the short-period analysis previously given."[10] In short, we established, by studying the intimate interplay of the financial system and the rest of the economy, that the trend movements in prices were not primarily the result of monetary factors.

The point is, of course, that if a large movement in the relative price of a major commodity occurs (for example, a quadrupling of the oil price) and the monetary system fails to impose the grotesque deflation required to hold the price level constant, by lowering other prices, then a rise in relative prices can yield a rise in "the price level." Thus, Paul Samuelson's recent unorthodox expostulation: "Microeconomic commodity inflation . . . refuses to remain microeconomic."[11] The obverse proposition holds, of course, for a sharp cost-induced decline of a heavily weighted commodity or service. The simple historical fact about the pre-1914 world is that monetary systems were sufficiently flexible to accommodate to rising costs except under circumstances of major war; and they were not geared to the objective of maintaining a constant price level.

An Aggregate Approach to the Rate of Increase in Productivity

Although the Tooke approach, with a passive, flexible money supply caveat, is, I believe, quite defensible, if systematically validated with empirical evidence on the short-run behavior of the monetary system, I sought to move beyond his somewhat ad hoc method and to deal with the problem in macro rather than merely micro terms. This involved focusing on the extent to which outlays other than those for consumption were productive or unproductive, the relative productivity of productive investment, and the average period of gestation of productive investment. The outcome for an index number representing "the price level" could be quite different depending on:

—The scale of resources which would otherwise be invested, allocated to military purposes (or whether the capital stock was absolutely diminished by war destruction)

—The scale of resources allocated to gold mining

—The scale of current investment resources allocated to sectors with long rather than short periods of gestation

—The productivity of current investment outlays, for example, whether they flowed to older sectors, where the rate of productivity increase had decelerated, or to newer sectors, usually involving the rapid exploitation of unfolding new technologies where productivity might be higher (the sectoral marginal capital-output ratio, lower).

In the later vocabulary of neoclassical growth models, I was asserting, in effect, that the rate of technical progress, usually assumed to be constant and Harrod-neutral, in fact varied considerably in the course of the past two centuries in various key countries (and the world economy), depending on the five variables cited above.[12] In addition, of course, changes in the proportion of income invested could also affect the result; for a given country, the course of the terms of trade could significantly affect the path of its price level; and, as is often argued in the 1970's, output per man-hour could be affected by changes in the constitution of the working force.[13]

In more general terms, this approach envisages the outcome for the price level as flowing from a dynamic race between demand and supply, that is, the pace at which a generalized demand curve (or rate of increase in money income) shifted to the right relative to the pace at which cost curves both shifted to the right and were lowered by the current rate of technical progress. The latter could, of course, be lowered not only by the productivity of current (or short period of gestation) investment but also by the

coming to completion of long-period-of-gestation investment undertaken in the past which, during its period of gestation, imparted an inflationary bias to the economy.

The Role of Cost Changes in the Movement of T

Here we come upon one of the key problems in translating a
treatment of prices in real terms into the quantity theory identity.
T (in the simplified equation $MV = PT$) subsumes within it both
changes in output and changes in costs due to technical progress;
that is, the shift of a supply curve downward and to the right can
simultaneously yield an increase in output and a reduction in
price depending on (a) the pace at which the relevant demand
curve is moving to the right and (b) its elasticity with respect to
price. The quantity theory does not permit one to get at this issue.
One of the few occasions when the problem was explicitly exposed was in a memorandum submitted by Alfred Marshall to the
Royal Commission on the Depression of Trade and Industry
(1886). After quoting Tooke on the fall in prices from 1814 to
1837, Marshall wrote: "I think, however, that there is an objection to Tooke's mode of wording, which applies also to many recent writings on the subject. He has not made it clear that the
diminution of the cost of production of commodities must not be
counted as an additional cause of the fall of prices, when its effects in increasing the supply of commodities relatively to gold
have already been allowed for separately. This is a point of some
difficulty, and its interest is theoretical rather than practical."[14]
As I have noted elsewhere: "More than anything else it was the
inability to deal analytically with T in quantity theory terms
which led to a concentration on the factors of the 'left-hand side,'
an identification of the quantity theory with a causal explanation
almost completely in terms of money."[15] Assuming, as we do up
to this point, that MV is passive and flexible, the outcome for P
can vary depending not only on the elasticity of demand but also
on the extent to which an increase in T is brought about by (a)
an expansion in demand with fixed supply curves, presumably
subject to diminishing returns; (b) an expansion in capacity with
existing technologies subject to constant returns or "economies
of scale"; (c) an expansion in production caused by a lowering
as well as outward shift of supply curves, due to the effective in-

troduction of new technologies.[16]

Evidently, we do not command the historical data to define with precision the role of each of these elements in any particular trend expansion of *T*. But it is possible to get a reasonable feel for their relative weight in different periods. That has been one objective of the analysis of trend periods I have conducted over the past forty years.

Put in simplest terms, my argument has been that there were three periods between 1790 and 1914 when, on balance, outlays above consumption levels in the world economy, taking lags into account, yielded a current "rate of technical progress" which, with the given trend increase in effective demand, yielded a rising trend in *P*: roughly, 1793–1815, 1848–1873, and 1896–1914. There were two periods when the obverse was true: 1815–1848 and 1873–1896. I attributed these shifts in the balance primarily to the changing requirements for long-period-of-gestation investment in food and raw materials, for military outlays, and for gold mining. The trend periods were, of course, not continuous; but my general explanation was, in fact, reinforced by the character of the periods when the trends temporarily reversed, for example, the large, long-period-of-gestation, extensive investments of the 1830's in the United States and in Argentina of the late 1880's which broke the continuity of the 1815–1848 and 1873–1896 trend periods in the world economy.

Thus, in a highly stylized way, the argument emerges as follows. In the monetary analysis of pre-1914 trends in prices, output (*T*) is determined exogenously by unexamined "real" factors; the quantity of money (*M* by one definition or another) is, under the gold standard, a dependent variable derived essentially from the monetary gold stock which, it is assumed, is a more or less stable function of gold production; therefore, with a given rate of increase in *T*, the trend in prices is determined by the course of the monetary gold stock and gold production. (We ignore here the deposit/currency and deposit/reserve ratios.)

With *T* and *MV* exogenously and independently determined, *P* is a dependent variable. What is happening to costs, including the rate of technical progress, is irrelevant except as changes in costs affect *T*.

In my formulation, the rate of change in costs helps determine the rate of change in prices as well as in *T*, creating a higher or lower demand for money to which the monetary system passively responds. Put another way, other things being equal, equivalent increases in effective demand or incomes can have quite different consequences for both prices and requirements for money, depending on the path of cost curves as determined by the scale, productivity, and period of gestation of current and past investment outlays, the scale of military outlays, the character of war disruptions, if any, and the scale of outlays for gold mining.

This way of looking at things is quite familiar in post-1914 discussions of incomes policy where, as in the present stage of the argument, the monetary system and fiscal policy are regarded as flexible. For example, E. F. M. Durbin argued early in the 1930's, after examining the alternatives, that the optimum policy was one of stable incomes with prices falling with the rate of increase of productivity.[17] Keynes, in *The General Theory*, examined a similar range of alternatives, using a similar analytic framework, opting in the end for money incomes rising with the rate of productivity increase and constant prices.[18] Something like this way of looking at things also emerges in modern econometric exercises where, rather starkly, it is assumed that "prices are basically determined as a markup on unit labor cost."[19] Changes in unit labor cost incorporate changes in the rate of technical progress as they affect labor productivity as well as short-run influences on the money-wage rate. For example, Edwin Kuh and Richard L. Schmalensee define the steady-state value of the money-wage as a constant times the product of the average real product of labor and the price level. The price level thus emerges as the money-wage level divided by the average real product of labor. The quantity theory of money, taken as an identity, can, in these terms, be re-written as $MV = K \frac{W}{AP} T$ with K a constant, W the steady-state money-wage, AP the average real product of labor, and T real national income. In this system, when dynamized, the rate of change of productivity is the driving variable, assuming still a flexible and passive monetary system.

As my argument above suggests, I would add to this equation, for a national economy, the price of imports.

It should be borne in mind, however, that in modern price analyses the stock of money is assumed to be flexible and capable of effective manipulation, over a significant range, by public authorities. It is, in effect, a control variable.

But Was the Pre-1914 Monetary System Passive and Flexible?

Now we come to the heart of the debate insofar as history is concerned: Is the assumption justified that the monetary system, as a matter of trend, was essentially passive in the pre-1914 world? Or, with a given T, did the money supply, independently determined, relentlessly impose its discipline, lifting or lowering the price trend? In the end, this is not a matter of theory. It is a matter of judgment about historical fact.

On what empirical grounds, then, did I conclude that the monetary system was not primarily responsible for the course of price trends in the pre-1914 world?

First, the phases of falling prices: 1815–1848, 1873–1896. As throughout the period 1783–1914, we are dealing with a world economy subject to fairly regular business cycles. The trends we measure in output and prices are the statistical outcome of one or another process of clearing the oscillating paths along which history actually unfolded. I did not perceive (and I do not perceive) any mechanism by which monetary systems could impose a trend decline in prices except by foreshortening periods of cyclical expansion, through premature imposition of monetary constraint, or by prolonging (or rendering abnormally acute) periods of cyclical contraction.

I explored the possibility of some such deflationary process operating in Britain in the periods of trend price decline by two methods: a laborious year-by-year and, for critical phases, week-by-week study of how monetary movements had their impact on the general course of the economy; and by comparing levels of unemployment, where available, or the length of phases of expansion and contraction during periods of falling and rising price trends.[20] Both methods yielded a negative result; that is, there was no evidence that the falling price trend was the result of the intrusion on the normal pre-1914 cyclical process of a monetary system inhibited by a chronic inadequacy of gold reserves. In the case of the United States, Germany, and France, where I have had to rely on secondary sources, rather than my own detailed investigations, I have found no reason to alter the conclusion to which the British data led me. Indeed, the fact that the world economy moved to uninhibited, even if brief, full employment in the 1820's, 1830's, 1840's, and round about 1890 is, in itself, prima facie evidence that a powerful secular demand constraint on the monetary side was not operative. Similarly, the behavior of one critical price is further prima facie evidence that monetary constraints did not operate to impose secular price deflations: the price of labor. The demographic forces operating on the supply of labor were quite different from the economic and technological forces operating on the supply of raw materials or manufactured goods. British money-wages did subside in the wake of the abnormal period of inflation during the Napoleonic Wars; and money-wages in the United States similarly declined after the Civil War. But, after these adjustments were completed, the trend of money-wages remained steady or fell only slightly during periods of secular price decline. This trend phenomenon cannot be attributed in this period to the power of unions and their capacity to impose inhibitions on the downward movement of money-wages. Wages, like most other prices, were determined, for the most part, in competitive markets, despite the rise of unions in the pre-1914 generation. It was, simply, the case that the trend expansion of capital and its rate of increase in productivity were greater than the increase in the labor supply; the marginal productivity of labor rose, and real wages reflected that fact. This is precisely what modern neoclassical growth models assume; and it happened, although it happened in a much more erratic way and with forces operating on the cost of living and real wages which such models screen out by assumption.

What about the Early 1880's?

The most promising case, from a monetarist point of view, is the international expansion which peaked in 1881–1882. In Britain, unemployment at the peak never fell below 2.3 percent (1882). The equivalent figures for the previous (and following) peaks were 0.9 percent (1872) and 2.1 percent (1890). The question is: Was the peaking out of this British boom, at a slightly higher than typical level of unemployment, caused by what might be called premature monetary stringency, induced by an international shortage of gold reserves? A variety of facts suggest this was not the case:

—The British peak (December 1882) comes later than those of France (December 1881), Germany (January 1882), and the United States (March 1882). As we shall see, the British recession was partially induced by prior upper turning points elsewhere.

—Detailed analyses of the upper turning point, including domestic and international pressures on the Bank Reserve, do not suggest that the boom was strangled from the monetary side: there was no monetary crisis in London equivalent to those of 1873 and 1890.[21]

—In substantial part, the relatively high level of British unemployment for a peak cyclical year can be attributed to the abnormally high level of unemployment in the building trades at the peak (3.5%). This stemmed, in turn, from the fact that Britain had just experienced an extraordinarily sustained housing boom in the period after the previous cyclical turning point: carpenters' and joiners' unemployment had averaged 0.8 percent for the period 1873–1877. Given the normally long rhythm of building cycles, one would not expect another great surge in the early 1880's. In addition, it should be noted that the unemployment figure for 1872 is uniquely low among the pre-1914 major cycle peaks: for example, 1899, 2.0 percent; 1907, 3.7 percent; 1913, 2.1 percent.

Pulling back from the behavior of the monetary system in relation to the rest of the economy, the central fact about the British expansion of June 1879–December 1882 is that it was primarily a domestic boom, with shipbuilding, now in the transition to steel, the principal leading sector, although electric light and power companies made their debut amidst some transitory excitement. There was no "mania" in London equivalent, say, to U.S. railroads in the early 1870's or Argentine railroads in the late 1880's. Net capital exports were, at the peak (1882), only two-thirds the level of the previous peak (1872). The long-term interest rate, as reflected in the price of fixed-interest securities, continued to fall throughout the expansion; and there is much qualitative evidence to support this finding. An ample supply of savings flowed to the long-term capital market, but the lenders were disappointed to find offerings where the expected rate of return over cost was modest. This is, simply, an expansion which peaked out before reaching an intense, inflationary stage of full employment; and, to put it cryptically, the weight of the evidence is that this happened because the marginal efficiency of capital curve was, for a time, relatively low, not because the rate of interest was high due to monetary stringency.

The gross structural distortions of the great inflationary boom of the early 1870's, notably in the United States and Germany, yielded a protracted depression. The milder expansion of the early 1880's yielded a briefer recession which gave way to a stronger boom in Britain, in no way inhibited by a gold shortage.

A part of the explanation for Britain's disappointment of the early 1880's clearly lies with the timing and character of the American boom. The American cyclical trough, as well as the peak, comes earlier than Britain's: March 1879 and March 1882, respectively. It was the revival of exports to the United States in 1879 which helped detonate the British expansion and the peaking out of exports to the United States which helped bring on the contraction.

There is, in turn, no great mystery about the nature of the American upper turning point. The 1879–1882 American expansion was based on a massive increase in railroad investment designed to double track and provide feeder lines for the transcontinental lines completed in the previous boom. In the course of 1881–1882 it became apparent that "railroads were multiplying too rapidly to be profitable."[22] The expected rate of return over cost declined, not because there was a rapid rise in interest rates or other costs, but because expectations of the rate of return became more sober than in 1879–1880. In particular, it was judged that the rate of expansion of traffic and short-run profits would, in fact, be less than that implicit in investment decisions made earlier. Although I did not have this American cycle specifically in mind, it conforms rather exactly to the following passage: ". . . there are also cycles in which the downturn occurs without any such dramatic arrival at a full-employment ceiling. The expected rate of return over cost in key sectors declines not because of a rise in costs but because it is perceived that the prior expansion in investment has brought capacity beyond the optimum level in those sectors; the expected rate of return on further expansion thus declines, without significant pressure from rising costs."[23]

It should also be borne in mind that the period 1879–1882 was an interval of extremely rapid rise in the U.S. monetary gold stock: a doubling in three years, accompanied by a 62 percent rise in M_2.

Another part of the explanation for the muted character of the British boom lies in the timing and character of the German expansion of the early 1880's. Investment in railroads dominated the boom of the 1870's, continuing to expand, in fact, down to 1876, long after the upper cyclical turning point (1872). In 1872 railroad investment was 35 percent of the total; in 1876, 29 percent.[24] As in the case of Britain, Germany experienced a post-upper-turning-point housing boom, peaking in 1875: the annual average level of housing investment (nonagricultural) was 250 million marks (1913 prices) in 1870–1873; 1,017 million for 1873–1876. The German expansion of the early 1880's was weak because railroad investment was running at about 75 percent of the level of the early 1880's, its proportion dropping in 1880–1884 to only 13 percent of total investment. Then came the steel revolution, in full force, lifting Germany from the phase of deceleration of the early 1880's. In the expansion of the late 1880's, industrial investment was 45 percent of the total, housing 28 percent, railroads only 6 percent. British exports to Germany rose by 50 percent in the boom of the early 1870's, by only 10 percent in the expansion of the early 1880's.

The central fact was that Europe was undergoing a transition decreed by the ending of the railway age. Railroad mileage had expanded at an average annual rate in Europe of 7.1 percent in the 1860's and 4.9 percent in the 1870's, but only 3.1 percent between 1880 and 1888.[25] The still-older leading sector, cotton textiles, also decelerated rapidly after a brief surge following the end of the American Civil War. By Michael Mulhall's calculations, European production of cotton cloth actually declined between the periods 1871–1880 and 1881–1887, the absolute decline being mainly confined to Britain.[26] New leading sectors were emerging, notably steel in all its variety of uses. But it is clear that the explanation for the muted expansion of the world economy in the early 1880's must be sought in its structural character rather than its monetary setting.

In concluding on the basis of detailed cycle-by-cycle analysis that, with certain specified exceptions, the behavior of the financial and monetary system was essentially passive, my judgment conformed, as we shall see below, to the later findings of Phillip Cagan on the United States from 1875 to 1960. Cagan relates the money stock and its components to reference cycles by using the National Bureau method. As one would expect, there is a strong tendency for the reserve ratio to decline under the optimistic circumstances of expansions, to rise during liquidity crises and the slackness of depression. A similar, but more erratic pattern marks the currency ratio, reflecting the expected positive pattern for the velocity of circulation of currency and money as a whole. The application of the National Bureau method to monetary and financial series in the Gayer study of British cycles over the period 1790–1850 led to a similar conclusion about the direction of causation and flexibility, although we did not have available money stock measurements of the kind Cagan commanded. The major exception to passivity—the strong reinforcing role in contractions of major financial crises—is similarly shared in the two studies, although the Gayer study contains a more explicit theory of the upper turning point, in which money plays a possible but ancillary role, but it is the upper turning point as a whole (not merely its monetary component) which triggers financial crises. Therefore, our view of the "independence" of financial crises and their monetary consequences somewhat differs from Cagan's.

What about Gold?

We turn now to the inflationary trend periods which occurred under the gold standard: 1848–1873 and 1896–1914. These the monetarists would link to the impact on the money supply of expanded gold production.

I have always regarded gold mining as an inflationary activity; and, since my views on this matter have occasionally been criticized, it may be useful to quote what I had to say about the impact of the gold discoveries in California and Australia in the middle of the nineteenth century:

> Gold, for those who mined it, was a useful product, capable of exchange for goods and services, including imports. The United States financed a part of its trade deficit and capital imports by mining and exporting gold, as did Australia. . . . The real effort required by Australia and the United States in mining gold was quite probably less than that necessary to purchase an equivalent volume of imports by growing and exporting, say, additional wheat or wool or cotton; although there were significant wastes of manpower and resources among the prospectors who did not strike it rich. On the whole, however, it is likely to prove the case, on close investigation, that in terms of the mining area

the production of gold was a thoroughly reasonable enterprise, in the nineteenth century. . . . Gold-mining in California and Australia, and the concurrent development of those territories in other directions, certainly constituted, at the time, a significant and attractive form of investment; and it was a form of investment tending to raise world prices, both because gold-mining was involved, and because of the considerable period of gestation involved in the opening up of new territories. On the other hand, the strictly monetary effects of the new gold, operating through central bank reserves and interest rates, do not appear to have been important.[27]

In placing primary emphasis on the direct and immediate inflationary effects of gold mining, I was, of course, arguing in an old tradition reaching back to the thoughtful efforts of Cairnes and Newmarch to sort out the routes of impact on the world economy of the mid-century discoveries in California and Australia and their exploitation.[28] Of the £27.5 million increase in British exports between 1850 and 1853, the increase to Australia accounted for £11.9 million (43%); the increase to the United States, for £10.7 million (39%). The gold rush dominated Australian economic life in these years with a flow of labor from other activities to mining, an explosive rise in money wages, a boom in land values, a heightened reliance on imports, and all the other characteristics rendered familiar in our time by the oil rush in Alaska of the 1970's and, indeed, by the extravagant, distorted pattern of growth in some OPEC countries. Much the same was true for California of the 1850's. For the United States as a whole, however, the expansion of the early 1850's was more widely based, including, notably, a more than tripling of railway mileage laid down over the decade—an additional 21,600 miles of track. These additions were mainly in the Middle West, where the period of gestation and the period of full exploitation were longer than in the case of the northeastern lines laid down in the 1840's. This was also the decade when railroadization proceeded rapidly throughout Europe, where an additional 17,420 miles were laid down. Finally, the world economy was marginally, but quite significantly, affected by war: the Crimean War (1854) and the Indian Mutiny (1857–1858). As one would expect, a period of rapid increase in effective demand induced by activities which either yielded no increase in the supply of goods and services (war, gold) or yielded their increase belatedly (the U.S. midwestern railways) was inflationary; money-wages surged up in the boom but failed to keep pace with the rise in retail prices; real wages fell away in Great Britain, France, and the United States.[29]

So much for a view of the 1850's in real terms. What about the monetary aspect of the great infusion of gold? J. R. T. Hughes' study of the 1850's is the only detailed modern analysis of the episode. His conclusion is the following:

> . . . the new gold came to Britain as payment for British goods and services (and in some cases as the property of British mining enterprises), but since the expansion of British manufactures needed increased supplies of raw materials much of the gold went out again in payments to foreign countries. Through this exchange between the gold producers on the one hand, and Britain, her foreign suppliers, and their commercial connexions on the other, the new gold of California and Australia supplied an expanding monetary base to economic activity throughout the world. This in turn engendered an expansion of the accompanying apparatus of credit which led to increased net investment and further increases in incomes.[30]

Hughes' final sentence in this passage is, in my view, a quite insufficient explanation for the international business expansion of the 1850's; and his argument in support of this judgment confronts a rather startling paradox of which he is fully aware: except for the year 1852, when the flow of gold to London clearly eased the money markets and brought down the Bank and market rates of interest, the 1850's was a period of high interest rates, a falling Bank ratio of bullion to liabilities, falling ratios of cash to deposits in joint stock banks, and chronic pressure on the monetary system. Indeed, the Bank of England's bullion holdings were substantially lower in 1860 than in 1850. Business expansion proceeded in the face of these obstacles down to the crisis of 1857 and the sharp recession of 1858. The necessary monetary expansion was accomplished by a massive increase in bills of exchange. The paradox of gold shortage at the Bank in a time of expanding gold production is accounted for mainly by a fact that Hughes does not take into account; that is, the British balance of payments was put under severe pressure by a 27 percent deterioration in the terms of trade between 1848 and 1855 (a 15% net deterioration between 1850 and 1860). This was also a decade of large capital exports; but we can assume the transfer was effected by the provision of British goods and services. Thus, although Britain expanded its gold coins in circulation substantially in the 1850's, in response to requirements imposed by expanding output combined with a sharp increase in prices and money-wages, it was under chronic pressure to disgorge the gold that arrived to pay for its relatively more expensive imports and to meet other obligations. In the United States there was some substitution of gold coins for bank notes.[31] France, bimetallist in the 1850's, imported gold and disgorged silver which flowed to the East in settlement of unbalanced trade accounts. Paris also served as a transshipment point for gold needed in Germany and northern Europe. In a table achieved after rather laborious calculations, Newmarch summarized his conclusions about the net addition to the world's monetary stock as shown in Table 5-1. As we all know, Newmarch rejected the proposition that the large additions of gold coins in circulation had a significant effect on the price level.

I would conclude as follows about this complex episode:

1. Without doubt, the diversion of manpower and resources to gold mining in California and Australia was one inflationary force operating in the world economy during the 1850's. In the short run, this diversion produced perfectly usable money and a radically increased demand for imports, but little else. The longer-run productive effects of expanding the economies of California and Australia lie mainly beyond the 1850's.

2. The inflationary effect of this diversion was compounded by three forces essentially independent of the gold discoveries:

a. The relative rise in a wide range of food and raw material prices, including a doubling in the American wheat price in two years, 1852–1854, which helped trigger the railroadization of Middle West

b. Significant military outlays for the Crimean War and Indian Mutiny

c. A strong industrial expansion in Western Europe, with railroads and heavy industry expansion the leading sectors

3. The interval of cheap money in Britain in 1852 (and the United States as well) was in no sense a fundamental cause of the subsequent expansion. Low interest rates were, indeed, help-

TABLE 5-1. Estimate of Extent to Which 174 Millions (British Pounds) of New Gold, 1848–1856, Have Been Absorbed in Gold Circulation of Various Countries

New supplies of gold 1848–1856		174 mlns.
Addition to Gold Circulation		
Of United Kingdom	20 mlns.	
Of France	60	
Of United States	50	
	130	
Of Australian colonies	10	
Of California	10	
Of Turkey & east of Europe	10	
Of Brazil, Egypt, & Portugal	10	
	40 mlns.	
		170 mlns.
Unaccounted for		4 mlns.

Source: Thomas Tooke and William Newmarch, *A History of Prices*, vol. VI (London: P. S. King [reproduced from the 1857 original text], 1928), p. 157.

ful, but they were typical of the late contraction and recovery stages of nineteenth-century business cycles. And the fundamental forces decreeing expansion proved sufficiently powerful to override chronic monetary stringency down to the crisis of 1857.

4. The availability of increased gold permitted Britain and others to expand their circulation of coins in an inflationary setting decreed by other factors; but the effective quantity of money necessary to finance the expansion of goods and services, at higher prices, required the evocation of enlarged credit instruments, notably bills of exchange. But the transmission of pressures on the Bank of England reserve through a high Bank rate simply did not work in constraining the money supply so long as business confidence remained high. For Britain, then, the 1850's was an interval of inflationary gold shortage.

In contemplating this story, monetary theorists should be clear that they cannot take refuge in the distinction between the short-run and long-run analysis of prices. As Table 5-2, below, indicates, of the 44 percent increase in British prices between 1850 and 1873, 31 percent occurred in the two years 1852–1854, that is, 71 percent of the total. Even more dramatic, from the trough in 1851 to the peak in 1857, 97 percent of the total increase in prices between 1849 and 1873 had occurred. Put another way, if we are to regard the price trend in this period as something other than the product of the convulsive events of the 1850's and the early 1870's, what happened in the former decade must be regarded as critical to any serious analysis. The quarter-century upward trend price increase turns out, in effect, to be very much the story of the 1850's.

We come now to the second major episode of expansion in gold production. It begins with the discovery in 1886 of the Witwatersrand deposits in South Africa and their subsequent exploitation but includes also substantial expansion over the next thirty years in gold output in the United States and Australia plus lesser increases in Russia and from other sources. Between 1890 and 1913 some £1,520 million in new gold may have been produced.[32] By Kitchin's well-known calculations the amount of the world monetary gold stock increased over these years (after deductions from total production for industrial uses and flows to India, China, and Egypt) from £720 to £1,579 million: an annual average rate of increase of 3.47 percent. This compares with annual average rates of growth of 3.43 percent for world industrial production, 3.94 percent for the volume of world trade.[33]

So far as the direct inflationary effect of gold production is concerned, the annual average production rate for the twenty-three years 1890–1913 is £66 million, as opposed to, perhaps, £19 million for the fifty-five years 1835–1889.[34] The direct inflationary process is most clearly perceived in the case of South Africa which, like California and Australia of the 1850's, was lifted into an intense mining boom followed by a wider process of economic development.[35] South Africa supplied perhaps half the increment in world gold production from the mid-1880's to the eve of the First World War. The South African boom was, however, somewhat different in character than those which began four decades earlier. There was no place for the romantic, individualistic prospector. The South African gold had to be extracted in minute particles, by capital-intensive methods, from a concentration of hard rock extending from the surface to a depth of many thousand feet; and a relatively larger local labor supply was available, reducing, to a degree, the role of immigration. But, as in the other cases, wages, rents, and the local price level in general rose disproportionately as labor was diverted to the mines; there was a favorable shift in the terms of trade; and a massive inflow of capital occurred—for the mines themselves, railroads, and other purposes. By 1910 the British may have invested about £350 million in South Africa.[30] Some capital also came from France and Germany. South African imports rose from an average level of £5–10 million per annum in the period 1874–1885 to £35–40 million on the eve of the First World War. Exports rose from £5–10 million to £60 million over the same period, a large export surplus emerging in the decade after the end of the Boer War. In that decade exports other than gold increased somewhat, but they were less than half of total exports in the immediate prewar years.

In short, the development of South Africa, like the concurrent development of Canada, Australia, and Argentina, was a major enterprise in the world economy during the pre-1914 generation. While the process was proceeding, these regions drew off capital in long-period-of-gestation investment. But, unlike the other cases, South Africa, in the end, mainly produced a product that added to the effective demand for goods and services but did not yield an increase in supply of goods and services, except for the industrial use of gold. In addition, tensions generated by the rapid development of South Africa triggered a rather costly war. The wartime increase in British military expenditures, from the average for 1895–1899 to the average for 1900–1903, was £65 million, 3.7 percent of net national income for the latter four years.

Without doubt, in these ways, South Africa was a distinct inflationary force in the world economy.

But gold mining was not the only inflationary force at work. As I have argued at length elsewhere,[37] there were in the pre-1914 generation:

—A series of small wars, other than the Boer War, plus a rise in the proportion of GNP devoted to military outlays by the major powers.

—A rise in the wheat price, as the U.S. wheat export capacity waned, leading to vast long-period-of-gestation investments to generate alternative sources of supply, notably in Canada, Australia, Argentina, and Russia. Although they ultimately provided wheat (and other useful resources) to the world markets, they experienced (excepting Russia), in their periods of expansion, disproportionate price and wage increases of the kind to be observed, in an exaggerated way, in South Africa.

—A waning of the rate-of-productivity increase in the leading sectors of the previous quarter-century (notably, railroads, steel, and shipbuilding) not fully compensated for by the emergence of the new leading sectors which were to shape a good deal of the economic history of the first three-quarters of the twentieth century (motor vehicles, electricity, and a new round of chemicals). A rise in the capital-output ratio is to be observed in all the major industrial economies between the 1890's and 1914.[38]

If one assumes that the world monetary system was sufficiently flexible and passive to permit these forces to operate in the normal cyclical manner of the century before 1914, they would certainly have produced, by themselves, an inflationary increase in prices.

What, in fact, was the situation in the money markets as the trends reversed from the mid-1890's? We shall focus first on Britain.

The British business-cycle expansion, which runs from a trough in February 1895 to a peak in June 1900, bears in three respects a family relation to that of the 1850's:

—It is nurtured (1894–1897) by an initial period of easy money (like 1852) to which a gold influx contributes. In this case the lull is rendered abnormally protracted by the uncertainties about the bullion standard in the United States.

—It is complicated in its latter stages by war (the Spanish-American and Boer Wars), as the 1850's were by the Crimean War and the Indian Mutiny.

—It is marked by sharp price increases (notably in coal) quite independent of the gold influx, as the 1850's were by a 78 percent rise in the British wheat price in 1852–1854.

—The boom is characterized in its latter stages, as in the 1850's, by an international "scramble for gold," and by high interest rates enforced by the Bank on the money market only with difficulty. Special price and other incentives were invoked to supplement interest rate increases to draw gold to or to hold it in London. As in the 1850's, there was a large flow of gold into domestic circulation, to finance expanded production and commerce at rising prices. There was also an important process of institutional change (like the expanded role of the bills of exchange in the 1850's): the movement toward consolidation of the private banks. To a degree, consolidation rendered the banks more independent of the Bank of England, since they held gold reserves of their own; but the process was accompanied by increased measures of cooperation which, in times of tension, rendered the banking system as a whole more cohesive.

The paradox of a gold shortage, at a time of massive increase of gold production, in the final years of the expansion is not quite as pronounced as it was in the 1850's. In substantial part, this was almost certainly due to a 10 percent favorable (rather than unfavorable) shift in the British terms of trade and to the fact that, for Britain, this was a boom based primarily on domestic investment rather than capital exports. The favorable shift in the terms of trade resulted primarily from a 90 percent increase in the export price of coal between 1897 and 1900. Britain benefited also from a 36 percent rise in shipping rates between 1897 and 1900, which was a powerful and general inflationary element in the rise of all prices of commodities internationally traded. In 1900 the Bank of England bullion reserve stood at £31.7 million as opposed to £42.0 million in 1896 (at the peak of bullion anxieties in the United States); in 1898, £31.2 million after the reflux to the United States had occurred.

The period 1897–1900 in Britain belongs with two other brief intervals between 1790 and 1914, when forces converged to produce a sharp convulsive rise in the price level, to which the monetary system accommodated, in one way or another, requiring thereafter a larger flow of money to conduct a given volume of transactions. Table 5-2 exhibits the proportion of the total price rise for Britain for three trend periods occurring within such brief intervals. The money-wage level also moved up in those brief intervals. In the case of 1897–1900, 67 percent of the total rise in British money-wages between 1897 and 1913 had occurred by 1900.

Friedman and Schwartz note that of the 49 percent rise in U.S. wholesale prices between 1897 and the close of 1914, two-thirds occurred between 1897 and 1902, the latter being the cyclical peak as opposed to 1900 for Great Britain.[39]

The reason for emphasizing these brief intervals in the present context is to underline two fundamental points made earlier:

—The analysis of prices in terms of broad trends can be quite misleading unless it is related to what actually occurred in the

TABLE 5.2. Intervals of Disproportionate Price Increase: Great Britain, 1793–1913

Trend Period	Price Increase	Interval	Price Increase	Percentage Interval Increase to Trend Period Increase
1793–1815*	75%	1798–1801	44%	66%
1850–1873	44	1852–1854	31	71
1897–1913	37%	1898–1900	21%	57%

* 1813, rather than 1815, is peak year. Range to peak year rather than 1815 is measured.

Source: B. R. Mitchell with collaboration of Phyllis Deane, *Abstract of British Historical Statistics* (Cambridge: At the University Press, 1971), pp. 470 (Gayer Domestic and Imported Commodities index) and 472–473 (Rousseaux overall index).

specific time periods when those trends found their way into history.

—Only by this kind of intense and general analysis, transcending the monetary variables, conducted over short time periods, can one hope to sort out the relative roles of monetary and nonmonetary factors.

In the late 1890's, gold mining, of course, played a role in the inflationary process, but it was a lesser factor than the nonmonetary factors set out earlier in this section. And if one takes into account these nonmonetary inflationary factors, yielding a sharp surge in prices and wages and imposing increased demands on the monetary system to conduct a given volume of transactions, a good deal of the mystery of the Gibson Paradox disappears. One does not have to evoke prescient operators in the money markets correcting the money rate of interest for the price trend. Anyone who has ever worked in a major financial center or read the daily and weekly reports knows that these institutions operated like not very bright, easily diverted bloodhounds, sniffing along the trail and off it, in response to exceedingly short run profit signals. Long-run rationality emerges only ex post, as forces operating persistently over short periods of time gradually produce what we can, looking back, triumphantly measure as a trend. The money markets were tight and interest rates relatively high at the end of the 1890's (as post-1852, forty years earlier) because they were forced to transact a sharply increased money value of business; and this phenomenon, reflecting sharp price and wage increases, was only to a modest extent the result of increased gold mining.

The question then arises: Even assuming that gold production was not the primary source of the price surges of the 1850's and 1890's, was not the increased supply of gold available to monetary authorities critically important in permitting the business expansions of those two decades?

In an earlier case, of course, without new gold flows, the system broke down under inflationary pressure, that is, in wartime Britain of the 1790's when the bullion standard was abandoned in 1797. But it is by no means clear that a protracted suspension was technically necessary.[40] By October 1797 the Bank was prepared to resume gold payments. The government, for understandable reasons at a time of major war, preferred the freedom of action suspension permitted. In the 1850's and 1890's increased gold was available, and, in the case of Britain, a good deal flowed into circulation, although the Bank's reserve did not increase. The United States did increase its gold holdings and circulation in this interval; but it was only after 1900—that is, after the big initial surge in world prices—that the Bank of France and the Reichsbank increased substantially their central reserves. It would take a detailed exercise in international counterfactual history to examine the monetary and financial alternatives open to the world economy in the pre-1914 generation if the increase in gold production had not occurred from the late 1880's but the other inflationary forces had operated. Certainly, an abandonment of the gold standard was not the only realistic option or a protracted depression of demand. The various national banking systems operated with quite different gold reserve ratios, and economies in the use of gold were evidently possible; the substitution of paper money for coin was a widely available option consistent with the gold standard; checks were, in any case, being rapidly substituted for currency. The only conclusion of which I am confident is that the pre-1914 world economy would not have enforced on itself a protracted constriction of demand due to a gold shortage.

Friedman and Schwartz, in dealing with this period, blow a marvelously certain blast on their trumpet: "The proximate cause of the world price rise was clearly the tremendous outpouring of gold after 1890."[41] Presumably they would assert a parallel proposition for the 1850's.

A close analysis of both periods indicates that the matter is by no means so clear. And, indeed, when Friedman and Schwartz shift, a few pages later, from gross measurements of trends in gold production, the components of the U.S. money stock, price, and output trends to how things actually unfolded between 1897 and 1914, clarity and simplicity disappear.[42] The price rise only begins after 1897; and there are two wars to be taken into account. And, if it did not violate their determination to take T as exogenous, there is a good deal more that ought to be taken into account in explaining price trends: the turnaround in the wheat price and the locus of wheat exports in the world economy; a vast surge in capital exports, with disproportionate inflationary effects in Canada and elsewhere; the marked deceleration in U.S. productivity, including an absolute decline in U.S. farm productivity after 1898; the rising peacetime allocations for military purposes among the major powers; and so on.

I conclude, in short, that expanded gold mining was in these years one of the inflationary forces at work; that the additional gold available permitted banking systems to accommodate to the rise in prices without greater structural changes in the monetary mechanism than those, in any case, proceeding; but that, for reasons that are quite clear in short-period supply and demand terms, this was, in general, an era of higher interest rates than the quarter-century that preceded and, in a curious way, a period of gold shortage.

The Positive Role of the International Monetary System

To assert that the price trends we observe in pre-1914 modern economic history were predominantly the product of nonmonetary forces is, of course, not to argue that the monetary system was wholly irrelevant to the price and output movements of that era. The international monetary system was an essential matrix for the network of linkages which makes the notion of a world economy a considerable reality.

The world economy was bound together by these three basic linkages:

—Massive international trade conducted in relative freedom, despite varying tariff barriers, including, especially, trade in certain basic commodities of heavy weight in virtually all domestic price indexes for which, essentially, international prices existed (e.g., cotton, wool and wheat)

—The existence of a network of large capital markets, among which short-term funds shifted sensitively in response to interest rate differentials or other factors determining expectations of profit

—The commitment of the major banking systems to buy and sell gold at fixed prices and to maintain a gold reserve which varied (relative to liabilities) as among the major countries, varied over time within countries, but nevertheless constituted a variable whose change affected interest rates and the supply of credit

In addition, of course, there was a considerable freedom to migrate.

These are the characteristics which, in a rough-and-ready way, kept the national economies in step with respect to both the business cycle and the prices of internationally traded goods, when corrected for transport costs, tariffs, and so on. National wage levels, despite the possibility of migration, varied considerably depending on demographic factors, the availability of good land, and national stages of growth (i.e., the extent to which then-modern technologies had been efficiently applied in their several economies). Therefore, goods and services not internationally traded varied considerably in price.

A major manifestation of the unity of the world economy was the international character of business cycles. The concordance with respect to time of business cycles from 1815 to 1914 among Great Britain, the United States, France, and Germany is striking but, of course, not exact.[43] For example, there are a number of minor cycles in the American experience not shared by the other major economies. There were even larger differences in the relative amplitude of the periods of expansion and contraction. For example, the expansion of the early 1870's was much less intense in France than in the three other economies primarily due to the payment of the indemnity resulting from the Franco-Prussian War; the American depression of the mid-1890's was deeper than the others due to the collapse of railroads as a leading sector and, probably, the monetary uncertainties of the time. Differences in the amplitude of expansion could reflect themselves in differential degrees of price inflation; but here the monetary system was usually involved. For example, it was normally the case that countries importing large amounts of capital could enjoy more intense business expansions, with greater degrees of price inflation, than the countries exporting capital. The discipline of the international gold standard was, to a degree, mitigated not only by the import of capital but also by a concurrent favorable shift in the terms of trade. Indeed, the import of capital, in several cases, was triggered by profit possibilities opened up by the rise in export prices which, simultaneously, yielded a favorable shift in the terms of trade.

In short, the conventional monetarist view that the world economy was kept in step by movements of gold, responding to differentials in national "price levels," is a gross and potentially misleading oversimplification. As one reads weekly accounts of the goings-on in the short-run capital markets, over the span of a cycle, one is impressed by the endless pulling and hauling of funds and gold, the alarms and excursions, the shifting of market and central bank short-term interest rates, and the intricate mechanics that went with a working international monetary system. In an upswing, movements toward tighter money were taken in stride so long as basic confidence in the profitability of the main lines of investment which powered the boom remained strong. As Arthur Lewis has observed, the connection between the stock of gold and the stock of money was "loose."[44]

In Britain, the ultimate international capital market of the era, the cyclical pattern tended to unfold as follows.

The early stages of revival were normally marked by easy money conditions and by falling rates of interest, short and long term, inside and outside the Bank of England. To this tendency abundant British harvests contributed in several important instances. Credit advanced in all forms outside the Bank probably increased mildly in most such early stages; but the falling tendency of prices made it possible to finance an increased volume of transactions with a given supply of money. Within the Bank, bullion increased, bills and notes discounted decreased, and the Bank rate fell or remained steady at a low level.

In the latter stages of expansion, there was a gradual tightening in the market and a tendency first for the market and then for the Bank rate to rise. Credit advanced outside the Bank rose sharply, and an increased amount of business came to the Bank as well, as other credit resources became more fully employed.

After the peak, interest rates continued to rise, but credit advances outside the Bank fell off. The Bank's discounts rose, often rapidly, as it fulfilled more or less adequately its role as last resort. Up to the turning point the Bank had been gradually coming to share a proportion of the burden of financing expansion; after the turning point it was meeting a crisis in confidence, an increase in liquidity preferences. The great financial crises of this era occurred, almost without exception, after the downturn of the cycle; and in fact they resulted largely from the change in profit expectations which can be taken, analytically if not statistically, to define the beginnings of the downturn. The nature of financial crisis, with its hasty liquidations and spreading of panic, accelerated the course of the decline in production and employment. It would, however, be incorrect to regard the financial crises of nineteenth-century Britain as the mechanism by which prosperity was turned into depression.

The question still remains, nevertheless, as to whether the gradual tightening of the money markets and the rise in interest rates in the latter stages of expansion, well before financial crisis, played a decisive part in causing a changed view of the future and the downturn. The evidence suggests that rising interest rates, like rising prices and money wages, symbolized an approach to an unstable position of full employment in the major cycles. They made cost conditions different from those which had been expected when various investment commitments were undertaken, and they carried psychological overtones as well. Meanwhile, the situation was also being altered by the completion of acts of investment previously undertaken. The expected rate of return over costs was being altered by a simultaneous fall in the expected rate of return and by a rise in costs. From these basic alterations in the complex of forces determining the volume of investment, rather than from a short-term credit shortage (or a deceleration of M), the turning point appears to have occurred. Like the supply of labor or commodities or fixed capacity, the short-term money supply set a limit to the extent to which expansion could proceed—a limit related in complex ways to the existence of an international monetary system. But that limit was certainly more elastic than for other factors of production, so long as confidence prevailed. Broadly speaking, these conclusions appear to apply to the other major economies of the era.

Certainly the most powerful role of the international monetary system was at times of financial panic. As suggested earlier, panics were the product of sharp downward revisions of profit expectations to which gradually tightening money and rising interest rates in the latter stages of expansion were a contributing but not a dominating factor. Once panic set in, however, the financial system reflected, transmitted, and then, to a degree, cushioned the impact of the radically increased liquidity preferences which, in a sense, operationally defined the crisis.

In downswings, of course, the international monetary system played a second significant cyclical role. After panic had subsided and the strains on the monetary system were eased by the reduced requirements decreed by falling output, prices, and, often, money-wages, interest rates fell. These periods of ease were a necessary but not sufficient condition for the emergence of a new upswing.

I would agree broadly with the summing up on this issue of Derek H. Aldcroft and Peter Fearon: "In sum, therefore, monetary forces varied in their influence from cycle to cycle, sometimes acting in a stabilizing manner, sometimes the reverse, but rarely did they initiate the turning points. In general, they operated in a passive manner, by aggravating or intensifying cyclical tendencies already present. Monetary restriction was probably more effective in damping boom tendencies than easy money conditions were in releasing the economy from recession."[45]

Six propositions flow from the perspective developed thus far; and it may be useful briefly to summarize them before turning to the monetarist literature.

1. The notion that a shift in relative prices cannot yield a rise or fall in "the price level" does not apply in a monetary system with significant flexibility. The hypothesis depends critically on fixed levels of the money stock (or money income) which force other prices to adjust to a change in the relative price of a single commodity. This is not a historically realistic assumption. Therefore, the analysis of price levels cannot be conducted simply on a macrobasis. The forces determining the movement of particular prices of heavy weight and/or amplitude of movement must be taken into account. Factors affecting costs and supply thus become directly relevant to price-level analysis.

2. The notion that the rate of increase in output can usefully be treated as exogenous in price analysis is gravely weakened by the fact that "the rate of technical progress" varies in response to

a wide range of complex forces which determine the pace at which cost curves are shifting down and to the right in relation to the movement and elasticity of demand curves. In addition to the rate of productivity increase, the price level for a given country is partially determined by import prices.

3. The analysis of national monetary systems and the workings of the international system conducted over short periods of time reveal, as a matter of fact rather than hypothesis, their considerable flexibility and justify the broad judgment that nonmonetary factors were paramount in determining price movements. And, indeed, monetarists concede, as we shall see, that, excepting cyclical declines in "deep depressions," changes in the monetary stock during business cycles originate from the side of the demand for money.

4. Increased gold mining was, indeed, an inherently inflationary activity in the world economy during the phases during which it occurred; but a useful explanation of its impact on prices must be couched in real rather than merely monetary terms. A close analysis of the 1850's and the 1890's, including gold mining and all the other forces which decreed an increased demand for money, removes a good deal of the mystery from the Gibson Paradox.

5. The manner in which price trends actually unfolded, with large price increases concentrated in a relatively few years, renders extremely doubtful the monetarist distinction between short-term and long-term price analyses.

6. A monetary analysis, by itself, cannot explain price movements, short run or long run. The monetary system in fact interacted endlessly, in complex ways, with the real factors at work. The role of money in the outcome cannot be delineated by a separate monetary analysis.

Friedman and Schwartz: Historical Analysis by Hypothesis

Against this background—with my presuppositions made explicit—we turn to consider how various modern analysts of pre-1914 price movements have dealt with the role of monetary and nonmonetary variables. We begin with Milton Friedman and Anna Jacobson Schwartz. Their *Monetary History of the United States, 1867–1960* yielded two major additions to knowledge: the various continuous statistical series measuring and bearing upon the stock of money; and interesting, often subtle, if occasionally debatable, analyses of monetary policy and other narrowly monetary episodes in economic history. These were based on qualitative as well as quantitative evidence. But the Friedman-Schwartz study reaches beyond its title: it seeks to explain the trend movement of prices in the pre–Federal Reserve period; in the post Federal Reserve period, notably in the 1930's, it seeks to explain output as well as price movements in terms of national policy toward the stock of money.

The theoretical foundations for the explanations offered in Friedman and Schwartz are not to be found in their *Monetary History*. As its opening sentence states, it is a "book about the stock of money in the United States." This is monetary history in an exceedingly narrow sense: "Throughout, we trace one thread, the stock of money, and our concern with that thread explains alike which episodes and events are examined in detail and which slighted." For the pre-1914 period, there are, for example, only two references in the book to interest rates, both in footnotes.[46]

Behind the obsessive focus on the stock of money, however, is a lucid doctrine, articulated and argued elsewhere, which Friedman has summarized as follows:

We have accepted the quantity-theory presumption, and have thought it supported by the evidence we examined, that changes in the quantity of money as such *in the long run* have a negligible effect on real income, so that nonmonetary forces are "all that matter" for changes in real income over the decades and money "does not matter." On the other hand, we have regarded the quantity of money, plus the other variables (including real income itself) that affect k [inverse of velocity of circulation] as essentially "all that matter" for the long-run determination of nominal income. The price level is then a joint outcome of the monetary forces determining nominal income and the real forces determining real income.

For shorter periods of time, we have argued that changes in M will be reflected in all three variables on the right-hand side of equation (6): k [inverse of velocity of circulation], P [price level], and y [real income]. But we have argued that the effect on k is empirically not to absorb the change in M, as the Keynesian analysis implies, but often to reinforce it, changes in M and k frequently affecting income in the same rather than opposite directions. Hence we have emphasized that changes in M are a major factor, though even then not the only factor, accounting for short-run changes in both nominal income and the real level of activity (y). I regard the description of our position as "money is all that matters for changes in *nominal* income and for *short-run* changes in real income" as an exaggeration but one that gives the right flavor of our conclusions.[47]

This positive, causal interpretation of the quantity theory of money, with its sharp distinction between the long and the short period, was adopted by Friedman and Schwartz with full awareness that neither the quantity theory identity nor the statistical correlation between the stock of money and the value of output (PT) can, in themselves, determine in which direction the lines of causation run. They address themselves to this critical point in the summation of the *Monetary History*:

> The close relation between changes in the stock of money and changes in other economic variables, alone, tells nothing about the origin of either or the direction of influence. The monetary changes might be dancing to the tune called by independently originating changes in the other economic variables; the changes in income and prices might be dancing to the tune called by independently originating monetary changes; the two might be mutually interacting, each having some elements of independence; or both might be dancing to the common tune of still a third set of influences. A great merit of the examination of a wide range of qualitative evidence, so essential in a monetary history, is that it provides a basis for discriminating between these possible explanations of the observed statistical covariation. We can go beyond the numbers alone and, at least on some occasions, discern the antecedent circumstances whence arose the particular movements that become so anonymous when we feed the statistics into the computer.
>
> One thing is abundantly clear from our narrative. Monetary changes have in fact often been independent, in the sense that they have often not been an immediate or necessary consequence of contemporaneous changes in business conditions.

The clearest example is perhaps the monetary expansion from 1897 to 1914, which was worldwide and reflected an increased output of gold. The increased output of gold was partly a consequence of earlier decades of declining prices, which encouraged gold production, and so speaks also for a mutual interaction between monetary and economic changes. But clearly the monetary expansion cannot be attributed to the contemporary rise in money income and prices. By itself, the rise in money income and prices made for a reduced output of gold in the world at large and for an outflow of gold from any single country in a gold-standard world. If the common movement of money and income was not purely coincidental, the direction of influence must run from money to income.[48]

No serious economic historian would deny that there have been independent monetary events in the sense defined here by Friedman and Schwartz, notably, changes in monetary standards and, in the American case, economically significant debates about such changes. The post–Civil War United States return to the gold standard, the adoption of the gold standard by other nations, the uncertainties about bimetallism in America of the mid-1890's, the interesting activism of Secretary of the Treasury Leslie M. Shaw in the early years of this century, the creation of the Federal Reserve system itself—these and other "independent monetary events" deserve a place in economic history. And, I would add, the major financial crises of the period, while primarily caused by other factors, played a significant quasi-independent role in the cyclical process. But, over the period 1869–1914, the only major monetary event cited, of a magnitude capable of affecting price trends, is the expansion of gold production and its alleged linkage to the price increase from the 1890's forward.

As I earlier indicated, I would regard the expansion of gold production from the late 1880's as one among other inflationary forces at work in the pre-1914 generation; but it is a much more complex case than the Friedman-Schwartz analysis would allow. They deal with it in a style for which Knut Wicksell once chided quantity theorists: "Any theory of money worthy of the name must be able to show how and why the monetary or pecuniary demand for goods exceeds or falls short of the supply of goods in given conditions. The advocates of the Quantity Theory have perhaps not sufficiently considered this point. They usually make the mistake of postulating their assumptions instead of clearly proving them."[49]

It is, I believe, not unfair to characterize the pre-1914 passages in *A Monetary History* as an exercise in postulating assumptions and arguing them on the basis of highly selective evidence, rather than trying to prove them on the basis of all the evidence. Temin's judgment about the Friedman-Schwartz treatment of the Great Depression after 1929 is in the same vein.

> Friedman and Schwartz's main conclusions are that the level of income fell as sharply as it did in the early 1930s because of a massive fall in the stock of money. This stock in turn fell primarily because of the sustained effects of multiple banking crises, that is, because of a restriction in the supply of money. But an account of the supply of money cannot be taken for an account of the stock of money unless it is known that demand plays no role. The *Monetary History* appears to have been designed to show just this—but it turns out to be a narrative based on such an assumption, not an argument for it. Friedman and Schwartz referred elsewhere to the *Monetary History* to show that the stock of money was historically determined independently of income and that the correlation between money and income therefore must be interpreted to mean that movements in the stock of money determine movements of income.[50]

How, then, do Friedman and Schwartz translate their theoretical presuppositions into historical analysis of price trends in the pre-1914 period? They do so by asserting two related but conceptually distinct propositions about the link between the money stock and the price trend. Both flow from Friedman's dual conclusions, quoted above, about the long-run meaning of the quantity theory of money: money has a negligible effect on the long-run trend in real income; the trend of the price level is, therefore, a joint outcome of monetary forces determining nominal income and the real forces determining real income.

1. First, there is the central theme, often reiterated, brought to bear on the three main periods dealt with, pre-1914:

—"The chain of influence [1865–1879] ran from expansion of output to price decline" (p. 41).

—"Resumption succeeded because the rapid growth of output brought a halving of the price level despite a mild rise in the stock of money" (p. 697).

—". . . the forces making for economic growth over the course of several business cycles [1879–1896, 1896–1914] are largely independent of the secular trend in prices" (p. 93).

—"The proximate cause of the world price rise [1896–1914] was clearly the tremendous outpouring of gold after 1890 that resulted from discoveries in South Africa, Alaska, and Colorado and from the development of improved methods of mining and refining" (p. 137).

2. Then there is a somewhat different conclusion for the period 1879–1896, namely, that a more rapid increase in the money stock would have been required if the price level were to have remained steady or declined less:

—". . . given the rapid rate of economic growth, the price decline could have been avoided only by a more rapid rate of rise in the stock of money" (p. 44).

—"Insofar as anticipations of falling prices lag behind the actual fall in prices, as they generally seem to do, interest rates will fall together with prices in the process of adjusting interest rates to the price decline. The lower interest rates, in turn, will make money more attractive as an asset relative to other fixed nominal-value assets and *so tend to mean that a larger rate of growth of the money stock is required to keep the price decline at any given level*" (p. 92, n. 5; emphasis supplied).[51]

As for the first conclusion, as I argued earlier, it is not sufficient to assert that the monetary system translated an exogenously given increase in output into a price decline. The mechanism of the process must be demonstrated.

As for the second proposition, it is not a statement of historical causation. It can even be read to mean that nonmonetary forces caused the price decline but that compensatory monetary action would have been necessary to yield a constant price level. I agree that a different monetary (or fiscal) policy might have modulated the secular price decline, principally by cushioning cyclical downswings and inducing more prompt cyclical recoveries. But that proposition tells us nothing about the cause of the secular price decline.

What mechanisms, then, do Friedman and Schwartz adduce

to explain how the monetary system translated a more or less constant rate of increase in output into a period of trend decline and then trend increase in prices?

One hundred and seventy-three pages are devoted to surveying the period 1867–1914 in three intervals: "The Greenback Period" (1867–1879), "Silver Politics and Price Decline" (1879–1898), and "Gold Inflation and Banking Reform" (1897–1914). One might have expected these examinations of relatively short periods of time to constitute a systematic vindication of Friedman's proposition that "changes in M are a major factor, though even then not the only factor, accounting for short-run changes in both nominal income and the real level of activity." The simple fact is that no such effort is made. So far as the analyses of money and prices are concerned, Friedman's long-run proposition is applied to short periods of time, with certain limited exceptions that we shall consider.

Take, for example, "The Greenback Period." Here, surely, there is an important short-period question: Did the readjustment of the war-distorted U.S. price level require a purposeful deflation, imposed by public authorities, more severe than those experienced elsewhere in the world economy between 1872 and 1879, before resumption could be carried out? Friedman and Schwartz supply the following answer: ". . . an unusually rapid rise in output converted an unusually slow rate of rise in the stock of money into a rapid decline in prices" (p. 41). They quite explicitly reject the analogy to the conventional interpretation of the deflationary pressure imposed on the British economy by the effort to maintain an overvalued pound between 1925 and 1931. I am inclined to agree that resumption was accomplished without an abnormal deflation induced for purposes of its achievement. As in Britain, after the Napoleonic Wars, the positive role of the government in creating the conditions for resumption was extremely limited. But I would make two observations. First, Friedman and Schwartz do not examine whether the American recession of the 1870's was more or less severe than those of, say, Britain and Germany. Lacking comparable unemployment data, this is a difficult but not impossible enterprise; for example, the decline in various real production, transport, and trade magnitudes could be compared. Second, and, for our present purposes, more important, no short-run mechanism is specified by which an extraordinarily rapid decline in prices could occur without such a demand deflation. Friedman's long-run proposition (making the price level dependent on exogenous movements in money and real output) is, simply, applied to short periods of time.

Now a short-period mechanism certainly did exist for adjusting the American price level to the world price level without a sharp deflation in demand; but it has no place in conventional monetary analysis. That mechanism was a rapid reduction in costs brought about by the ending of wartime inhibitions on production and interregional trade and of the wartime diversion of resources above consumption levels, combined with the positive cost-reducing effects of productive investment undertaken after hostilities had ceased. Fundamental to the American adjustment, for example, were radical immediate postwar reductions in raw cotton and wheat prices and in the consumers' price index. The decline in the latter permitted a decline in money-wages to be consistent with a rise in real wages, down to the peak of the boom of the early 1870's. Table 5-3 suggests the nature of the adjustment which had, evidently, mainly taken place by 1873. The United States at peace had reassumed its normal place in the world economy, and its price and wage structures reflected that fact. The relative behavior of British and American money and real wages between 1873 and 1879 suggests the possibility, at least, that, for whatever reasons, the American depression may have been more severe than the British.

My point here, however, is not to assert or explain the possibility that the American depression of the second half of the 1870's went deeper than that in Britain. It is to indicate that the Friedman and Schwartz analysis of this interval is dealt with in terms of long-run rather than short-period monetary analysis and to argue again that the short-run analysis of prices, and the effort to segregate monetary from nonmonetary influences on prices, requires close attention to what actually happened in the course of particular cycles, including what happened to costs.

We confront similar, but not identical, problems in the Friedman and Schwartz treatment of the period 1879–1897. Again, the basic treatment is in terms of the long-run determination of the price trend by exogenously introduced trends in output and the stock of money. As throughout the book, changes in the components of the latter are specified in some detail in passages of

TABLE 5.3. *Prices and Wages: United States and Great Britain, 1865, 1873, 1879 (all magnitudes reduced to 1873 = 100)*

	Raw Cotton Price		Wheat Price	
	U.S. (1)	U.K. (2)	U.S. (3)	U.K. (4)
1865	819	260	165*	113**
1873	100	100	100	100
1879	69	60	68	77

 * 1866, peak year.
 ** 1867, peak year.
 *** Allowing for unemployment.

great value. But there is no systematic effort to demonstrate that short-run changes in the stock of money determined substantially fluctuations in both money and real income.

There is, however, something else: an analysis of the four cyclical phases which make up these eighteen years in terms of the workings of the international gold standard and monetary "disturbances."

Between 1879 and 1897 we are dealing with two major business cycles in the world economy. With some eccentricities in timing and circumstance, they were shared by the American economy. Friedman and Schwartz analyze the sequence of expansions and contractions in a rather special way. They do not assert that the cycles were inherently monetary phenomena. Nor do they specify or analyze the investment surges and contractions which, as a matter of historical fact, lay at the heart of these cycles. There is, for example, nothing of consequence about American railways in the 1880's, the investment and trade aspects of the opening up of the gold mines in South Africa, the steel and shipping revolution, or the important preparatory laying down of railway lines in Canada and Australia and only a misleading reference to British investment in Argentina.[52] From 1879 to 1891 the story is told in terms of a highly simplified, aggregate version of "the classical gold-standard mechanism in operation,"[53] with the focus almost exclusively on the United States and Great Britain. In this version, the American price level rises (1879–

Money-Wages		Cost of Living		Real Wages	
U.S.	U.K.***	U.S.	U.K.	U.S.	U.K.***
(5)	(6)	(7)	(8)	(9)	(10)
104	86	133	88	79	88
100	100	100	100	100	100
77	89	82	84	94	103

Sources: *Historical Statistics of the United States, Colonial Times to 1970* (Washington, D.C.: GPO, 1975), cols. 1 and 3, pp. 208–209; cols. 5, 7, and 9, p. 165. Mitchell, *Abstract of British Historical Statistics*, col. 2, p. 491; col. 4, pp. 488–489; cols. 6, 8, and 10, pp. 343–344.

1882) relative to Britain's when gold flows in, responding to a favorable trade balance and capital imports; it is disciplined into line by the depression of 1882–1885, when abnormal grain exports and capital imports cease. Britain is portrayed between 1879 and 1882 as constrained by its gold outflow. One would never guess from this account that British unemployment declined from 11.4 percent in 1879 to 2.3 percent in 1882; or that real national income rose 11 percent in these three years; or that a large and persistent gap between Bank of England and market interest rates existed throughout the boom, cushioning the domestic economy substantially from the international pulling and hauling in London.

From the point of view of the present analysis, however, the central point is this: the highly stylized portrait of the British and American economies under the gold standard in the early 1880's in no way explains the declining price trend, which is the main problem Friedman and Schwartz address in their chapter. And the authors do not pretend that it does.

The business expansion of 1885–1891 is dealt with in a different way: as simply "unremarkable." The period is introduced with this statement: "There is little that requires special mention about this segment, which is to say that the fluctuations within it seem attributable to no special 'disturbing' factors, and, we do not know how to explain them."[54]

There is, in fact, a good deal that is remarkable about the

American cyclical pattern in the late 1880's and early 1890's: the recession of 1887–1888, not shared in the other major economies, and the expansion of 1891–1893, similarly unshared. There is also the peaking out of U.S. railway investment in the late 1880's and the beginnings of the adjustment of the American economy to a new pattern and level of investment as a proportion of GNP. But all this and much else of interest to more conventional business cycle analysts is irrelevant to the authors' concern with "monetary disturbances," although it can be argued that these nonmonetary phenomena had significant monetary consequences.

Finally, there is an analysis of "the disturbed years," 1891 to 1897, in which great emphasis is given to the effect on international capital movements of uncertainty about the American monetary standard. The authors are explicit, however, that they are considering only limited monetary aspects of the deep post-1893 depression which had unexamined other causes.

The analytic treatment of the cyclical phases from 1897 to 1914 is, similarly, dominated by Friedman's long-period rather than short-period doctrine, that is, by a treatment of prices as the outcome of autonomous movements in output and the money stock. There are also rather unilluminating speculations on the switch of the United States at the turn of the century to the role of capital exporter, an interesting passage on the efforts of Secretary of the Treasury Shaw to behave as a central banker, a lively account of the panic of 1907, and a useful summary of the banking reform movement leading up to the creation of the Federal Reserve system.

To understand sympathetically what Friedman and Schwartz were trying to accomplish in these uneven historical passages, it is useful to turn to their 1963 paper in the *Review of Economics and Statistics*, "Money and Business Cycles."[55] They begin, again, with a statement of awareness that the close correlation of the stock of money with the cyclical behavior of the economy tells us little about the direction of causation; and they pose this question:

> Is the cyclical behavior of money primarily a reflection of the cyclical behavior of the economy at large, or does it play an important independent part in accounting for the cyclical behavior of the economy? . . . The key question at issue is

not whether the direction of influence is wholly from money to business or wholly from business to money; it is whether the influence running from money to business is significant, in the sense that it can account for a substantial fraction of the fluctuations in economic activity. If the answer is affirmative, then one can speak of a monetary theory of business cycles or—more precisely—of the need to assign money an important role in a full theory of business cycles. The reflex influence of business on money, the existence of which is not in doubt in light of the factual evidence summarized above, would then become part of the partly self-generating mechanism whereby monetary disturbances are transmitted. On the other hand, if the influence from money to business is minor, one could speak of a cyclical theory of monetary fluctuations but not of a monetary theory of business cycles.[56]

Clearly, the kind of evidence adduced in *A Monetary History of the United States* for the pre-1914 period is not sufficient to vindicate "a monetary theory of business cycles." And in a further passage in "Money and Business Cycles," it becomes clear that Friedman and Schwartz judge that what they have thus far accomplished in their empirical work is to demonstrate that, in certain specific cases, "the influence running from money to business is significant."

For the pre-1914 period their specific cases of an independent and "significant" monetary role are of three kinds:
—Wartime inflations
—The effect of expanded gold production on prices
—The role of monetary factors in three deep depressions (1875–1878, 1892–1894, 1907–1908)

With respect to wartime inflation, I assume no historian or economist would quarrel with the assertion that prices can be raised by one form or another of money creation in substantial excess of tax collections, notably at a time when manpower and capital are being substantially diverted from productive activities.

With respect to enlarged gold production, I, at least, would not disagree that it played a role in the price increases of the mid-century and pre-1914 periods, although I would assign, in the latter case, a less exclusive role to gold than Friedman and Schwartz and trace out a somewhat different route of impact.

With respect to the three deep depressions cited, I have no

doubt that post-upper-turning-point crises and bank failures yielded a rush to liquidity reflected in declines in the deposit-currency and deposit-reserve ratios; and these movements, once under way, reacted back on the level of consumption and investment outlays, output, employment, and prices. And, so far as the 1890's are concerned (I am less sure about the late 1870's), uncertainty about the monetary standard almost certainly played a role in deepening and prolonging the American depression. But we are dealing here with the monetary system as a living part of the whole interacting economic process, not as a unique initiating force. In my view, and that of most business-cycle analysts, the basic source of the pre-1914 deep and prolonged depressions is the scale of the structural distortions in the previous intense boom.[57]

I conclude, then, that, aside from its measurement of the American monetary stock and its changing components, the limited aim and achievement of *A Monetary History*, with respect to the short-period role of money, was to dramatize that there were, indeed, some episodes when impulses derived from the monetary standard and the monetary mechanism did "matter"; that is, they had some significant impact on the course of real output and/or prices. And, as one who has systematically included sections on money and finance in all his various analyses of short-run business fluctuations, I am quite prepared to assign money a systematic if limited role in a full theory of business cycles without accepting either the vulgar or modulated versions of the dictum that "money is all that matters for changes in *nominal* income or for *short-run* changes in real income."

It is important to be aware that *A Monetary History* does not attempt to vindicate that dictum, although Friedman appends to "Money and Business Cycles" a "tentative sketch" of the central mechanism for a monetary theory of business cycles, to which we shall refer later.[58]

As for the Friedman and Schwartz analysis of long-period price trends as a dependent variable, responding to independently determined trends in real output and the money stock, *A Monetary History* is in no sense a demonstration. It is, simply, an assertion by hypothesis of the direction of causation in the quantity-theory identity. And, for reasons I shall summarize in Section III of this chapter, I reject, on this issue, the distinction between short- and long-run analysis.

Cagan: Analysis by Correlation

Professor Phillip Cagan's *Determinants and Effects of Changes in the Stock of Money, 1875–1960*, like *A Monetary History*, adds significantly to knowledge about movements in the stock of money in the United States. It is, in particular, a study of the cyclical and trend movements in the three chosen determinants of the money stock: high-powered money, the currency ratio, and the reserve ratio. But, like Friedman and Schwartz (who used Cagan's findings), he moves from the specialized terrain of monetary analysis to conclusions on larger matters.

Cagan's basic method is functional rather than historical; that is, he examines for the whole period of his study the contribution of the three components to movements in the total stock of money and then the cyclical and trend behavior of each component. Nevertheless, in dealing with both cyclical and trend behavior, changes are often explained in historical terms. And, admirably, he not only presents cyclical behavior in the form of averages but also provides the reader with the patterns for individual cycles. Moreover, his trend measurements distinguish different periods, for example, 1877–1913 and 1918–1953. For our purposes—the analysis of pre-1914 price trends—it is unfortunate that he does not systematically break down the pre-1914 period (as he does, for example, in Tables 4 and 11) into subperiods ending in 1896 and 1913.

Behind Cagan's painstaking research is a desire to settle the question of which way causation runs within the quantity-theory identity:

> There are basically two ways to clarify the source of covariation between money and business activity. One is to examine the effects of changes in the money stock on business activity. These effects, though studied extensively, have proved difficult to trace. Even when large, they are likely to involve distributed lags and so to affect various parts of the economy at different times. Identifying cause and effect is then extremely difficult and hazardous. An alternative approach is to examine the factors affecting the amount of money supplied. The more they reflect fluctuations in business activity, the less reliance can be placed on the importance of money-stock effects in explaining the observed co-

variation—and conversely. The belief that this approach can shed light on the importance of the two directions of influence is the main motivation for the present study.[59]

The first proposition he asserts relates the rate of change of the money stock to reference cycles in business activity. He finds an intriguing monetary lead of about a quarter of a reference cycle which "suggests that the effect of changes in monetary growth on business activity is largely responsible for the covariation between them."[60] But, somewhat wistfully, he notes that the lags "would undoubtedly be less" if the comparison were made with the rates of change in business activity. And so they have proved to be.[61]

Indeed, Cagan's most general conclusion on the cyclical relation between money and business activity is, broadly, negative from a monetarist perspective and differs markedly from Friedman's dictum on the short-run, quoted above. "It seems highly probable that cyclical fluctuations in business activity account for most of the cyclical variations in growth of the money stock, although many variations in particular years can be traced to special monetary developments largely unrelated to concurrent business conditions."[62]

As in Friedman and Schwartz, the "special monetary developments" come to rest on the role of money in major wars and periods of contraction in major cycles.[63] The now-familiar argument is that severe panics had monetary consequences which justify the proposition that money was an independent force in producing "severe cycles."

Cagan's speculations about the behavior of the monetary stock in relation to the severity of business contractions cover a good many possibilities, including the hypothesis that panics result "from the severity of the accompanying business contractions."[64] Cagan rules out this possibility because panics come at different stages of the downswing. This is dubious ground for rebuttal. Although changing expectations of profit in the leading sectors of a boom did produce some panics shortly after the upper turning point, there is no reason why the dynamics of contraction itself could not cause later dramatic failures and liquidity crises. He also finds two severe contractions, accompanied by sharp declines in the money stock, with no panic: 1921 and 1937–1938. Since the latter was initiated by a sharp rise in the reserve ratio, he is left with one case. On this frail basis he concludes: "The evidence is therefore consistent with and, taken as a whole, impressively favors emphasis on the decline in the rate of monetary growth as the main reason some business contractions, regardless of what may have initiated them, became severe."[65]

Quite aside from the possibility of differences in judgment about the strength of the evidence, this sentence contains an ambiguity about causation similar to some of the Friedman and Schwartz propositions about the 1879–1896 period of price decline. Is Cagan arguing that the severe declines were caused by other factors and could only have been arrested by a different policy toward the monetary stock, or does he take the path of the monetary stock as the fundamental cause of the deep depression?

But the basic problem with Professor Cagan's analysis is one that runs through the whole monetarist literature. He refuses to ask and try to answer the critical questions: What causes business cycles? What causes the upper turning point? How do monetary and nonmonetary factors relate to each other in the course of business cycles? The possibility of nonmonetary factors at work is not excluded—indeed, often explicitly accepted. And Cagan, in particular, bluntly accepts for minor cycles and, implicitly, for the expansion stages of major cycles the initiating role of "business activity" in determining the movement of the money stock. But, like his monetarist colleagues, he stays rigorously within the bounds of his monetary vocabulary. All else is exogenous, never to be discussed in substance or analyzed. That is why monetarist conclusions, in their scholarly rather than crusading mode, emerge as suggestive or in the form of correlations others are challenged to disprove. I asserted earlier that there is no way to conduct a serious analysis of price movements wholly in monetary terms. Cagan's analysis demonstrates that the same proposition holds for business-cycle analysis, although, as we shall see, he flirts a bit in Appendix D with a pure monetary theory of business cycles.

Cagan also deals, at various points, with one of Friedman and Schwartz' central historical themes: the role of gold and gold mining in determining the pre- and post-1896 price trends in the years before the First World War.[66] Some of Cagan's specific historical observations are distinctly questionable; for example, he refers to the period 1882–1896 as one of "declining prices reflecting worldwide deflation."[67] Unless this statement is meant as a tautology, it is wrong. There was a powerful worldwide boom in the second half of the 1880's, including a price rise counter to trend. Later he asserts, in the same vein, that the Baring crisis of 1890 "had roots in the world wide deflation of prices which accompanied the comparatively low output of gold."[68] I would have thought it was agreed that the Baring crisis arose from a gap familiar in the story of manias and financial crises: in this case the gap between the flow of expected profits from Argentine railway building (and Argentine capacity to meet its repayment commitments) and the time it actually took to expand agricultural production (and freight receipts) on the pampas.

Cagan's central proposition about price trends is, essentially, identical with that of Friedman and Schwartz: down to the mid-1890's, "the growth of world trade and of gold use was outpacing the growth of the world stock and so was depressing price levels";[69] the price decline induced, after a long lag, the rise in gold production from the late 1880's;[70] and the rise in gold production caused the subsequent rise in prices down to 1914. These propositions emerge even more starkly than in Friedman and Schwartz since there is no effort, in Cagan's analytic study, to deal historically with the short phases into which the two trend periods decompose. What we do have are cycle-by-cycle data permitting us to observe in different columns the rates of change in wholesale prices, the money stock, and the three chosen components of the money stock; and some correlations for all years (1877–1954) and for two nonwar periods (pre-1914 and post-1919).[71] T, the course of real output, never appears, let alone the forces operating on costs and productivity.

Aware of the indecisive character of findings derived from correlation analysis, Cagan makes an effort to argue analytically against those who take a different view of the causes of pre-1914 price trends.[72] This is a somewhat baffling and grossly incomplete passage. The major direct quotation is from a redoubtable advocate of the link between gold and price trends, W. Stanley Jevons.[73] Critics of the monetarist view (never clearly paraphrased or quoted) are alleged to have hinged their argument on nonexistent or imperfect monetary data when, in fact, they were usually offering, from the side of costs and productivity, a quite different explanation for the direction of causation within a quantity-theory equation accepted as a tautology. Then comes an argument which, if I correctly understand it, asserts that the short run and long run must be separated sharply because of the possibly long (but unspecified) lags between monetary changes and their effects. Finally, there is a passage summarizing Cagan's interesting but explicitly inconclusive efforts to test various theories of the Gibson Paradox, an exercise elaborated with respect to Irving Fisher's theory, in Appendix B. There is a footnote reference to the work of E. H. Phelps Brown and myself,[74] but no substantive effort to deal with our views. Cost and productivity changes, as in the rest of the monetarist literature, remain naughty words.

Despite Cagan's finding that, in cyclical fluctuations, the money stock was primarily a reflex of business activity, there is a sketch (Appendix D) of a "purely monetary cycle" which we shall examine briefly later.

Cagan's study, in the end, results in a paradox. He concludes: "Although the cyclical behavior of the three determinants is not easy to interpret, it seems safe to conclude that most of their short-run variations are closely related to cyclical fluctuations in economic activity—the opposite of the conclusion reached for the long run."[75] As in the exposition of my argument in the first part of this paper, the monetary and financial system emerges from Cagan's study as responding passively to demands induced by fluctuations in business activity; but Cagan never examines the forces determining such fluctuations. In the long run, he is left with fluctuations in gold output, responding, in part, to inducements set up by price trends. In the period of trend price decline within the scope of his study, he offers, like Friedman and Schwartz, no recognizable mechanism by which the alleged gold shortage could have caused the price decline. For the period of increased gold availability, he is simply content, again like Friedman and Schwartz, to exhibit the association of increased gold supplies and rising prices without investigating the mechanism at work or exploring the other forces at work making for the rising price trend of the pre-1914 generation.

Higonnet and the British Monetary Data

There is no doubt that we are all in the debt of René Higonnet for having had the wit to go back to semiannual banking supplements of the *Economist* and construct a more complete and consistent series for banking deposits than that devised merely from the reporting banks. Moreover, Higonnet admirably indicates both the statistical and the analytic limitations of his reconstructed series.[76]

Higonnet's central conclusion is that the total of "bank money," as best he can measure it, increased more in the period of rising than of falling prices. His trend calculation is flawed by his measurement from cyclical peak to trough for the first period (1873–1894), from trough to peak for the second (1894–1913).[77] It is also useful to examine the behavior of his series by cycles and shorter phases in the two trend periods (see Table 5-4).

What emerges is significant irregularity in how each trend period unfolded. Bank deposits fall sharply in the period 1873–1879 in the face of deep depression and the rapid decline of prices from their inflationary peak of 1873. Deposits rise substantially in the expansion of 1879–1883 when prices, after an initial speculative surge (1879–1880), fall away to slightly below their 1879 level. They hold steady in the cyclical decline of 1883–1886, when prices again fall sharply. They rise at their maximum rate for the whole period 1873–1913 in the boom of 1886–1890, before the large influx of gold occurs but when price trends temporarily reverse. They rise during the decline of 1890–1894, when prices are falling rapidly.

It is clear that the overall measures of bank deposit trends for the period Higonnet measures (1873–1895) tell us little about what really happened: three periods of business decline in which bank deposits, respectively, fell sharply, remained constant, and increased while prices fell at rapid if not uniform rates; two periods of business expansion in which bank deposits increased at quite different rates with prices falling slightly in the first expansion, increasing rapidly in the second.

There is a similar irregularity during the trend upswing. There is a major expansion in the late 1890's in bank deposits and a sharp price rise, mainly confined to the years 1898–1900. As with the price peak of 1873, it is inextricably bound up with a coal shortage with wide-ranging price consequences. Bank deposits level off as prices fall away, on balance, to 1904. The two subsequent phases of business expansion (1904–1907 and 1908–1913) are each associated with price increases, although the association evidently differs. In 1908, the price decline is associated enigmatically with a sharp rise in bank deposits.

I draw two conclusions from this sequence: first, considerable violence is done by looking at the course of bank deposits and

TABLE 5-4. *Cyclical and Trend Growth Rates: Bank Deposits in the United Kingdom, 1877–1914, and Price Movements*

	Cyclical Phase	Trend Measure		Price Trend
1873–1879ᶜ	−2.60%			−4.73%
1879–1883ᴱ	1.85			−0.30
1883–1886ᶜ	0.00			−5.59
1873–1883		−0.84%	P-P	−2.98
1879–1886		1.05	T-T	−2.60
1886–1890ᴱ	4.16			1.07
1890–1894ᶜ	1.29			−3.28
1886–1894		2.71	T-T	−1.13
1879–1894		1.94	T-T	−1.82
1894–1900ᴱ	3.19			2.95
1900–1901ᶜ	0.00			−6.67
1901–1903ᴱ	0.00			−0.72
1903–1904ᶜ	0.00			1.45
1894–1904		1.90	T-T	1.06
1904–1907ᴱ	2.12			4.55
1907–1908ᶜ	3.35			−8.75
1904–1908		2.29	T-T	1.05
1908–1913*ᴱ	3.67%			3.09
1907–1913*		3.15	P-P	1.02
1900–1910*		1.44		0.39
1873–1895		1.00		−2.61
1895–1913*		2.54%		1.77%

Note: C designates phase of cyclical contraction; E, cyclical expansion; P–P, measurement from peak to peak; T–T, from trough to trough.

Sources: Bank deposits calculated from René P. Higonnet, "Bank Deposits in the United Kingdom, 1870–1912," *Quarterly Journal of Economics* 72, no. 3 (August 1957): 330, col. 1, except for figures marked by asterisk (*) which are sum of cols. 2 and 3. The figure for 1873 is taken as Higonnet's rough estimate for that year: £600–£630 million (p. 347). In all cases the mean figure within Higonnet's ranges is used to calculate growth rates. Price movements calculated from overall Sauerbeck-Statist indexes, Mitchell, *Abstract of British Historical Statistics*, pp. 474–475.

prices in simple trend-period terms; second, an explanation of these irregular cyclical and trend patterns would require, from my perspective, a full economic history of the period, including the course of production, productivity, and terms of trade. Indeed, Higonnet observes rather in the spirit of Cagan's short-run analysis: "The influence of the business cycle on the series is obvious . . . . the growth of bank money is not constant but is strongly affected by current economic conditions."[78] But the sharp expansion of deposits and prices in the period 1886–1890 should, by itself, caution analysts from making any easy association between gold production and prices.

Higonnet moves on from his analysis of trends in bank deposits in relation to price trends to consider those who have disagreed with the gold hypothesis. Without quite saying so, he implies that those counterarguments hinged crucially on the trend in British bank deposits. One would never know from Higonnet's account, for example, that Phelps Brown based his argument substantially on changing rates of productivity increase.

But the fundamental weakness in Higonnet's argument is that he appears insensitive to the fact that a simple correlation between bank deposits (or even the monetary stock) and national income (embracing output as well as prices) tells us nothing about the direction of causation.[79] And this is true of his narrower argument that the period 1873–1895 was a time of "stagnation of credit." The decline of bank deposits over the period 1873–1883 (peak to peak) could reflect a fall in prices, from the side of costs and productivity, just as the rise of the late 1880's or late 1890's could reflect a rise in prices induced from the side of costs and productivity.

In short, while adding to our knowledge of British banking statistics, Higonnet did not advance our understanding of the relation between money and prices.

Subsequent work by British, Japanese, and American scholars has both altered Higonnet's calculations and yielded approximations of the British money stock from 1871 to 1913 and for subsequent years.[80] Table 5-5 sets out the new calculations for selected years, as well as Higonnet's.

Evidently, Nishimura and Schwartz believe Sheppard's data for the 1880's are too low. The full details of the argument are not germane to this chapter. But briefly, so far as bank deposits are concerned, Nishimura argues that Sheppard's figures, drawn directly from the balance sheets of the joint stock banks published in the Banking Supplements of the *Economist*, are underestimates on two counts: undercoverage of joint stock banks (by 9% in 1880) and an inadequate allowance for the ratio of deposits at reporting joint stock to deposits in private banks. Sheppard took the ratio back to 1880 at the 1891 level (1.135). Nishimura, in constructing his series for the 1870's, from wider data, solved the problem of the missing private bank data by multiplying the number of branch offices by the average of deposits per known branch, dealing separately with the London and country offices.

Sheppard holds that, for the 1870's, this procedure leads to an overestimate since many private country bank offices were not seriously engaged in the deposit business in the 1870's.

Schwartz, by an ingenious extrapolation backward of the 1891–1914 trend in the proportion of private to joint stock bank deposits and forward extrapolation of Nishimura's ratios for 1870–1880, produced a series which roughly reconciles at the year 1891, when, it is assumed, underestimation of private bank deposits in Sheppard's series is eliminated.

Sheppard, Nishimura, and Schwartz all sought to eliminate the element of double-counting acknowledged as possible by Higonnet, in his figures, which included interbank deposits. Nishimura and Schwartz also take into account nonbank deposits in the Bank of England.

Evidently, the Schwartz deposit estimate, for the 1880's, is closer to Nishimura's than that suggested by Sheppard's 1880 figure.

There was an extremely sharp expansion of the money supply in the latter stages of the boom which peaked in 1873, marked as it was by a coal bottleneck and a more general inflationary spurt. The money supply subsided in the 1870's as prices declined rapidly and heavy unemployment was experienced in 1878–1879. (The level of activity was quite well maintained down to 1877 by a boom in housing construction, aided by the low interest rates which followed the decline in capital exports after 1873.)

A curious result emerges if one then compares the evolution of the money stock and the price level. In the period of price decline the money stock expands faster than in the period of price increase: the average annual rate of growth from 1883 to 1896 is, by Sheppard's calculations, 3.06 percent; by Schwartz', 2.41 percent. For the period 1896 to 1913, the figures are, respectively, 2.25 percent and 1.92 percent. In part, this anomaly results from the flow of gold to London in the 1890's compounded to a degree by the flight of funds from a United States uncertain about its monetary standard. But monetarists cannot have it both ways. The U.S. trend in the money stock also behaves in an unexpected

TABLE 5-5. *U.K. Money Supply, Prices, and Output: Alternative Estimates, Selected Years, 1870–1913 (£ million)*

	Economist Estimate of Bank Deposits (Higonnet) (1)	Annual Average Growth Rate %	Gross Deposits All Commercial U.K. Banks (Sheppard) (2)	Annual Average Growth Rate %	Total Deposits (Nishimura) (3)	Annual Average Growth Rate %	Total Deposits (Schwartz) (4)
1871	—	—	—	—	443	—	372
1873	615	—	—	—	512	7.51	448
1879	525	−2.6	342 (1880)	—	498	−0.46	438
1883	565	1.85	392	4.65	—	—	489
(1873–1883)	—	(−0.84)	—	—	—	—	—
1890	665	2.36	499	3.51	—	—	570
1896	775	2.58	701	5.83	—	—	690
1900	845	2.19	799	3.33	—	—	779
(1890–1900)	—	(2.42)	—	(4.82)	—	—	—
1907	895	0.82	862	0.95	—	—	848
1913	1,085	3.26	1,059	3.49	—	—	1,017

Note: Dates are major cycle peaks with the following exceptions: 1871 is included as an initial date, at an intermediate point in the upswing which began from a trough in 1868; 1879 is included as the trough of a particularly severe cyclical depression; 1896 is included as the approximate trough in the secular movement of prices. The 1873 estimate by Higonnet is drawn mainly from an ad hoc estimate for that year made by John Dun. The mid-point in the ranges offered by Higonnet are taken in each case. His 1913 figure is the sum of the *Economist* totals for joint stock and private banks that reported their deposits; but by 1913 the reporting was virtually complete; only 21 banks did not publish their balance sheets by that time.

way with respect to price trends if the special circumstances of the mid-1890's are eliminated. From the cyclical peak in 1882 to the peak in 1892 the rate of increase (M_3) is 5.35 percent,[81] while the wholesale price index (Warren and Pearson) fell at an annual rate of −7.1 percent; from 1892 to 1913 the money stock figure rose at a quite similar rate—5.68 percent; but this time prices rose at an annual rate of 1.3 percent.[82]

In both the British and American cases the explanation of these superficial anomalies lies in basic developments in the economy which altered the relation between income and the money supply as well as institutional changes which altered bank reserve ratios. And it is on these that A. A. Walters focuses in his examination of

Annual Average Growth Rate %	Net U.K. Money Supply (Sheppard) (5)	Annual Average Growth Rate %	Money Stock (Schwartz) (6)	Annual Average Growth Rate %	Overall Price Index (1867– 1877 = 100) (7)	Annual Average Rate of Change %	Real GNP (1900 Prices) (8)	Annual Average Growth Rate %
—	—	—	502	—	100	—	1,106	—
9.62	—	—	583	7.77	111	5.36	1,092	−0.63
−0.35	495 (1880)	—	573	−0.29	88	−3.80	1,187	1.40
2.72	548	3.45	616	1.83	82	−1.75	1,363	3.52
(0.86)	—	—	—	(0.55)	—	(−2.08)	—	(2.24)
2.25	624	1.87	698	1.80	72	−1.84	1,510	1.47
3.23	811	4.47	840	3.13	61	−2.73	1,740	2.39
3.08	939	3.73	919	2.27	75	5.30	1,904	2.28
(3.17)	—	(4.17)	—	(2.79)	—	(0.41)	—	(2.35)
1.22	985	0.69	997	1.17	80	0.9	2,109	1.5
3.08	1,183	3.10	1,160	2.56	85	1.0	2,374	2.0

Sources: Col. 1, Higonnet, "Bank Deposits in the United Kingdom," pp. 330 and 347; cols. 2 and 5, David K. Sheppard, *The Growth and Role of U.K. Financial Institutions, 1880–1962* (London: Methuen, 1971), p. 182; col. 3, Shizuya Nishimura, "The Growth of the Stock of Money in the U.K., 1870–1913," unpublished paper, Hosei University, Tokyo, 1973, p. 11, table 9, col. 5; cols. 4 and 6, privately supplied by Anna J. Schwartz; col. 7, Sauerbeck-*Statist* Overall Price Index, Mitchell, *Abstract of British Historical Statistics*, pp. 474–475; col. 8, C. H. Feinstein, statistical tables of *National Income Expenditures and Output, 1885–1965* (Cambridge: At the University Press, 1976), T14–T15 (at 1900 factor cost).

the British pre-1914 experience, notably, the rise in the use of checks and the course of the velocity of circulation.[83]

For our limited purposes, however, the relevant point is that subsequent research has not confirmed Higonnet's belief that revised bank deposit statistics demonstrated the primacy of gold production in determining the course of British prices.

Thomas: The Core and the Periphery

In the second edition of his *Migration and Economic Growth*, Brinley Thomas undertakes to introduce a monetary dimension to his analysis of economic interaction within a world economy, as well as to integrate the findings of the Kuznets long-cycle literature.[84] Having discussed in Chapter I my view of various long-cycle theories, I shall confine myself here to the monetary aspects of Thomas' latest formulation.[85] In an analysis for which I have considerable sympathy, Thomas sets up a model in which capital flows, in successive cycles, from an advanced industrial nation (C) to the new-country periphery of the world economy (D); and then, after a recession, capital flows in the next expansion to C's domestic capital stock, notably to domestic residential construction.[86]

Thomas weaves together real and monetary factors in the following way to explain the upper turning point of a cycle in which there are large capital exports from C to D during the expansion:

> In the early part of the upswing in D there is not likely to be trouble. To simplify, let us ignore saving and postulate that the lending is entirely at the expense of home investment in C and that the borrowings are entirely spent by D; then the transfer will be effected without price or income adjustments if the marginal propensities to import add up to unity. A moderate degree of under-effected transfer will entail adjustments which will slow down the boom in D, but the infrastructure investment projects already launched are unlikely to be much curtailed.

> In the later stage of the boom the situation changes. As the export upswing gathers momentum in C, a turningpoint is reached. Investment induced by the growth of exports increases rapidly, and at the higher level of employment marginal costs rise, while demand is running high in construction activity in D. Productivity in C's export sector has ceased to go up and may be falling, and export prices rise relatively to import prices. Meanwhile, C investors are receiving an increasing flow of interest and dividends on their foreign securities. This wealth effect is likely to promote further *ex ante* lending which now reaches a very high level. The population variable, emigration, is also at a high level but its rate of growth is already declining for demographic reasons and after a short lag this entails an upturn in construction from the low point reached in C.

> At this stage transfer becomes seriously under-effected; the growth of the current trade balance cannot keep up with

the *ex ante* lending. The monetary authority in C is faced with an external drain of gold to D and an internal drain due to a combination of export-induced investment and a revival in construction. This means severe monetary instability. The central bank must take drastic action to replenish its reserves and raises the interest rate to a punitive level. This attracts a large flow of short-term balances and gold from D, and there is a fall in purchases of D securities. The representative investor in C, impressed by the increasing risk attached to D securities and attracted by the marginal efficiency of investment in home construction, will now optimize by increasing his stock of domestic securities at the expense of his foreign portfolio.

The monetary cobweb thus set in motion breaks the infrastructure boom in D. The large loss of gold reduces D's money supply or sharply reduces its rate of growth and this precipitates a downturn. . . . In short, our view of the pre-1913 Atlantic economy is that the inverse cycle was propelled by real determinants but that, in the crucial phases when expansion gave way to contraction, changes in the stock of money played a significant independent part in influencing the course of the economy.[87]

My objection to this formulation is that the upper turning point in such cycles was not a pure product of a "monetary cobweb." On the upswing, short-run expectations of profit were exaggerated in many (not all) cases. Without the element of "mania," one cannot understand, for example, the capital export boom to the United States of the early 1870's, Argentina of the late 1880's, or, indeed, such earlier cases as 1809–1810 (Latin America), 1824–1825 (Latin America), and 1834–1836 (United States).[88] The fundamental perception that yielded the upper turning point in such cases was that profits would be less than expected in the short run. A number of factors could bring about this change in short-run profit expectations: a peaking in D's key export price, a rise in costs, or an awareness that the period of gestation of the investments undertaken was longer than had been earlier anticipated. Indeed, at a later point Thomas quotes A. G. Ford on the crisis of 1890: ". . . the slow maturing of investment projects for which the service charges were immediate was a main cause of the Baring crisis."[89] As I indicated earlier, I would not rule out the role of rising interest rates as part of the setting in which upper turning points occurred; but the major financial crises and panics of the pre-1914 era took place after the downward revision of profit expectations, usually in one of the leading sectors sustaining the boom. My central comment on Thomas, then, is essentially the same as those made earlier with respect to Friedman and Schwartz and Cagan, with respect to the role of money in major contractions. In his summing up, Thomas, in fact, turns to Cagan on this point.[90]

Dickey: The Quantity Theory and Cost Reductions

George Edward Dickey's doctoral thesis, *Money, Prices and Growth*, is a serious and original effort to introduce cost changes into the quantity-theory analysis of prices. He almost—but not quite—solves two of the central problems posed by quantity-theory formulations: the problem of relative price changes in relation to "the price level," and the introduction of cost changes in the analysis of Q (the volume of transactions).

Dickey's analysis covers 1869–1896 in the United States. His central thesis is the following: "Cost reduction in the production and distribution of goods which occurred during the period 1868–1896 resulted in reduced product prices and increased output and investment. Given the actual growth of the money supply and movements in velocity, the economy was able to experience both rapid growth and a decline in the price level. This deflation which can be characterized as supply- rather than demand-induced was for that reason compatible with rapid expansion of output."[91]

He develops his thesis in three steps:

—A general theoretical argument indicating the conditions under which a shift of cost curves downward and to the right can yield reduced prices, increased output, and maintained or increased profit levels. This case is illustrated within his period with reference to the Bessemer process, the exploitation of the Mesabi iron range, and transport innovations.

—An empirical test of whether price changes were supply or demand induced for seventeen basic commodities. Of 439 observations, 45.1 percent were cases of supply-induced deflation; only 15.7 percent, demand-induced. When price movements in peak and trough cyclical years are examined, the shares were 36.9 percent and 8.1 percent, respectively; for trough years, 53.1 percent and 17.7 percent, respectively. When relative prices are calculated, in 74.3 percent of the cases where the money price of a commodity fell its relative price also fell.

—An empirical examination of profits during the period of trend price decrease indicating, by various measures, that real earnings rose and the spirit of enterprise remained strong. He concludes: "We found that, even in a time of pronounced deflation, price changes were influenced much more by supply factors than by aggregate demand. Consequently, profits remained intact. Changing costs and technology peculiar to each market are much more important in providing investment opportunities than the monetary factor (within wide variations in the rate of change of the money supply) working in all markets through aggregate demand."[92]

Despite his redoubtable effort to dramatize the role of costs in determining price changes, Dickey struggles, not without difficulty, to remain loyal to monetary doctrine, namely, that cost changes can only shift relative prices but not "the price level." His difficulties are of two kinds. First, he is aware that some of the changes he is examining (notably, transport costs) are so substantial and pervasive that they are a bit difficult to fit into the rubric of relative price shifts: "Transportation is an important factor in contributing to adjustments in the price structure as it is an input into almost every production process."[93] Nevertheless, he sticks with the monetarist notion that the price level is a dependent variable resulting from exogenously determinined rates of increase in MV and Q. He never asks whether it was possible that MV adjusted itself to the money requirements set up by an expanding Q under conditions of rapidly reduced costs. For that reason, he criticizes my formulation for assuming that MV was, essentially, passive.[94] And when he sets down his own theoretical formulation, his critical assumption is that M and V are exogenously determined and fixed and, therefore, PQ must remain constant under the condition of a price cut, in a particular sector, brought about by reduced costs.[95] Only under such a rigid assumption will a fall in the relative price of a major commodity not result in a decline in the price level. His system, like that of most other monetarists, requires that money prices adjust around the existing mean in the face of a sharp relative movement of a significant major commodity. Our difference thus clearly hinges on the passivity and flexibility of the pre-1914 monetary system.

Here Cagan's cyclical views on the United States and mine on Britain substantially converge—a fact Dickey does not take into account. But Dickey does leave the door ajar: "To the extent that forces creating changes in relative prices also act on the determinants of the aggregate price level (M, V, and Q), changes in relative prices will be accompanied by changes in the aggregate level of prices."[96] In the period he examines, the rapid decline in costs and relative prices reduced, in my view, the demand for money below the level which would otherwise have obtained, and the path of M responded.

Dickey's second difficulty is that he twice confuses an analysis of the reasons for the price decline with statements which imply, simply, that a different policy toward the money supply would have been required to keep the price level constant or reduce the severity and duration of recessionary periods.[97] As noted earlier, this kind of ex post reasoning about policy tells us nothing definitive about causation.

Although monetarists have no reason to complain of Dickey's formal orthodoxy, his introduction of cost and supply changes as well as the lucidity with which he states the unlikely conditions under which a relative price change will not yield a change in the price level are likely to leave them uneasy. And, although I would argue that I have not ignored the influence of money, he is broadly correct, I believe, in the assertion which shaped his research: "In the context of the equation of exchange, MV = PQ, the defenders of monetary explanations of the price level have concentrated on M and V, giving scant attention to Q; while the proponents of alternative explanations concentrate on the components of Q and ignore the influences of M and V. Only an explanation which recognizes the effect of all three variables can fully relate economic growth and the price level."[98]

III

A Few Reflections on Theory

Before summarizing the theoretical conclusions which emerge from this review of my perspective in relation to others, it may be useful to recall the context in which the revived debate on money arose over the past generation. Milton Friedman, in a reply to his critics, breaks off to evoke vividly something of his own intellectual history, the tradition of the Chicago school, and its link to his later work on money.[99] In a world almost dominated by Keynesian analysis, Friedman and his associates felt both righteous and beleaguered. They brought to bear talent and energy in a sustained counterattack, in which a passionate motivation was disciplined but not wholly concealed by loyalty to high intellectual standards. And all this was heightened, of course, by the possible relevance of the theoretical and historical debate to current economic policy. The faith that a proper monetary policy, based on a tightly controlled rate of increase in the money stock, could provide steady, noninflationary growth gave a special thrust to both the theoretical and the historical debate. One cannot escape the sense that both the monetarists and their Keynesian critics felt they were playing for high stakes in terms of influence on public policy.

There is nothing unique in the history of the social sciences about a debate of this kind, in which conflicts about ideas and policy are interwoven with strong human feelings. Such multifaceted controversies have been, in fact, a central part of the process by which the body of economic thought has been built and enriched. But in this case, the debating context has had two particular consequences. First, monetarists vacillate between the proposition that money has mattered more than some may have supposed in determining the course of income and prices and the proposition that money has been a unique and overriding factor. There is also the vacillation, often noted in this review, between whether money was a unique and overriding factor or whether it could have been or could be made to be such a factor by a correct monetary policy. The first, more modest proposition could lead to the harmonization or, at least, to an agreed cross-translation of theoretical vocabularies and the sorting out in economic history of monetary and nonmonetary factors within a larger theoretical framework including both. The second proposition results in nonnegotiable demands and confrontation. This is unfortunate because, as we have seen, monetarists, read carefully, are not arguing that nonmonetary forces did not exist in history or, even, that monetary forces were systematically overriding. It is when the issue of fiscal versus monetary policy is joined that the question of whether money is exogenous, endogenous, or the product of complex interaction becomes an enflamed battlefield.

A second, distorting consequence of the debate results from the fact that the most intense analytic and policy confrontation has been between the monetarists and the Keynesians as they argued the relative virtues of fiscal and monetary policy in dealing with unemployment and inflation. Both are, essentially, framed by Marshallian short-period assumptions. Therefore, what I, at least, regard as the gravest weakness of monetary analysis—the failure to deal effectively with changing costs and productivity and fluctuations in the relative price of basic commodities—has not been properly identified or explored in the course of the protracted debate.

The vacillation in monetarist writing between money being significant (or playing an important independent role) and money playing a unique, overriding role in both the cyclical and trend behavior of economic systems has, then, the following important effect. When monetarists argue on relatively modest grounds, we may accept, as I have long accepted, a place for money in the dynamics of prices and production; but so long as we use the quantity theory of money as our primary analytic prism, we are left without a theoretical structure capable of integrating money with the rest of the economy. How can a serious economic historian, for example, take T as an exogenously given variable? How can he work usefully with a system where changes in technology and in the supply of food and raw materials (and their changing relative prices) have no discernible place? It is useful for Cagan to confirm what every historian of business cycles already knew, namely, that, on the upswing, the monetary system exhibited great flexibility, responding to the needs of an economy confident in its commitments, and that, on the downswing, financial crises had significant further monetary consequences, affecting production and prices. But as the matrix for a business cycle analysis which would actually deal with the interplay of real and monetary factors, the quantity theory of money is a virtually useless instrument. Business cycles were the form that economic growth assumed in the pre-1914 world. Each cyclical expansion was carried forward by surges of investment in particular directions, determined by areas of profitability opened up by the coming of particular new technologies; or by increased requirements for foodstuffs and raw materials signaled, in turn, by the price movements of particular commodities; or by neglected requirements for housing and other infrastructure. There was a rough-and-ready logic in the sequence of cyclical leading sectors which the quantity theory of money does not permit us to grip.

Thus, quite aside from the specific arguments adduced in the first two sections of this chapter, indicating my differences with the monetarists in dealing with money and prices, I would conclude that, if the more modest assertions of the monetarists are accepted, we are still left with the grand theoretical problem of integrating real and monetary analysis.

Professor Friedman's answer to this argument is, presumably, that he has made the linkage via a Walrasian "real" system.[100] But that is just the problem: a Walrasian system lacks precisely the kind of supply-side dynamism we require to analyze cycles, trends, or the movement of modern economies even over short periods of time. As I have often said, the Marshallian long period is with us every day of our lives.

When, in an exploratory way, monetarists leave the world of historical evidence and strive to outline a pure monetary theory of a business cycle, the inadequacy of their theoretical base becomes even more clear.[101] Friedman and Schwartz, for example, trace out what might be described as a portfolio theory of a business cycle. An initial exogenous force (say, an increase in open market purchases by a central bank) accelerates the rate of increase of the monetary stock. Those who sold securities to the central bank will, if a commercial bank, become more liquid and lend more, creating further deposits, and thus accelerate the growth rate in high-powered money. The nonbank seller will find himself with redundant money balances and look about for assets to supplant those sold to the central bank, bidding up the price of such assets. The process becomes progressive: the range of assets acquired spreads from fixed-interest securities to capital expansion of plants, houses, durable consumer goods, and so on. This happens because, as the prices of financial assets are bid up, they become expensive relative to nonfinancial assets. But the subsequent bidding up of prices of existing nonfinancial assets tends to raise wealth relative to income and to increase the attraction of purchasing current services. Thus, a general business expansion gets under way which is checked by a decline in the deposit-currency ratio as redundant cash balances shift from the financial community to the rest of the community; by a lag in the perception of money holders of the consequences of price increases which leads them to overestimate the extent of the monetary redundancy in their portfolios; and by distortions in the relation of high-powered money to the monetary stock and in the deposit-currency ratio away from their long-run equilibrium levels. Thus, the system contracts, reverting to its previous proportioning of balance sheets.

I would make the following observations on this exercise:

—Expansion begins with an increase in the money supply and the subsequent argument is rooted in the lag between the rate of increase in the money stock and business activity which even monetarists now agree is not satisfactory evidence of a causal connection. In fact, we know a great deal about what detonates a cyclical upswing: good harvests, increased exports, a favorably revised view of the profitability of investment in railways, housing, a new technological possibility, and so forth. All would have monetary consequences; but aside from a prior condition of monetary ease, there is no empirical foundation for a monetary shock acting as the initiating force in business expansions.

—The extension of the portfolio concept from financial markets to business inventories, long-term capital expansion, housing construction, durable consumer goods, and, even, investment in human capital misconstrues the process which, in fact, leads to their expansion and contraction, that is, expected rates of return over cost for business firms, changes in real income, and expected changes for consumers.

Evidently, it is possible to construct, with appropriate lags and interactions, a monetary cycle. Friedman's is an ingenious scheme designed to keep the whole economic process within the portfolio adjustment mechanism and to be consistent with the cyclical behavior of the monetary variables, as he interprets them. But no effort is made to establish whether the cycle that emerges is consistent with the total evidence on business-cycle behavior, including the nonmonetary variables.

Cagan's cycle is a more conventional model. Although his evidence does not firmly identify an independent role for money in cycles beyond panics and their monetary effects in "severe" downswings, he posits, at the close of his chapter on cause-and-effect relations, the possibility that a general mutual dependence exists between the money stock and economic activity.[102] On this hypothesis he produces an equation relating business activity to the past rate of change in the money stock and another equation relating the past rate of change in the money stock to the current level of business activity. He assumes that the latter lag is shorter than the former. When the two equations are combined, this version of a multiplier-accelerator analysis reaches its upper turning point, not when physical bottlenecks are reached, but when the monetary system reaches the limit of its expansionary capabilities and the rate of growth of the money stock slows down, leading to an absolute decline, with a lag, in business activity.

Unlike Friedman and Schwartz with their all-embracing portfolio approach, Cagan does not, in the end, pretend that his construct is sufficient:

If one accepts the interpretation of the evidence presented here—or goes somewhat further than this evidence can justify—and designates the preceding monetary model of the cycle as a full explanation, the validity of many other models of the business cycle is not necessarily thereby denied, though the rationalizations for them would then be different in some respects. The reason is that such models can be more or less descriptively accurate even though incomplete. There is nothing in the preceding model that rules out, or even makes unlikely, cyclical relations between income, consumption, investment in plant and equipment or inventories, and other variables depicted in the well-known multiplier-accelerator model in all its versions. Indeed, the latter model seems quite consistent with the purely monetary model just described. One can make a long list of other relations that might hold for cyclical movements, whatever the initial source of instability. If the preceding monetary model is valid (in the sense of descriptive accuracy), these other models may or may not be valid; the case is in no way prejudiced. Nevertheless, given the validity of the monetary model, these other models must be incomplete—in the sense of omitting "important" elements of the cyclical process—as also the purely monetary model would be if any of the other models proved to be valid.

Business cycle research has found so many sources of instability in our economy that it would be rash to suggest that money-stock changes are the main one. Aside from possible government stabilization, an industrial economy will undergo fluctuations stemming from the ubiquitous lags and rigidities, which prevent instantaneous adjustments to changes in demand. Lagged adjustments tend to be accentuated and prolonged by the interdependence of many economic variables, a process that the various "multipliers" and "accelerators" help to describe.[103]

My criticism of both the long-term and the cyclical application of the quantity theory comes to rest, then, on its inability to bring into play the changes in technology, industrial capacity, infrastructure, and supply of foodstuffs and raw materials which, in my view, are critical to an understanding of both long-term price trends and business cycles. We need a dynamic theory of production and prices to explain price trends and business cycles: for trend analysis, an exogenous T is insufficient; for cycle analysis, the implicit or explicit Marshallian short-period framework does not capture reality.

It follows from this view—that the Marshallian long-period factors are in movement even over short periods of time and must be introduced into useful analyses—that the distinction between short-period and long-period analyses can be illusory. There is, of course, an almost textbook exception, that is, the possibility that protracted periods of falling price trends increased the incentive to find and mine gold, under an international gold standard regime. I do not believe the connection has ever been documented for the pre-1914 gold discoveries, and the lags were very long indeed. The response of gold production to a rise in its real price (a decline in the price level) was extraordinarily delayed: from 1815 to mid-century; from 1873 to the late 1880's. But, barring evidence to the contrary, I am inclined to allow for the possibility of this palpably logical but unproven linkage.[104]

But putting this case aside, I would hold that movements in prices, production, and, indeed, the components of the money stock must be tracked and explained over short periods of time, with long-period forces introduced into short-term analysis. The operation of long-period forces should not be isolated in separate analyses: long-period forces should be detected and identified as they interwove with cycles and other short-period phenomena. This judgment flows from a conclusion, based on much empirical research, that the cyclical process itself was inextricably linked to long-term change. The problem is not solved by the introduction of such concepts as exogenous investment.[105] This judgment also flows from a fact dramatized, for example, by Tables 5-2 and 5-4; that is, long-term trends were not continuous. We enter an unreal world of our own fabrication when we abstract trend relations from their erratic, unfolding short-period historical context. That, for example, is the lesson of the 1850's and 1890's, where careful short-period analysis, taking all relevant factors into account, can explain why times of great gold inflow could also be, in a sense, times of gold shortage.

These strictures apply equally to the neo-Keynesians who have been the principal antagonists of the monetarists. The great debates of the pre-1914 world were mainly about the causes of price trends and their mechanisms; the great debates of our time have been over the causes of short-term movements in output and prices and their mechanisms. The more recent debates have generated a vast theoretical literature.[106] It is not appropriate to review that literature here because it is informed by the explicit or implicit assumption that the stock of money is flexible and manipulable by public authorities, although there is serious difference of view about the freedom of action monetary authorities actually enjoy. Our concern in this chapter has been almost exclusively with the pre-1914 world where the control of prices and output by public authorities was not a generally accepted objective. And although much of the contemporary debate focuses on the appropriateness of one or another theoretical approach to the problem of income and price analysis, the ultimate cutting edge of the argument concerns policy: Is monetary policy an efficient and sufficient tool for controlling the level of income and price or should the tools of fiscal policy be deployed as well? It is my impression that, policy differences aside, the monetarist and neo-Keynesian analytic vocabularies could be quite easily reconciled; and, indeed, one of our most famous and widely used elementary textbooks does the job quite well.[107] When the contestants debate, it is true, the old question of whether money is endogenous or autonomous re-emerges, but that is because the central recommendation of the monetarists is that the money supply be rendered autonomous and expanded at a fixed rate, as an act of public policy. A major complaint of the monetarists is, in fact, that monetary authorities are permitted to respond excessively to "the needs of trade." But as a matter of analysis, rather than advocacy, there is nothing in the historical findings of the monetarists, in their theoretical structure, or in the evidence their research has generated on the post-1945 world to prevent their acceptance of one of the options set out in Friedman and Schwartz' *Monetary History*, namely, that "changes in income and prices . . . might be mutually interacting, each having elements of independence."[108]

But neither neo-Keynesian nor monetary analysis deals satisfactorily with the factors that emerge as of critical importance to the course of prices in our review of the pre-1914 world, that is, changes in the relative prices of basic commodities, changes in the rate of increase in productivity associated with the character and rhythm of introduction of new technologies, and changes in the pattern and average period of gestation of new investment. In short, both neo-Keynesian and monetarist analyses of prices and output are conducted essentially within a Marshallian short-period framework or with the long-period factors exogenously determined and treated as fixed trends.

This is not only an unsatisfactory way to go about the analysis of the pre-1914 world; it is also a grossly insufficient way to deal with the world economy of the 1970's and 1980's where radical shifts in relative prices have occurred and are likely to continue to occur, where many major economies have experienced deceleration in the rate of productivity increase, and where radical changes in the direction of investment will be required to reachieve structural balance and resumed rapid growth.

Now, briefly to summarize:

1. The new monetarist literature has provided us with valuable additional historical data in interesting and useful forms. The three major elements of "independence" in the role of money that the monetarists identify (wartime inflations, gold discoveries, and financial crises which exacerbate severe depressions) are legitimate, but in no sense new; and, in each case, their arguments are incomplete. Wartime inflations were caused by changes on the side of supply as well as by government expenditures in excess of revenue; financial crises were not wholly independent of the cyclical process as a whole and, especially, the not wholly monetary mechanism of the upper turning point; and the role of increased gold production in the price rise from the mid-1890's to 1913 is both overestimated and its mechanism inadequately explained in the new monetarist literature.

On the other hand, the monetarist literature (notably, Cagan) has re-affirmed the flexibility of the pre-1914 money supply in the cyclical process and its responsiveness to business activity.

There is nothing in the new monetary literature to lead me to alter the views at which I had earlier arrived about the relation between money and prices.

2. If we are to achieve a reconciliation between monetary and nonmonetary perspectives in price analysis, a first condition is to separate historical analysis from contemporary policy advocacy. However understandable, the two lines of activity have mixed poorly.

3. Analytically, the central problem is to recognize that the monetary systems of the pre-1914 world, as well as those which have evolved since the end of the First World War, were flexible over a wide range. This means that shifts in relative prices could and did translate themselves into movements in "the price level." No mechanism existed pre-1914, or subsequently, to force the compensatory price changes required to maintain a constant price level in the face of major changes in relative prices. It follows directly that changes in the rate of productivity increase, in the relative prices of foodstuffs and raw materials (as well as in money-wages), must be taken into account in a modified quantity-theory equation. And this modification, in turn, means that the distinction between the Marshallian short and long period cannot be sustained. Movements in prices over short periods of time must take into account the supply-side, Marshallian long-period factors operating on costs.

4. Since output and price are jointly determined, it follows that we need a general theory of prices and output to conduct serious price analyses. The quantity theory, with T (or Q or Y) exogenously given, is a poor instrument for this purpose. Walrasian general equilibrium system is also inadequate, because it does not provide for changes in the rate of productivity increase or changes in the relative prices of basic commodities. Conventional neoclassical growth models are also inadequate: they provide for rates of productivity increase but usually under rigid simplifying assumptions which rule out a realistic examination of the implications of changes in the rate of productivity increase, and they do not provide for changes in the relative prices of basic commodities, including the lags and differing periods of gestation which were often the cause of such changes. Such models are, in fact, usually formulated in real terms without a price component. We require disaggregated growth models, with possibilities for

changes in the rate of productivity increase and in relative prices, linked to the monetary mechanism. Chapter 2 goes some distance in these directions. But in the end, price movements are only to be understood as part of a general, sectorally disaggregated theory of growth, embracing cycles and trends, as well as the growth process itself, linked to the monetary mechanism. Since the monetary mechanism varied greatly over the past two centuries of modern growth, by both countries and time periods, it follows that such analyses must be conducted in historical terms rather than merely by the application of universal models.

6

Growth Rates at Different Levels of Income and Stage of Growth: Reflections on Why the Poor Get Richer and the Rich Slow Down

I

We turn now to a particular application of the role of technology in the economic process—the subject of Chapter 4. At its core, modern economic growth consists in the progressive absorption of new technologies which raise the level of productivity. The pace at which this process proceeds depends on the size and productivity of the pool of unapplied technologies available, the capacity and will of a society to exploit that pool, and the relevance of that pool to a society's level of income and tastes as reflected in the income elasticity of demand. This chapter explores how these factors, taken together, determine growth rates at different levels of income and stages of growth.

Two recent cross-sectional analyses have underlined a fact familiar to economic historians: the late-comers to modern economic growth tend to catch up with the early-comers. The widely held notion that the rich typically get richer, the poor relatively poorer, is supported neither by evidence from the contemporary scene nor by that from the longer past.[1]

Using World Bank data, Thorkil Kristensen, for example, has calculated the 1960–1970 real GNP per capita growth rates for seven income groups defined in 1967 U.S. dollars, embracing 122 countries, set out in Table 6-1. Growth rates accelerate from Group 7 to Group 3 and then decelerate.

Hollis Chenery underlines the same basic proposition.[2] Using a vocabulary of stages, rather than real income per capita group-

Note: The bulk of this chapter was first published in *Research in Economic History* 3 (1978).

ings (Table 6-2), he emerges with a pattern of growth rates for the period 1960–1973 essentially similar to Kristensen's.[3] Again, one can observe a sequence of accelerating and decelerating growth with the "centrally planned" economies exhibiting growth rates roughly equivalent to Chenery's "transitional" stage.

Historically, the catching-up tendency can be demonstrated in

Table 6-1. *Income Levels and Growth Rates, 1960–1970*

	Population 1967 (millions)	GNP per Capita 1967 U.S. $	Average Annual Growth Rate 1960–1970
United States	199	$3,670	3.2%
Group 1 ($1,750–$3,670)	307	3,120	3.4
Group 2 ($1,000–$1,750)	238	1,490	3.5
Group 3 ($700–$1,000)	444	930	6.5
Group 4 ($400–$700)	161	550	4.4
Group 5 ($200–$400)	299	270	2.9
Group 6 ($100–$200)	376	130	2.6
Group 7 ($50–$100)	1,580	90	1.7
World	3,391	$ 610	3.2%

Source: Thorkil Kristensen, *Development in Rich and Poor Countries* (New York: Praeger, 1974), pp. 156–159.

Table 6-2. *Annual Average Growth Rates per Capita GDP, 1960–1973*

Stage	%
A. Old developed	
1. United States	3.1%
2. Other	3.7
Total	3.4
B. Newly developed	7.0
C. Transitional	3.9
D. Less developed	1.8
Total market economies	2.8
E. Centrally planned	3.6%

Source: Hollis Chenery and Moises Syrquin, *Patterns of Development, 1950–1970* (London–New York: Oxford University Press for the World Bank, 1975), table 2b.

a simple, rough-and-ready way; but there are difficulties, as we shall see, in reconstructing a satisfactory historical table like Kristensen's or Chenery's.

As for the simple demonstration, Table 6-3 exhibits growth rates from the beginning of take-off to a five-year period centered on 1967 for fourteen countries with reasonably long spans of sustained modern growth.[4]

Canada, Australia, and Argentina are, at first sight, something of a puzzlement. They moved into industrialization relatively late, from initially high levels of income per capita based on extremely favorable resource-population balances, but they subsequently experienced relatively low average growth rates compared to other late-comers. In part, this was evidently due to the low level of ex-

Table 6-3. *Per Capita Growth Rates, Take-off to 1967: Fourteen Countries* (1967 U.S.$)

	Take-off Date	Take-off Date	Approximate GNP per Capita: Beginning of Take-off	GNP per Capita 1965–1969	Number of Years	Annual Average Growth Rate
Great Britain	1783		$183	$2,018	184	1.31%
United States*	1843		451	3,995	124	1.77
France	1830		173	2,343	137	1.92
Germany	1850		249 (1851)	2,148	116	1.87
Sweden	1868		239	3,244	99	2.67
Japan	1885		158 (1886)	1,207	81	2.54
Russia–USSR	1890		246	1,594	77	2.46
Italy	1895		300	1,333	72	2.09
Canada	1896		796	2,962	71	1.87
Australia	1901		923	2,106	66	1.26
Argentina	1933		418	741	34	1.70
Brazil*	1933		144	323	34	2.40
Mexico	1940		224	545	27	3.35
Turkey	1934		$171	$ 331	33	2.02%

* Regional take-offs are judged to have occurred beginning in the 1820's in New England, and in the São Paulo region from 1900 to 1920.
Source: Appendix 1, this chapter.

port prices for Argentina and Australia in the 1920's and the impact on all three countries of the depression of the early 1930's.[5] In the case of Argentina, economic policy and political instability decreed an erratic stop-and-go growth pattern after 1945. But a protracted reliance on raw material as opposed to manufactured exports may have affected the outcome, as Chenery argues in general (see below, Section IV), as well as the tendency of high income per capita countries to increase disproportionately their allocations for services (see below, Section V).

Britain, the pioneer, grows most slowly (1.31%); the countries whose take-offs began in the second quarter of the nineteenth century move more briskly (unweighted average, 1.85%); those who entered sustained growth in the last quarter of the nineteenth century do still better (average, 2.44%); and the three who began in the period 1933–1940 average a shade better (2.59%), although the outcome is determined by Mexico's performance. But we know that the developing nations of the post-1945 world, which have moved into Kristensen's intermediate real income levels (or to Chenery's "transitional" status), have generally enjoyed higher growth rates than were typical either of the pre-1914 world or of the older industrialized countries of the West during the 1950's and 1960's.

II

The question then arises: Can we construct historical tables relating, like Kristensen, growth rates to income levels per capita? Table 6-4 sets out the results of this kind of exercise for the fourteen countries included in Table 6-3, based on the data in Appendix 1.

The following observations on Table 6-4 can be made:

1. Excepting the highest income range, which embraces the uniquely high growth rates of the post-1945 period, the historical averages are systematically lower than those for the 1960–1970 period whose special features are discussed below (see Section V).

2. Like the cross-sectional data on the 1960's, the historical averages exhibit acceleration up to the level of $700–$1,000, then deceleration, excepting the highest income range—mainly a product of recent times.

3. Looked at more closely, however, the rates for individual

TABLE 6-4. *Historical Annual Average Growth Rates and Real GNP per Capita: Fourteen Countries (1967 U.S.$)*

	$100–$200	$200–$400	$400–$700	$700–$1,000	$1,000–$1,750	$1,750–$3,670
Great Britain	0.30%	1.57%	1.60%	0.94%	1.14%	2.23%
United States		1.56	1.31	2.56	1.68	1.96*
France	1.56	1.87	2.24	1.90	1.36	4.45
Germany		2.17	1.09	3.85	1.28	4.13
Sweden		1.70	2.90	1.83	2.92	3.28
Japan	2.99	1.73	2.37	7.69	9.92	7.24
Russia–USSR		1.89	1.87	5.21	4.11	3.88
Italy		0.80	1.38	5.23	3.61	2.08
Canada			1.83	2.22	1.63	2.28
Australia				1.98	0.67	2.68
Argentina		3.79	1.04	3.66		
Turkey	0.98	3.26				
Brazil	2.04	3.06	7.40			
Mexico	1.43	1.90	3.19			
Historical average (unweighted)	1.55	2.07	2.35	3.28	3.12	3.42
Kristensen average	2.60%	2.90%	4.40%	6.50%	3.50%	3.40%

* U.S. rate of 1.96% is for movement from $1,779 to $4,696; rate from $1,779 to $3,723 is 1.77%; from $3,723 to $4,696, 2.94%.

Note: Years chosen are nearest approximation to Kristensen's real GNP per capita ranges; e.g., rate for Great Britain in $100–$200 range is from $152, when first estimate is available, to $199 (1702–1793). An unweighted average is appropriate here because country data are given and discussed in the text and because, in historical analysis, when countries passed through these income ranges at different times and in different international environments, one can assume less uniformity of growth rate behavior in particular income ranges than in cross-sectional analysis.

Source: Appendix 1, this chapter.

countries reflect (and sometimes mask) the impact of specific periods of acceleration or deceleration associated either with conditions in the world economy during certain periods of the past or with peculiarities in their domestic evolution. For example:

a. The British movement through the $1,000–$1,750 range covers two quite distinct experiences over the years 1914 to 1961: an average growth rate of −0.25 percent from 1914 to 1932, embracing, as it does, the worst of the interwar years; a 2.0 percent rate from 1932 to 1961.

b. The U.S. movement through the $1,750–$3,670 range straddles the depressed 1930's and covers a much longer period (42 years) than for, say, Sweden (23 years), whose depression experience was somewhat less acute.

c. Australia, after an exuberant pre-1914 expansion, does not regain its GNP per capita level of 1912 until 1940 due to the impact of the First World War and the low export prices and sluggishness of its major export market, Great Britain. Thus, it required Australia eighty-two years to transit the income range $1,000–$1,750 as against five years for Japan. Canada's deceleration in the $1,000–$1,750 range, covering the years 1906–1942, is similarly affected by its ties to the United States. It does better than Australia in the 1920's, worse in the 1930's. These and similar problems in the country data are inherent in historical, as opposed to cross-sectional, calculations. In the latter case, one can assume a somewhat more uniform international environment. In historical analysis the income ranges fall in different periods for the several countries.

4. In the four cases where rough GNP per capita estimates exist for pre–take-off (or pre–modern growth) decades, there is an acceleration not revealed by the Kristensen real income ranges used in Table 6-4. The take-off rates are, evidently, higher, and progressively higher with the passage of time in this extremely limited sample (see Table 6-5).

III

This brings us to the critical difference between real income per capita analysis and the kind of stages of growth analysis I have developed. The latter centers on the degree to which the pool of modern technology, at any particular period, has or has not been efficiently absorbed in a given economy.[6] The progressive absorption of increasingly sophisticated technologies and the application of such technologies to an increasing number of the economy's sectors (including agriculture) do, indeed, have major implications for the large aggregates, for example, the level and rate of growth of real income, the proportion of income invested, the proportion of the working force engaged in modern industry, and so on. But levels of real income and stages of economic

TABLE 6-5. *Growth Rates at Early Stages: Four Countries*

	Growth Rate by Income Range	Growth Rate Pre–Take-off (within time period of income range)	Growth Rate Post–Take-off (within time period of income range)
Great Britain ($100–$200)	0.30% (1702–1793)	0.22% (1702–1782)	0.84% (1783–1793)
Russia ($200–$400)	1.19 (1871–1913)	0.91 (1871–1890)	1.43 (1890–1913)
Italy ($200–$400)	0.80 (1863–1909)	0.18 (1863–1895)	2.22 (1895–1909)
Mexico ($200–$400)	1.90% (1920–1957)	1.03 (1920–1940)	3.53% (1940–1957)

Source: Appendix 1, this chapter.

growth are not rigorously related. It is possible to have relatively rich pre–take-off countries like pre-1901 Australia or contemporary Libya and relatively poor countries which have acquired command over a wide range of quite sophisticated technologies like contemporary China and India. The latter are, by my definition, in the drive to technological maturity, although the modernization of their massive low-productivity agricultural sectors will, evidently, require considerable time and the scale of those rather sluggish sectors, relative to the more dynamic industrial sectors, is likely to decree rather low aggregate growth in real income per capita for a further protracted period.

Against this background, growth rates for the take-off and the pre-1914 portion of the drive to technological maturity are set out in Table 6-6. Measurement here is confined to the pre-1914 period (excepting Japan, to 1920) to screen out the effects of the First World War and the interwar pathology.

Acceleration in income per capita occurs in the drive to technological maturity in all cases except Germany. The German outcome is the result of two phenomena: the depth of the depression following upon the extraordinary boom of the early 1870's, and the deceleration of the prewar generation which, in differing degrees, was shared by Britain, the United States, and Germany.[7] German growth rates for shorter periods moved as follows between 1851 and 1912:

TABLE 6-6. *Stages of Growth, Income Ranges, and per Capita Growth Rates: Nine Countries, Pre-1914 (1967 U.S. $)*

	Take-off Dates	Income Range
Great Britain	1783–1830ᵃ	$183 –$ 345
United States	1843–1870	451 – 641
France	1830–1870	173 – 337
Germany	1840–1870	249ᵇ– 344
Sweden	1868–1890	239 – 389
Japan	1885–1905	158 – 215
Russia–USSR	1890–1905	246 – 293
Italy	1895–1913	300 – 427
Canada	1896–1913	$796 –$1,184
Unweighted average		

ᵃI would now date the end of the British take-off in 1830 with the opening of the railway age and divide the "Drive to Technological Maturity" into two phases, the first ending in 1870, the second the age of steel, running concurrently with the similar stage for the United States, France, and Germany. The average annual growth rate for Britain in the second phase is only 0.84%.

1851–1874	2.05%
(1868–1874	3.16)
1874–1883	0.34
1883–1890	2.02
1890–1900	1.64
1900–1912	1.16%

There is another family of nations where historical comparison may be of some use, that is, those whose take-offs occurred between the 1930's and 1960's and which had entered the drive to technological maturity by the end of the 1960's. The impact of the Second World War varied as among those which entered modern economic growth before 1945 (e.g., Turkish growth was damped more sharply than in the case of the three Latin American states); but no gross violence is done by comparing the relative growth rates, by stages, for the seven countries set out in Table 6-7.

Although its degree varies, there is, without exception, accel-

| Average Annual Growth Rate | Drive to Technological Maturity | | Average Annual Growth Rate |
	Dates	Income Range	
1.36%	1830–1870[a]	$345–$ 662	1.64%
1.31	1870–1910	641– 1,419	2.01
1.68	1870–1913	337– 950	2.44
1.72	1870–1913	349– 658	1.49
2.24	1890–1913	389– 757	2.94
1.63	1905–1920[c]	215– 314	2.56
1.17	1905–1913	$293–$ 341	1.91
1.98	—	—	—
2.36	—	—	—
1.72%			2.14%

[b]The initial date available for German income and investment data is 1850.

[c]The Japanese drive to technological maturity is here extended to 1920, since Japan was not significantly involved in the First World War.

Source: Appendix 1, this chapter.

eration in the drive to technological maturity. As in all other comparisons of recent decades with the pre-1914 world, the growth rates are higher for both stages in Table 6-7 than in Table 6-6.

IV

With these data in hand we are in a position to come to grips with the central analytic problems posed by the tendency of both historical and contemporary growth rates to accelerate and then decelerate, whether measured against real income per capita or by stage of growth as defined either by Chenery or by myself.[8]

Kristensen's fundamental propositions bearing on the rising and falling sequence of growth rates come to this: economic growth depends on the rate of absorption of the existing and unfolding stock of relevant knowledge; the rate of absorption depends on the availability of both trained men and capital; the reason for the accelerated growth among his middle-income

TABLE 6-7. *Stages of Growth, Income Ranges, and per Capita Growth Rates: Seven Countries, 1933–1972 (1967 U.S. $)*

| | Take-off | |
| | | Income |
	Dates	Range
Argentina	1933 –1950	$418 –$544
Turkey	1933 –1961	171ª– 262
Brazil	1933 –1950	144 – 221
Mexico	1940 –1960	224 – 432
Iran	1955ᶜ–1965	201 – 246
Taiwan	1953 –1960	142 – 178
South Korea	1961 –1968	$120 –$175
Unweighted average		

Note: The drive to technological maturity has, evidently, not been completed in these seven countries.
ªInitial date available, 1934.
ᵇFinal date, 1970.

countries is that they have built up the stock of trained manpower (including entrepreneurs) to a position where they can accelerate the rate of absorption of the existing stock of knowledge, so long as they generate at home or acquire from abroad the requisite capital to incorporate that knowledge; the reason for the subsequent slowdown in growth rates is that the high-income countries, having absorbed the backlog of existing knowledge, must rely for subsequent growth on the rate at which new knowledge is created.[9] He concludes: "Thus, if there is something that can be called the typical growth curve for GNP per capita, it is not an exponential curve but rather an S-shaped curve that may or may not approach an upper limit."[10]

On the basis of this quantitative but not directly measurable hypothesis, Kristensen proceeds to indicate how his S-shaped path of technological absorption is reflected in a wide range of more or less measurable economic and social indicators which he associates with real income per capita, for example, the distribution of the working force, urbanization, income distribution, food and energy consumption, health services, demographic variables, education, foreign trade, and so forth. His data for the level and change in the distribution of the working force during the 1960's

| Average Annual Growth Rate | Drive to Technological Maturity | | Average Annual Growth Rate |
	Dates	Income Range	
1.56%	1950–1972	$544–$875 [d]	2.29%
1.54	1961–1972	262– 380 [b]	4.22
2.55	1950–1972	221– 450	3.29
3.34	1960–1972	432– 608 [b]	3.48
4.12	1965–1972	246– 335 [b]	6.37
3.28	1960–1972	178– 388	6.71
5.54	1968–1972	$175–$245	8.78
3.13%			5.02%

[c] Initial date, 1960.
[d] Final date, 1971.
Source: Appendix 1, this chapter.

and for the relative level of productivity in agriculture in 1970 are set out by income groups in Table 6-8.

Evidently, the most rapid rate of increase in industrial employment (and a rapid rate of decline in agricultural employment) comes in the movement from Group 6 to Group 4. It is in the movement from Group 4 to Group 3 that the gap between agricultural and nonagricultural productivity (and income distribution) most sharply narrows. The movement from Group 2 to Group 1 is accompanied by a relative decline in industrial employment and a rise in service employment, while the relative level of agricultural employment falls dramatically from Group 2 to Group 1. Thus, the movement up to the maximum overall growth rate of Group 3 is accompanied by a rise in the proportion of the work force in industry, strengthened finally by a diffusion of high-productivity methods to agriculture; the subsequent subsidence of growth rates is accompanied by a shift of manpower to services and a further sharp decline in the relative level of employment in agriculture. A relative decline in industrial employment emerges at the highest income levels. These results roughly conform to the well-known analyses of Kuznets and Chenery-Syrquin.

TABLE 6-8.   *Changes in Distribution of Labor Force by Type of Activity, 1960 and 1970*

	No. of Countries	Population 1967 (millions)	Agriculture (%)	
			1960	1970
Group 1 ($1,750–$3,670)	4	274.2	9.9%	7.1%
Group 2 ($1,000–$1,750)	4	136.2	20.9	20.0
Group 3 ($700–$1,000)	3	119.5	27.2	20.6
Group 4 ($400–$700)	2	41.5	41.1	28.8
Group 5 ($200–$400)	2	25.8	58.1	47.9
Group 6 ($100–$200)	3	174.6	68.9	63.9
Group 7 ($50–$100)	—	—	—	—
Total	18	771.8	29.1%	24.7%

* Relative Level I compares GDP per capita in agriculture with that in "nonagriculture," the latter equaling 100. Level II compares GDP per capita in agriculture with that for the economy as a whole (including agriculture).

Chenery does not ignore the absorption of the stock of knowledge and technology or the build-up of human capital required for that absorption. But in focusing on the accelerated growth rates of the transitional period, his hypothesis is more direct than Kristensen's: "The transformation of the production structure from primary production to industry lies at the heart of transitional growth."[11] His broad conclusion about the typical S-shaped path of growth is much like Kristensen's. He finds considerable uniformity of industrial structure at the lowest and highest income levels which supports "the concept of a 'transition' and leads to the description of many aspects of structural change by a logistic or other function having lower and upper asymptotes."[12]

Chenery defines the transition itself in statistical terms (1973

Industry (%)		Services (%)		Relative Level *	
1960	1970	1960	1970	I	II
34.5%	33.7%	55.6%	59.2%	53.7%	55.4%
42.6	36.9	36.5	43.1	51.5	54.1
31.4	34.3	41.1	45.1	49.8	58.1
28.4	35.3	30.5	35.9	28.6	37.7
15.2	15.7	26.7	36.4	21.9	36.5
9.7	10.2	21.4	25.9	13.4	33.0
—	—	—	—	32.1	61.5
30.0%	29.7%	40.9%	45.6%	12.8%	20.9%

Source: Kristensen, *Development in Rich and Poor Countries*, pp. 39 and 49. Groups are defined in 1967 U.S. $.

U.S. $) using the production and trade patterns developed in the Chenery-Syrquin study as touchstones:

> The transition can be usefully divided into an earlier and a later phase by measuring the halfway point in each development process. For example, on average, the share of industry (manufacturing plus construction) in GNP increases from an average of 12.5% for underdeveloped countries to 38% for developed ones. This process is half completed at an income level of about $450 [300 1967 U.S. $] which is close to the average for all processes. On the other hand, the rise in the share of manufactured exports in GDP [gross domestic product] (from 1.1% to 13%) takes place

much later in the transition and is half completed only at an income level of $1000 [625 1967 U.S. $]. In the following discussion the countries that have completed more than half of the normal changes in the structure of production and trade will be classed as "transitional" and those that have not reached this point as "less developed."[13]

The transitional countries, in turn, are grouped in three categories: "large" countries, with populations of 15 million or more in 1960, substantial domestic markets for manufactures, and relatively low ratios of foreign trade to GNP; small countries relatively specialized in primary exports; small countries relatively specialized in the export of manufactured goods and services.[14]

Chenery also embraces within the transitional category two further types of economies which exhibit higher growth rates than either the least-developed or old developed nations: "newly developed market economies" and "newly developed centrally planned economies."[15] All had levels in 1973 of GNP per capita over $1,000 (1967 U.S. $) and productive structures more or less typical of that real income level.

In thus defining the transition process, Chenery embraces nations in subcategories containing about 52 percent of the world's population as of 1973: newly developed market (7%), newly developed centrally planned (9%), transitional market economies (13%), transitional centrally planned (35%, including China, 23%). The old developed countries contained only 13 percent of the world population; the other developing countries, 35 percent.

Since one of Chenery's principal objectives in this analysis was to underline the increasing role of manufactured exports in the foreign trade of transitional nations, he applies a dynamic theory of comparative advantage to his data. The large transitional countries expand their manufacturing sectors in response to the expanding domestic market, enjoy economies of scale, and then translate their virtuosity into enlarged, sophisticated manufactured exports. The small manufacture-oriented countries, lacking either a big domestic market or exportable natural resources, substitute for the latter sophisticated manufactured exports in proportions not very different from those typical of the large transitional countries. The small primary-oriented countries tend to rely too long on their natural resource endowments. They are

Growth Rates 273

slower to acquire sophisticated industrial structures. Their industrial and overall growth rates are lower than for the small manufacture-oriented countries. Ultimately, however, the inadequacy of their raw material exports to satisfy their foreign exchange requirements pushes them toward export diversification.

Thus, in Chenery's view, domestic demand and foreign exchange requirements, in differing proportions and at different phases of growth, mainly determine industrial structures in developing countries in a manner roughly approximating profit maximization under dynamic circumstances. From this perspective, changes in the structure of employment and technological progress are "essentially by-products" of the changes in industrial structure and the composition of exports.[16] Behind the whole process, however, is the assumption that self-sustained economic growth is under way; capital and human skills (via education) are expanding more rapidly than unskilled labor; and the outcome is not merely a rise in real income per capita (which, through the income elasticity of demand, alters industrial structure) but also a shift in factor proportions, which leads to an expansion in manufactured exports.

In a larger sense, both Kristensen and Chenery are asserting that growing economies, viewed in cross-section, alter their structures and their allocations of resources in a roughly uniform way, once they begin to move forward in modern (or self-sustained) growth. The pattern that emerges reaches beyond conventional economic variables to birth and death rates, educational levels, social welfare allocations, and income distribution. The average cross-sectional pattern is, as one would expect, subject to considerable deviation; and, as Chenery's exploration of manufacture- and primary-oriented small countries indicates, some of those deviations are systematic. But what we have here is a rather grand assertion of the ultimate imperatives of balanced growth. As Chenery and Syrquin say, "the model implicit in our analysis is one of general equilibrium."[17]

Their cross-sectional view is, essentially, similar to what I have long asserted in dynamic, historical terms, namely, that growing economies follow an approximation of optimum sectoral paths:

> When the conventional limits on the theory of production are widened, it is possible to define theoretical equilibrium

positions not only for output, investment, and consumption as a whole, but for each sector of the economy.

Within the framework set by forces determining the total level of output, sectoral optimum positions are determined on the side of demand by the levels of income and of population, and by the character of tastes; on the side of supply, by the state of technology and the quality of entrepreneurship, as the latter determines the proportion of technically available and potentially profitable innovations actually incorporated in the capital stock.

In addition, one must introduce an extremely significant empirical hypothesis: namely, that deceleration is the normal optimum path of a sector, due to a variety of factors operating on it, from the side of both supply and demand.

The equilibria which emerge from the application of these criteria are a set of sectoral paths, from which flows, as first derivatives, a sequence of optimum patterns of investment.

Historical patterns of investment did not, of course, exactly follow these optimum patterns. They were distorted by imperfections in the private investment process, by the policies of governments, and by the impact of wars. . . . The historical sequence of business cycles and trend-periods results from these deviations of actual from optimal patterns; and such fluctuations, along with the impact of wars, yield historical paths of growth which differ from those which the optima, calculated before the event, would have yielded.

Nevertheless, the economic history of growing societies takes a part of its rude shape from the effort of societies to approximate the optimum sectoral paths. . . . In essence it is the fact that sectors tend to have a rapid growth-phase, early in their life, that makes it possible and useful to regard economic history as a sequence of stages rather than merely as a continuum, within which nature never makes a jump.[18]

The major analytic difference as among Kristensen's, Chenery's, and my views of the process of growth centers on the role of technological progress. Kristensen regards the diffusion of old and new technological knowledge as fundamental to growth. Chenery regards the progressive absorption of new technologies, as one moves up the income per capita ladder, as a by-product of the expansion of manufactures of increasing sophistication; and this perspective is understandable in cross-section analysis, with a given pool of working technologies assumed to exist accessibly in the old developed countries. From a historical perspective, I would side with Kristensen on the critical role of the diffusion of technologies, but I would add two points. First, the subtly interconnected world of science and technology must be regarded as an economic sector to which resources are allocated and which yields, like any other sector, a conceptually definable, if difficult to measure, rate of return over cost, with appropriate lags. Second, the sequence in which technologies have been created followed a logic of necessity, although necessity was not always a fertile mother. One reason for underlining the importance of technological generation and diffusion is that for two centuries it was essential to hold diminishing returns at bay with respect to agriculture and raw material production, an aspect of the story of growth which falls out in a cross-sectional view of the complacent 1950's and 1960's, when the prices of basic commodities were relatively low.[19] A cross-sectional analysis as of, say, the 1790's, the 1850's, 1900–1910, 1945–1951, or the mid-1970's could certainly not ignore the effects on income and growth rates of relative prices. A further reason for emphasizing the role of technology and its diffusion is because it affects the growth paths of particular sectors, requiring, however, a higher degree of disaggregation to capture than the broad manufacturing categories ("early," "middle," and "late") employed in the Chenery-Taylor model.

V

In this setting, it is possible to address the three large questions which emerge from this analysis as a whole:

—Once take-off (or modern growth) has begun, why does growth accelerate in Kristensen's middle income range, Chenery's transition, and my drive to technological maturity?

—Why does growth decelerate in Kristensen's two highest income ranges, Chenery's old developed countries, and those far along in my stage of high mass-consumption?

—Why were average growth rates for all income levels and stages higher from, say, 1950 to 1972 than in the pre-1914 world?

One obvious element in the answers to all three questions lies in the behavior of investment rates. Historically, investment rates, having risen during take-off, rise again in the drive to technological maturity, then increase slowly. In the case of the United States and Germany, they actually declined from their peaks in the railway age before 1914. In the post-1945 world, as Table 6-9 shows, in all cases except the United States, investment rates in the advanced industrial countries reached levels never before attained. The pattern emerges clearly in the Chenery-Syrquin cross-sectional calculations covering countries over the period 1950–1970.[20] They are compared in Table 6-9 with roughly equivalent pre-1914 data for eight countries.

In both the cross-section for the period 1950–1970 and the pre-1914, the investment proportions rise to a peak at $1,000 per capita, although the historical sample beyond $1,000 consists only of the United States. Pre-1914 investment rates (like per capita growth rates) are systematically lower than for the 1950–1970 period.

Why, then, did the investment rate rise to, say, $1,000 per capita?

The conventional answer would focus on two factors. First, the shape of the consumption function. We can assume that as income per capita rises, notably under the conditions of increasingly skewed income distribution which typically marks the early stages of modern growth, the proportion of total income saved and invested will rise. Second, the rise in per capita income and tax revenues (accompanied by increasingly modern and efficient administration) permits governments to play an enlarged relative role in meeting the educational, infrastructure, and other investment processes designed to sustain an increasingly urbanized and industrial society. To these basic factors linking the rise in per capita income to a disproportionate rise in private and public investment, one can add the emergence or expansion of institutions for the more effective channeling of private savings into productive investment[21] and, in some cases, increased access to capital imports.[22]

But there is another way of viewing the rise in the investment rate which would link its path not merely to the rise in income per capita but also to the deeper process of technological absorption proceeding as modern growth unfolds. One can argue in general terms, as I did in *The Stages of Economic Growth*, that the rise of the investment rate during take-off is as much a result

TABLE 6-9. *Gross Domestic Investment as Percentage of Gross Domestic Product at Different Income per Capita Levels, 1950–1970, and Approximate Pre-1914 Historical Equivalents*

Income Level*		$\dfrac{\text{GDI}}{\text{GDP}}$ Cross-Section: 1950–1970	**Pre-1914 Investment Proportions
Mean under	$ 100	13.6%	—
	$ 100	15.8	—
	$ 200	18.8	10.4%
	$ 300	20.3	12.6
	$ 400	21.3	13.0
	$ 500	22.0	14.9
	$ 800	23.4	15.2
	$1,000	24.0	20.9
Mean over	$1,000	23.4	17.0% ($1,500 U.S. only)
Total change		9.8%	
Income at midpoint		$200	

* Income levels are in 1964 U.S. $. The correction for comparison with Kristensen's calculations in 1967 U.S. $ is 1.09. The mean value for countries under $100 is approximately $70; for those over $1,000, approximately $1,500.

** These historical data are unweighted averages of eight countries for which reasonably reputable investment proportions as well as real income per capita have been calculated: Great Britain, United States, France, Germany, Sweden, Japan, Italy, and Canada. The British data include capital exports. Only three achieved $1,000 per capita real incomes pre-1914 (1967 U.S. $): Great Britain, United States, and Canada. Only the United States reached $1,500. The year chosen for measurement is the nearest approximation to the indicated real income per capita in 1967 U.S. $. Data sources for the investment proportion are given in Appendix 2, this chapter.

Source: Cross-Section, 1950–1970: Chenery-Syrquin, *Patterns of Development*, pp. 20–21. Pre-1914: Appendix 2, this chapter.

as a cause of the innovations which, ultimately, lift income per capita.[23] The case can be put more narrowly by examining the mechanism of expansion in leading sectors. As new technologies were brought efficiently within the economic structure, they set in motion rapidly growing sectoral complexes much larger than the new industries, narrowly defined. The role of corporate as opposed to private saving expanded. These complexes, embracing many subsectors, reflected the new leading sector's backward, lateral, and forward linkages to the rest of the economy. The rapid expansion of these new sectoral complexes, suffusing substantial regions within countries, generated both expanded demand for capital and, through the plough-back of profits, a part of the requisite supply of capital. In their periods of rapid expansion a disproportionate amount of investment flowed to these sectors, where a high marginal rate of savings typically prevailed. Commenting on post-1945 Europe, M. M. Postan makes this observation on the link between technological innovation and investment.

> In almost every European country the industries heading the list, i.e., those with the largest infusion of capital, were the "modern" or the modernized industries. The chemical and petroleum industries, with their joint offspring in petrochemicals, plastics, and man-made fibres, developed a voracious appetite for new capital as they grew and renewed their equipment. Equally voracious for capital were the engineering and metal-working industries, especially their newer branches, such as electro-mechanical, electronic, and motorcar. On the other hand, new investment was low relatively to output, and also grew rather slowly, in such industries as cotton and wool, coal-mining (except where they were in the process of wholesale modernization as in the United Kingdom), wood-working, or in such older branches of the engineering and metal-working industry as manufacture of railway equipment and milling machinery.[24]

He then illustrates his proposition from data bearing on several European countries.

The extent to which rapid growth within a technologically new sector in its rapid expansion phase generates the profits to supply by plough-back its own capital is difficult to measure.[25] If one regards innovation as generating a whole sectoral complex rather than merely a new industry, the concept of plough-back must widen to embrace all those (often within a particular region) sharing the disproportionate expansion of income and willing to direct their savings (or profits) to the complex further expansion. In a sense, all of Manchester was, in one way or another, caught up in the cotton textile revolution, as was Detroit with the automobile some 130 years later. How far plough-back, thus broadly defined, can initiate and carry forward an innovational industry depends, evidently, on its capital intensity. Historically, for example, the British and other modern textile industries could expand mainly through the plough-back of profits. The more capital intensive railways—some with long periods of gestation and pay-off —evidently required the initial mobilization of capital from wider sources and, in some cases, public support for a considerable period until freight and passenger traffic built up and profits permitted the industry to be more self-sustaining. The subsequent series of major innovating industries varied in this respect.[26]

The link among technological innovation, rapid sectoral growth, and the generation of profits for re-investment is an important, if still somewhat obscure, subject; but it helps, I believe, to explain the high growth rates of the late-comers to modern growth. They had a larger backlog of technological possibilities to bring within the economy than the early-comers of the North Atlantic world who, aside from Britain's initial precocious advantages in cotton textiles, the steam engine, and coke-manufactured iron, acquired the new technologies roughly together, as they emerged, that is, railroads, steel, electricity, modern chemicals, and the internal combustion engine. As the late-comers absorbed this large backlog, they generated a good part of the supply of investment resources. The consumption function, under conditions of rapid rise in real income per capita, generated the balance, including the contribution of the public sector.

Given the modest proportion of industrial to total investment and the relatively small proportion of total value added by rapidly expanding, technologically new sectors, narrowly defined, one might conclude, prima facie, that overall investment patterns and rates could be affected only modestly by the pace of technological absorption. The railroads were, in this respect, unique and something of an exception. They alone accounted for about 15 percent of total U.S. gross investment in the 1850's, about 23 percent of British gross domestic capital formation in the period 1856–1865. But one can be confident that the proportion of total investment to be thus directly accounted for by the rapid expansion of a new innovating industry was normally much lower. On the other hand, we lack the data to measure the effects on investment patterns and rates of the full sectoral complexes set in motion by the introduction of new technologies. One can only guess, for example, at the massive investment consequences of the rapid diffusion of the private automobile in the United States from, say, 1916 to 1929 and in Western Europe and Japan in the 1950's and

1960's; for what is involved is not merely the backward linkages (to the production of steel, rubber, petroleum products, electrical equipment, etc.) but also the housing and other supporting services for the expanded working forces in this sectoral complex, road-building, the emergence of new suburban areas, automobile service and repair facilities, and so forth.

In any case, the argument here is that the rise in the investment rate flows not merely from the familiar savings-supply variables (rising real income per capita, modernized financial institutions, and rising tax revenues available for public investment) but also from the dynamics of the rapidly expanding leading-sector complexes set in motion by the introduction of new technologies which, as it were, expand both the demand for and the supply of investment resources.

One would, therefore, expect the investment rate to rise as modern technology came to be applied over a widening range of sectors; and one would expect investment and growth rates to be higher when late-comers had mobilized the human and institutional capacity rapidly to introduce the backlog of available but unapplied technologies.

Why, then, did investment rates level off? In part, the logic of the preceding argument would suggest that investment rates would level off when nations had fully applied the backlog of existing technologies and had come to rely on the flow of new technologies coming forward. But here, surely, the consumption function, as decreed by both private and political decisions, is also a determining if not the decisive factor. In more or less free enterprise, democratic societies, limits on savings and investment emerge as individuals decide, within households, business firms, and as voters, the proportion of their income that will be allocated, on the one hand, to private consumption and public services (the latter rising relatively with increases in income per capita) and, on the other hand, to savings and private and public investment. At particular periods of time various kinds of investment have had to compete against each other for scarce resources, for example, railroads and housing against other forms of investment during the great railroad-immigration booms of the United States during the nineteenth century and capital exports versus home investment in the pre-1914 decade in Britain.[27] The ultimate savings limits vary from country to country but they do appear to approach an asymptotic ceiling. Under political dictatorships the ceilings may be higher as consumption is constrained; but the imperatives of political stability, even under the disciplines of a police state, set limits on the resources that can safely be diverted from current consumption.

If investment rates merely leveled off and incremental capital-output ratios for the economy as a whole remained constant, one would expect growth rates to level off at high income per capita ranges rather than to decline. The question therefore arises: Does the course of incremental capital-output ratios in the process of economic growth (as well as investment rates) help determine the S-shaped path of growth in real income per capita? Here we are in a terrain of great complexity, incompletely explored. Indeed, so many variables bear on the overall incremental capital-output ratio of an economy that we may never command sufficient data to sort out with confidence why the historical ratios, as nearly as we can estimate them, moved the way they did. And the interpretation of their movement, even in contemporary economies, where data are more complete, is an art rather than a science.[28]

Some of the factors bearing on the incremental capital-output ratio are these:

—The degree of utilization of capacity

—The wide dispersion of sectoral capital-output ratios and, therefore, the sensitivity of incremental capital-output ratios in various countries to differences in structure, including the age of the capital stock in the various sectors

—The rate of population increase and urbanization as they affect requirements for housing and infrastructure, where capital-output ratios are high

—The capital-intensity of the leading-sector complexes and their phase of evolution, as the latter affects the productivity gains they are incorporating into the economy

—The scale of the backlog of unapplied technologies relevant to the economy's stage of growth and resource endowments

—The current flow of new technologies resulting from prior investment in research and development

—The quality of entrepreneurship, including the efficiency with which capital is allocated and employed in the public sector or in response to public policies, and the quality of the working force, as determined by educational and skill levels

Commenting on the historical tendency of incremental capital-output ratios to rise (at various rates and levels) in advanced industrial countries, Kuznets concluded:

> The explanation for these rising and rather variable capital-output ratios, as well as for the differences in their level among countries, must be sought in the diverse conditions that influence the use of material capital—investment in man, technological peculiarities of the detailed industry-mix, relative supplies of capital and labor, and organizational structure of economic units and country—and permit the attainment of the same product by different combinations of labor and capital, total or incremental. It would be a gross oversimplification to assume that purely technical constraints make for a fixed capital-output ratio, even within narrowly defined industrial subdivisions, let alone a complex and changing mixture like a country's economy.[29]

In fact, only close, detailed analysis of a particular national economy at a particular time is likely to provide reasonably satisfactory insight into the multiple variables determining the level and changes in its incremental capital-output ratio. We cannot expect a great deal of wisdom from staring at capital-output ratios for many countries over long periods.

It may, nevertheless, be useful to array (Table 6-10) the incremental capital-output ratios implicit in the growth and investment rates previously cited (Tables 6-1, 6-4, and 6-9).

Only limited observations can be drawn from Table 6-10:

—The tendency of capital-output ratios to rise with higher levels of income per capita is broadly evident in both the cross-sectional and the historical columns, confirming the Kuznets finding.

—Capital-output ratios were systematically lower in the period 1950–1970 than pre-1914, and this may be due to the larger backlog of unapplied technologies available and, perhaps, to higher relative allocations of resources to education.

—One can only speculate about the cause for the transient decline in cross-section for the $500–$800 income range. I would guess that it is a result of the technologies associated with the first mass phase of the motor vehicle, durable consumer goods revolution which generally comes in modern times at about that income range.

—The pre-1914 decline in the $300–$400 range is the result

TABLE 6-10. *Average Incremental Capital-Output Ratios by Income per Capita Levels (1964 U.S. $)*

Income Level	Cross-Section 1950–1970	Pre-1914
Under $100	3.8%	—
$100–$200	3.4	4.6%
$200–$300	3.4	4.7
$300–$400	4.0	3.7
$400–$500	4.3	5.1
$500–$800	2.6	5.6
$800–$1,000	3.4	5.4%
$1,000–$1,500	4.2%	—

Note: Evidently, the growth rates used in this table to derive incremental capital-output ratios are total, not per capita. They are drawn from Kristensen and the sources in Appendix 1. In the construction of the cross-sectional column in this table, Kristensen's real growth rates by real income per capita level have been regrouped to conform to the somewhat different Chenery-Syrquin income-range categories to take advantage of the Chenery-Syrquin calculation of investment rates at different income levels. Kristensen's calculations, in 1967 U.S. $, and the historical data have also been converted in this table to 1964 U.S. $, to match the Chenery-Syrquin data. The conversion factor is 1.09. The pre-1914 column includes, where the income levels are appropriate, Great Britain, United States, France, Germany, Sweden, Japan, Italy, and Canada. The figures are unweighted averages of the relevant number of countries. The investment rates are to be found in Appendix 2.
Source: Appendixes 1 and 2, this chapter.

of the sharp but transient decline of the capital-output ratios of Germany, during the great boom of the early 1870's (1868–1873), and of Sweden, during its drive to technological maturity (say, 1890–1914).

Kuznets' explanation for the rising tendency in incremental capital-output ratios comes to rest on the rising stock of long-lived capital goods and an assumed declining marginal yield from capital, as the following passage makes clear:

If capital formation proportions rise, incremental capital-output ratios can remain constant only if the rate of growth of countrywide product rises proportionately. If population grows at a decreasing rate, as it has in many developed countries, product per capita grows at an increasing rate even if total product grows at a constant rate; and if the total product has to accelerate to keep the capital-output ratio constant, with rising capital formation proportions, acceleration in the rate of growth of per capita product must be all the more marked. Such accelerated growth in per capita product should result in higher savings and hence in higher capital formation proportions—which means that the rate of growth of total and per capita product must accelerate further, if the incremental capital-output ratio is to be kept from rising. Since the extent of such self-acceleration is limited in conditions of a declining rate of growth of population, and since the increased supply of capital funds makes for a larger stock of long-lived goods and a lower marginal yield of capital, a *rising* incremental capital-output ratio, gross or net, is plausible in the course of economic growth. Such a rise would be even more prominent if we were to add investment in man to capital formation, for then the capital formation proportion would be rising even more appreciably while the rate of growth of countrywide product would be unaffected.[30]

This explanation may be more persuasive if one widens "investment in man" to embrace the relative rise of services in general, that is, services other than education and health to which, presumably, Kuznets was primarily referring. Service sectors are generally believed to have low capital-output ratios, although automation has rendered some of them capital intensive in recent times. On the other hand, they are usually characterized by lower productivity per man-hour than manufactures. One instinctively feels that the rising tendency in incremental capital-output ratios for more affluent economies is, somehow, related to the rising role of the service sectors and the declining role of the manufacturing sectors where high productivity innovations have been historically concentrated. But on this matter I, at least, am not prepared to be dogmatic. For our present purposes it is sufficient to note empirically that a combination of an investment rate which levels off (or declines) and a rising incremental capital-output ratio—for whatever reasons—is sufficient to explain the declining growth rates at high income per capita levels.

But these generalizations appear to have been violated by the extraordinary growth rates of the world economy from the Second

World War down to 1973, notably the accelerated growth rates of the high-income countries of Western Europe and Japan. All the elements cited in this analysis, operating on the side of the supply of and demand for investment resources and their productivity, appear to have played a part in the emergence after 1945 of the highest per capita growth rates the world economy has experienced over the past two centuries.

1. The postwar commitment of governments to maintain relatively full employment, in an environment of ample investment opportunities and a wide range of instruments for affecting the total level of effective demand, permitted growth to assume the form of variations in growth rates or shallow cycles in employment as compared to the pre-1914 era or the pathological interwar years. The upshot was markedly higher average per capita growth rates in Western Europe and Japan than any previously experienced for such a sustained period, while the United States, with a lower growth rate, nevertheless enjoyed for a quarter-century an average unemployment rate approximating that of the prosperous 1920's. On average, capital was more regularly and fully employed than in the historical past.

2. Western Europe and Japan enjoyed for a time the role of late-comers; that is, they absorbed efficiently the backlog of technologies associated with the rapid diffusion of the automobile and durable consumer goods, as well as the migration to suburbia, a process in which they had somewhat lagged behind the United States.[31] It was the stimulating effect of exploiting this differential technological backlog which, in my view, mainly decreed the surge in Western European and Japanese investment ratios relative to the United States in the post-1945 boom. The phenomenon emerges clearly in Table 6-11. As the new technological complexes were rapidly absorbed in Western Europe and Japan, the lift to productivity they afforded may have waned, while outlays on education, health, and certain other services expanded disproportionately.[32] These factors may help account for the rising tendency in Western European and Japanese capital-output ratios in the course of the 1960's.

Special circumstances evidently affect the level and course of these ratios; for example, the rapid postwar recovery (and utilization of idle capacity) in countries which had suffered considerable physical damage yielded abnormally low ratios for 1950; the full utilization of U.S. capacity brought down the capital-output

TABLE 6-11. *Post-1945 Incremental Capital-Output Ratios (ICOR) and Growth Rates: Eight Countries (five-year averages centered on indicated years)*

	1950 ICOR	1950 Growth Rate	1955 ICOR	1955 Growth Rate
Great Britain	5.5*	2.7%	6.1	2.5%
United States	6.2	3.8	5.3	3.0
France	2.4	8.4	4.1	4.6
Germany	3.5*	6.5	2.7	7.4
Sweden	4.4	4.8	6.5	3.6
Italy	2.3	8.8	3.5	5.6
Japan	2.2	13.3	2.3	9.4
Canada	4.7	4.9	4.9	5.1
Unweighted average	3.9	6.6%	4.4	5.1%

* 1952.

ratio in the mid-1960's, and so forth. The extraordinarily high capital-output ratios for Great Britain are the result of a special complex of forces, best elucidated by Postan.[33] But, without exception, there is an increase during the second half of the 1960's. They have, almost certainly, risen farther in the first half of the 1970's under the impact of increased allocations to contain pollution, the effects of high energy prices, and an increase in idle capacity.

3. In the developing regions of Latin America, Africa, the Middle East, and Asia, the sustained high momentum of the advanced industrial countries, their own purposeful efforts to increase investment rates and absorb new technologies, and a significant margin of public and private capital flows yielded average per capita growth rates never before experienced for sustained periods, despite much unevenness among them and the special problems imposed by high rates of population increase.

4. The postwar global boom was carried forward in an environment of relatively falling energy prices and, from 1951 to 1972, of relatively falling or low prices of foodstuffs and raw materials. The subsequent unfavorable shift in the terms of trade for energy and food importers not only struck, in general, at the rise in real incomes but also inhibited directly the further expansion of the energy-intensive leading sectors of the previous period. A restruc-

1960		1965		1970	
ICOR	Growth Rate	ICOR	Growth Rate	ICOR	Growth Rate
5.7	3.1%	5.6	3.2%	8.6	2.1%
4.6	3.2	3.3	5.0	4.3	3.3
4.3	5.0	4.3	5.5	4.5	5.7
2.7	9.3	4.6	5.1	4.7	5.4
6.0	4.2	5.5	4.3	5.9	3.7
3.3	6.7	4.2	4.6	4.4	4.6
2.8	11.3	3.0	10.3	3.4	10.2
5.5	4.0	4.0	5.9	4.9	4.4
4.4	5.8%	4.3	5.5%	5.1	4.9%

Source: Appendixes 1 and 2, this chapter.

turing of investment patterns (and, perhaps, some rise in investment rates) will be required to regain previous growth rates as well as efforts to overcome, by new technologies, the drag on growth imposed, notably, by high energy prices.

In short, the remarkable growth rates of the quarter-century after the Second World War depended in part on two inherently transient phenomena: the catching up of Western Europe and Japan with the United States in the technologies of high mass-consumption and relatively cheap energy and the increased capacity of governments to design programs of full employment and growth, as compared to earlier times, which remains available if successfully geared to appropriate sectoral investment patterns. The current evidence on their effective will to do so is mixed.

Cross-sectional and historical analysis among countries (as well as interregional analysis) suggests that late-comers to the process of modern growth tend to catch up with early-comers. The acceleration of growth in the drive to technological maturity (and middle income ranges) is seen as the dual result of an increased capacity to raise private and public investment rates with the rise in per capita income and to absorb and diffuse the backlog of modern technology as education is expanded and economic institutions acquire increasingly sophisticated abilities. The tendency of investment rates to level off is judged the result of private and public decisions which, in effect, set a limit on the society's willingness to sacrifice current consumption for future productive capacity and the diminishing backlog of unapplied technologies. The broad, well-documented tendency of capital-output ratios to rise with the rise in income per capita may be a result of both the changing structure of the capital stock and the shift to services. The postwar boom in Western Europe and Japan emerges as the result of a transient interval when a major backlog of unapplied technologies was available under circumstances of relatively low prices for energy and other basic materials. Capital-output ratios tended to rise in the second half of the 1960's. A substantial change in the directions of investment and, perhaps, a rise in investment rates may be required to re-achieve the growth rates of the two previous decades, in the wake of the price revolution of 1972–1979.

APPENDIX I. *Real GNP per capita (1967 U.S. $: Five-year moving averages)*

Decade	1	2	3	4	5	6	7	8	9	0
Argentina										
190–	309	292	321	343	375	381	377	401	409	425
191–	421	443	435	380	378	358	321	375	380	398
192–	400	418	450	465	450	463	478	494	503	465
193–	427	406	418	444	457	451	481	480	490	470
194–	486	502	495	537	501	535	598	590	550	544
195–	554	507	534	545	570	570	589	619	575	609
196–	642	619	588	627	663	731	741	768	823	849
197–	875									
Australia										
186–		735	727	768	729	746	813	822	804	833
187–	777	840	900	902	975	942	946	1,006	988	1,007
188–	1,045	954	1,043	1,009	1,039	1,016	1,089	1,058	1,118	1,050

Decade	1	2	3	4	5	6	7	8	9	0
Australia										
189–	1,099	944	878	891	825	873	809	923	911	952
190–	923	902	1,046	1,006	1,031	1,122	1,097	1,150	1,220	1,253
191–	1,172	1,233	1,224	989	1,061	1,125	1,090	1,090	986	1,180
192–	1,179	1,153	1,171	1,261	1,181	1,178	1,141	1,117	1,106	1,005
193–	994	1,047	1,075	1,090	1,133	1,173	1,236	1,181	1,208	1,235
194–	1,262	1,290	1,315	1,339	1,361	1,378	1,392	1,400	1,457	1,486
195–	1,490	1,438	1,503	1,558	1,601	1,601	1,585	1,662	1,694	1,742
196–	1,719	1,800	1,885	1,980	1,974	2,065	2,106	2,241	2,320	2,368
197–	2,392									
Brazil										
192–								137	137	138
193–	138	139	144	149	153	158	161	169	177	174
194–	187	169	170	175	183	197	209	217	219	221
195–	233	237	241	256	268	273	278	277	286	294
196–	306	307	309	309	315	318	323	344	365	388
197–	419	450								
Canada										
187–	514	523	545	553	560	581	588	608	614	619
188–	637	640	657	659	676	678	694	695	712	712
189–	735	742	763	770	791	796	817	822	843	847
190–	913	962	955	956	994	1,034	990	1,001	1,081	1,071
191–	1,146	1,121	1,184	1,145	1,137	1,143	1,134	1,140	1,119	1,085
192–	964	1,030	1,083	1,069	1,092	1,159	1,255	1,342	1,320	1,239
193–	1,061	942	871	967	1,033	1,069	1,166	1,154	1,229	1,390
194–	1,576	1,852	1,894	1,953	1,877	1,797	1,829	1,846	1,830	1,925
195–	1,978	2,081	2,144	2,048	2,184	2,310	2,293	2,277	2,310	2,324
196–	2,350	2,456	2,542	2,656	2,790	2,924	2,962	3,090	3,204	3,239
197–	3,369									
France										
182–						166	168	170	171	173
183–	175	177	179	180	182	188	194	200	206	212
184–	218	223	228	233	238	243	248	252	256	259
185–	263	267	271	274	278	282	284	286	288	291
186–	293	296	300	302	305	308	315	322	330	337
187–	344	352	366	379	392	405	419	432	445	458
188–	471	485	493	501	509	517	526	535	544	553
189–	562	570	587	603	619	635	651	666	679	692
190–	705	704	723	780	770	787	806	810	835	834

Decade	1	2	3	4	5	6	7	8	9	0
France										
191–	867	949	950	927	904	881	858	835	811	788
192–	730	881	946	1,088	1,088	1,128	1,083	1,141	1,254	1,231
193–	1,173	1,090	1,095	1,072	1,025	1,014	1,054	1,047	1,125	933
194–	741	666	635	538	586	895	959	1,020	1,142	1,227
195–	1,292	1,326	1,354	1,408	1,475	1,550	1,613	1,639	1,659	1,769
196–	1,824	1,912	1,966	2,058	2,153	2,250	2,343	2,440	2,608	2,738
197–	2,855									
Germany (West Germany after 1945)										
185–	249	260	248	255	240	267	273	275	276	304
186–	287	300	317	315	316	319	317	347	325	344
187–	356	390	399	426	417	407	399	415	399	383
188–	396	395	414	430	438	442	445	462	476	487
189–	464	486	518	516	530	547	562	594	578	563
190–	548	502	581	600	614	605	625	617	624	612
191–	636	659	658	658	658	659	659	659	660	660
192–	660	661	651	641	631	627	718	730	683	654
193–	581	564	634	691	758	827	907	996	1,006	1,016
194–	1,027	1,040	1,054	1,070	1,088	1,109	1,017	939	868	803
195–	881	940	997	1,082	1,164	1,237	1,280	1,305	1,376	1,592
196–	1,716	1,841	1,932	2,095	2,134	2,173	2,148	2,280	2,444	2,546
197–	2,573									
Great Britain										
170–		152	153	154	156	157	158	160	161	162
171–	162	162	162	161	161	160	160	159	159	159
172–	158	158	158	157	157	157	157	156	156	156
173–	156	156	157	157	157	158	158	158	158	159
174–	160	161	162	163	164	165	166	167	168	169
175–	171	173	174	176	177	179	180	181	182	184
176–	182	180	178	177	175	173	172	170	168	167
177–	168	170	171	173	174	175	177	178	180	181
178–	182	182	183	184	185	185	186	187	187	188
179–	192	196	199	203	207	210	214	217	220	224
180–	227	230	231	233	236	236	239	240	241	242
181–	244	247	251	255	258	259	262	266	270	271
182–	273	282	290	298	306	314	322	330	337	345
183–	355	350	349	360	376	385	376	393	407	390
184–	425	368	363	388	407	429	432	440	449	446
185–	468	474	491	504	514	533	536	520	543	547
186–	564	558	578	587	618	622	623	636	645	662

Decade	1	2	3	4	5	6	7	8	9	0
Great Britain										
187–	697	683	677	710	709	711	711	710	687	738
188–	733	737	766	753	745	750	785	790	799	801
189–	825	802	786	825	842	875	867	911	947	920
190–	940	948	945	940	950	967	958	924	950	974
191–	990	987	947	1,034	1,174	1,198	1,224	1,208	1,035	910
192–	817	906	933	956	1,011	960	1,026	1,047	1,066	1,055
193–	997	989	1,002	1,071	1,107	1,136	1,174	1,208	1,236	1,409
194–	1,490	1,494	1,508	1,426	1,320	1,309	1,272	1,298	1,329	1,378
195–	1,424	1,412	1,471	1,519	1,557	1,584	1,606	1,599	1,642	1,708
196–	1,758	1,765	1,827	1,922	1,966	1,993	2,018	2,096	2,124	2,152
197–	2,191									
Iran										
195–										201
196–	209	215	220	227	246	254	276	293	317	335
Italy										
186–			283	292	308	210	277	294	300	302
187–	298	292	399	299	309	304	301	301	303	304
188–	290	301	299	302	303	304	307	303	291	306
189–	305	394	300	396	300	304	290	304	307	326
190–	341	336	344	342	353	360	388	390	408	385
191–	406	411	427	419	467	521	535	537	456	422
192–	409	429	453	457	476	478	474	502	512	488
193–	485	493	487	485	517	514	545	548	583	572
194–	564	547	482	383	304	395	463	501	541	583
195–	627	645	687	719	766	689	834	867	926	978
196–	1,051	1,142	1,188	1,212	1,234	1,255	1,333	1,408	1,477	1,542
197–	1,554									
Japan										
188–						158	168	171	179	173
189–	188	183	193	200	209	205	201	207	219	213
190–	218	213	211	231	215	216	208	227	229	241
191–	239	238	236	234	245	263	282	303	318	314
192–	329	316	298	330	316	313	318	334	331	328
193–	326	333	360	389	404	406	445	458	472	483
194–	438	433	433	410	322	216	230	261	265	293
195–	239	356	370	383	417	453	493	511	556	638
196–	743	778	845	951	985	1,076	1,207	1,366	1,511	1,650
197–	1,727	1,852								

Decade	1	2	3	4	5	6	7	8	9	0
Mexico										
189–						143	150	156	147	146
190–	156	143	158	159	173	169	177	175	178	178
191–	180	182	185	187	189	192	194	196	199	201
192–	204	205	209	201	210	223	214	215	205	187
193–	191	157	171	179	188	199	201	202	227	224
194–	244	259	266	278	281	284	285	289	300	325
195–	338	342	333	356	376	387	404	414	413	432
196–	431	438	463	498	504	532	545	568	583	608
Russia–USSR										
187–	207	209	210	212	213	214	215	216	217	217
188–	218	219	219	220	221	226	231	236	241	246
189–	250	254	257	261	264	268	271	273	276	278
190–	281	284	287	290	293	295	297	299	301	303
191–	315	328	341	350	360	370	380	390	401	413
192–	413	414	415	406	400	395	388	382	384	396
193–	394	386	397	414	478	504	542	540	561	560
194–	540	520	499	479	458	459	514	587	655	722
195–	788	844	875	894	967	992	1,043	1,104	1,157	1,200
196–	1,252	1,305	1,333	1,410	1,455	1,533	1,594	1,647	1,668	1,796
197–	1,886	1,938								
South Korea										
195–				99	105	110	115	118	113	118
196–	120	121	128	134	139	152	159	175	198	212
197–	230	245								
Sweden										
186–		248	252	250	252	250	242	239	236	284
187–	291	312	325	343	311	343	328	321	327	331
188–	343	335	352	355	365	360	365	370	384	389
189–	404	400	411	450	428	485	486	488	491	517
190–	519	501	555	564	560	626	615	620	634	661
191–	688	660	757	725	753	850	762	712	729	815
192–	718	669	724	780	855	876	917	919	996	1,030
193–	917	893	904	993	1,042	1,099	1,172	1,215	1,282	1,249
194–	1,226	1,230	1,292	1,343	1,464	1,593	1,662	1,728	1,774	1,910
195–	1,977	1,933	1,993	2,126	2,184	2,241	2,298	2,324	2,445	2,520
196–	2,647	2,730	2,836	3,025	3,105	3,163	3,244	3,358	3,503	3,654
197–	3,638									

Decade	1	2	3	4	5	6	7	8	9	0
Taiwan										
195–		135	142	149	155	157	163	167	174	178
196–	184	192	203	220	240	252	270	289	303	325
197–	355	386								
Turkey										
193–				171	171	177	174	185	192	196
194–	189	196	177	173	142	183	179	198	173	197
195–	220	232	251	222	231	240	248	269	272	262
196–	262	270	282	286	304	318	331	345	365	380
United States										
178–									202	211
179–	218	223	225	232	235	239	242	246	253	260
180–	262	267	269	272	276	279	279	279	283	295
181–	297	293	295	300	309	314	318	323	325	327
182–	325	332	334	341	348	355	358	365	367	374
183–	383	390	399	404	416	425	430	434	441	446
184–	446	446	451	458	467	478	490	499	499	504
185–	513	513	523	525	527	534	525	534	541	539
186–	536	543	553	562	574	583	597	613	627	641
187–	653	669	683	692	699	708	722	739	757	778
188–	797	818	822	827	834	857	883	901	917	964
189–	987	1,061	992	945	1,038	999	1,073	1,078	1,154	1,166
190–	1,275	1,261	1,301	1,259	1,326	1,452	1,449	1,303	1,435	1,419
191–	1,442	1,489	1,517	1,375	1,396	1,568	1,512	1,651	1,649	1,598
192–	1,533	1,598	1,779	1,798	1,816	1,907	1,900	1,900	1,965	1,749
193–	1,603	1,359	1,324	1,433	1,565	1,770	1,851	1,744	1,879	2,021
194–	2,325	2,597	2,901	3,066	2,982	2,599	2,529	2,594	2,555	2,750
195–	2,922	2,959	3,040	2,947	3,112	3,117	3,105	3,019	3,159	3,173
196–	3,180	3,333	3,419	3,556	3,723	3,928	3,995	4,151	4,220	4,146
197–	4,241	4,469	4,696							

Sources:

Argentina, Gross Domestic Product per Capita (1960 billion pesos)

1900–1934: Carlos F. Díaz Alejandro, *Essays on the Economic History of the Argentine Republic* (New Haven: Yale University Press, 1970), table 19, pp. 418–420.

1935–1965: Ibid., table 11, pp. 407–408.

1966–1971: *United Nations Yearbook of National Account Statistics* [UNYNAS], 1972, vol. I, p. 6. (Linkage years: 1935, 1965.)

Australia, Gross National Product per Capita (1966 million pounds)

1861–1937: N. G. Butlin, *Australian Domestic Product, Investment and Foreign*

Borrowing, 1861–1938/39 (Cambridge: At the University Press, 1962), table 269, pp. 460–461.

1938–1948: B. D. Haig, "National Income Estimates," *Australian Economic History Review* 7, no. 2 (September 1967): 180.

1949–1956: Commonwealth Bureau of Census and Statistics, *Australian National Accounts: National Income and Expenditure* (Canberra: Australian Government Publishing Service, 1963), table 10, p. 32.

1957–1959: *UNYNAS*, 1967, p. 10.

1960–1971: *UNYNAS*, 1972, vol. I, p. 12.

(Linkage years: 1938, 1948, 1957, 1960)

Brazil, Gross National Product per Capita (1953 million cruzieros)

1927–1937: Alexander Ganz, "Problems and Uses of National Wealth Estimates in Latin America," in *The Measurement of National Wealth*, ed. Raymond Goldsmith and Christopher Saunders (London: Bowes & Bowes, 1959), p. 225.

1939–1954: United Nations, *Análysis y Proyecciones del Desarrollo Económico: El Desarrollo Económico del Brasil* (Mexico City: United Nations Publication, 1956), table 1, p. 12.

1955–1966: *UNYNAS*, 1967, p. 71.

1967–1973: World Bank, "Basic Economic Data Sheet, World Table 1," *1975 World Tables* (Washington, D.C.: World Bank, 1976), p. 84.

(Linkage years: 1942, 1953, 1966)

Canada, Gross National Product per Capita (1961 million dollars)

1870–1925: Angus Maddison, *Economic Growth in the West* (New York: Twentieth Century Fund, 1964), table A-2, pp. 201–202.

1926–1971: Minister of Industry, Trade and Commerce, *Canadian Statistical Review, Historical Summary 1970 [CSRHS]* (Ottawa: Information Canada, 1972), sec. 3, table 1.3, p. 16.

(Linkage Year: 1929)

France, Gross National Product per Capita (1959 million francs)

1825–1898: Institut National de la Statistique et des Etudes Economiques, *Annuaire statistique de la France, résumé retrospectif [ASFR]*, 1966 (Paris: Institut National de la Statistique et des Etudes Economiques), table 13, p. 555.

1901–1958, 1960–1964: Ibid., table 14, p. 556 (Sauvy's estimates).

1959: Ibid., table 8, p. 553.

1966–1971: *UNYNAS*, 1972, vol. I, p. 353.

(Linkage years: 1959, 1963)

Germany, Gross National Product per Capita (1913 million marks)

1850–1959: Walther G. Hoffmann, *Das Wachstum der Deutschen Wirtschaft Seit der Mitte des 19 Jahrhunderts* (Berlin: Springer-Verlag, 1965), table 249, pp. 827–828.

1960–1964: *UNYNAS*, 1965, p. 124.

1966–1971: Ibid., 1972, p. 385.

(Linkage years: 1959, 1963)

Great Britain, Gross National Product per Capita (1958 pounds)

1700–1821:* Phyllis Deane and W. A. Cole, *British Economic Growth, 1688–1959*

(Cambridge: At the University Press, 1962), table 19, p. 78; table 72, p. 282.

1830–1869: Phyllis Deane, "New Estimates of Gross National Product for the United Kingdom 1830–1914," *Review of Income and Wealth*, ser. 14, no. 2 (June 1968): 106–107.

1870–1965: C. H. Feinstein, *National Income Expenditure and Output of the United Kingdom, 1855–1965* (Cambridge: At the University Press, 1972), table 5, T14–T17.

1966–1971: Central Statistical Office, *Annual Abstract of Statistics* (London: Her Majesty's Stationery Office, 1972), table 318, p. 297.

* Linkage procedures: For the period 1700–1821, GNP per capita estimates were derived from a GNP index (1958 = 100) created from the following sources: 1700–1821, Deane and Cole, *British Economic Growth*, table 19, p. 78, and table 72, p. 282. Linkage year 1801 was derived from table 19, assuming an annual rate of growth of 2.82 percent for total real output during the decade 1790–1800. 1830–1912, Deane, "New Estimates of Gross National Product," table B, pp. 106–107. Deane's estimates were transformed into index numbers and the data were linked in 1831 with the GNP index derived from Deane and Cole, table 72, p. 282. 1913–1965, Feinstein, *National Income Expenditure and Output*, table 6, Compromise Estimate, T18–T20. All index numbers were standardized to base year 1958 = 100. GNP estimates for 1700–1821 were calculated by multiplying the yearly index number by Feinstein's 1958 estimate for GNP at factor cost (20, 396; see table 5, T17).

Iran, Gross Domestic Product per Capita (1959 billion rials)

1959–1970: Jahangir Amuzegar and M. Ali Fekrat, *Iran Economic Development under Dualistic Conditions* (Chicago: University of Chicago Press, 1971), table 1.5, p. 96.

Italy, Gross Domestic Product per Capita (1954 million lira)

1861–1964: Giorgio Fia, *Notes on Italian Economic Growth, 1861–1964* (Milan: Editore Guiffie, 1965), table 3, pp. 60–63; table 4, p. 64.

1966–1972: *UNYNAS*, 1972, vol. I, p. 581.

(Linkage years: 1952, 1960)

Japan, Gross National Product per Capita (1963 billion yen)

1885–1904: Kuzushi Ohkawa et al., *Estimates of Long Term Economic Statistics of Japan since 1868* (Tokyo: Toyo Keizai Shinpo Sha, 1974), table 18, p. 213.

1905–1962: Kazushi Ohkawa and Henry Rosovsky, *Japanese Economic Growth* (Stanford: Stanford University Press, 1973), table 6, pp. 288–289.

1963–1973: World Bank, "Basic Economic Data Sheet—World Table I," p. 12.

(Linkage years: 1905, 1963)

Mexico, Gross National Product per Capita (1950 million pesos)

1895–1910: Enrique Pérez López, "The National Product of Mexico: 1895 to 1964," in *Mexico's Recent Economic Growth: The Mexican View*, trans. Marjory Urquidi, Latin American Monographs, no. 10 (Austin: University of Texas Press, 1970), table 2, p. 28.

1921–1939: Ibid., table 3, p. 29.

1938–1965: Clark W. Reynolds, *The Mexican Economy* (New Haven: Yale University Press, 1970), table D5B, pp. 371–373.

1966–1970: *UNYNAS,* 1972, vol. II, p. 100.
(Linkage years: 1939, 1963)

Russia–USSR, Gross National Product per Capita (1937 million rubles)
1870–1913: Raymond W. Goldsmith, "The Economic Growth of Tsarist Russia,
1860–1913," *Economic Development and Cultural Change* 9, no. 3 (April 1961):
441–475.
1928–1965: Angus Maddison, *Economic Growth in Japan and the USSR* (New
York: W. W. Norton and Company, 1969), app. C, table B-1, p. 155.
1966–1969: Stanley Cohn, "General Growth Performance of the Soviet Economy,"
in *Economic Performance and the Military Burden in the Soviet Union,* Joint
Economic Committee (Washington, D.C.: GPO, 1970), sec. D-31, table 1, p. 17.
1970–1972: *UNYNAS,* 1973, vol. II, p. 639.
(Linkage years: 1913, 1965, 1969)
The GNP estimates were derived from an index (1937 = 100) and multiplied by
Richard Moorsteen and Raymond Powell's GNP estimate for 1937. See Moorsteen
and Powell, *The Soviet Capital Stock, 1928–1962* (Homewood, Ill.: Richard D.
Irwin, 1966), table 1, p. 622.

South Korea, Gross Domestic Product per Capita (1960 billion won)
1953–1964: *UNYNAS,* 1965, p. 212.
1965–1975: *United Nations Statistical Yearbook* [UNSY], 1973, p. 550.
(Linkage year: 1963)

Sweden, Gross National Product per Capita (1959 million kronor)
1861–1954: Östen Johansson, *The Gross Domestic Product of Sweden and Its Composition, 1861–1955* (Stockholm: Almqvist & Wicksell, 1967), table 56, pp. 152–
153.
1955–1965: *UNYNAS,* 1967, p. 628.
1966–1971: Ibid., 1972, vol. II, p. 454.
(Linkage years: 1955, 1965)

Taiwan, Gross National Product per Capita (1966 million N.T. dollars)
1952–1970: Lin Shu-ting et al. (eds.), *China Yearbook, 1972/73* (Taipei: China
Publishing Company, 1973), p. 207.
1971–1972: *Statistical Abstract of the Republic of China, 1973,* Directorate General
of Budget, Accounting and Statistics Executive Yuan (Republic of China, 1974),
table 257, p. 672.

Turkey, Gross Domestic Product per Capita (1948 million Turkish lira)
1933–1962: Oktag Yenal, "Development of the Financial System," in *Four Studies
on the Economic Development of Turkey,* ed. Frederick C. Shorter (New York:
Augustus M. Kelley, 1967), table 4, p. 103.
1963–1964: *UNYNAS,* 1965, p. 369.
1966–1970: Ibid., 1972, vol. II, p. 563.
(Linkage years: 1962, 1963)

United States, Gross National Product per Capita (1929 dollars)
1789–1973: Thomas S. Berry, "U.S. Product and Income Accounts since 1789:
Revised Annual Estimates," unpublished manuscript (n.d.), table 38B, p. 22.

APPENDIX 2. *Gross Investment as Percentage GNP (Five-year moving averages)*

Decade	1	2	3	4	5	6	7	8	9	0
Canada										
186–										11.9
187–	12.1	12.2	12.4	12.6	12.8	13.1	13.3	13.5	13.6	13.7
188–	13.6	13.6	13.4	13.2	13.1	12.9	12.7	12.5	12.6	12.8
189–	13.2	13.8	14.6	15.4	16.2	17.0	17.9	18.7	19.5	20.3
190–	21.1	21.9	22.7	23.6	24.4	25.3	25.9	26.5	26.8	26.9
191–	26.9	26.8	26.4	25.9	25.2	24.3	23.4	22.6	21.7	20.9
192–	20.0	19.1	18.3	17.4	17.1	17.3	18.1	18.9	19.1	18.0
193–	16.1	13.6	11.9	10.9	11.7	12.7	13.7	14.5	15.2	15.5
194–	16.1	16.7	17.3	17.9	18.5	19.1	19.7	20.3	20.8	21.2
195–	21.7	22.0	22.2	23.0	24.1	24.6	24.8	24.9	24.0	22.8
196–	21.8	21.4	21.5	22.0	22.4	22.6	22.5	22.2	21.7	21.4
197–	21.0									
France										
181–			5.9	6.0	6.1	6.3	6.5	6.6	6.8	7.0
182–	7.1	7.3	7.5	7.7	7.8	8.0	8.1	8.3	8.5	8.7
183–	8.8	9.0	9.2	9.3	9.5	9.7	9.9	10.0	10.2	10.4
184–	10.5	10.7	10.7	11.0	11.3	11.5	11.7	12.0	12.3	12.6
185–	12.7	13.1	13.4	13.7	14.0	14.2	14.5	14.8	15.1	15.3
186–	15.6	15.9	16.2	16.4	16.7	16.9	17.1	17.3	17.4	17.5
187–	17.7	17.8	17.9	18.1	18.2	18.3	18.5	18.6	18.8	18.9
188–	19.0	19.2	19.3	19.4	19.5	19.6	19.7	19.7	19.8	19.8
189–	19.8	19.8	19.9	19.9	19.9	19.9	20.0	20.0	20.0	20.0
190–	20.0	20.0	19.9	19.9	19.9	19.9	19.9	19.8	19.6	19.4
191–	19.2	19.0	18.8	18.6	18.3	18.1	17.9	17.7	17.4	17.2
192–	17.0	16.8	16.5	16.3	16.1	15.7	15.7	15.4	15.2	15.0
193–	14.8	14.5	14.3	14.1	13.9	13.6	13.6	13.7	14.0	14.5
194–	15.2	15.9	16.5	17.2	17.8	18.5	19.2	19.5	19.7	19.6
195–	19.1	18.6	18.4	18.6	19.1	19.9	20.2	20.5	20.8	21.0
196–	21.1	22.0	22.8	23.4	24.0	24.6	24.8	25.2	25.4	25.7
197–	26.0									
Germany (West Germany after 1945)										
185–	9.3	10.7	8.7	9.5	8.1	8.4	7.9	9.9	8.8	10.1
186–	11.4	12.1	11.5	11.9	10.8	10.8	9.9	10.3	10.5	12.1
187–	11.8	13.8	14.0	14.6	13.6	13.0	11.0	9.8	9.0	8.6
188–	8.6	9.3	9.8	10.1	10.6	10.9	11.5	12.2	11.9	12.2

Decade	1	2	3	4	5	6	7	8	9	0
Germany (West Germany after 1945)										
189–	12.3	11.8	11.2	12.0	12.3	13.3	14.6	15.5	15.3	14.6
190–	14.1	13.8	13.8	14.6	15.9	15.7	15.3	14.9	14.6	14.4
191–	14.8	15.2	15.5	15.4	15.0	14.8	14.5	14.3	14.0	13.8
192–	13.6	13.4	13.2	11.8	12.1	12.1	11.0	9.1	8.9	6.7
193–	4.8	4.8	6.1	7.3	9.6	11.8	13.2	14.1	14.9	14.8
194–	15.0	15.3	15.5	15.7	16.0	16.2	16.4	16.7	17.5	17.6
195–	17.2	17.5	18.4	18.3	19.2	20.6	21.6	22.0	23.0	23.8
196–	24.4	25.1	25.6	25.7	25.2	24.8	24.4	24.4	24.7	25.7
197–	26.8									
Great Britain										
182–										3.9
183–	4.1	4.2	5.1	5.4	5.8	6.4	6.8	6.4	6.2	5.9
184–	5.7	5.6	6.0	6.9	8.0	8.6	8.9	8.9	8.4	8.1
185–	7.7	7.6	7.6	7.8	8.0	8.3	8.8	8.8	8.5	8.1
186–	8.3	8.2	8.8	9.4	10.0	10.1	10.3	10.2	10.8	11.6
187–	12.3	12.8	12.9	12.3	11.0	10.1	9.3	8.8	9.3	9.8
188–	10.5	11.0	11.3	11.3	11.4	11.7	11.7	12.2	12.0	11.6
189–	10.8	10.2	9.4	9.4	9.3	9.3	9.6	9.8	9.7	9.8
190–	9.9	9.9	10.2	10.9	11.7	12.1	12.4	12.7	12.8	12.8
191–	13.2	13.2	13.0	12.7	12.5	12.2	12.3	12.5	12.6	12.4
192–	12.2	11.7	11.1	10.4	10.2	10.3	10.4	10.3	9.8	8.9
193–	8.0	7.5	7.6	8.2	8.9	9.5	9.5	6.0	2.6	−0.3
194–	−3.3	−6.0	−4.5	−1.7	0.7	4.4	8.3	11.4	12.4	13.8
195–	14.2	14.5	14.2	15.3	15.7	16.1	16.2	16.5	16.7	16.6
196–	16.4	16.8	17.1	17.3	17.8	18.4	18.4	18.4	18.4	18.1
197–	17.8									
Japan										
188–					12.2	13.0	13.4	14.9	14.2	14.5
189–	14.1	14.5	14.8	15.6	17.0	18.1	18.1	18.1	17.5	16.1
190–	14.9	14.1	14.1	14.1	15.0	15.6	16.3	16.4	16.9	16.9
191–	16.8	17.3	17.1	16.8	17.7	19.0	19.4	20.8	21.2	20.7
192–	19.4	19.3	18.0	17.7	17.5	17.4	17.1	16.9	16.3	15.7
193–	15.7	15.6	16.1	17.0	18.8	21.3	24.1	26.9	27.2	26.1
194–	24.8	23.2	16.9	16.1	16.4	15.8	14.9	18.1	18.9	18.9
195–	19.3	19.9	20.6	21.3	22.6	23.4	24.4	26.5	28.4	29.9
196–	31.2	32.4	32.5	32.0	31.7	31.9	32.4	33.2	33.6	33.6
197–	34.0	33.8	33.7							
Italy										
186–					2.3	2.8	3.2	3.8	4.4	5.0

Decade	1	2	3	4	5	6	7	8	9	0
Italy										
187–	5.7	6.3	6.9	7.5	8.0	8.4	8.8	9.1	9.4	9.7
188–	10.1	10.4	10.7	10.9	11.0	10.9	10.8	10.6	10.3	10.1
189–	9.9	9.6	9.4	9.2	9.2	9.2	9.3	9.6	9.8	9.9
190–	10.0	10.2	10.7	11.5	12.5	14.0	15.3	16.1	16.3	16.2
191–	15.5	14.9	14.3	14.1	13.8	13.6	13.5	13.3	12.9	12.9
192–	13.1	14.1	15.3	16.8	17.6	18.0	17.9	17.6	17.0	16.1
193–	15.7	15.3	15.2	15.8	16.5	16.8	16.9	16.7	16.2	16.1
194–	16.3	16.4	16.5	16.6	16.8	16.9	17.0	17.1	17.4	17.9
195–	18.3	18.8	19.3	19.7	20.1	20.3	20.6	21.0	21.4	21.7
196–	22.4	22.6	22.2	21.4	20.6	19.9	19.6	19.8	20.2	20.5
197–	20.8									
Russia–USSR										
192–								8.5	9.3	10.3
193–	11.9	13.7	15.6	17.1	18.1	18.5	18.1	17.2	16.2	15.1
194–	14.3	13.8	13.9	14.5	15.5	16.7	18.2	19.5	20.6	21.5
195–	22.0	22.3	22.5	22.8	23.2	23.8	24.4	25.1	25.6	26.0
196–	26.3	26.4	26.4	26.4	26.4	26.3	26.3	26.3	26.3	26.4
197–	26.6	26.8	27.0							
Sweden										
186–		8.8	8.1	8.4	8.0	7.3	7.1	7.0	6.6	6.9
187–	8.4	9.5	11.0	12.0	12.7	12.5	11.8	11.0	10.5	9.8
188–	9.5	9.7	9.8	10.1	9.9	9.9	9.7	9.8	9.0	9.0
189–	8.5	8.2	8.4	8.9	9.6	10.7	11.8	12.3	12.6	12.5
190–	12.6	12.5	12.5	12.8	13.1	12.9	12.2	11.8	11.5	11.1
191–	11.3	11.8	11.8	11.6	11.7	11.7	11.7	12.3	12.6	12.6
192–	12.7	12.7	12.7	12.8	12.9	13.1	13.3	13.9	14.4	14.4
193–	14.1	14.0	14.1	14.5	15.4	16.7	17.9	18.0	17.8	18.0
194–	18.1	18.0	18.0	18.8	19.5	19.5	19.4	20.0	20.1	20.3
195–	21.0	21.8	22.6	23.6	24.4	24.7	24.8	25.2	25.1	24.5
196–	24.4	24.5	24.2	24.1	23.9	23.6	23.0	22.6	22.0	21.6
197–	21.1									
United States										
178–									11.2	12.2
179–	11.8	12.0	12.8	13.2	13.8	14.4	14.4	14.0	13.6	13.0
180–	12.8	13.2	13.8	14.2	14.8	15.6	15.6	14.8	14.0	13.8
181–	13.2	13.8	14.8	16.4	17.0	18.2	18.4	17.8	16.6	16.2
182–	15.4	14.8	14.8	15.0	14.6	14.8	15.0	14.8	15.0	15.4
183–	15.6	16.0	17.0	17.8	18.2	18.4	18.8	18.0	17.2	16.4

Decade	1	2	3	4	5	6	7	8	9	0
United States										
184–	15.6	14.8	15.0	14.8	15.0	15.2	15.4	15.6	16.0	16.6
185–	17.4	17.8	18.0	18.2	18.2	17.8	17.8	18.0	16.8	14.2
186–	12.2	10.6	9.4	11.0	14.2	17.2	19.6	21.2	21.6	22.0
187–	22.0	21.8	21.8	21.4	20.6	19.6	19.0	18.8	18.8	19.2
188–	19.8	20.2	20.0	20.0	20.0	20.2	19.8	20.6	20.8	21.4
189–	21.0	21.2	20.8	20.2	19.2	18.8	18.6	18.2	18.4	18.6
190–	19.0	18.8	18.6	18.8	18.6	17.8	18.2	18.2	17.4	17.0
191–	17.6	16.2	15.0	14.8	13.8	12.0	12.8	14.4	13.6	14.0
192–	15.8	15.4	15.0	16.2	16.6	15.8	16.2	14.8	12.8	10.0
193–	7.8	5.6	5.2	5.8	8.0	9.0	10.0	10.8	11.6	10.2
194–	9.2	7.8	6.2	6.4	8.2	11.2	13.4	16.2	16.8	16.8
195–	16.0	16.0	15.6	15.4	15.4	15.4	15.8	15.4	14.8	14.8
196–	15.0	14.8	15.0	15.4	15.4	15.4	15.4	15.0	14.8	15.0
197–	15.2	15.6	16.0							

Sources:
Canada
1870–1913: Maddison, *Economic Growth in the West*, p. 238.
1926–1960: Ibid., table 12, p. 240.
1961–1971: *CSRHS*, 1972, sec. 3, table 1.2, p. 15.

France
1813–1908: J. Marczewski, "The Take-Off Hypothesis and French Experience," in *The Economics of Take-Off into Sustained Growth*, ed. W. W. Rostow (New York: St. Martin's Press, 1963), table 2, p. 121.
1938: *ASFR*, 1961, table 4, p. 356.
1949–1959: Ibid., 1966, table 8, p. 553.
1960–1971: *UNYNAS*, 1973, vol. III, p. 47.

Germany
1850–1956: Hoffmann, *Das Wachstum*, table 248, pp. 825–826.
1957–1966: *UNYNAS*, 1967, pp. 238, 240.
1967–1971: Ibid., 1972, vol. I, p. 384.
(Beginning in 1960, figures include Saar and West Berlin)

Great Britain
1830–1914: Deane, "New Estimates of Gross National Products," table A, pp. 104–105 [(GFDC + NFI) • / • GNP_{tc}].
1920–1959: Deane and Cole, *British Economic Growth*, app. 3, table 91, pp. 332, 333.
1960–1966: *UNYNAS*, 1967, p. 697.
1967–1971: Ibid., 1973, vol. III, table 2A, p. 52.

Italy

    1865: Shepard B. Clough, *The Economic History of Modern Italy* (New York: Columbia University Press, 1964), app., table 7, p. 372; table 10, p. 375.

    1875–1959: Maddison, *Economic Growth in the West*, app. I, pp. 239–240.

    1960–1971: *UNYNAS*, 1972, vol. I, p. 580.

Japan

    1885–1904: Ohkawa et al., *Estimates of Long Term Economic Statistics*, table 1, p. 178.

    1905–1970: Ohkawa and Rosovsky, *Japanese Economic Growth*, table 5, pp. 286–287 (col. 3 • / • col. 6).

    1971–1973: World Bank, "Basic Economic Data Sheet—World Table I," p. 12.

Russia–USSR (1937 prices)

    1928–1967: * B. R. Mitchell, *European Historical Statistics* (New York: Columbia University Press, 1975), pp. 788, 794.

    1967–1972: *UNSY*, 1974, p. 620.

    1973: Ibid.

    1967–1973: * Unpublished U.S. government calculations.

    *Linkage procedures: For the period 1955–1967, estimates were obtained in 1937 prices using 1955 linkage year index from Mitchell, *European Historical Statistics*, p. 794. For the period 1967–1973, the United Nations current figures and U.S. government gross investment estimate in 1969 prices were transformed into index numbers, and the data were linked in 1967 with the 1937 transformed prices above. The Soviet consumer price index is constant. Although it is not an adequate index for the prices of capital goods, I have judged it legitimate to assume capital goods prices essentially constant over these years. The investment proportions which emerge by this method differ only marginally from those to be derived for 1970–1973 from Central Statistical Board of the Council of Ministers, *The USSR in Figures for 1973* (Moscow: Progress Publishers, 1975), pp. 144, 175.

Sweden

    1861–1969: Mitchell, *European Historical Statistics*, pp. 782, 789, and 795.

    1970–1972: *UNSY*, 1973, p. 565.

United States

    1789–1973: Berry, "U.S. Product and Income Accounts since 1789," table 5B, p. 3.

7

How to Break the Impasse in North-South Multilateral Economic Negotiations

I

Given the global character of the problems thrown up by the coming of the fifth Kondratieff upswing and the tendency toward convergence among early- and late-comers to industrialization analyzed in Chapter 6, North-South economic negotiations, looking toward common action, ought to flourish. In fact, they are now stuck; and, with minor exceptions, they have proved sterile. It is the thesis of this chapter that a different conceptual framework and, derived from it, a different negotiating agenda, as well as a different cast of negotiators, will be required if such negotiations are to achieve the large purposes which the facts of global interdependence rationally dictate. A revision in the domestic economic policies of the advanced industrial countries of the North will also be required.

We have arrived at the present negotiating impasse by a path which is now tolerably clear. Calls for a New Economic Order from the South antedate the quadrupling of the oil price by OPEC; but that event set the initial tone of the negotiations. It did so by inducing the political leaders of the South to believe that a time had come when their command over the flow of raw materials necessary to the more industrialized North provided the leverage to exact important concessions which would enlarge the North-to-South flow of foreign exchange and technology.

For many intellectuals and politicians in the developing world, the success of OPEC in asserting its power in the autumn of 1973 was a memorable and heartening event. Here were nations— mostly small, in some cases poor, in all cases not fully modernized—using their control over a basic raw material to shake the foundations of the rich and comfortable societies which had based their post-1945 prosperity on cheap energy. Hitherto weaker states successfully asserted their capacity to divert more resources to themselves. At last, they could feel that the unfair allocation of the benefits that their raw materials had provided in the past was redressed. Whether that allocation was, in fact, fair or unfair, OPEC's action was a demonstration of power through a disciplined cooperation the developing nations had never before been able to generate.

The impulse to emulate OPEC by political pressure, where producers' cartels were not a realistic option, was heightened by another fact. The progress in modernization made in a good many developing nations in the 1950's and 1960's had yielded a generation quite as capable of sophisticated analysis of the world scene as those who provided the staff work for OPEC. Leaders of that generation felt themselves much more nearly the technical equals of their opposite numbers in the North than the pioneers of development in the previous generation. They were quite right.

And so they went on the attack in 1974. It was tactically as well as psychologically understandable that they should do so. On the one hand, the North was shaken by the rise in the oil price and looked weak and uncertain after two decades of majestic, confident growth; on the other hand, the world economy, for part of the year at least, was experiencing high raw material prices. The foreign exchange position of a good many producers of raw materials, other than oil, was strong as a result of the several previous years of global economic expansion.

If one reviews the major international conferences of 1974, one might guess that North-South relations had already polarized and that the world faced inevitably a protracted neomercantilist struggle. There were the acrimonious United Nations General Assembly debate of April 1974, the population meeting at Bucharest, the food conference at Rome, and the sterile session on the law of the seas at Caracas. In all of them, the air was filled with rhetoric about imperialism; with claims for the unilateral transfer of resources from the rich to the poor; and with the ardent assertion of national sovereignty by the less developed nations, combined with equally ardent demands that the more developed states surrender sovereignty and behave in terms of the requirements of the international community. In the face of this verbal and political onslaught, the more developed nations mainly reacted defensively.

The special United Nations session of September 1975 was, in tone and substance, markedly less contentious than those of 1974. Three factors appear to account for the change. First, the United States arrived with rhetoric of reconciliation and a working agenda for North-South cooperation. Although the American commitment of resources was limited, the rhetoric, the headings for action, and the assumption of leadership were useful. Second, and perhaps more important, the OECD recession over the previous year had badly damaged prospects in many parts of the developing world, demonstrating in a rather painful way the reality of North-South interdependence. In 1974, close to the peak of the previous boom, there had been much talk from the South about the North's excessive consumption of raw materials: in 1975 the South was concerned about foreign exchange losses from declining raw material sales and prices. Third, the damage done the developing world by OPEC's oil price increase was better understood and the somewhat artificial 1974 unity of the developing nations was thereby strained despite the formal maintenance of a common front against the industrial North.

A package of resolutions emerged from this session on September 16, 1975, which still shapes the agenda of North-South negotiations. It covers four main headings: a variety of measures to enlarge the foreign exchange earning capacity of developing countries through international trade, increased aid, the accelerated transfer of technology, and measures to accelerate agricultural production in the developing nations and to provide international grain stocks as a hedge against poor harvests in developing nations.

This agenda was pursued for the better part of two years in the Conference on International Economic Cooperation and Development in Paris. The tone of the negotiations was temperate; but the New Realism, in Maurice Williams' phrase, yielded only meager results: a promise to raise a special $1 billion fund to aid the most hard pressed developing nations, a commitment to consider at a later time the creation and financing of buffer stocks and commodity price stabilization, a commitment to consider debt rollovers on a case-by-case basis, and the offer of long-term support for transport and communication development in Africa.

The North was willing to do something about the worst manifestations of disarray in the developing world (the aid fund and selective debt rollovers); but the grand vision of a New Economic Order incorporated in the resolutions of September 16, 1975, had all but disappeared.

This happened, I believe, for three reasons: the South lacked the power to enforce its will on the North; politicians in the North lacked a political base to meet even the legitimate claims of the South, due to the state of the northern economies; the ideological mood of 1974 yielded an agenda substantially inappropriate to the true state of affairs in the world economy: its key problems and the potentialities for fruitful North-South cooperation. I shall deal with these three matters in reverse order of their statement and conclude by considering whether what I propose contains a basis for practical politics and diplomacy.

II

First, then, the negotiating agenda and the underlying concept which informs it. The agenda is now structured in a way so familiar as to be regarded by most as tediously inevitable: how much more is the North prepared to give the South in trade concessions, aid, and technology? It is strictly a one-way street. Its appeal, if any, in the North is to those like myself and other old crusaders on behalf of the developing nations who do, indeed, believe in the notion of a world community, in the responsibilities of the early-comers to industrialization to the late-comers, and in the real, if oblique and sometimes distant, advantages to the early-comers of sustained economic and social progress among the late-comers. But it is simply a fact of life that the appeal to northern conscience and vaguely articulated long-run self-interest is now an insufficient basis for serious progress in North-South multilateral economic negotiations. It would be a false realism to eliminate from the North-South dialogue the authentic element in the North of responsibility and concern of the more advantaged for the less advantaged; but that abiding strand in Northern thought, feeling, and politics is, by itself, incapable of bringing a North-South partnership to life.

The situation recalls an observation Jean Monnet made in Washington early in 1946 in the wake of the negotiation of the first British postwar loan. He said the British were wrong to make their appeal to Americans in terms of memories of the gallant stand on behalf of the West when Britain stood alone. It would not last. On the other hand, Americans could not resist joining in a promising enterprise. Therefore, he would seek aid by first laying out the whole modernization plan, emphasizing what the French aimed to do for themselves. He was confident that, in such a constructive setting, Americans would be prepared to help meet the plan's foreign exchange requirements. He got his loans; and, indeed, it was some such approach that rendered the Marshall Plan politically viable in 1947–1948.

Conceptually, then, I believe we now need a different approach: the definition of a common enterprise, with explicitly recognized common interests, to which all parties, North and South, might contribute. At its core, such a common enterprise requires a commitment by nations, North and South, to act, in a significant degree, each within its own capacities, in terms of the requirements of the international community. I would suggest that such an approach flows naturally from an assessment of where the world economy now stands and from certain quite specific common interests the North and South share in its future. Surely, in the end, we shall get back to trade, aid, and all the rest, as Monnet got back to U.S. loans in 1946. But we ought to start with the state of the world economy, its problems and possibilities.

The central fact about the world economy is that we have come to a phase when, for a quarter-century at least, the inputs to sustain an increasingly industrialized global civilization will have to be enlarged and conserved: food to meet the population bulge of perhaps 2 billion over the next quarter-century, 90 percent of which will occur in the southern continents; energy in a variety of old and new forms to help transit the period until, one hopes, science and technology yield a new essentially infinite (breeder or fusion) or renewable (solar) energy source; raw materials to support a rate of industrialization of 7.5 percent per annum in the developing continents (if the rates of the 1950's and 1960's are re-attained), 5.0 percent in the northern industrial world; policies and resources to contain or reduce air and water pollution and to maintain, in general, a viable environment; and new technologies, to render these and other shared objectives viable not only over the next generation but also in the following century, for the time lags in the creation of new technologies are long.

As Chapters 1, 2, and 3 suggest, we have entered the fifth period in the past two centuries of relatively high prices for the basic commodities necessary to sustain expanding populations in increasingly urban industrial settings. In the four previous periods the world economy cooperated to ameliorate or solve problems of relative shortage in the sense that investment flows responded to the profit possibilities created by high prices for basic resources; and governments permitted this to happen. New resource-rich areas were opened up and new technologies were created. Indeed, on the four previous occasions the response was overdone, and sustained periods of relatively cheap basic commodities resulted. But such cooperation in the past was mainly through the working of the private markets. This time, public policy will have to be involved because, for good or ill, governments are deeply involved in family planning, agriculture, energy, raw materials, the environment, and research and development.

I am asserting, then, that a first approximation of a North-South negotiating agenda should be functional; focused around the global resource agenda; addressed, in the first instance, not to negotiations but to these two questions: What has to happen in the world economy over the next quarter-century or so if economic and social momentum is to be maintained in both the North and the South? What can each nation contribute to a successful outcome?

Behind this notion of the agenda and an appropriate approach to it is a larger conception. I would argue that we have been wrong to divide the world, in our minds, into rich and poor countries and, especially, to let ourselves believe that the normal pattern in the world is for the rich to get richer, the poor to get poorer. As Chapter 6 argues, both history and a cross-sectional view of the contemporary scene tell us that the opposite has generally been true.

Two things follow from the view developed in Chapter 6. First, evidently, the developing nations are not a homogeneous group in terms of real income per capita, stage of growth, or capacity to act effectively on the resource agenda all nations now confront. Second, the appropriate perspective on North-South relations is not one of income redistribution from the rich to the poor, but of so maintaining the growth process in the world economy that the normal catching-up process operates on behalf of the late-comers. It is historically, technically, and ideologically more correct and illuminating to regard the world as made up of nations that entered modern growth (or take-off) at different periods than of the rich and the poor. As shall emerge, this perspective in no way reduces the importance of aid, liberalized trade, and accelerated transfer of appropriate technologies. But it does put those familiar functions in a different and, in my view, more accurate and wholesome perspective.

The proposed conceptual basis for multilateral North-South negotiations is, then, quite simple: the North and South share equally an interest that the world economy so operate as to permit and encourage growth rates in both regions roughly like those of the 1950's and 1960's—if possible, even higher than the 1960's in the South; and this requires the North and the South to cooperate intimately over the next quarter-century to assure that the resource problems of the world economy are effectively dealt with.

III

The question then arises: If the proper approach is for the nations of the North and South to examine how common problems are to be solved, how does the old agenda of aid, trade, and the transfer of technology re-enter the picture? The answer is, I believe, that it re-emerges quite naturally from a functional approach to common problems.

Take, for example, the fields of population and food. Assume that a group of North-South representatives were to conclude that it is in the common interest of the world community that, on average, gross birth rates in the developing world should be at or below 20 per 1,000 by the year 2000 and that an average annual expansion of agricultural production in the developing world of 4 percent should be achieved and maintained. (Put aside, for the moment, the familiar resistance of representatives of developing nations to acknowledging a birth rate target in multilateral forums.) Given the implications of birth rates for current and future (especially post-2000) requirements for food, health and education services, income distribution, unemployment levels, the political viability of developing nations, and the possibilities for minimal tranquility on the world scene, some such overall target for the reduction of birth rates ought, rationally, to be accepted. Less contentious is the target for a 4 percent annual increase in agricultural production in developing nations, a rough figure estimated as necessary to permit standards of diet to be improved in the South as well as to avoid gross malnutrition on a large scale.

What might rational North-South representatives agree about the respective responsibilities and tasks of the two regions in achieving some such agreed objectives?

Surely, the responsibility for family planning rests initially with the governments and peoples of Latin America, Africa, the Middle East, and Asia. Only they can radically enlarge the investment of political and administrative capital to reach effectively into the life of families in the villages and cities; only they can decide to invest more resources in creating a social environment, notably in health services and education, conducive to an accelerated decline in birth rates. But once such commitments are made, enlarged economic assistance, in aid and trade, can help substantially to support the necessary diversion of domestic resources.

As for technology, the scientists of the developing and developed world should, evidently, cooperate intimately to try to create birth control devices that are cheaper, longer lasting, and psychologically more acceptable than those now available.

As for the agricultural target, there is a similar natural convergence. Again, the initial primary responsibility falls on the governments and peoples of the developing nations. Without a will and commitment to raise agricultural production, including the sometimes painful decision to provide adequate price incentives to the farmer and to reduce the number of middlemen between the farmer and the urban market, external assistance is merely pushing on a string. But external aid can be of critical importance once the domestic decisions are made to enlarge acreage, increase irrigation, expand production or inputs of chemical fertilizers and pesticides, and expand local extension services and research facilities.

It should be noted that the modernization of rural life, which serious agricultural programs require, converges fully with the requirements of effective programs to reduce birth rates.

With respect to energy and raw materials, developing nations evidently have a strong interest in enlarging domestic production at times when prices are relatively high. And, with respect to raw materials, a common North-South interest in principle has been recognized in mitigating price fluctuations for all parties and income fluctuations for producers. The missing element in the domains of energy and raw materials lies in the failure of the international community to establish mutually acceptable rules of the game for private foreign investment which would also provide for the efficient development of such resources on behalf of the world economy as a whole. That failure is already distorting investment patterns toward politically hospitable regions which do not necessarily contain the most productive resources. The costs of this distortion with respect to raw materials (other than energy) are currently mitigated by the deceleration of growth in the world economy since 1974; but inadequate or misdirected investment in raw materials could become a serious brake on expansion if something like the growth rates of the 1960's were recaptured.

We are all aware of the nationalist sensitivities which surround the question of foreign private investment in basic resources. I shall merely note the issue here and return to it later.

So far as energy is concerned, however, there is a good deal more to the common agenda than finding new gas and oil reserves and exploiting them. Over the next quarter-century, the developing nations confront the task of disengaging from reliance on gas and oil while building an alternative energy base. This is, incidentally, true for most OPEC countries, as well as for the major oil- and gas-producing regions of the United States. Most developing countries will require external capital and/or technical assistance to make that transition efficiently and in good time. The new technologies and technological refinements in the production and use of various forms of energy, which will be required over the next generation, should not be—and are, in fact, unlikely to be—solely the product of scientists and inventors from the industrial North. The world economy should benefit, for example, from the ingenuity of southerners in developing solar energy where, by and large, the developing continents command a comparative advantage. And there are other energy possibilities where the South could lead the way, for example, energy derived from certain abundant forms of biomass. For some time, however, the developing nations making the energy transition will have to depend substantially on technologies generated in the North: nuclear power plants, including, in time, breeder reactors; synthetics from coal; photovoltaic cells for solar electricity, assuming their continued cost reduction brings them into economical range; methods for harnessing geothermal energy; and so forth.

The central point here is, simply, that the energy problem is inherently global; oil-importing nations of the South, as well as the North, feel the weight of high energy prices; they all are endangered by the probable peaking out of OPEC production capacity in the 1980's; they all (and the members of OPEC as well) confront the transition to a new intermediate energy base and, then, to a new long-term energy base.

If ever an array of common problems existed justifying intimate, sustained long-term North-South cooperation, including the OPEC nations, it lies in the fields of energy and raw materials. In a rational world, it would involve greatly enlarged capital and technological flows from North to South, enlarged exports from South to North, and an increasing technological contribution of the South to the world economy as a whole.

As for pollution control and the protection of the environment, there is an understandable tendency in the South to regard large outlays to maintain clean air and water as a luxury only the rich North can afford. A good deal of pollution control is a matter of welfare economics trade-offs where judgments will legitimately differ among countries, within countries, and even among towns sited on the same lake or river. But there are aspects of environmental protection which cannot be brushed off with such welfare economics agnosticism, for example, the safe management of nuclear power plants and their waste, the control of pollution in waterways shared by more and less industrialized countries (the Mediterranean), and the containment or reversal of the dangerous attrition of arable land. The latter includes a considerable array of problems: rapid deforestation is not only reducing timber and firewood supplies but also accentuating flooding and erosion problems; the abuse of land, notably by overgrazing, is extending the deserts in northwest India and the Middle East, as well as in several parts of Africa; the same forces are rapidly degrading three major mountain zones and their adjacent lowlands (the Himalayas, the Andes, and the East Africa highlands); inadequate drainage is reducing the productivity of some of the major areas of irrigated land through water-logging and salinity and by the accelerated silting of reservoirs and canals. Large investments are required to halt and reverse these trends. They are unlikely to be undertaken except in a context where developing countries, often in cooperation with one another, have focused sharply on the tasks of agriculture and are being strongly supported by the international community.

Evidently, then, a wide range of environmental problems have implications which transcend national borders and lend themselves to North-South cooperation. But such cooperation is unlikely to happen except in a larger context of partnership within which common North-South objectives have been identified over a wider front. Hard-pressed developing nations, in an increasingly neomercantilist world setting, are likely to continue to operate on short-run, highly nationalistic criteria, even if those criteria prove costly over the long term. And the long term can be upon us in very short periods of time, indeed, as the state of pollution in the Mediterranean and the situation in the Sahel demonstrate.

The time ahead is one where research and development, in particular as they relate to problems of resources and the environment, will rise in priority. In a sense, new technologies will have to substitute for the great open physical frontiers of the past. As suggested earlier, contributions to the world's stock of modern technology are likely to come increasingly from the latecomers to industrialization with the passage of time. To historians, the process is familiar. The initial round of modern technologies (textile machinery, the cotton gin, iron production using coke, the steam engine, the railroad, and steel) was generated by the first group of nations to enter take-off: Great Britain, the United States, Belgium, France, and Germany. In the twentieth century, those whose take-offs came between 1870 and 1900 (Sweden, Hungary, Japan, Russia–USSR, Italy, Spain, and Canada) made increasing contributions to the expanding global pool of technologies, for example, modern chemicals, the internal combustion engine, electricity, electronics. It is certain that the presently more advanced among the developing nations will extend that pattern. Nevertheless, for some considerable time the bulk of new technologies will be generated in and diffused from the North. The sense of dependence this situation generates—

even if transient by a historian's standards—is understandable. And so the issue of the transfer of technology has emerged as a major item on the North-South agenda.

There is, however, an aura of unreality about much of the discussion of this question. There are, of course, types of external assistance which can increase a developing nation's scientific and technological base, for example, through the education abroad of individuals, the strengthening of local educational institutions, the setting up of specialized research institutions. And there is legitimate scope of re-examining the potentialities for transferring technologies controlled by governments as well as in reviewing private patent arrangements for elements of monopoly and other inequities. But the central fact is that the bulk of new technologies have been absorbed in developing nations by the creation of industrial firms which incorporate them in their production. Local, foreign, or joint entrepreneurship capable of putting the technology to work efficiently in the production process has been the critical factor rather than the transfer of the technology itself. This has been true since, say, Francis Cabot Lowell in 1814 set up his mill in Massachusetts on the basis of pirated British technology. Some developing nations, like the United States in its early days, have generated cadres of domestic entrepreneurs capable of bringing into effective use new technologies drawn from abroad. In other cases, foreign firms and entrepreneurs are initially required. And there is a wide spectrum of local capacities and external needs in between, including the possibility of management contracts. Thus, for the flow of technology to be accelerated, what is required in many cases is a stable resolution within developing countries of the criteria for accepting foreign firms or managers and stable rules of the game for their profitable survival on terms economically and politically acceptable to host governments. This is extremely important, for example, if chemical fertilizer capacity is to be expanded rapidly in many developing countries which now lack management and technological skills on a requisite scale. One can explain psychologically and politically why this issue periodically becomes enflamed within developing countries; but one can explain equally why such reactive nationalism produces, in turn, grave responses in the parliaments, congresses, and board rooms of developed countries. These responses, in turn, limit the possibilities of generating political support for increased aid and liberalized trade.

By discouraging private investment from abroad, they also reduce the flow of new technology and the building of badly needed industrial capacity.

This is a tough and complex set of issues; but it is capable of rational resolution, as many existing bilateral arrangements demonstrate. No multilateral North-South partnership will be truly serious until it is faced and resolved. This judgment is not only a recognition that any partnership must be a two-way street; it is also rooted in the narrower circumstance that the most efficient arrangements for the progress of developing nations must be based on the realities of economic interdependence, including the absorptive capacity of developing nations with respect to new technologies.

IV

Before examining the practical negotiating implications of this argument, I turn to a barrier to successful North-South negotiations at least as serious as a faulty concept and agenda, that is, the chronic sluggishness of the OECD economies since 1974.

That sluggishness gravely inhibits the capacity of the North to respond to the possibilities of multilateral negotiations in four distinct respects.

—First, the legitimate claim of the South for enlarged export markets in the North is directly inhibited by the latter's average slow growth rates. The volume of southern exports and the prices of many of those exports are intimately tied to the rate of growth of the North.

—Second, this source of southern foreign exchange is further weakened by the emerging pattern of trade policy. The trend in the North is, in fact, regressive: toward protectionism of the old-fashioned kind, or "controlled trade"—a euphemism for "protectionism."

—Third, the failure of the OECD world to generate effective energy policies, which would bring under control and reduce their OPEC oil imports, reduces also the possibilities of generating a setting and a bargaining position capable of bringing OPEC and the energy problem in general within the orbit of North-South negotiations. As shall emerge, OPEC could play an important role in such negotiations as a whole.

—Fourth, the broad political consequences of chronic stagflation and unresolved energy problems reinforce the technical effects of the other forces at work. With acute and urgent domestic problems and strained national budgets, parliamentary bodies are likely to put a lower priority on external aid than on social outlays to cushion the domestic consequences of chronic stagflation. And stagflation is, evidently, a poor political setting in which to seek a liberalization of foreign trade.

Put another way, the first duty of the North to the South (as well as to its own citizens) is to overcome stagflation and resume growth rates similar to those of the 1950's and 1960's.

As I have argued at length elsewhere, this resumption of high growth rates cannot occur in the old pattern.[1] The leading sectors in the North in the 1950's and 1960's were the rapid diffusion of the private automobile and durable consumer goods; the migration to suburbia; and the disproportionate expansion of certain services (notably higher education, medical care, and travel). All have been decelerated by the rise in the relative price of energy and the consequent deceleration in the growth of real private income. In addition, some of these leading sectors were decelerating quite rapidly in the latter half of the 1960's for what one might call normal reasons, as they moved toward their natural limits. Trees do not grow to the sky; and the automobile industry in the North, for example, showed the signs of deceleration which had, in the past, been exhibited, after prior heroic periods of rapid expansion, by the cotton textile industry (the 1870's), the railroads (1890's), and so on. In short, a conventional neo-Keynesian stimulus to effective demand is most unlikely to bring us back to an approximation of regular full-employment growth rates of the kind enjoyed in the North over the past generations.

In my judgment, the leading sectors for the generation ahead, as in other periods of relatively high prices for basic commodities, are going to be in resource-related fields: energy, energy conservation, raw material expansion and conservation, water supply development and conservation, agriculture (notably in the developing continents), transportation, pollution control, and research and development over a wide front. To generate the requisite expansion in investment in these sectors will require considerable changes in public policy, both to create a setting in which private investment will expand appropriately and to generate, where the private sector cannot do the job, the necessary public investment funds.

If that assessment is roughly correct, an important conclusion bearing on North-South negotiations follows; that is, the concentration on resource problems in the North required to regenerate rapid economic growth would also lead to a clarification in the North of its serious international interests in resource development and conservation through an effective North-South partnership. Put another way, North-South negotiations are likely to appear a potentially costly and substantially irrelevant diversion in the OECD world so long as the governments are concentrated on trying to get back to full employment by manipulating the simple neo-Keynesian tools of monetary and fiscal policy in a frustrating and inherently losing game; but such negotiations will come closer to the center of northern concern when the North takes the measure of its resource problems and the potentially benign effects on employment and growth of dealing with them vigorously.

V

Now a few words about the power of the South to impose solutions on the North or otherwise to shape its destiny without cooperation from the North.

Although OPEC-type monopolies are not easy to reproduce, there have been a few efforts in this direction. The Caribbean producers of bauxite have managed through export taxes, accompanied by long-term agreements with foreign firms committed to operating in their territories, to achieve an impressive rise in prices; similar efforts have been canvassed or attempted in other fields, including coffee, phosphates, bananas, and copper. In addition, raw materials production has been nationalized in many developing countries. The cost to all parties of these trends is a sharp drop of foreign investment in the exploration and production of raw materials in, for example, Latin America. The Latin American nations do not yet command the capital, technology, and expertise to compensate fully for this decline. The upshot may be a concentration of raw material expansion in more hospitable areas with less productive deposits, yielding higher prices; for example, the U.S. government is already financing research and development in the production of aluminum from abundant clays in possible substitution for imported bauxite.

The exact benefit and cost, short run and long run, to the South in pursuing OPEC-type policies are difficult to calculate; and they would, of course, vary from commodity to commodity, country to country. What is clear is that the order of magnitude of net gains is likely to prove trivial as compared to the benefits of reasonably wholehearted North-South cooperation over a wide front embracing trade, aid, and the transfer of technology. And, of course, relatively few countries in the South command the leverage over raw material supply even to attempt to exercise an OPEC-type option.

It is also worth asking if the South is capable of generating sustained momentum on its own, without the cooperation of the North. After all, the South cannot guarantee that the North will hit upon the new economic concepts and policies and demonstrate the will to implement them required to overcome stagflation and reachieve the high sustained growth rates from which all parties could benefit. Here the answer appears to be that some developing nations have made rather impressive adjustments in the face of high energy prices and northern sluggishness. Some, of course, contain promising energy resources of their own, even if they are not substantial exporters. Others have exploited with vigor and imagination the potentialities of exporting goods and services to the rapidly expanding OPEC nations. Latin America, as a whole, might do reasonably well if its governments could, at last, overcome the political and other barriers which have for so long prevented it from achieving an effective common market. In general, this resilience has been exhibited most strongly by the more advanced among the developing nations, that is, those who have moved beyond the range of consumer goods industries, in substitution for imports, to chemicals, metal-working, and the simpler forms of electronics. And I would guess that, if the North continues to wallow along myopically with low growth rates and grossly inadequate energy policies, the South will find ways to continue somehow to move forward, even if at diminished rates of growth in real income per capita. The determination of the South to modernize its societies should not be underestimated.

But this would be a second-order solution at best and not available to a good many developing countries at early stages of development, for example, most of the African nations. Almost all the nations of the South face a generation when the strains of excessive population increase will be at their maximum. Most will be hit hard if the arrival of an OPEC production capacity ceiling in the 1980's causes a further rise in the real price of oil and an absolute shortage in relation to total global requirements for oil imports. Even the most advanced of the developing nations need, for another generation at least, a rich flow of technology from the North to make the adjustment to a new energy base and for many other purposes.

The right solution, therefore, is to try to overcome the impasse in North-South multilateral negotiations and achieve the partnership between the early- and late-comers to modern growth which a serious concern for the welfare of human beings everywhere would dictate.

VI

If the argument of this chapter is broadly valid, two things ought to happen concurrently.

First, a North-South conference ought to reconvene on a new basis, with radically altered structure, procedures, and personnel as compared to the ill-fated Conference on International Economic Cooperation. Its committee structure should be broken out by functional areas: a combined group working on population and agriculture; special groups on energy, raw materials, water supply, pollution control, research and development. Each committee should devote itself initially to receiving and absorbing expert opinion on the nature of the problems confronted over, say, the next quarter-century and the character of the policy options open to the world community. The fact is that a good deal of the expert staff work has already been done. For example, there is the report of a responsible group of international experts, *Energy: Global Prospects, 1985–2000*, directed by Professor Carroll Wilson of MIT. Similar studies are available in all the other fields except research and development as a whole, where the considerable body of existing material is fragmented by functional areas. Research and development should, evidently, be considered in each committee as it relates to that subject matter; but, in my view, a separate committee should take a hard look at the area as a whole.

The committees would find, of course, that many appropriate courses of action should be (and in some cases are being) taken on a national or regional basis. Their task, in the first instance, would be to seek agreement on certain specific global objectives in each field and to isolate the appropriate terrain for concerted international action.

With such targets defined, the committees could then proceed, in each field, to discuss, debate, and, if possible, resolve what each side, North and South, could and ought, in equity, to contribute to the global objective. They would find that the North-South dichotomy was by no means always the appropriate framework to define responsibilities; but, if progress had been made in setting common objectives, the necessary flexibility would no doubt emerge.

Above the functional groups a top-level committee should monitor the exercise as a whole; assess the pattern of policies that were emerging with respect to capital flows, trade, and technical assistance; look for equitable trade-offs; and isolate tough, intractable problems for special examination and negotiation. It would also have the responsibility to collect, as it were, the results from the functional committees and translate them into general policies on aid, trade, capital movements, and the transfer of technology.

More important, even, than a changed structure is the matter of different negotiating personnel. If North-South negotiations are to be serious, the men and women who bear responsibility in the relevant domestic ministries ought also to bear responsibility in multilateral negotiations. One reason that bilateral economic negotiations have been systematically more serious and productive than multilateral negotiations is that they are usually conducted between officials in ministries bearing day-to-day responsibility for one aspect or another of the domestic economy. Put another way, North-South multilateral negotiations have come to be conducted by specialized diplomats, learned in the peculiar ideology and procedures of such negotiations but substantially divorced from the serious business of running a country. Such negotiations are likely to succeed only when they are conducted by officials who bring to them the same practical sense they apply to domestic problems or bilateral negotiations.

In addition to a reorganized North-South negotiation, a second enterprise should concurrently be under way in the OECD. A special group should be summoned with a mandate to outline a policy which would break the OECD world definitively out of stagflation. OECD committees have operated over recent years in a cautious neo-Keynesian framework, implicitly assuming that their task was to tread a narrow line along some fictitious Phillips curve, balancing stimulus to demand against demand-pull inflation. Neither resource problems (notably energy policy) nor the problem of controlling wage-push inflation was seriously on their agenda. The best they could achieve were recommendations that the stronger economies pull the weaker economies toward higher growth by generating export-led expansions. This has not worked. Therefore, a new group of experts should now be asked to outline a strategy for sustained higher growth embracing energy and other resource problems (including the urgency of bringing down OECD oil imports from OPEC) and the problem of wage-push inflation, with all its sharp edges, complexities, and sensitivities.

As I argued earlier, nothing less than resumed high and stable OECD growth is likely, in the end, to make viable a North-South partnership. The view of resource requirements and policies under such circumstances should flow into the restructured work of the new North-South negotiating institution.

If all this should work, the international community would emerge with a concerted effort to deal with its major resource problems, in an environment of resumed high growth rates, with liberalized trade (a positive inflation-damping force under conditions of rapid growth), enlarged aid directly and indirectly linked to common resource problems, enlarged international flows of private capital, as well as enlarged public and private North to South flows of technology. Moreover, OPEC would be wholly within the international club, not an economic superpower wooed by the oil importers, North and South, but essentially making arbitrary monopolistic decisions.

VII

Now, finally, is this a utopian dream or is there, within it, a germ of political and diplomatic reality?

If one examines the present cast of mind and rhetoric of multilateral economic diplomacy, the vested interests and bureaucratic habits that have grown up around it, the domestic audiences to which it caters, one would have to conclude that the proposal is, indeed, unrealistic.

But five circumstances argue that it is worth articulating lucidly and making the case before the world.

—First, North-South multilateral negotiations are now stuck, and the political base in the North for serious assistance to the South is weak and fading.

—Second, many of the elements in the analysis I have laid out here are recognized de facto in the pragmatic network of bilateral economic relations which bind particular northern to particular southern countries. For example, some southern countries have found politically acceptable ways to receive private flows of capital and technical assistance and to develop their production and exports of raw materials needed in the North. There is, in short, a gap between the southern stance in multilateral as opposed to bilateral negotiations.

—Third, in their national policies, an increasing number of southern countries are already moving with some vigor in policies addressed to family planning and agricultural self-sufficiency. It should be easier than it was at Bucharest in 1974 to move toward international targets in the closely linked population-food area.

—Fourth, the OPEC nations, looking a bit further down the line, are beginning to perceive that they, too, face the task of creating a new energy base for the future if their hopes of building and sustaining sophisticated industrial structures are to be fulfilled; and this requires close cooperation with the industrial North. In fact, this perception is already evident in the bilateral relations of some OPEC members with the major industrial nations.

—Fifth, the state of the OECD economies as of 1979, their grim energy prospects, and their dismal performance over the past six years ought to produce a burst of fresh thought and policy, if the North has not lost its resilience and decided, in effect, to go down in the neo-Keynesian style to which it has become accustomed.

It is clearly possible that these forces will not triumph; that North-South multilateral negotiations will lapse or continue on a desultory sterile path; the erosion of northern support for southern aid and trade concessions could persist; the slide toward quasi-protectionism could continue; the OECD could more or less passively await the arrival of the OPEC production capacity ceiling in an environment of greater or lesser stagflation. In that case, we can expect very serious economic and political crises ahead. But it is barely possible that perceptions and courses of action now embedded in some bilateral and national policies could be elevated to a multilateral level and North-South negotiations endowed with a new thrust and vitality.

8

The Chapter That Keynes Never Wrote

All of us deeply regret that the meeting scheduled earlier could not take place because of a determined and well-organized minority. Nevertheless, what I was going to say to my fellow students in economics is now being recorded; and, as an old teacher, I am quite as happy with a small class as a big class.

I made notes today reflecting on my travels in Latin America and on the work that I've been doing in CIAP [Inter-American Committee on the Alliance for Progress]; and I decided to talk tonight about a problem which I believe is fundamental to the future of democracy and the future of economic development in almost every part of the world.

I

A title for what I have to say might be: "The Chapter That Keynes Never Wrote."

Briefly, the problem is this: The Keynesian revolution taught us all that unemployment is an act of man and not of God; that it is within our own powers to prevent the terrible discipline of depression, or recession, which was a means of keeping a certain order in growth during the nineteenth century. This was the period and the problem I first studied. But what Keynes did not teach us was how in a democracy you maintain full employment without inflation.

Note: Remarks made to nine Argentine students, Buenos Aires, Wednesday, February 24, 1965.

At the moment, in the postwar world, there is—and I believe there properly is—a feeling among our people that they will not accept severe depression any longer as a fact of political life. Out of this feeling arises the problem that confronts us all. It is not a problem of underdeveloped countries, nor a problem of Latin America alone. It is a problem for the United States and for all economically advanced democracies. It is: How do we maintain full employment without inflation and without the kind of stop-and-go policies that we have seen, for example, in England and in Argentina and in the United States of the 1950's?

II

One must first establish why it is that democratic political and economic procedures tend to yield inflationary pressures.

The answer arises from the fact that prices and wages are set in two separate operations in our society, neither of which conforms to classic competition as we all learned it in our textbooks. We have moved—and there are good reasons why we have moved—toward collective bargaining. In a collective bargaining arrangement between industry and labor, there are limits and disciplines on both sides. But those are the disciplines of the situation in that industry. If labor has good bargaining leverage and presses hard, and if the situation of industry is such that it feels that it cannot get a lower level of wages, it does two things: it accepts a wage increase which goes beyond the increase in productivity in that industry, and then, to protect its profits and its viability, it raises prices.

The second part of the process is, of course, in price-setting itself, independent of labor bargaining. In many countries industrial prices are not set on the simple model of competitive operations which we learn in our textbooks. You do not necessarily have pure monopolies; but you do have groups of industries setting prices on what we economists call oligopolistic terms, which means, simply, that each firm takes into account the effect of its own actions on the market.

Moreover, in an inflationary situation, where people have come to expect prices to rise and wages to rise, business then proceeds to anticipate these rises; and by its anticipating them, prices in fact do rise. This forces up the cost of living. Thus, the case for an increase in wages in the next round of negotiation is very strong.

The banking system, faced with this kind of collective bargaining, where there is no relation between wages and productivity, and faced with price-setting which may anticipate inflation, has the choice either of checking the process at the cost of unemployment and slowing down the rate of growth or of simply validating the process and permitting growth and inflation.

The problem as I've roughly defined it, as I say, is not a problem for Argentina alone or for Latin America alone. It's a problem in the United States. It's a problem now—in Western Europe.

III

Before I discuss how one deals with this problem in more specific terms, I might say briefly what the answer is that we have begun to find in some countries—and that I think we must find in the second half of this century in all countries if democratic methods are to prove viable. The answer is to make, in effect, a kind of social compact in the society, in which the setting of wages is disciplined in terms of productivity, protecting the real wages of labor and permitting labor to share in productivity increases but keeping wages from going beyond that norm; a compact in which prices are set in terms of the real cost situation and do not seek to anticipate inflation and thereby set in motion a circular process. (I may say that in many countries where I have observed the process of inflation I have the feeling that a large part of the process resembles a dog chasing its tail.)

IV

That was precisely the problem President Kennedy faced when he came to responsibility in Washington in January of 1961.

In the latter years of the 1950's, although it is not generally understood abroad, we in the United States had our own version of what we can see quite often in Latin America, namely, unemployment and rising prices.

President Kennedy understood that, unless he could solve this problem, his two most important objectives and responsibilities were endangered.

Our rising prices were weakening our balance of payments position. That meant, in turn, that our ability to maintain military forces and to meet our commitments around the world might be endangered. There was the danger of our being forced by balance of payments pressures to retract from our commitments and responsibilities on the world scene.

And there was a second danger. If we tried to meet those international commitments under this kind of inflationary pressure, we would have to forego doing in the United States those things President Kennedy had set his heart on doing. We would have had to maintain such high interest rates and monetary restraints that we would continue to have severe unemployment and a low rate of growth. It would have been impossible to get from the Congress, under those circumstances, the resources we wanted for urban reconstruction, for education, and for those other domestic objectives of both President Kennedy and President Johnson.

Certain key industrial leaders were brought together with labor leaders and with representatives of the consumer and agriculture. Out of those White House talks emerged what we call wage guidelines, which is, simply, that we try to keep the average money wage increase in the United States at a level no higher than the average increase in our productivity.

This means, of course, that industry also had to avoid price increases. It could not try to take advantage of this new wage discipline. It had to follow price policies that fitted these guidelines.

This acceptance of wage guidelines without formal legislation was a tour de force, an act of extraordinary leadership in our society. And, in the end, after some rather famous difficulties with the steel industry, wage and price guidelines have come to be built into our country's economy. But it will take endless vigilance and self-discipline on all sides to maintain them. But that is always the way with a democracy.

Of course, we in the United States are not the only ones to face this problem. Italy, in the great adjustment after 1962 when at last there was no longer a surplus of labor from the south, has had to face exactly this problem; Britain now faces it; France faces it; Germany in time will face it. The Netherlands and Scandinavia for some time have conducted interesting experiments in this kind of basic social compact which permits the reconciliation in a democratic society of the imperatives of both full employment and relatively stable prices.

V

In Latin America the problem is, perhaps, more difficult than it has been for the United States and Western Europe. Latin America is, as I have said on other occasions, at the end of its first generation of sustained industrialization. That process has brought new people into the cities from the countryside. It has brought a shift of political, social, and economic power from the countryside to the cities. These events in the first generation—this coming in to a new circumstance, the beginnings of modern industrial life—have led the people in the cities to push hard for their advantage, since they did not have many advantages in the earlier historical situation.

At the same time, for technical reasons, industry has been governed by monopolistic pricing. The technical reasons are two. First, private industry has worked behind high tariff barriers with small markets. This meant almost inevitably in the early stage, when there weren't many firms, that they found themselves in a monopolistic situation. Then, of course, the governments took over and operated a certain number of industries which were inherently monopolistic; and that was one of the reasons why they felt nationalization might be socially necessary and justified.

But the problem is that there is a resultant tendency—a systematic tendency—to move toward inflation. And inflation endangers the whole future modernization of Latin America.

In the first generation inflation was, in a sense, bearable, not because it helped Latin American development but because it was not inconsistent with a boom based on import substitution. The fact that you could have an import substitution boom under inflationary conditions led some to believe that inflation was some kind of special device which avoided the normal disciplines of economics and politics and social organization. But the experience of Latin America in recent years—in Uruguay, the experience goes back almost a decade—the experience of a combination of inflation and stagnation, and sometimes inflation and severe unemployment—has led to a profound rethinking of this problem in Latin America.

VI

We in CIAP have taken this matter seriously. CIAP is, as you know, a group which consists of a chairman, who is Carlos Sanz de Santamaría of Colombia, and seven other members, all of whom are Latin American except myself. We have all agreed that we must try, within our possibilities, to help the nations of Latin America reconcile stability with development. Our report in October [1964], which went to the ministers' meeting at Lima, has a long section on inflation. It represented the most serious and systematic thought that all of us, representing very different experiences, could bring to bear on the problem of Latin American inflation.

We began by listing the damage that inflation does. Inflation distorts the direction of investment; it sets up exchange rates which tend to lag behind their real level and make exports difficult; it tends to make men seek in business not to maximize their output at lowest prices but to find that type of output and that price level which are the best hedges against inflation. It creates an atmosphere among devoted laborers, with great skills and a desire to do something for their country, in which they lose the sense of the relationship between productivity and their income; and they, too, struggle, like businessmen, to hedge against inflation.

The last of the eight points we made is, I think, the most profound and serious. It is the one that I wish to talk about now.

The last point we made was that inflation sets every element in the society against the other. It prevents that coming together of people around a national objective and a national program which is essential for the serious modernization of the whole society. This is not a question of one group's being more wicked than the other. When you live in an inflationary environment, and you are uncertain about the possibilities of stabilization, you are driven inevitably to take out the best insurance policy you can for yourself, your family, your group. The fact that this effort to take out insurance policies leads and forces further inflation is a fact that each individual and group, operating alone, is in no position to take into account. In the CIAP report, which you can all get from the OAS (Report No. CIAP-170), we then set out a three-point program to bring inflation to a halt. I summarized it at a press conference today; it's available to you, and I'll just list the headings and we can go on.

VII

The first heading is, of course, that you must cut the government deficits and bring the budgets into balance. Deficits are a direct inflationary impulse; but, beyond that, when the government does not move toward balance, the confidence that inflation can be controlled is lost in the society. Men assume inflation and, by assuming it, bring it about.

So you have two effects: a direct monetary effect of the deficit and what you might call a confidence effect.

To end these deficits means getting greater efficiency in the government-owned corporations, the *autarquías*, the railroads, and so on. And it means more people must pay their taxes. There is no way for a truly modern society to develop if men don't pay their taxes.

It also means thinking about rates which really represent the cost of the service provided by a government corporation.

The second category is less familiar (and we in CIAP have been crusading for it because we think there are so many unfamiliar, unexploited possibilities): it is to attack the cost of living from the supply side by improving the marketing arrangements between the countryside and the city. You know in Latin America—perhaps not so much in your country, but generally in Latin America—the farmer often gets only 15 percent of the price of food in the city, due to the existence of five or six intermediaries.

This means that food prices are high, but what the farmer gets is low. We must try to help governments and private organizations cut this margin. A reduction in this margin could play an important role in damping down inflation.

On the industrial side there are possibilities of getting industrialists to begin to produce with a mass-market mentality rather than a small-market mentality; that is to say, they must seek to accept small profit margins and seek big turnovers.

I remember saying this to a group of businessmen in Venezuela. This was a good group who had put out a proclamation in support of the Alliance for Progress. I told them that I was pleased to see their support for the social objectives of the Alliance: health, housing, education, and so on. But I felt that as businessmen they had an additional and distinct obligation. Their obligation as businessmen is to stop regarding the poor folk in their country as a social problem and begin to look at them as potential customers, and to end the game of big mark-ups and low turnovers and begin to become modern businessmen who play for small profit margins and high turnover.

Now for the third part of the CIAP program. In addition to the attack on the deficit from as many directions as is necessary; in addition to the government's setting a good example of efficiency in its operations, in the government corporations and elsewhere; in addition to the attack on the cost of living from the supply side, a social compact must be sought.

VIII

Now what is the substance of this compact? For each country it may be difficult to negotiate, but its essence is quite simple.

Labor must be given confidence that its real wage will be protected and that it will get a fair share of the increases in productivity. Now labor struggles in an environment of inflation to get a wage increase beyond the last increase in the cost of living. But I don't think there is any member of a working-class family who, in his heart, doesn't know that further inflation will take that away and that the trend of his real wage will decline. There is no group in the population of a country which has a greater stake in price stability than the working class. The systematic history of inflation is that the working class is least able to defend itself in an inflationary environment.

In return for a firm link between wages and cost of living changes, labor must accept the fact—which every serious working man knows—that what he will get in real terms over a period of time depends on how much work he does; that is, he must also accept a link between productivity and wages. I myself was brought up close to working people. I worked in my father's small factory. I have never believed that working men were too ignorant to know their own interest and to know it with great wisdom. I believe that, if this contract could be put to them in a way in which they had confidence, they would accept it.

Now on the side of industry. Industry must be given confidence that the level of wages will not rise beyond productivity increases. It must also develop confidence that the wage guidelines will be held and that it will be able to operate in a stable environment. In return, industry must, of course, pay its taxes, which is necessary as part of monetary stabilization; and it must follow price policies that do not anticipate increases in wages: industry must forego inflationary price policies. Industry must also play its part in the attack on the cost of living from the supply side. And this goes not only for men of industry but also for men of commerce.

Then, finally, there is the question of government. In all this, government must, of course, lead the way. It must, where it is involved in negotiations with labor, show that the line linking wages to increases of productivity will be held. The government must be resolute in collecting taxes. And, as I said earlier, it must, above all, set an example of efficiency where it has production responsibilities and in government expenditures so as to demonstrate at the heart of national life that the objective of the economy is to use resources efficiently.

The most basic definition of economics remains, I think, still the best: it is the art of allocating scarce resources with alternative uses, in the light of individual and communal objectives. All of our countries, no matter how rich, are dealing with the problem of scarce resources. If these resources are not expanded the society cannot really benefit. And no group really can benefit for long, even though it may think, in the short run, that it has a pretty good deal. There is no substitute for increased productivity in economic development.

IX

Now I know very well that it is not easy for political parties in the United States and in Western Europe to make this kind of social compact. Our political parties have tended to build up, between the opposition and the government, a dialogue sometimes based on ideological slogans and concepts out of the past. It is hard in the United States and Western Europe to get the degree of consensus that is required, in the face of outmoded political concepts and commitments.

What is the consensus we seek? It says, "Yes, we shall have competitive political parties, we shall debate, we shall argue; but we shall argue within an agreed framework in the society which permits us to reconcile stability and full employment."

In Latin America the development of this great continent with enormous potentials and a great destiny on the world-scene hinges on finding an answer to that question. And the Latin American political parties, of course, like our own, have their roots in old quarrels and old debates that go back, some of them, to the French Revolution and to ancient local quarrels. (For example, I was well educated today at lunch about the jockeying between Buenos Aires and La Plata.) Every country has a basis for its party structure in the issues of the past—in its own country and elsewhere. But the modern problem, the problem of developing a foundation in a society which will reconcile stabilization and growth, is the problem of finding a consensus on these critical issues and having politics go forward within that frame.

People often ask what the relationship is between stabilization and development. We have tended to put the two parts of our work in economics in separate chapters. The monetary experts generally talk about the money supply, exchange rates, and prices; while the others talk about investment, capital output ratios, and GNP. That split in economics was never sound. But now it leads us in the wrong direction; for when one goes deeper into the problem either of development or of inflation, he finds that both stabilization and development hinge on the same kind of compact in a society. On the stabilization side it is a compact of the kind I described, in which each one is given an incentive to do the thing he knows to be in his long-run interest and to forego the thing he is tempted to do in his short-run interest. And he can only do that if each element in the society plays its part. But equally, as I was saying today at the press conference, development also requires a deep social compact. Economists have a proud role to play in economic development. But I would say about economists and development what Clemenceau said about generals. He said that war was too serious a matter for generals; just so, economic development is too serious a matter for economists—at least, for economists alone.

In the end, a development plan has to be an agreed vision of where a country wishes to be in five or ten years. It must be understood by each sector and each region of the country; it must be debated by each sector and region until each part of the society comes to an understanding and an acceptance of where its own part fits in the total scheme; and then the society can go forward.

We can see in many Latin American countries the beginning of an important effort to take the national development plans out of politics. I don't know enough about Argentina to say whether this is possible or wise. Every nation's politics is uniquely its own. An outsider should not try to be too wise about it. But I also know that the struggle is going forward in many nations to do just that —that is, take the development plan out of economics and out of conventional politics and put it into the nation. This requires also a consensus and a social compact.

And this is right, because we economists are and should be rather humble people.

I quoted today the medieval story of "Le Jongleur de Notre Dame." We're jugglers. But we're juggling for a great purpose. That purpose is to generate the material resources, the social institutions, which will provide a better life for the men and women and children of the countries with which we work.

All of us who work in the Alliance for Progress are conscious that whether we are playing with statistics or arguing capital-output ratios, or doing other technical things, this is really what the game is about.

I began by saying that these were rough notes for a chapter that Keynes never wrote. But I should like to end by reminding you of the statement Keynes made in his toast to the Royal Economic Society in 1945. What I have tried to say to you tonight is in the spirit of that toast.

Keynes said: "To economics and economists who are the trustees, not of civilization, but of the possibility of civilization."

Thank you very much for coming.

Notes

PREFACE

1. The phrases here, enclosed in single quotation marks, are drawn from Ilya Prigogine, "Order Out of Chaos," a public lecture delivered at the University of Texas at Austin, November 18, 1977, on the occasion of the announcement of his Nobel Prize award.

CHAPTER 1. *The Long Cycle*

1. N. D. Kondratieff, "The Long Waves in Economic Life," *Review of Economic Statistics* 17, no. 6 (November 1935): 105–114. See, also, George Garvy, "Kondratieff's Theory of Long Cycles," *Review of Economic Statistics* 25, no. 4 (November 1943): 203–220; and the discussion of Kondratieff's views in Simon Kuznets, *Secular Movements in Production and Prices* (Boston and New York: Houghton Mifflin Company, 1930), pp. 263–265. Kondratieff published his views in three versions between 1922 and 1928. His concept of capitalist economies oscillating around a long-run dynamic-equilibrium position came to be regarded, in Stalin's time, as anti-Marxist heresy. In 1930 he was sent to a Siberian prison camp where, according to Solzhenitsyn's *Gulag Archipelago*, he died.
2. Kondratieff, "The Long Waves in Economic Life," pp. 112–115.
3. Schumpeter evidently knew and was respectful of Kuznets' *Secular Movements in Production and Prices* and A. F. Burns' *Production Trends in the United States since 1870* (New York: National Bureau of Economic Research, 1934). Significant work on sectoral patterns was also done in the 1930's by Walther Hoffmann, *Stadien und Typen der Industrialisierung* (Kiel: Institut fur Weltwirtschaft, 1931).
4. Kuznets, *Secular Movements*, p. 329.
5. Ibid., pp. 4–5.

6. Ibid., pp. 206–259.
7. Ibid., p. 258.
8. Simon Kuznets, *National Product since 1869* (New York: National Bureau of Economic Research, 1946), especially pp. 87–90; "*Quantitative Aspects of the Economic Growth of Nations*," I: "Levels and Variability of Rates of Growth," *Economic Development and Cultural Change* 5, no. 1 (October 1956): 44–51; and "Long Swings in the Growth of Population and in Related Economic Variables," *Proceedings of the American Philosophical Society* 102, no. 1 (1958): 25–52. Between Kuznets' *Secular Movements* and his *National Product since 1869*, Arthur F. Burns (1954) had moved the analysis of trend cycles in growth in the United States from a sectoral to an aggregate basis (see, especially, Chapter 6 in his *Production Trends in the United States since 1870*).
9. Brinley Thomas, *Migration and Economic Growth* (Cambridge: At the University Press, 1954; 2d ed., 1973), especially pp. 102–113; A. K. Cairncross, *Home and Foreign Investment, 1870–1913* (Cambridge: At the University Press, 1953), especially pp. 187–221. It should be noted that, still earlier, Walter Isard and Norman J. Silberling had demonstrated an association between migration and construction in the United States, as well as with transport cycles (Walter Isard, "A Neglected Cycle: The Transport-Building Cycle," *Review of Economic Statistics*, November 1942, pp. 149–158; Norman J. Silberling, *The Dynamics of Business* [New York and London: McGraw-Hill, 1943], especially pp. 175–238).
10. For a rather full listing of the Kuznets cycle literature, see the bibliography in Richard A. Easterlin, "Economic-Demographic Interactions and Long Swings in Economic Growth," *American Economic Review* 16, no. 5 (December 1966): 1100–1104.
11. Kuznets, "Long Swings," p. 33.
12. Ibid., p. 36. In his various expositions of the Kuznets long cycle, Moses Abramovitz has sometimes listed price movements as related to them; but he did not establish a firm and lucid linkage. See, for example, Abramovitz' colloquy on this subject before the Joint Economic Committee, *Employment, Growth, and Price Levels*, 86th Congress, 1st Session, Part II (Washington, D.C.: GPO, 1959), pp. 458–459.
13. In addition to Abramovitz' 1959 statement before the Joint Economic Committee, see his "The Nature and Significance of Kuznets Cycles," *Economic Development and Cultural Change* 9, no. 3 (April 1961): 225–248; and "The Passing of the Kuznets Cycle," *Economica*, November 1968, pp. 349–367.
14. Allan C. Kelley's widest ranging paper in this field is "Demographic Cycles and Economic Growth: The Long Swing Reconsidered," *Journal of Economic History* 29, no. 4 (December 1969): 633–656.
15. Richard A. Easterlin, *Population, Labor Force, and Long Swings in Economic Growth* (New York: National Bureau of Economic Research [distributed by Columbia University Press], 1968). Easterlin has carried forward his analysis of the links between U.S. demo-

graphic patterns and the course of economic growth in "Demographic Influences on Economic Stability: The United States Experience," *Population and Development Review* 4, no. 1 (March
1978): 1–22, a paper written jointly with Michael L. Wachter and
Susan M. Wachter.

16. Arthur I. Bloomfield, *Patterns of Fluctuation in International Investment before 1914*, Princeton Studies in International Finance, no.
21 (Princeton: Princeton University Press, 1968), p. 5. Conversely,
P. J. O'Leary and W. Arthur Lewis conclude that British capital
movements were perverse—motivated merely by dissatisfaction
with low rates of return in domestic capital markets and supplying
excessive capital to agricultural regions at a time when their export
prices were falling, in the period 1883–1896 ("Secular Swings in
Production in Trade, 1870–1913," *Manchester School* 23 [May
1955]: 145–146). This judgment is based, I believe, on an insufficient view of the motives for pre-1896 capital exports. The opening
of highly fertile areas could be profitable even in a general environment of falling prices, notably at a time of rapidly falling transport
costs. But, on the face of it, the build-up of Argentine, Canadian,
and Australian infrastructure in the 1880's was a fortunate preparation for the period of rising prices and production that followed,
roughly, 1896. Nevertheless, the O'Leary-Lewis analysis must be accounted a major effort to take into account price and international
capital movements in assessing long cycles. The problem of explaining increased capital exports to peripheral agricultural areas at
times of declining price trends continued to trouble Lewis (*Growth
and Fluctuations, 1870–1913* [London: George Allen and Unwin,
1978], pp. 180–181). There were more solid grounds for London's
investing in Australia and Argentina of the 1880's than "the band-
wagon effect . . . Foreign lending was in the air" that Lewis adduces.
See, for example, W. W. Rostow, *The World Economy: History and
Prospect* (Austin: University of Texas Press, 1978), pp. 185–193.

17. Jeffrey G. Williamson, *American Growth and the Balance of Payments,
1820–1913* (Chapel Hill: University of North Carolina Press, 1964);
A. G. Ford, "British Investment in Argentina and Long Swings,
1880–1914," *Journal of Economic History* 31, no. 3 (September
1971): 650–663.

18. Bloomfield, *Patterns of Fluctuation*, p. 5.

19. The lag of capital imports behind series reflecting domestic expansion
can be traced out in the economic history of particular foodstuff
and raw-material-producing regions, but it is caught statistically in
general terms by Bloomfield, ibid., p. 34.

20. E. H. Phelps Brown with Sheila V. Hopkins, "The Course of Wage-
Rates in Five Countries, 1860–1939," *Oxford Economic Papers* 4,
no. 3 (October 1952): 226–296; E. H. Phelps Brown and B. Weber,
"Accumulation, Productivity, and Distribution in the British Economy, 1870–1938," *Economic Journal* 63, no. 250 (June 1953): 263–
288; Bernard Weber and S. J. Handfield-Jones, "Variations in the
Rate of Economic Growth in the U.S.A., 1869–1939," *Oxford Eco-*

nomic Papers 6, no. 2 (June 1954): 101–131. For earlier specu-
lation on retardation in older sectors, compensated (to an un-
measurable extent) by rapid growth in sectors incorporating new
technology, see Burns, *Production Trends,* especially pp. 276–281.
Also G. T. Jones, *Increasing Return* (Cambridge: At the University
Press, 1933).

21. The first of these quotations is from Abramovitz, "The Nature and
Significance of Kuznets Cycles," p. 226; the second is from his "The
Passing of the Kuznets Cycle," p. 351. On this point, see also O'Leary
and Lewis, "Secular Swings in Production in Trade," pp. 116–118:
"One may be tempted to deny that there is fundamentally a Kuznets
cycle, and may prefer to say that all that happens is that once every
twenty years one of the Juglar depressions gets out of hand, and
lasts for 6 to 8 years, instead of lasting for 1 and 2 years only." This
point relates to Arthur F. Burns' emphasis on the "sharp divergence
of production trends" and "the strain and loss of industrial balance"
during the upward phase of a trend-cycle movement, yielding a
protracted downward phase of a re-adjustment and recovery of
balance (*Production Trends,* pp. 248–249). It is also connected to
Kuznets' finding, cited above, that the amplitude of secondary cycles
is associated positively with the momentum of a sector, as measured by its primary trend. Lewis develops his view at length in
Growth and Fluctuations, 1870–1913, chap. 2, in which Kuznets
cycles emerge as super-Juglar booms and slumps.

22. Burns, *Production Trends,* p. 248.

23. Thomas, *Migration and Economic Growth,* p. 249.

24. Simon Kuznets, "Long Swings," p. 33. This proposition does not, of
course, exclude capital imports or the typical rise in the investment
proportion during the early phase of modern growth.

25. James B. Shuman and David Rosenau, *The Kondratieff Wave* (New
York: Delta Publishing Company, 1972), p. 99.

26. Ernest Mandel, *Late Capitalism,* tran. Joris De Bres (London: NLB
[Verso edition], 1978). My review of *Late Capitalism* is to be found
in the *Journal of Economic History* 40, no. 2 (September 1979).

27. Nathaniel J. Mass and Jay W. Forrester, *Understanding the Changing
Basis for Economic Growth,* prepared for the Joint Economic Committee, U.S. Congress (Washington, D.C.: GPO, August 9, 1976),
p. 17.

28. Ibid., pp. 20–21.

29. Joseph Schumpeter, *Business Cycles* (New York: McGraw-Hill, 1939),
vol. II, especially pp. 1032–1050.

30. Ibid., p. 1050.

31. W. W. Rostow, *Getting from Here to There* (New York: McGraw-Hill,
1978; London: Macmillan, 1979), p. 168.

32. Charles P. Kindleberger, "The Aging Economy," *Weltwirtschaftliches
Archiv* 114, no. 3 (1978): 407–421.

33. W. W. Rostow, *The Process of Economic Growth* (Oxford: Clarendon
Press, 1953, 1960), pp. 107–108.

CHAPTER 2. *A Simple Model of the Kondratieff Cycle*

1. Edward A. Hudson and Dale W. Jorgenson, "U.S. Energy Policy and Economic Growth, 1975–2000," *Bell Journal of Economics and Management Science* 5, no. 2 (Autumn 1974): 461–514. See, also, Alan S. Manne, "ETA: A Model for Energy Technology Assessment," ibid., 7, no. 2 (Autumn 1976): 379–406; and Michael Kennedy and E. Victor Niemeyer, *Energy Supply and Economic Growth*, Discussion Paper, no. 4-76 (Austin: Department of Economics, University of Texas at Austin, n.d.) For an effort to establish the routes and order of impact on oil-importing countries of the rise in oil prices of 1973–1974, employing various short-term U.S., West European, and Japanese econometric models, see, notably, Edward R. Fried and Charles L. Schultze (eds.), *Higher Oil Prices and the World Economy* (Washington, D.C.: Brookings Institution, 1975). See, also, Charles J. Hitch (ed.), *Modeling Energy-economy Interactions: Five Approaches* (Washington, D.C.: Resources for the Future, September 1977); and Energy Modeling Forum, *Energy and the Economy*, vol. I (Palo Alto, September 1977). Chapter 3 contains further observations on some of the energy-economy models developed in the 1970's.

2. The price revolution which began at the end of 1972 stirred up a fresh theoretical effort on a different aspect of the basic materials problem from that dealt with here, that is, the optimum rate of depletion of exhaustible resources. See, for example, Robert M. Solow, "Intergenerational Equity and Exhaustible Resources," in *Symposium on the Economics of Exhaustible Resources*, special issue of *Review of Economic Studies*, 1974, pp. 29–45.

3. John H. Williams, "The Theory of International Trade Reconsidered," *Economic Journal* 154, no. 39 (June 1929): 196. Although not in revolt, a distinguished modern builder of growth models concludes with a similar point: "It should be quite obvious to any careful reader of this book that our analysis so far is based on a very large number of assumptions, some of which can be justified only on the grounds of their analytic tractability . . . further work may require some radical reconsideration of the premises underlying the present type of inquiry" (Sukhamoy Chakravarty, *Capital and Development Planning* [Cambridge, Mass.: M.I.T. Press, 1969], p. 246).

4. Paul A. Samuelson, "Prices of Factors and Goods in General Equilibrium," *Review of Economic Studies* 21, no. 54 (February 1954): 1–20.

5. Hirofumi Uzawa, "On a Two-Sector Model of Economic Growth," *Review of Economic Studies* 29, no. 78 (October 1961): 40–47.

6. R. W. Shephard, *A Theory of Cost and Productions Functions* (Princeton: Princeton University Press, 1970).

7. Kuznets, "Long Swings," pp. 25–52.

8. It is somewhat surprising that real GNP in the K case actually overtakes the BG path. This results from the interplay of relative price

changes, investment demand, and saving behavior. Our saving assumption, equation (11), which was nominal saving as a fixed-expenditure share-saving function, then implies higher physical quantities purchased. Since physical saving must equal physical investment in a full-employment model, the cost of capital falls until the additional *I* goods are purchased by firms. Thus, total capital accumulation in the K case slightly exceeds that in the BG case, and terminal period GNP is slightly (about 2%) higher in the K case.

Professor William H. Hogan pointed out this phenomenon to us and suggested instead either a fixed real share savings function or saving behavior which adjusts so as to maintain a constant real rate of return on capital. Either of these changes in assumptions would slightly decrease GNP in the final periods. However, the main results of the model, namely the cyclicality present due to changes in N availability, would be unaffected by any reasonable modifications of the saving function.

9. A seeming anomaly in the W case is the relatively high growth rate of real GNP in the second half of the cycle, leading to a higher compound rate than in the S2 case. This is due to the extremely high level of the relative price of basic to industrial goods in the first years of the W case, along with the fixed-value share-saving function, as explained in note 8, above. Thus, there is a very large accumulation of capital in the early part of the period, which pays off in GNP terms later on. In fact, of course, a great deal of savings and industrial production is drained off for war purposes. Savings available for productive purposes are reduced. Since our model does not provide for a war production sector, this piece of reality is not captured here.

10. Abba P. Lerner uses implicitly a model much like that presented here in "Stagflation," *Intermountain Economic Review* 6, no. 2 (Fall 1975): 1–7. For a comment on its inadequacies, see W. W. Rostow, "The Bankruptcy of Neo-Keynesian Economics," *Intermountain Economic Review* 7, no. 1 (Spring 1976): 1–12.

11. Hudson and Jorgenson, "U.S. Energy Policy and Economic Growth," pp. 461–514. See, also, D. B. Humphrey and J. R. Moroney, "Substitution among Capital, Labor, and Natural Resource Products in American Manufacturing," *Journal of Political Economy* 83 (February 1975): 57–82.

12. J. H. Clapham, *The Economic Development of France and Germany, 1815–1914* (Cambridge: At the University Press, 1928), p. 158.

13. Benedetto Croce, *Historical Materialism and the Economics of Karl Marx*, tran. C. M. Meredith (New York: Russell and Russell, 1966), pp. 3–4.

CHAPTER 3. *Energy, Full Employment, and Regional Development*

1. Executive Office of the President, Energy Policy and Planning, *The National Energy Plan* [NEP] (Washington, D.C.: GPO, April 29, 1977),

pp. 97–98. This theme was reiterated in the *Economic Report of the President to the Congress* (Washington, D.C.: GPO, January 1978), p. 194.

2. NEP, p. 97.

3. See, for example, Hitch (ed.), *Modeling Energy-Economy Interactions*, especially pp. iii–iv (Hitch), and Lester B. Lave's summation, pp. 278–300. Also, Energy Modeling Forum, Institute for Energy Studies, Report 1, vol. 1, *Energy and the Economy* (Stanford, September 1977). For a lucid nonmathematical exposition of an energy-economy model, see Spurgeon M. Keeny, Jr. (Chairman), *Nuclear Power Issues and Choices*, Report of the Nuclear Energy Policy Study Group (Cambridge, Mass.: Ballinger Publishing Company, 1977), chap. 1, "Energy and the Economic Future," pp. 41–70. To a degree, the Energy Supply Planning Model developed by Bechtel National, Inc., is exempt from these criticisms. It traces back the investment requirements (including types of hardware and labor) of various energy targets and specifies their regional implications. It also embraces realistic time lags.

4. W. W. Rostow, W. L. Fisher, and H. H. Woodson, *National Energy Policy: An Interim Overview* (Austin: Council on Energy Resources, University of Texas at Austin, September 12, 1977), pp. 8–12.

5. The estimates are those of Sidney Pollard, reprinted in François Crouzet (ed.), *Capital Formation in the Industrial Revolution* (London: Methuen, 1972), p. 33. See, also, Phyllis Deane, "Capital Formation in Britain before the Railway Age," reprinted in ibid., pp. 101–103, on agricultural investment.

6. Arthur Hope-Jones, *Income Tax in the Napoleonic Wars* (Cambridge: At the University Press, 1939), chap. 6, "The Yield on the War Income Tax," pp. 72–110.

7. Ibid., p. 103.

8. Douglass C. North, *The Economic Growth of the United States, 1790–1860* (Englewood Cliffs, N.J.: Prentice-Hall, 1961), p. 244, charted on p. 93. It should be noted that the United States enjoyed an almost OPEC-like burst of prosperity in the 1790's when wartime price movements and transient status as an unchallenged neutral permitted the United States to exploit a doubling of its terms of trade from 1793 to 1799. See also Jeffrey G. Williamson, *American Growth and Balance of Payments, 1820–1913* (Chapel Hill: University of North Carolina Press, 1964).

9. North, *Economic Growth*, pp. 244, 257 (southern land sales), and 259 (western land sales).

10. Alvin Hansen, "Factors Affecting the Trend in Real Wages," *American Economic Review* 15 (March 1925): 32.

11. See, for example, Cairncross, "Investment in Canada, 1900–1913," chap. 3 in *Home and Foreign Investment*, pp. 37–64. See, also, Rostow, *The World Economy*, pp. 171–172 and 449–450, where other sources are indicated.

12. In fact, the convergence between rapid industrialization and a boom centered on relatively high agricultural prices (favorable terms of

trade, large capital imports, and immigration) occurred in the United States of the 1850's as well as during the pre-1914 generation in Russia (excepting immigration), Australia, and the São Paulo region of Brazil. See, for example, Rostow, *The World Economy*, pp. 427–430, 462–463, and 483–486.

13. C. H. Feinstein, *Statistical Tables of National Income, Expenditure and Output of the U.K., 1855–1965* (Cambridge: At the University Press, 1976), pp. T48 (domestic investment) and T38 (foreign investment).

14. See Rostow, *The World Economy*, pp. 174–194.

15. For a more detailed analysis, see W. W. Rostow, "A National Policy towards Regional Change," *New England Economic Indicators* (Federal Reserve Bank of Boston), May 1977, pp. 5–11. Also, see chap. 10 ("Regional Change: Conflict or Reconciliation") in Rostow, *Getting from Here to There*.

16. The paper *Energy and the Economy* of the Energy Modeling Forum, p. iv, is admirably explicit about the limitations of the conventional models.

17. Remarks prepared for delivery at the twenty-fifth anniversary meeting of the Council for Financial Aid to Education, New York City (news release, Department of Defense), p. 3.

18. Rostow, *The Process of Economic Growth*, p. 90.

19. For a detailed analysis in these terms, see Rostow, *The World Economy*, pp. 247–286.

20. See Hajo Hasenpflug and Mathias Lefeldt, "Structural Changes in World Trade since the Oil Crisis," *Intereconomics* (Hamburg), July–August 1977, pp. 187–191. A shift of this order of magnitude only occurred twice before in modern economic history: to Great Britain during the French Revolutionary and Napoleonic Wars when it dominated overseas trade; and to the United States between the years immediately before the Second World War and those immediately afterward.

21. Federal Energy Administration [FEA], *National Energy Outlook* (Washington, D.C.: GPO, 1976), pp. 43–44 and 293–323. See, also, the array of estimates presented in J. Michael Gallagher and Ralph G. J. Zimmermann, *Capital, Manpower, Materials, and Equipment Requirements for a Department of Commerce Projection* (San Francisco: Bechtel Corporation, December 1976), pp. 3–7.

22. Since the Kozmetsky-Konecci calculations are estimates for the whole period 1977–1985, they lend themselves only to average investment rates. The proportions in the text are, therefore, not comparable to those in Table 3-5 for the years 1977 and 1985.

23. Barry Bosworth, James S. Duesenberry, and Andrew S. Carron, *Capital Needs in the Seventies* (Washington, D.C.: Brookings Institution, 1975).

24. The best analyses of regional shifts combining income, population, and structural change are those of William H. Miernyk, for example, "Regional Shifts in Economic Base and Structure in the United States since 1940," paper prepared for the Conference on a National

Policy towards Regional Change: Alternatives to Confrontation, University of Texas at Austin, September 24–25, 1977. For a thoughtful preliminary exploration of energy in relation to this process, see Irving Hoch, "The Role of Energy in the Regional Distribution of Economic Activity," a paper prepared for the same conference. Among the many studies of recent population movements, including the astonishing movement away from metropolitan areas, see Peter A. Morrison, "Current Demographic Change in Regions of the United States," also prepared for the Austin regional conference. It should be noted that one study of a non-American region is framed by an approach similar to that taken here: T. M. Lewis and I. H. McNicoll, *North Sea Oil and Scotland's Economic Prospects* (London: Croom Helm, 1978). The authors provide detailed investment and employment estimates for energy-related activities and explore potentialities for industrialization which might be stimulated by the regional presence of energy supplies.

25. For further vivid expositions of the dangers to the American economy implicit in this situation, see Charles Schultze, remarks before the American Council of Life Insurance Annual Meeting, New York, November 30, 1977; and Richard N. Cooper, a speech before the Annual Business Forecasting Conference at the University of California, Los Angeles, December 8, 1977.

26. FEA, *National Energy Outlook*, 1976, p. 43.

27. Richard Nehring and Benjamin Zycher, with contributions from Joseph Wharton, *Coal Development and Government Regulation in the Northern Great Plains: A Preliminary Report* (Santa Monica, Calif.: Rand Corporation, August 1976), p. 122.

28. See, notably, James W. McKie, "The Effects of the Proposals for Natural Gas Pricing in the National Energy Plan on the Energy Economy of Texas," in *Preliminary Assessment of the President's National Energy Plan* (Austin: University of Texas, May 11, 1977), pp. 179–201.

29. William R. Kaiser and Hal B. H. Cooper, Jr., "The Impact of Coal Utilization in Texas under the National Energy Plan," in *National Energy Policy: A Continuing Assessment* (Austin: University of Texas Council on Energy Resources, January 1978), pp. 121–181.

CHAPTER 4. *Technology and the Price System*

1. Alfred Marshall, *Principles of Economics* (London: Macmillan, 1930), p. 461.

2. C. E. Ayres, *Toward a Reasonable Society* (Austin: University of Texas Press, 1961), pp. 27–28.

3. In the case of Ayres, a part of the difficulty was his strong and complex emotional reaction to modern science and scientists, a theme which dominates *Science: The False Messiah* (Indianapolis: Bobbs-Merrill Co., 1927). In his conclusion (p. 294) he asserts that "machine technology was not derived from science, but crept upon us after a fashion of its own." He also denies a link between necessity and

invention with this aphorism: "Inventions are provided not to suit the needs of civilization but according to the development of science and invention" (p. 295). It is not difficult to see how these propositions, taken together, led Ayres to deal with the flow of technology as an autonomous phenomenon not lucidly linked to either science or incentives set up by the working of the economic system. Later he referred to science and technology as "inseparable," but he did not pursue this theme (*Toward a Reasonable Society*, p. 7).

4. This point is developed fully in W. W. Rostow, *How It All Began: Origins of the Modern Economy* (New York: McGraw-Hill, 1975).

5. Dwight H. Perkins, "Government as an Obstacle to Industrialization: The Case of Nineteenth Century China," *Journal of Economic History* 27 (December 1967): 485.

6. C. E. Ayres, *The Theory of Economic Progress*, 2d ed. (New York: Schocken Books, 1962), pp. xvi–xvii.

7. For a subtle discussion of this weakness in Smith's analysis, see R. Koebner, "Adam Smith and the Industrial Revolution," *Economic History Review*, 2d ser. 11, no. 3 (1959): 381–391. The quoted sentence is from p. 382. See, also, C. P. Kindleberger, "The Historical Background: Adam Smith and the Industrial Revolution," paper presented at the Adam Smith Bicentennial, April 2, 1976.

8. See Adam Smith, "Effects of the Progress of Improvement upon the Real Price of Manufactures," chap. 11 in *Wealth of Nations*, bk. 1 (London: George Routledge and Sons, 1890).

9. Alfred Marshall, *Principles of Economics*, 8th ed. (London: Macmillan, 1930), p. 461.

10. As I noted in *The Process of Economic Growth*, p. 6, Marshall also dealt with the problem of increasing returns in Appendix J, pars. 8 and 10, in *Money, Credit, and Commerce* (1923; reprint ed., Clifton, N.J.: Augustus M. Kelley, Publishers, 1975). These paragraphs are entitled, significantly: "Hindrances to the isolation for separate study of tendencies of Increasing Return to capital and labour in the production of a country's exports" and "Diagrams representing the case of Exceptional Supply, in which the exports of a country show strong general tendencies to Increasing Return, are deprived of practical interest by the inapplicability of the Statical Method to such tendencies." Marshall was impressed by the wide range of forces that might affect the long-period course of output and price. In both Appendix H and his treatment of the case of Exceptional Supply, he referred to the impact on demand of prior dramatic lowering of supply curves—i.e., of consumption habits built up over time by the nature and cheapness of supplies available. He noted, for example, the price inelasticity of British demand for cotton during the American Civil War, which in part could be attributed to the previous decline in price and growth in the habit of cotton-using it induced. More generally, long-period analysis troubled him because demand and supply became interdependent and historical developments were not fully reversible. Equilibrium could not, therefore, be exhibited in terms of a static analysis.

11. Marshall, *Principles of Economics*, pp. 378–379.
12. Ibid., p. 460.
13. Ibid.
14. Allyn Young, "Increasing Returns and Economic Progress," *Economic Journal* 38 (December 1928): 527–542. A. C. Pigou dealt with the case of increasing returns extensively in his *The Economics of Welfare* (London: Macmillan, 1920). His interest was primarily in how this case disrupted the rules of general equilibrium, related to monopoly, and bore on tax policy. It was this study which led to J. H. Clapham's "Of Empty Boxes," *Economic Journal* 32 (September 1922): 305–314. Clapham's target was Pigou's use of the concept of increasing and diminishing returns industries. His attack set off a first-class controversy, fruitful in a number of directions—notably Piero Sraffa's fathering of the modern theory of imperfect (or monopolistic) competition ("The Law of Returns under Competitive Conditions," *Economic Journal* 36 [December 1926]: 535–550). But the relation of technology to the price system, as considered here, was not much advanced.

    Among the participants in the "Empty Boxes" debate, D. H. Robertson sedulously kept the unresolved issue of increasing returns alive. See, for example, his "Those Empty Boxes," *Economic Journal* 34 (March 1924): 16–31, and his later observations in *Lectures on Economic Principles* (London: Staples Press, 1957), especially pp. 116–121. I record in the Introduction to *The Process of Economic Growth* (p. 6) Robertson's salutary warning to me about the pitfalls of the Marshallian long period as I began work on that book in 1949.

    It should also be noted that G. T. Jones, in an original and creative study, tried to give rigor to the notion of increasing returns and to measure its operation in a selected group of British and American industries over the period 1850–1910 (*Increasing Return*, ed. Colin Clark [Cambridge: At the University Press, 1933]). But, following Marshall, Jones excluded the "epoch-making discoveries (e.g., the steam engine, the electric motor, the internal combustion engine) . . . Such discoveries are the creators of new industries rather than economies reaped from the growth of the old" (p. 15).
15. Young, "Increasing Returns and Economic Progress," p. 533.
16. Ibid., p. 535.
17. Ibid., p. 534 n. 2.
18. Ibid., p. 534.
19. Ibid., p. 535.
20. For a further discussion and criticism of multiplier-accelerator analysis, see Rostow, *The Process of Economic Growth*, pp. 92–96.
21. Richard M. Goodwin, "Secular and Cyclical Aspects of the Multiplier and the Accelerator," chap. 5 in *Income, Employment, and Public Policy: Essays in Honor of Alvin H. Hansen* (New York: W. W. Norton and Co., 1948), pp. 124–132; quotation on p. 129.
22. For a more thorough exploration of Harrod's limiting assumptions, see Rostow, *The Process of Economic Growth*, pp. 86–91. J. E. Meade's

346 *Note to page 164*

A Neo-Classical Theory of Economic Growth (London: Allen and
Unwin, 1961) is developed under similar inhibiting assumptions,
explicitly excluding "economies of large-scale production, external
economies, market forms other than the perfectly competitive, and
so on" (p. v). It should be noted that Harrod's formulation triggered
a lively exploration of the conditions required for the long-run neutrality of innovations and the long-run approximate stability of the
shares of labor and capital in the distribution of income (see,
notably, Charles Kennedy, "Induced Bias in Innovation and the
Theory of Distribution," Economic Journal 74 [September 1964]:
541–547; Paul A. Samuelson, "A Theory of Induced Innovation
along Kennedy-Weisacker Lines," Review of Economics and Statistics 47 [November 1965]: 343–356; Charles Kennedy, "Samuelson
on Induced Innovation," and Paul A. Samuelson's "Rejoinder," Review of Economics and Statistics 48 [November 1966]: 442–444,
444–448).

The Kennedy-Samuelson exchange does, in a highly abstract way,
relate a part of the process of innovation to the market process. But,
in the special perspective of this chapter, it suffers three weaknesses. First, innovation emerges, once again, as a diffuse incremental process, with no serious attention devoted to the relations
among science, invention, and innovation, except for Samuelson's
observation in "A Theory of Induced Innovation" (pp. 353 and 355)
that, after some major breakthrough, creative scientists have an
instinct as to where the next promising line of inventive activity
lies. Second, the character of invention and innovation is dealt with
only as it relates to a capital- or labor-saving bias, leaving, as in
other analyses of this type, a critical unexamined role for "exogenous technical changes." Third, the theoretical conditions for
approximate long-run stability in distributive shares in a technically
advancing economy with the supply of capital increasing faster
than the supply of labor are explored with no empirical reference
to the process by which that (very rough) stability has been
achieved. In fact, the trend in distributive shares has varied—for
example, in Britain between, say, the periods 1873–1896 and 1896–
1914 (see W. W. Rostow, British Economy of the Nineteenth Century [Oxford: Clarendon Press, 1948], chap. 4, "Investment and
Real Wages, 1873–86," and the Appendix, "Mr. Kalecki on the Distribution of Income, 1880–1913").

While recognizing the theoretical validity of the issues examined
in the Kennedy-Samuelson exchange, I would suggest that the relation between patterns of investment and innovation, on the one
hand, and distributive shares, on the other, are more likely to be
illuminated by a study of how these relationships have unfolded by
sectors through time than by a specification of the conditions for
their aggregate stability—among other reasons because of the substantial role played by the relative prices of foodstuffs in income
distribution, a factor which does not figure in the highly aggregated

Kennedy-Samuelson formulations. Only a much more disaggregated and more dynamic model (of the kind laid out in Sections IV–VII of this chapter), embracing opportunities and pressures for invention and innovation arising from the income elasticity of demand and diminishing returns in the input sectors of the economy, is capable of rendering invention a truly induced phenomenon. The assumption of a higher rate of increase in capital than labor in a two-factor single or dual commodity model does not suffice, either for that purpose or for a realistic explanation of distributive shares.

23. Paul A. Samuelson, *Economics*, 7th ed. (New York: McGraw-Hill, 1967).

24. Janos Kornai, *Anti-Equilibrium* (Amsterdam-London: North-Holland Publishing Co., 1971), p. 373.

25. Nicholas Kaldor, "The Irrelevance of Equilibrium Economics," *Economic Journal* 82 (December 1972): 1237–1255.

26. Ibid., p. 1240.

27. Ibid., p. 1246.

28. Ibid., p. 1255.

29. Ibid., p. 1249.

30. The way of looking at science, invention, and innovation outlined here is more fully developed in Rostow, *The Process of Economic Growth*, especially chaps. 2 and 3.

31. A curve of this kind is implicit in the analysis of Thomas S. Kuhn, *The Structure of Scientific Revolutions* (Chicago: University of Chicago Press, 1962 and 1970). For a sustained debate on Kuhn's propositions and his response, see Imre Lakatos and Alan Musgrave (eds.), *Criticism and the Growth of Knowledge* (Cambridge: At the University Press, 1970). For formulation of a similar sequence, see Rostow, *The Process of Economic Growth*, pp. 62–63, including the relevant footnotes, where the difficulty of defining the economic yield from fundamental science is discussed.

32. See, notably, Jacob Schmookler, *Invention and Economic Growth* (Cambridge, Mass.: Harvard University Press, 1966). For earlier discussions of invention as an economically induced phenomenon, see A. P. Usher, *History of Mechanical Inventions* (New York: McGraw-Hill, 1929); S. C. Gilfillan, *The Sociology of Invention* (Chicago: Follett Publishing Co., 1935); R. S. Sayers, "The Springs of Technical Progress in Britain, 1919–1939," *Economic Journal* 60, no. 238 (June 1950): 275–291, especially p. 282; and T. S. Ashton, *The Industrial Revolution, 1760–1830* (London: Oxford University Press, 1948), pp. 91–92. J. Schumpeter's indecisive discussion of this question should also be noted (*Business Cycles* [New York: McGraw-Hill, 1939], vol. I, p. 85 n.). Schumpeter allows not only for the existence of inventions and innovations induced by necessity but also for inventions not related to any particular requirement or not related to the requirement met by the particular innovation that incorporates them. Schumpeter states: "It might be thought that innovation can never be anything else but an effort to

cope with a given economic situation. In a sense this is true. For a given innovation to become possible, there must always be some 'objective needs' to be satisfied and certain 'objective conditions'; but they rarely, if ever, uniquely determine what kind of innovation will satisfy them, and as a rule they can be satisfied in many different ways. Most important of all, they may remain unsatisfied for an indefinite time, which shows that they are not in themselves sufficient to produce an innovation." The issue is discussed in Rostow, *The Process of Economic Growth*, pp. 83–86.

33. Nathan Rosenberg has discussed this point thoughtfully—and the limits it set on Schmookler's basic thesis—in "Science, Invention, and Economic Growth," *Economic Journal* 84, no. 333 (March 1974): 90–108.

34. Rostow, *How It All Began*, chap. 4.

35. Schmookler, *Invention and Economic Growth*, p. 200.

36. I. D. Burnet, "An Interpretation of Take-Off," *Economic Record*, September 1972, pp. 424–428. The quotation is from p. 424 and the figure from p. 425.

37. Ibid., p. 425.

38. Kuznets, *Secular Movements*, pp. 4–5. Also, Rostow, *The Process of Economic Growth*, pp. 80–103. Kuznets did not relate his study to the theoretical literature on increasing returns. *The Process of Economic Growth* is presented as "an effort to explore a method for permitting the introduction of (Marshallian) long-period factors into economic analysis," including increasing returns (pp. 5–8).

39. In developing this system at greater length in Rostow, *The Process of Economic Growth* (chap. 4), formal difficulties with the concept of an ex ante optimum pattern are examined, stemming from the impossibility of predicting precisely the content of new inventions and shifts in the social and political framework of the economy (pp. 97–98). The concept of an ex post equilibrium is also introduced and illustrated, and its usefulness discussed (pp. 98–103). For present limited purposes, this distinction between ex ante and ex post is not necessary, for we are assuming the stock of science and inventions as given, as well as the political and social framework of the economy, notably as it affects public policy and the quality of entrepreneurship by sectors.

40. Kuznets, *Secular Movements*, especially pp. 11–35.

41. See, for example, Kuznets' calculations of the changing ratio of value added to the cost of raw materials in a number of industries, ibid., pp. 41–49.

42. Robertson, *Lectures on Economic Principles*, pp. 116–117.

43. The literature in this field is well summarized in the Selected Bibliography set out in Larry E. Westphal, *Planning Investments with Economies of Scale* (Amsterdam-London: North-Holland Publishing Co., 1971), pp. 365–370. See also references attached to David A. Kendrick's chap. 8, "Systems Problems in Economic Development," in *Economics of Engineering and Social Systems*, ed. J. M. English

(New York: Wiley, 1972), pp. 323–324. To these listings should be added the work of Janos Kornai, notably *Mathematical Planning of Structural Decisions* (1967) and *Anti-Equilibrium* (1971), both published by North-Holland Publishing Co., Amsterdam-London. In particular, Kornai's analysis of the planning implications of increasing returns in a particular industry (man-made fibers) (*Mathematical Planning*, pp. 99–107) belongs in the same family of studies as Westphal's analysis referred to above.

44. David A. Kendrick, "Systems Problems in Economic Development," p. 216.

45. It should be noted that the shape of disaggregated Chenery-Taylor curves is not merely a function of GNP per capita levels (and the income elasticity of demand for consumer goods): like Kuznets' secular trend production curves, the Chenery-Taylor curves also reflect factors on the supply side (including increasing returns) which, in time, yield retardation in particular sectors, as new technologies are introduced into an economy and progressively exploited.

46. For a discussion of this model in relation to the possibilities of inflation and unemployment, see Rostow, *The Process of Economic Growth*, especially pp. 86–96, and chap. 5, "Growth and Business Cycles." Development planning models have, from the beginning, been sensitive to the foreign balance, given the critical role of imports of capital equipment and the implicit or explicit interest of the analysts in the level of foreign aid.

47. W. W. Rostow, *Politics and the Stages of Growth* (Cambridge: At the University Press, 1971), p. 19.

CHAPTER 5. *Money and Prices*

1. These analyses appear in Rostow, *British Economy of the Nineteenth Century*, especially chaps. 1, 3, 4, and 7. These chapters, in turn, drew heavily on my doctoral thesis, "British Trade Fluctuations, 1868–1896: A Chronicle and a Commentary," Yale University, 1939, and from work done in the study by A. D. Gayer et al., *The Growth and Fluctuation of the British Economy, 1790–1850* (Oxford: Clarendon Press, 1953; 2d ed., Harvester Press, 1975), especially vol. II, chaps. 4 and 5.

2. See, notably, Thomas, *Migration and Economic Growth*, 2d ed., pp. 246–248. The references are to René P. Higonnet, "Bank Deposits in the United Kingdom, 1870–1912," *Quarterly Journal of Economics* 72, no. 3 (August 1957): 329–367; Milton Friedman and Anna Jacobson Schwartz, *A Monetary History of the United States, 1867–1960* (Princeton: Princeton University Press, 1963); and Phillip Cagan, *Determinants and Effects of Changes in the Stock of Money, 1875–1960* (New York: Columbia University Press, 1965). Efforts to deal with the causes of the trend decrease in U.S. prices are also made in George Edward Dickey, *Money, Prices and Growth: The American*

Experience, 1868–1896 (New York: Arno Press, 1977); and Roger Edward Shields, *Economic Growth with Price Deflation, 1873–1896* (New York: Arno Press, 1977).

3. Chapter 1 of this book reflects a part of the review of theories of long-term trends.

4. Rostow, *The World Economy*, p. xliii.

5. See Gayer et al., *The Growth and Fluctuation*, vol. I, pp. 459–528, for the construction and behavior of the price indexes generated by that study. The weights for the domestic and imported price indexes are given on p. 484. As the authors emphasize, the indexes are, like most wholesale commodity price indexes, strictly confined to foodstuffs and raw materials.

6. For charted data, see ibid., vol. II, p. 818 (domestic price index), p. 826 (price of wheat), and p. 950 (cost of living and real wages, London artisans).

7. See, for example, Thomas Tooke, *A History of Prices and of the State of Circulation from 1793 to 1837* (London: Longman, 1838), vol. I, pp. 118–173.

8. Gayer et al., *The Growth and Fluctuation*, vol. I, pp. xii–xiii.

9. Ibid., vol. II, p. 642.

10. Ibid., vol. II, pp. 656–657. Aside from the financial sections of the history in vol. I, the debate about price movements is canvassed and the evidence summarized in vol. II, pp. 623–658. Peter Temin uses a somewhat similar method to test the monetary explanation for the U.S. business recession of 1929–1930 in *Did Monetary Forces Cause the Great Depression?* (New York: W. W. Norton, 1976), pp. 103–137.

11. Paul A. Samuelson, "Worldwide Stagflation," *Intermountain Economic Review* 6, no. 2 (Fall 1975): 9.

12. The implications of these variations, except gold production, are systematically formalized in Chapter 2 of this volume.

13. I have in mind here the alleged role in decelerating the U.S. rate of increase of output per man-hour of the increased proportion of women and teenagers in the working force. See, for example, John Kendrick, "Productivity Trends and Prospects," in *U.S. Economic Growth from 1976 to 1986: Prospects, Problems, and Patterns*, vol. I, *Productivity*, Studies prepared for the use of the Joint Economic Committee (Washington, D.C.: GPO, October 1, 1976).

14. Alfred Marshall, *Official Papers* (London: Macmillan, 1926), p. 5. The work of George Edward Dickey (discussed pp. 246–248) is a major effort to solve this problem on a theoretical and empirical level.

15. Rostow, *British Economy of the Nineteenth Century*, p. 151 n. 1.

16. Since economists generally use the term "increasing returns" to define the case where "economies of scale" are at work, with existing technologies, we cannot unambiguously designate technological change as yielding increasing returns. For discussion, see Chapter 4.

17. E. F. M. Durbin, "Money and Prices," chap. 7 in G. D. H. Cole (ed.), *What Everybody Wants to Know about Money* (New York: Alfred A. Knopf, 1933), pp. 272–274.

18. J. M. Keynes, *The General Theory of Employment, Interest, and Money* (New York: Harcourt Brace, 1936), pp. 269–271.

19. Edwin Kuh and Richard L. Schmalensee, *An Introduction to Applied Macroeconomics* (New York: American Elsevier Publishing Company, 1973), p. 144; the price equations in the authors' model of the U.S. economy are presented on pp. 143–146. Ray C. Fair includes the price of imports as well as the wage rate in the price equation of his econometric model in *A Model of Macroeconomic Activity*, vol. II, *The Empirical Model* (Cambridge, Mass.: Ballinger, 1976), pp. 121–122.

20. See, especially, Rostow, *British Economy of the Nineteenth Century*, pp. 44–50; and Gayer et al., *The Growth and Fluctuation*, vol. II, pp. 634–638.

21. See, especially, Rostow, "British Trade Fluctuations," pp. 177–191. Also W. Edwards Beach, *British International Gold Movements and Banking Policy, 1881–1913* (Cambridge, Mass.: Harvard University Press, 1935), pp. 105–111. In 1881–1882 the Bank's reserve was under pressure from time to time both from abroad and to meet internal requirements in a period of business expansion. But brief periods of high interest rates drew gold to London; and, as often, the gap between bank and market rates of interest shielded the domestic credit structure, as long as profit expectations remained favorable.

22. Rendigs Fels, *American Business Cycles, 1865–1897* (Chapel Hill: University of North Carolina Press, 1959), p. 126. Fels' full account of the upper turning point in this cycle is on pp. 124–128. Friedman and Schwartz are content with the following simple conclusion about the American upper turning point: "The level of prices and money income reached in the United States by the end of 1882 was higher than could be maintained at the fixed exchange rates" (*A Monetary History*, pp. 99–100). With respect to Britain, they note the rise in the bank rate to 6 percent in January 1882. They fail to note that it began its decline three weeks later and that the upper turning point for Britain is in December 1882.

23. Rostow, *The World Economy*, p. 309.

24. Walther Hoffmann, *Das Wachstum der Deutschen Wirtschaft seit der Mitte des 19. Jahrhunderts* (Berlin: Springer-Verlag, 1965), pp. 451–452.

25. Rostow, *The World Economy*, p. 152.

26. Michael G. Mulhall, *Dictionary of Statistics* (London: George Routledge, 1892), p. 157.

27. Rostow, *British Economy of the Nineteenth Century*, pp. 21–23. I would cite this passage in pleading innocent of D. H. Robertson's charge that my debunkery was excessive in this matter. Robertson wrote: "I am still obscurantist enough to believe that if you dig holes in the ground it probably does make some difference to money prices whether what comes out is simply dirt, or is a money metal which the diggers can use for purchase of goods and services" ("New Light on an Old Story," *Economica*, n.s. 15, no. 60 [Novem-

ber 1948]: 297). Evidently, I agree, as the reference to gold as "a useful product, capable of exchange for goods and services, including imports" indicates. On the complex, sometimes paradoxical, but limited effects of gold imports on money markets, interest rates, and so forth, see Robertson's *A Study of Industrial Fluctuation* (London: repr. London School of Economics and Political Science, 1948), pp. 228–235 ("Gold, —Medicine, Poison, and Intoxicant"). See, also, Knut Wicksell's consideration of the same problem (to which Robertson refers with approval) in *Lectures on Political Economy,* vol. II, *Money* (New York: Augustus M. Kelley, 1967), pp. 159–168 ("The Defects of the Quantity Theory: An Attempt at a Rational Theory").

28. Thomas Tooke and William Newmarch, *A History of Prices,* vol. VI (London: P. S. King [reproduced from the 1857 original text], 1928), especially pp. 135–236; J. E. Cairnes, *Essays in Political Economy: Theoretical and Applied* (London: Macmillan and Co., 1873). The contemporary analysis of the *Economist* is also valuable on this matter; for example, *Economist,* 1849, pp. 4–5, 320–321; 1850, pp. 1010–1011, 1317–1318, 1373–1374; 1851, p. 1425; 1852, pp. 1, 6–7, 557–558, 1061–1062; 1853, pp. 193–194, 221–222, 642–643, 985; 1855, pp. 977–979. For a modern analysis in this vein, see J. R. T. Hughes, *Fluctuations in Trade, Industry, and Finance* (Oxford: Clarendon Press, 1960), pp. 10–17 and 241–256. The latter pages constitute Hughes' effort to account for the effect of increased gold production on the behavior of the monetary variables in Britain during the 1850's.

29. Rostow, *The World Economy,* p. 157.

30. Hughes, *Fluctuations,* p. 17.

31. W. B. Smith and A. H. Cole were also struck by the paradox of the accretion of gold accompanied by high interest rates in the United States of this period; see *Fluctuations in American Business, 1790–1860* (Cambridge, Mass.: Harvard University Press, 1935), p. 127: "Again, one sees portrayed the generally high level of money rates throughout most of these two decades—especially during the years 1846–57, a period in which there was a constantly increasing gold supply! If such levels—and possibly higher—be taken as the experience for the country as a whole, one can conclude only that, though gold supplies may have increased and though they may have had effect on commodity prices and the like through the expansion which they made possible in total purchasing power, the pressure of the demand for accommodation at the banks was steadily too large and too insistent to permit softening of money rates for any considerable periods. Even the concomitance of enlarging gold supplies, of increasing bank capitals, and of swelling imports of foreign capital could not satisfy the credit needs of a young country whose mixture of productive factors was so specially compounded as that of the United States in the 'forties and 'fifties of the last century."

32. Joseph Kitchin, "Production and Consumption of Gold—Past and Prospective," annex VII, table I (following p. 62), in *Interim Report*

of the Gold Delegation of the Financial Committee (Geneva: League of Nations, September 8, 1930).

33. Rostow, *The World Economy*, pp. 665 and 669.
34. Joseph Kitchin, "Production and Consumption of Gold," p. 57.
35. See, notably, Donald Wood Gilbert, "The Economic Effects of the Gold Discoveries upon South Africa: 1886–1910," *Quarterly Journal of Economics* 47 (1933): 553–597.
36. This is the estimate of Sir George Paish, quoted by Gilbert, ibid., p. 561. Money calls for portfolio investment in Africa as a whole for the period 1886–1910 came to £331 million (Matthew Simon, "The Pattern of New British Portfolio Foreign Investment, 1865–1914," reprinted in *The Export of Capital from Britain, 1870–1914*, ed. A. R. Hall [London: Methuen, 1968], p. 40). The approximation of the two figures can only be suggestive, since they are not strictly comparable in either category or coverage, although the bulk of British investment in Africa over these years was in South Africa. To give these sums a certain proportion, £331 million was about twice British gross domestic capital formation for the mid-year of 1898, 19 percent of GNP.
37. Rostow, *The World Economy*, pp. 169–194.
38. See, for example, Simon Kuznets, *Modern Economic Growth* (New Haven: Yale University Press, 1966), pp. 252–255.
39. Friedman and Schwartz, *A Monetary History*, pp. 138–139.
40. Gayer et al., *The Growth and Fluctuation*, vol. I, especially pp. 51–53.
41. Friedman and Schwartz, *A Monetary History*, p. 137.
42. Ibid., pp. 138–188.
43. For data and discussion, see Rostow, *The World Economy*, pp. 323–330.
44. Lewis, *Growth and Fluctuations*, p. 90.
45. Derek H. Aldcroft and Peter Fearon (eds.), *British Economic Fluctuations, 1790–1939* (London: Macmillan, 1972), p. 56. The quotation in the text is from the editors' introduction.
46. Friedman and Schwartz, *A Monetary History*, pp. 91–92 and 98–99.
47. In Robert J. Gordon (ed.), *Milton Friedman's Monetary Framework: A Debate with His Critics* (Chicago: University of Chicago Press, 1974), p. 27. Equation (6) referred to in this passage is as follows: $M = k\,Py$, where M is the money stock; k, the ratio of the money stock to income; P, the price level; y, national income in constant prices. Other formulations of Friedman's monetary doctrine are to be found in "The Quantity Theory of Money—A Restatement," in Milton Friedman (ed.), *Studies in the Quantity Theory of Money* (Chicago: University of Chicago Press, 1956); *A Theory of the Consumption Function* (Princeton: Princeton University Press, 1957); "The Lag in the Effect of Monetary Policy," *Journal of Political Economy* 69 (October 1961): 447–466; "The Role of Monetary Policy," *American Economic Review* 58 (March 1968): 1–17; *The Optimum Quantity of Money, and Other Essays* (Chicago: Aldine, 1969); with David Meiselman, "The Relative Stability of Monetary

Velocity and the Investment Multiplier in the United States," in *Stabilization Policies,* Studies for the Commission on Money and Credit (Englewood Cliffs, N.J.: Prentice-Hall, 1963); with Anna J. Schwartz, "Money and Business Cycles," *Review of Economics and Statistics* 45 (February 1963): 32–78.

48. Friedman and Schwartz, *A Monetary History,* p. 686.

49. Wicksell, *Lectures on Political Economy,* vol. II, *Money,* pp. 159–160. The reference is apt in the present context. Wicksell uses as his example (pp. 160–165) interpretations of the impact of the mid-century gold discoveries in California and Australia, tracing out their consequences in a manner not unlike the sequence outlined in the section entitled "What about Gold?"

50. Temin, *Monetary Forces,* pp. 30–31. For a judgment along similar lines, see A. B. Camp, "Does Money Matter," *Lloyds Bank Review,* no. 98 (October 1970), pp. 22–37.

51. The passage from which this quotation is excerpted constitutes one of the two substantial references to pre-1914 interest rate movements in the book. It appears in a footnote in which it is implied, by reference to a third party, that my explanation of the price decline of the final quarter of the nineteenth century hinges decisively on the concurrence of falling prices and interest rates—the Gibson Paradox. I did, indeed, refer to this phenomenon; and I do not believe the monetarists have successfully disposed of it by references to the real as opposed to money rate of interest, or to lagged anticipation of falling price trends. But my central argument (summarized in the early sections of this chapter) has, to the best of my knowledge, never been addressed by the monetarists who remain strictly within their own vocabulary and theoretical framework.

52. Friedman and Schwartz, *A Monetary History,* p. 104. The key statement is: "A shift of British investment to the Argentine in mid-1890 caused a loss of gold from New York." British investment in Argentina expanded from 1886 to 1889, declining in 1890 in the context of the Baring crisis and the events leading up to it. It is true that Argentina drew bullion from London in 1890; but this had happened in the second half of the three previous years (see, for example, *Economist,* 1887, p. 933; 1888, p. 1309; 1889, p. 1129).

53. Friedman and Schwartz, *A Monetary History,* p. 99. I find it somewhat surprising that the authors do not exploit, for example, the fine-grained, sophisticated scholarship of W. Beach, R. S. Sayers, and A. G. Ford bearing on the workings of the international gold standard in this period, as well as the earlier work of Taussig's famous students whose research cast grave doubts on the classical view of the adjustment mechanism under the pre-1914 gold standard.

54. Ibid., p. 102. A footnote is then attached (p. 102 n. 20): "One possibility is that they reflect partly the secondary and tertiary waves from the reaction mechanism referred to in footnote 15 above." Footnote 15, dealing with the alleged mechanism accounting for the behavior of the British and American economies from 1879 to 1882—including the balance of trade, capital movements, gold

flows, and relative price levels—is as follows: "We are indebted to Clark Warburton both for calling our attention to this see-saw movement and for the term. Note that the reaction mechanism alluded to is one that would convert a random shock affecting conditions of international trade into a series of cycles. Note also that the cycles on the two sides of the Atlantic would have predictable differences in phase" (pp. 98–99 n. 15). The argument here is, I suspect, to be understood in terms of the authors' speculations about the possibility of a pure monetary theory of the business cycle, in their 1963 *Review of Economics and Statistics* article, pp. 58–63.

55. Friedman and Schwartz, "Money and Business Cycles," especially pp. 48–56.

56. Ibid., pp. 48–49.

57. See, for example, Burns, *Production Trends*, especially pp. 248–249. But see, also, Lewis, *Growth and Fluctuations*, pp. 33–68, and his version of Kuznets cycles, with superbooms and "great depressions."

58. Friedman and Schwartz, "Money and Business Cycles," pp. 58–63. One rather troubling aspect of the debate about the role of money in price and output determination is the tendency of some monetarists to imply that Friedman and Schwartz demonstrated propositions they did not even pretend to demonstrate. For example, D. E. W. Laidler and J. M. Parkin, "Inflation—A Survey," *Economic Journal* 85, no. 340 (December 1975): 752 and 779: "The studies of Friedman and Schwartz (1963) and Cagan (1965) . . . show that, although in certain episodes the supply of money did respond passively to demand, in most cases the direction of causation was clearly from supply side factors to demand side factors. . . . causation has primarily run from money to income and prices over most time periods."

59. Cagan, *Determinants and Effects of Change*, p. 1.

60. Ibid., p. 4.

61. See, for example, John Kareken and Robert M. Solow, "Lags in Fiscal and Monetary Policy," Research Study One in *Stabilization Policies*, prepared for the Commission on Money and Credit (Englewood Cliffs, N.J.: Prentice-Hall, 1963), pp. 14–96. Kareken and Solow demonstrate for the period 1939–1959 in the United States that no systematic lag appears if the rate of change of the money stock is compared with the rate of change of total production. See, also, James Tobin, "Money and Income: Post Hoc Ergo Propter Hoc?" *Quarterly Journal of Economics* 84, no. 2 (May 1970): 301–317; Milton Friedman, "A Comment on Tobin," ibid., pp. 318–327; and Tobin's "Rejoinder," ibid., pp. 328–329. In his comment on Tobin, Friedman, in effect, drops the lagged correlation between the rate of increase of the money stock and business activity from his arsenal, without abandoning his basic position, arguing that he had long held the view that the timing evidence was "suggestive" but not "decisive" (pp. 320–321). He also provides his argument for studying the lag (pp. 321–322), namely, that for purposes of policy

or prediction the lag ought to be understood. Here again is the problem that arises often in the monetarist literature between the analysis of money as a causal factor in the past and the potentialities for control over prices and output of a purposeful monetarist policy.

62. Cagan, *Determinants and Effects of Change*, p. 272. Cagan follows this passage with indecisive speculations on possible lagged or otherwise more complex relations between the rates of change in the money stock and business activity, mainly designed to keep alive the notion that, by some route, the causal chain might run systematically from money to business activity. As Cagan acknowledges (p. 273), the rather rigid nature of his method of correlation precludes a satisfactory exploration of the possibility of a more complicated relationship between money and business activity.

63. Ibid., pp. 262–268.

64. Ibid., p. 265.

65. Ibid., p. 267. Surely, we know enough about the sharp global depression of 1920–1921 to be confident that it was a response to the overstocking of inventories in the first excessively optimistic phase of peace.

66. See, especially, ibid., pp. 51–52, 59–67, 75–76, 96–98, and 235–260.

67. Ibid., p. 51.

68. Ibid., p. 62.

69. Ibid., p. 75.

70. Cagan hedges, a bit, the rigid, if lagged, causal connection between declining price trend and the subsequent increase in gold production, allowing for the fortuitous discovery of mines and for the emergence of new technologies not linked to the incentive provided by a falling price level in a gold standard world (e.g., ibid., p. 97). R. S. Sayers has taken the flat view that the gold discoveries in California and Australia were fortuitous ("The Question of the Standard in the Eighteen-Fifties," *Economic History* 2 [1930–1933]: 597–598): "This notion [that the gold discoveries were induced by a prior period of falling prices] seems very strained when the actual history of the gold discoveries is remembered. In California a man building a saw-mill had occasion to dig a trench, and found he was digging out gold. True, if prices had not been so low in England there might not have been so many people in California, and the *chances* would accordingly have been less than they were. But however much we strain our imaginations to justify *Blackwood's* explanation of the California discovery, no stretch of the imagination can justify the application of such an explanation to the Australian discoveries. For as long ago as 1844 Murchison, in an address to the Royal Geographical Society, had shown the probable existence of gold in Australia, basing his argument on the similarity between the gold-bearing Urals and the mountains of Australia. The result was a continual search for gold until it was found, in one place after another. When there was talk of gold deposits in the nineteenth century, people did not stay to consider costs. Really it is

difficult to see a great and precise 'natural law' working here."

71. Cagan, *Determinants and Causes*, pp. 236–237. Tables 28 and 29 are, in effect, a summary of a good deal of Cagan's argument.

72. Ibid., pp. 249–260, "Some Long-Standing Objections Reconsidered."

73. It should be noted, however, that Jevons introduces an important notion the monetarists never consider: "The normal course of prices in the present progressive state of things is, I think, downwards." Behind this observation (on the period 1815–1848) is a concept of the role of productivity in long-run price trends highly relevant to both of the trend periods included in Cagan's study.

74. Cagan, *Determinants and Causes*, p. 254 n. 14.

75. Ibid., p. 261.

76. See, especially, Higonnet, "Bank Deposits in the United Kingdom," pp. 333–345.

77. Ibid., p. 347. Friedman and Schwartz make a similar distorting error (*A Monetary History*, p. 91). Inexplicably, Higonnet associates the "spectacular increase" in bank money of 1895 with "the break in the price trend" at the time. British prices did not begin to move up significantly until 1898. The rise in bank money in 1895 was, in part, a result of a large flow to London from other financial centers plus a substantial accretion of gold from the Rand (*Economist, Review of 1898*, p. 4).

78. Higonnet, "Bank Deposits in the United Kingdom," pp. 337 and 340.

79. Ibid., see, notably, pp. 354–358.

80. See, notably, David K. Sheppard, *The Growth and Role of U.K. Financial Institutions, 1880–1962* (London: Methuen, 1971). Sheppard's calculations for bank deposits for the 1880's have been criticized as too low by Shizuya Nishimura, who also extends back to 1870 bank deposit calculations and suggests revisions of Sheppard's figures for gold coin in circulation in "The Growth of the Stock of Money in the U.K., 1870–1913," unpublished paper, Hosei University, Tokyo, 1973. Anna Jacobson Schwartz not only called my attention to the Nishimura paper but also graciously made available her calculations (as of 6/2/78) of the British money stock from 1871 forward. These are a component of the forthcoming Friedman-Schwartz comparative study of the British and American monetary experiences and their wider economic meaning.

81. The National Bureau of Economic Research cyclical turning point for the United States is January 1893. The money stock figure available in that year is for June, already reflecting the recession. Therefore, the June 1892 figure is chosen to reflect the cyclical peak in that cycle.

82. Lewis reflects on the anomaly, its causes (notably, changes in the velocity of circulation) and its implications for the gold-price linkage in *Growth and Fluctuations*, pp. 87–93.

83. A. A. Walters, *Money in Boom and Slump* (London: Institute of Economic Affairs, 1969), especially pp. 25–35.

84. Thomas, *Migration and Economic Growth*, pp. 244–289.

85. To clear the ground for more substantive matters, I should note two

errors in Thomas' assessment of my views. First, he appears to believe that I was unaware of the rise in British foreign investment in the late 1880's (p. 188 n. 1). In my *British Economy of the Nineteenth Century* (pp. 25 and 85–88), I discuss at some length this "meaningful break" in the pattern of the Great Depression. Second, like Higonnet himself, Thomas grossly overestimates the extent to which my analysis of the causes of the post-1873 British price decline hinged on data about British bank deposits.

86. As noted in Chapter 1, my sympathy with Thomas' analysis would be stronger if he had included explicitly the factors which tended to raise the marginal efficiency of capital in the C regions, that is, price and relative price movements; technological developments, such as barbed wire and the refrigerator ship; political or policy developments in C areas, such as those which led to the demand in the pre-1896 period for Canadian, Australian, and Argentine railroads; and so on. To summarize briskly the historical case for Thomas' proposition: the British boom of the 1820's was primarily internal, despite a flyer in Latin American mining investment in 1824–1825; the boom of the 1830's saw large outflows to the United States; in the boom of the 1840's, capital mainly stayed home building the British railway net; in the 1850's, American railways drew large funds from London; the British boom of the 1860's was primarily internal; the boom of the early 1870's saw large British capital exports; that of the early 1880's was mainly internal, with diminished capital exports; but the strong expansion of the late 1880's saw large capital exports, notably to Argentina; the British boom of the late 1890's was primarily internal; the expansion from 1904 to 1913, interrupted in 1907–1908, saw unexampled levels of capital exports, notably to Canada.

87. Thomas, *Migration and Economic Growth*, pp. 263 and 283.

88. For a lively revival of this old strand in cyclical analysis, see, notably, C. P. Kindleberger, *Manias, Panics, and Crashes* (New York: Basic Books, 1978).

89. Thomas, *Migration and Economic Growth*, p. 276.

90. Ibid., pp. 282–283.

91. Dickey, *Money, Prices, and Growth*, p. 21.

92. Ibid., p. 92.

93. Ibid., p. 32.

94. Ibid., p. 11. Dickey does not examine my empirical argument for the passivity of the money supply, summarized in the section entitled "But Was the Pre-1914 Monetary System Passive and Flexible?"

95. Ibid., pp. 39–41. The key passage is the following: "Assume that the money value of national income is fixed; i.e., M and V are exogenously determined; from the equation of exchange, $MV = PQ$, it follows that money national income, PQ, is also fixed. PQ is the sum of the values of all of the currently produced goods and services: $PQ = p_1 q_1 + p_2 q_2 + \ldots \ldots + p_n q_n.$
"Consider the effect of an increase in the quantity supplied brought about by a downward shift in the supply curve of product

j. The result of this shift in supply is to lower the price of good j and to increase the quantity supplied. Depending upon the elasticity of demand, the percentage decline in the price of good j will be more or less than the percentage increase in the quantity supplied. However, the new price of the commodity must be consistent with monetary conditions which require that PQ remain constant. This means that the aggregate price level must fall since, *cet par*, output has increased.

"If the demand for the product is elastic its price will not fall sufficiently as a result of the shift in supply alone to lower the price level and maintain monetary equilibrium. Thus, general deflationary forces will be set up to lower all prices until the correct price level emerges. ($p_{j1}q_{j1} > p_{j0}q_{j0}$; thus $P_1Q_1 > P_0Q_0$, and P_1 must fall.)

"If the demand for the product is unitary elastic then the fall in the price of the product will just balance the increased output, and there will be no need for further adjustments in the prices of other products to maintain monetary equilibrium. If the demand for the product is inelastic, the demands of monetary equilibrium will require all prices to rise until the proper, albeit lower, price level is restored."

96. Ibid., p. 29.
97. Ibid., pp. 11–12 and 91.
98. Ibid., p. 15.
99. Gordon (ed.), *Milton Friedman's Monetary Framework*, pp. 162–168.
100. Ibid., especially pp. 32 n. 19, 145–146, 150.
101. See Friedman and Schwartz, "Money and Business Cycles," pp. 59–63, and Cagan, *Determinants and Effects of Change*, app. D, pp. 313–316. It should be noted that James Tobin has produced a rather elegant monetary cycle ("Money and Income," pp. 310–314). Tobin uses the model to argue that an ultra-Keynesian model can yield the same kind of lags between the rate of growth of the money supply and business activity as a monetarist model.
102. Cagan, *Determinants and Effects of Change*, pp. 276–278, formalized in App. D, pp. 313–316.
103. Ibid., pp. 277–278.
104. Lewis (*Growth and Fluctuations*, p. 93), however, makes the following relevant observation: "It was both true and important that a declining price level increases the profitability of mining gold, and so expands the output of existing mines, whereas a rising price level reduces the output of the mines. However, the big changes in gold production were due to new discoveries rather than to changes in the output of existing mines. More people look for gold when mining is more profitable because of falling prices than look when mining is less profitable because of rising prices. But looking is not the same as finding. The finding of new large and rich deposits of gold, like those of California, Australia and South Africa, includes such a large random element that one must not incorporate it mechanically into a self-generating theory of prices. We accept neither that changes in gold supply caused the changes in prices

nor that changes in prices caused the changes in gold supply. History is full of fortuitous coincidences, and this was such an occasion." See, also, the view of R. S. Sayers in note 70.

105. My disaggregated, dynamic theory of production and prices, applied to growth, business cycles, and trend periods, is more fully set out in *The Process of Economic Growth*. That book is the theoretical matrix for *The World Economy*. The inadequacy of the concept of exogenous investment is dealt with explicitly in *The Process of Economic Growth*, pp. 86–96.

106. A good many of the main themes, findings, and unresolved problems in that literature are reflected in Gordon (ed.), *Milton Friedman's Monetary Framework*, and Laidler and Parkin, "Inflation—A Survey."

107. Paul A. Samuelson, *Economics*, 10th ed. (New York: McGraw-Hill, 1976), especially chap. 18, "Synthesis of Monetary Analysis and Income Analysis."

108. Friedman and Schwartz, *A Monetary History*, p. 686.

CHAPTER 6. *Growth Rates at Different Levels of Income*

1. As Jeffrey G. Williamson has demonstrated, the long-run tendency within nations (as well as on the world scene) is in the direction of income equality ("Regional Inequality and the Process of National Development: A Description of the Patterns," *Economic Development and Cultural Change* 13, no. 4, part II [July 1965]: 3–84). This is the basic historical process underlying the much discussed rise of the Sunbelt in the United States, a trend vigorously under way since 1940 at least.

2. Hollis Chenery, "Transitional Growth and World Industrialization," paper presented to the Nobel Symposium on the International Allocation of Economic Activity, Stockholm, June 8–11, 1976. See also Hollis Chenery and Moises Syrquin, *Patterns of Development, 1950–1970* (London–New York: Oxford University Press for the World Bank, 1975), especially pp. 135–136.

3. Chenery and Syrquin, *Patterns of Development*, table 2b. Chenery's stage criteria relate, essentially, to the proportion of GNP derived from industry and the share of manufactures in total exports, the latter lagging the former as growth proceeds. For example, the share of manufacturing in the "old developed" countries for 1973 is 30.7 percent; the "newly developed," 29.6 percent; the "transitional," 21.7 percent; the "less developed," 14.4 percent; the "centrally planned," 39.8 percent. As noted below (Section IV), the character as well as the relative scale of industry plays a role in Chenery's analysis, as does the character of exports. In general, the "transitional" countries are in the process of absorbing the basic heavy industry sectors (steel, light engineering, chemicals); the "newly developed," the more sophisticated technologies associated with motor vehicles on a mass scale, durable consumer goods, heavy engineering, electronics, and so on.

4. The historical per capita income series in 1967 U.S. $ used in Table 6-3 and the sources from which they are derived are given in Appendix 1. The figures for GNP per capita are five-year averages centered on the indicated years. They have been derived by converting real income per capita series in local currencies to 1967 U.S. $, with 1967 the linkage year. The dates chosen for the beginning of take-off represent my judgment from the full range of statistical and qualitative evidence available. A few of the dates differ from those set out tentatively in *The Stages of Economic Growth*. These revisions and the rationale for them are presented in Part Five of *The World Economy*. Despite the debate during the 1960's on the concept of stages of growth (reviewed and responded to in the 1971 edition of *The Stages of Economic Growth*), there are, in fact, only marginal differences about when take-off or modern growth or the first industrial revolution began in particular cases. Compare, for example, Simon Kuznets' dates for the beginning of modern growth (*Economic Growth of Nations* [Cambridge, Mass.: Belknap Press of Harvard, 1971], p. 24) with my tentative approximate dates for the beginning of take-off (*The Stages of Economic Growth*, p. 38). For the inescapable difficulties in using long-term measurements of real income and the case, on balance, for using them, see Kuznets, *Economic Growth of Nations*, pp. 1–10.

5. Growth rates for shorter periods for these three countries are set out below, including pre-take-off rates for Argentina, from 1901 to 1933:

	Canada Average Annual Growth Rate	Australia Average Annual Growth Rate	Argentina Average Annual Growth Rate
1896–1920	1.30%	1.30%	1.34%
1920–1929	2.20	−0.72	0.55
1929–1933	−9.87	−0.71	−4.52
1933–1945	6.61	1.99	1.52
1945–1967	2.10	2.00	1.79
Average growth rate (1896–1967)	1.87%	1.26%	1.33%

6. For discussion of this point, see, for example, Rostow, *The Stages of Economic Growth*, pp. xiii–xiv, 180–181, and 196–198.

7. For discussion of this phenomenon, see Rostow, *The World Economy*, pp. 177–185.

8. It should be noted that the difference between Chenery's and my stage conceptions is reduced when he moves from association of real GNP per capita with the aggregate share of GNP generated by industry to the association of GNP per capita with periods of acceleration and deceleration in certain "early," "middle," and "late" industry groups. The latter method was developed most fully in H. B. Chenery and L. Taylor, "Development Patterns: Among Countries and over Time," *Review of Economic Statistics* 50, no. 4 (November 1968): 391–416. We are, nevertheless, left with the anomalies

where real GNP per capita and industrial virtuosity do not match: the relatively rich but technologically underdeveloped nations (e.g., Libya); the poor but technologically rather advanced nations (e.g., China and India).

9. Thorkil Kristensen, *Development in Rich and Poor Countries* (New York: Praeger, 1974), especially chap. 4, pp. 24–36. In Kristensen's analysis, it is the current rate of growth of knowledge which determines the slope of the S-curve at the highest income levels.

10. Ibid., p. 29.

11. Chenery, "Transitional Growth and World Industrialization," p. 7.

12. Ibid., p. 4.

13. Ibid., pp. 5–6. The basic table, including production and trade patterns in relation to real income per capita levels, is to be found in Chenery and Syrquin, *Patterns of Development*, pp. 20–21. These calculations were done in 1964 U.S. \$. Chenery's 1976 paper uses (income per capita) ranges in 1973 U.S. \$. The conversion factor for 1973 from 1964 U.S. \$ is given by Chenery as 1.61; from 1967 U.S. \$ the figure would be 1.48.

14. The large transitional countries as of 1973 include South Africa, Yugoslavia, Mexico, Iran, Brazil, Turkey, Colombia, and South Korea. The small primary-oriented countries include Venezuela, Saudi Arabia, Jamaica, Uruguay, Iraq, Chile, Costa Rica, Malaysia, Algeria, Nicaragua, Dominican Republic, Guatemala, Zambia, Rhodesia, Paraguay, Syria, Ivory Coast, and Ecuador. The small industry-oriented countries include Lebanon, Panama, Taiwan, Peru, Tunisia, and El Salvador. Chenery places China among the "transitional centrally planned" countries, India among the "developing countries." I am inclined to view them both as in the drive to technological maturity—or "transitional." See *The World Economy*, chaps. 43 and 44.

15. The "newly developed market economies" include (large) Japan, Italy, Spain, Argentina; (small industry-oriented) Israel, Puerto Rico, Ireland, Greece, Singapore, Hong Kong, and Portugal. Venezuela and Saudi Arabia are excluded. Their real income per capita would qualify them for this group, but their production structure would place them in an earlier "transitional" category. "Newly developed centrally planned economies" include the Soviet Union and six Eastern European countries with a 1973 population of 105 million, undifferentiated in Chenery's tables for lack of comparable data.

16. Chenery, "Transitional Growth and World Industrialization," p. 17.

17. Chenery and Syrquin, *Patterns of Development*, p. 10.

18. Rostow, *The Stages of Economic Growth*, pp. 13–14. This passage, in turn, was rooted in my *The Process of Economic Growth*. See also my "The Bankruptcy of Neo-Keynesian Economics," especially pp. 9–11.

19. The complacency was, of course, confined to the advanced industrial countries importing large quantities of basic commodities. A Latin American analysis of growth rates in the 1950's, for example, would not have omitted the impact of relative prices.

20. Chenery and Syrquin, *Patterns of Development*, pp. 20–21.
21. See, notably, Raymond W. Goldsmith, *Financial Structure and Development* (New Haven: Yale University Press, 1969).
22. In cross-sectional analysis for 1950–1970, however, Chenery and Syrquin (*Patterns of Development*, p. 20) find the proportion of GNP acquired through capital imports at a maximum at lowest income levels (under 100 1964 U.S. $). It is probable that pre-1914 the proportion was also at a maximum, on average, in the earliest phases of modern growth.
23. Rostow, *The Stages of Economic Growth*, especially, pp. 19–26, 46–58.
24. M. M. Postan, *An Economic History of Western Europe, 1945–1964* (London: Methuen, 1967), p. 128. The point is made statistically for an earlier period in the United States by Daniel Creamer and Israel Borenstein, assisted by Martin Bernstein, in *Capital in Manufacturing and Mining* (Princeton: Princeton Universtiy Press, 1960), pp. 24–31 and 106.
25. For a measurement of the role of plough-back financing in the United States in manufacturing and mining over the period 1900–1953, see Sergei Dobrovolsky, assisted by Martin Bernstein, "Long Term Trends in Capital Financing," part II of Daniel Creamer et al., *Capital in Manufacturing and Mining*, pp. 109–191. Dobrovolsky finds that gross internal financing as a percentage of the total varied with the size of firms but approximated for this period two-thirds.
26. In an evocative passage on historical capital-output ratios, Simon Kuznets raises the "notion of distinct economic epochs, associated with epochal innovations that are the major sources of growth during each epoch—innovations that are revolutionary enough to require several centuries for exploitation and general enough to affect a number of large societies. Within each epoch, after some passage of time, the areas, nations, or regions that are 'developed,' i.e., have taken sufficient advantage of the growth potential of the current epochal innovation, emerge; and we can then search for some common characteristics of such growth, e.g., capital formation proportions of more or less similar level, trend or bearing on rates of growth of product" (*Population, Capital, and Growth* [New York: W. W. Norton, 1973], pp. 137–138). What I am suggesting here is that somewhat similar, distinctive patterns of investment proportions and marginal capital-output ratios may have accompanied the introduction and diffusion of the major "epochal innovations" which mark the era of modern growth itself, for example, cotton textiles, railroads, steel, the internal combustion engine, electronics, and so on.
27. For reference to these cases, see above, Chapter 1.
28. For a perceptive exercise in the art of interpreting incremental capital-output ratios in post-1945 Western Europe, see, for example, Postan, *An Economic History of Western Europe*, pp. 133–142, exploring implications of table 12 on p. 115. For suggestive but inconclusive efforts to explain the rising tendency in the American capital-output ratios since the late 1960's, see, for example, *Economic Re-*

port of the President, January 1976 (Washington, D.C.: GPO, 1976), pp. 41–47; and *U.S. Economic Growth from 1976 to 1986: Prospects, Problems, and Patterns,* vol. 1, *Productivity,* Studies prepared for the use of the Joint Economic Committee (Washington, D.C.: GPO, October 1, 1976): John Kendrick, pp. 7–11 and 20; Edward F. Renshaw, pp. 21–56. The latter two studies, dealing with productivity as a whole, touch on factors beyond those determining incremental capital-output ratios. A valuable compendium of capital-output ratios, including historical data and references to detailed analyses, is Chapter 6 in Centrum Voor Economische Studien, *A Bank of Econometric Knowledge* (Louvain: Katholike Universitut te Leuven, 1974), pp. 87–147 ("Capital Productivity and Related Ratios").

29. Kuznets, *Modern Economic Growth,* pp. 260–261. The historical data on which Kuznets commented are on pp. 252–256.

30. Ibid., pp. 261–262. Postan, *An Economic History of Western Europe,* pp. 134–135, argues persuasively against placing excessive weight on the age of the capital stock as a factor in determining incremental capital-output ratios.

31. On Western European versus U.S. growth rates, see, for example, E. F. Denison, *Why Growth Rates Differ* (Washington, D.C.: Brookings Institution, 1967), especially pp. 236–237. An analysis of the postwar boom in Western Europe and Japan in these terms is presented in detail in Rostow, *The World Economy,* chap. 17.

32. For a useful measurement of the rise in public expenditure and its major components, see Joseph E. Pluta, "National Defense and Social Welfare Budget Trends in Ten Nations of Postwar Western Europe," *International Journal of Social Economics* 5, no. 1 (1978): 3–21. It should be noted that there was a systematic tendency of capital-output ratios to rise in the pre-1914 decade in the then-advanced industrial countries. It may have been associated with a waning of productivity gains as the steel revolution in all its manifestations came to maturity.

33. Postan, *An Economic History of Western Europe,* pp. 133–142. Postan puts particular weight on abnormally high and chronic excess capacity in certain older sectors of the British economy and on differences in the quality of management as among the sectors.

CHAPTER 7. *How to Break the Impasse in North-South Multilateral Economic Negotiations*

1. See, in particular, Rostow, *Getting from Here to There.*

Author Index

Subject Index

Printed and bound by CPI Group (UK) Ltd, Croydon, CR0 4YY

16/04/2025

14658534-0003